Evolution in an Anthropological View

~

D0707348

Evolution in an
Anthropological View

~

C. Loring Brace

A Division of
ROWMAN & LITTLEFIELD PUBLISHERS, INC.
Walnut Creek • *Lanham* • *New York* • *Oxford*

ALTAMIRA PRESS
A Division of ROWMAN & LITTLEFIELD PUBLISHERS, INC.

Published in the United States of America
by AltaMira Press
A Division of Rowman & Littlefield Publishers, Inc.
1630 North Main Street, Suite 367
Walnut Creek, CA 94596
http://www.altamirapress.com

Rowman & Littlefield Publishers, Inc.
4720 Boston Way, Lanham, Maryland 20706

12 Hid's Copse Road
Cumnor Hill, Oxford OX2 9JJ, England

British Library Cataloguing in Publication Information Available

Library of Congress Cataloging-in-Publication Data

Brace, C. Loring.
    Evolution in an anthropological view : collected essays / C. Loring Brace.
        p. cm.
    Includes bibliographical references and index.
    ISBN 0-7425-0262-7 (cloth : alk. paper) — ISBN 0-7425-0263-5 (pbk. : alk. paper)
    1. Human evolution. 2. Physical anthropology. 3. Fossil hominids. I. Title.
GN281 .B668   2000
599.93'8—dc21   99-056212

Printed in the United States of America

∞™ The paper used in this publication meets the minimum requirements of American National Standard for Information Sciences—Permanence of Paper for Printed Library Materials, ANSI/NISO Z39.48–1992.

Editorial Management by Jennifer Robin Collier
Project Management by Lisa Auer
Production Services by ImageInk, San Francisco
Cover Design by Raymond Cogan
Cover Art by Mary L. Brace. The skull is a drawing of the best-known French Neanderthal, La Chapelle-aux-Saints, done at the Musée de l'Homme in Paris in September 1988, with the permission of M. Jean-Louis Heim.

Table of Contents

~ Dedicated ~

To the Memory of
John C. Donaldson, 1888–1969
My favorite uncle, and probably the only person past or present
who would really understand what I have tried to do.

Foreword

I have been publishing on human evolution for more than 40 years now, and, while one or two of my essays are occasionally referred to in retrospect by practitioners in the field, the evolutionary perspective that runs through all of them is largely missing from biological anthropology today. This, then, is the excuse for assembling them in a single volume. With the dawn of a new millennium, there is always the hope that a recognition of the principles of organic evolution may yet filter into the anthropological outlook.

As one contemplates the strange world of paleoanthropology at the present time, one is tempted to reverse Dorothy's wondering comment after landing in Oz. Given the curious stance of the majority of those who purport to deal with what they claim to be human evolution, I would have to say that I don't think we are in the realm of the biological sciences any more. There is something of a chance, however, that we are actually in Kansas where the Board of Education has made it contrary to policy for science teachers to consider the dynamics by which the living world has been shaped so as to attain its present form. The current President of the American Association for the Advancement of Science and celebrated science writer Stephen Jay Gould entitled his Viewpoint column in the August 23, 1999, issue of *Time Magazine* "Dorothy, It's Really Oz." As Gould wrote, "They still call it Kansas, but I don't think we're in the real world anymore." He could just as easily have been writing about the intellectual realm inhabited by the students of human evolution. Certainly a concern for the processes by which the form of living human beings emerged from non-modern-appearing ancestors is almost entirely missing from paleoanthropology today.

Here it is appropriate for me to give my thanks to the many curators and collection managers who have given me access to the materials under their care, from New York to New Zealand, by way of Adelaide, Bangkok, Beijing, Berkeley, Cambridge (both), Canberra, Chengdu, Dunedin, Edinburgh, Florence, Fukuoka, Geneva, Hobart, Hong Kong, Indiana, Jakarta, Johannesburg, Kuching, Kyoto, Lisbon, London, Marseilles, Monaco, Nairobi, Oslo, Paris, Quebec, Rome, Shanghai, Sydney, Tel Aviv, Tokyo, Tübingen, Verroia, Washington, Xi'an, Yogyakarta, Zagreb, Zürich, and many, many other places. Here also I wish to express my gratitude to my brother Gerry's college classmate and my friend for 50 years, Dr. Richard J. Kaplan of the Rand Corporation in Santa Monica, California, for providing me with a continuous flow of clippings from *The Times Literary Supplement, The American Scientist,* and a range of other published sources that I would not otherwise encounter on a regular basis. My lexicographic brother Gerry Brace, who has toiled as a translator for the Institut Français du Pétrol at Nanterre for four decades, has given me a similar set of clippings from popular French publications that would not normally have come my way. These two have provided invaluable support for my efforts to see the issues in my field from a truly international perspective. In addition, my brother Gerry and also my wife, Mary L. Brace, have used their proofreading skills to help remove the rough spots in some of my less well-schooled efforts at phrasing.

Finally, I want to extend my gratitude to Brian M. Fagan for interceding on my behalf with AltaMira Press. In the mid-1960s when I was teaching at the University of California–Santa Barbara, we sought to strengthen our young Department of Anthropology by adding to our number, and Brian Fagan was one of the promising young scholars we added. But that was just before the Governor of California, Ronald Reagan, fired the President of the University of California with the reproof that "The State of California has no business subsidizing intellectual curiosity." To those of us who had been trying to build an enterprise whose whole justification was based on an appeal to intellectual curiosity, it seemed quite evident that our presence in a state-supported school in California was no longer welcome. So we left for other states where the role of stimulating and feeding intellectual curiosity was actually considered a desirable thing.

When Brian arrived to take up his position the next year, we had all departed. I have always felt a twinge of guilt about having gone through the process of hiring him, and then leaving him in the lurch before he even had the chance to work with us. So I felt a little sheepish when I returned to Santa Barbara as a visiting lecturer in spring 1998. This was the first time I had been back since bailing out in 1967. Brian, bless his soul, held no grudge, and when I told him that I had been having no luck in finding a publisher for this manuscript, he immediately called up AltaMira Press himself, and that was how the arrangements were made. I had actually been queried by three other publishers about my intentions in regard to producing a book, but each had recoiled with horror when they actually discovered what it was to be about. Thanks to the intercession of Brian Fagan, my manuscript received sympathetic attention, and that is how this book actually came to be.

Except for the last one, all these essays have been published previously. As they appear here, they have been edited to ensure "consistency" of style which may or may not represent an improvement. The consistency preferred would require me to use "that may or may not" in the previous sentence. This is in accordance with the convention imposed by American arbiters of English usage who insist that a restrictive clause should not be introduced by a "which." Winston Churchill, no mean stylist in the mother tongue, responding to a grammarian's complaint about his use of a preposition to end a sentence, declared that this was the kind of rule-bound fussiness "up with which I will not put." The American restrictive clause rule would rewrite his sentence to read "up with that I will not put." Just so that my sentences did not contain an endless string of "that" and "that" and "that," I had originally made a considered substitution of a "which" for a "that" where I felt that the situation warranted. My intent, as was true for the original versions, was to maintain some kind of readable flow to the stilted academic plod that is so often encountered in the books and journals where they initially appeared. I am grateful to the people at AltaMira Press for allowing me to keep my original phrasing in a significant number of instances.

In their original published form, each essay was accompanied by a full list of the sources cited. Just this past summer one very influential biological anthropologist, writing for an e-mail list, observed that "there are few practicing paleoanthropologists who have much respect for [Brace's] more extreme views these days" (Eric Delson, August 19, 1999). Since I had been aware, even as I was in the course of writing them in the first place, that the essays represented here could be regarded as just those that present my "more extreme views," I had made a considerable effort to provide more than the usual quantity of documentation in their support. The list of sources cited for each, then, tends to be quite a lot longer than is usual for the field. When all are combined in a single integrated bibliography, this runs to more than 250 pages. The author, year, and page (where necessary) of each citation is retained in the appropriate places in the text of each reprinted article to serve as documentation for the points being made, and the reader who is really interested in checking up on the sources cited can go back to the original publications and look them up in the bibliography. A complete bibliography is not appended, since it would have made the book half again as long as it is, but the citations mentioned in each of the Prologues and Epilogues are recorded in full at the end of this volume.

C. Loring Brace
Ann Arbor, Michigan
September 23, 1999

Introduction

Forty years ago, when I was finishing course work as a graduate student, I became consciously aware that the outlook and expectations of evolutionary biology were simply missing from biological anthropology. Scholars who were recognized as being involved in the study of "human evolution" paid virtually no attention to the actual course taken by which human form had arisen and why. Instead, their efforts were almost exclusively devoted to denial. Virtually all the hominid fossils that did not look just like living humans were discounted for one reason or another.

The Australopithecines, bipedal "man-apes" with barely more than one-third the brain size of *Homo sapiens* then known only from South Africa, were considered to be Middle Pleistocene in age. The half a million years by which it was assumed that they were removed from living humans was simply not enough time to allow for their transformation into fully human form. An interesting sideline, no doubt, but one that became extinct without issue. Now that Australopithecines of more than one variety have been found in an arc of ancient African savanna land deposits from the Chad Basin in the interior of western Africa eastward to Ethiopia and south via Tanzania and Mali to South Africa and dating back more than five million years, those earlier denials have given way to the concession that one such form almost certainly was the root from which all subsequent humans had evolved. But which? The realm of Australopithecine paleoanthropology is populated by a roster of prima donnas—well, actually, most of them are male—and each sings the praises of his own particular discovery as the one true progenitor of us all.

Then there is the phenomenon represented by the fossils first uncovered in Java starting in the years just after 1890, through the efforts of the Dutch physician Eugene Dubois. He had christened his find *"Pithecanthropus" erectus*. That generic name has not stood the test of time, and, along with similar Chinese specimens found in the decade before the outbreak of World War II, these are now generally referred to as *Homo erectus*. Paleoanthropologists have always been somewhat ambivalent about the status of that group in the spectrum of human evolution. "Awfully crude," has been one reaction, and then of course they were found in Asia, which according to general opinion was not where the main show of human evolution had taken place anyway. Many then concluded that these also were just another sideline that had become extinct without issue.

Recently there has been a return to the earlier enthusiasm for giving each newly discovered specimen a new species name justified by an enamel wrinkle in a molar or a bony squiggle in the jaw joint or on the side of the skull behind the ear. One might call this the parable of multiplying droves of species, but, rather than being a nurturing enterprise, it is more in the nature of the paleoanthropologist's being a "sorcerer's apprentice," giving each new figurative broomstick a separate specific name.

Finally there were the fossils that immediately preceded the earliest specimens that could be accepted as full *Homo sapiens* (even if that *sapiens* was itself a bit on the crude side). These robust predecessors, named after the first such to be discovered in Germany in 1856, were the Neanderthals. Without exception, paleoanthropologists looked at these with a palpable shudder and simply dismissed as a flat impossibility the idea that they could have evolved into modern human form, and reinforced their rejection by considering the fossils in question to constitute a completely separate species, *Homo "neanderthalensis."* In general, the practitioners in the field were convinced that it was only a matter of time before "ancient true man" would be discovered, disqualifying the candidacy of such bestial manifestations as Neanderthals or Pithecanthropines as potential ancestors.

It struck me as most curious that a profession that, in the abstract, accepted a hypothetical fur-covered, projecting-canine-toothed, tree-going primate as the ultimate human ancestor would balk at a Neanderthal with a brain every bit as large in proportion to body size as our own. Conversion of Neanderthal to living human form would only have required a modest average reduction in robustness, whereas converting an arboreal ape into a hairless terrestrial biped had to have involved a substantial makeover. Yet that major retooling was accepted in theory while the minor tinkering needed to generate a modern out of a Neanderthal was considered beyond the pale. It seemed to me that anthropology simply could not bring itself to apply evolutionary thinking to the question of the emergence of modern human form.

During my student years, we were encouraged to read Franz Weidenreich's splendid descriptive monograph on the *erectus* material discovered during the decade before the Japanese invaded China and put a halt to excavations in 1937 (Weidenreich, 1943b; White, 1974:22). Franz Weidenreich (1873–1948), who had earlier been fired by the French when they removed the German-speaking faculty at the University of Strassburg/Strasbourg after regaining Alsace-Lorraine at the end of World War I, had fled Hitler's Germany to become Honorary Director of the Cenozoic Research Laboratory associated with the Geological Survey of China, and he was also

Visiting Professor of Anatomy at the Peking Union Medical College in Beijing, China. Subsequently, he became a refugee once again as war engulfed eastern Asia, and he spent the last years of his life in New York where he wrote up his Chinese material at the American Museum of Natural History (and see the account of his life and work by W. K. Gregory in Washburn and Wolffson, eds., 1950). The Chinese *erectus* collection was the largest assemblage of such specimens ever found. Unfortunately, the originals were all lost when Japanese troops captured the U.S. Marine detachment trying to take them back to America for safekeeping the very day that the bombs fell on Pearl Harbor bringing the United States into the war with Japan—December 7, 1941 (though that was actually December 8 in China, since that is west of the international date line). Weidenreich's monograph, "The Skull of *Sinanthropus pekinensis*" (Weidenreich, 1943b), is a masterpiece of careful Germanic-style scholarship written at the American Museum of Natural History in New York from his notes on the originals and with the help of a fine set of casts, photographs, and the superb drawings prepared by his staff of Chinese illustrators. We were told to read it for its splendid description but to skip his efforts at interpretation, which were considered "questionable" and "unreliable" (and see Hooton's review, 1943:327).

Indeed Weidenreich had tried to do something that is still absent from what continues to be orthodoxy in paleoanthropology. He had engaged in a conscious effort to place the earlier hominid skeletal remains into a systematic evolutionary perspective. Not only did he regard the available Middle Pleistocene hominid fossils as representatives of a "stage" in human evolution, but he also treated the subsequent Neanderthal material as a morphological intermediate between *erectus* and "modern" human form consistent with the fact that it was intermediate in time as well. To be sure, Weidenreich specifically rejected a Darwinian view of evolution in favor of one that had overtones of orthogenesis—straight-line evolutionary momentum—with a retrospective bow to a Lamarckian faith in the inheritance of acquired characteristics. Still, it was the only effort to put the hominid fossils into some sort of evolutionary framework, and it had never been given a full-scale critique let alone a rebuttal.

Only later did I discover that the Czech-American scholar Aleš Hrdlička—the first biological anthropologist at the Smithsonian Institution in Washington—had previously defended the view that the Neanderthals could be regarded as representatives of an actual stage or "phase" of human evolution (Hrdlička, 1927, 1929, 1930). Like Weidenreich's subsequent view, this was a well-thought-out evolutionary treatment but it was not articulated within the context of the Darwinian paradigm. It too is rarely more than mentioned in passing, and the issues it raised have never been given a full discussion or rebuttal. (For an effort at such a discussion see Chapter 2, "The Fate of the 'Classic' Neanderthals".)

As my graduate student years were coming to a close, I resolved to try to resuscitate that attempt to deal with the human fossil record from an evolutionary perspective and try to make a deliberate effort to use the outlook of neo-Darwinian expectations that had come to characterize evolutionary biology over the previous two decades (Dobzhansky, 1937; Huxley, ed., 1940; Mayr, 1942; Simpson, 1944, 1953).

As I surveyed the various efforts to treat the course of human evolution available in English (Keith, 1915, 1925; Hooton, 1931, 1946; Howells, 1944, 1959; Clark, 1955a), I was struck by the fact that the logic of Darwinian evolution was simply missing. Instead, the authors of all the available treatments of the fossil evidence for human evolution seemed to be marching to the beat of a different drummer. Rather than taking the available fossils as indicating the course that evolution had actually taken, the crucial events were invariably said to have taken place somewhere else for reasons that were beyond our ability to discover. Then, after "modern" human form was assumed to have sprung into existence elsewhere by what amounted to a kind of "special creation," its exemplars tramped forth and, because of their assumed "superiority," supplanted the various archaic manifestations that had lingered on in such Old World peripheries as Europe, China, and Australia.

It did not take a great deal of rooting to discover the source of that "different drummer" and how biological anthropology came to acquire the curious non-Darwinian outlook that has continued to characterize the field. The full manifestation of that stance was first expressed by the French paleontologist Marcellin Boule (1861–1942), in his extended treatment of the Neanderthal skeleton from La Chapelle-aux-Saints, found in Corrèze in Southern France in 1908 (Boule, 1911–1913). Boule subsequently produced a general treatment of human "evolution" in *Les hommes fossiles* (1921), later revised and translated into English as *Fossil Men* (Boule and Vallois, 1957).

The basic model for the emergence of modern form by unknown means "elsewhere" and its subsequent invasion and replacement had all been laid out in Boule's La Chapelle-aux-Saints monograph, but this in turn was only a latter-day application of the paradigm that had received its full development in nineteenth-century French paleontology (Gaudry, 1878). That approach, for its part, was the direct continuation of the treatment of succession in the fossil record established in the first third of the nineteenth century by the founder of the whole field of paleontology, the distinguished French scientist Georges Cuvier (1769–1832). In dealing with change in the geological and bio-logical record of the past, Cuvier had invoked a series of cataclysmic causal events that were beyond the capacity of science to understand (Coleman, 1964). It was a view that was labeled "catastrophism" by the Cambridge philosopher of science William Whewell (Whewell, 1832).

In contrast, natural science in England operated under the assumption that the forces that had shaped the world were the same as those which continue at the present day, and that these were capable of being understood by the powers of human reason. The Edinburgh geologist James Hutton (1726–1797), in the context of the Scottish Enlightenment, had first articu-lated this approach to dealing with the events of the past (Hutton, 1794), and this was picked up and expanded by Sir Charles Lyell (1797–1875) in systematic fashion as he worked to establish geology as a full-fledged science (Wilson, 1972). Charles Darwin (1809–1881) then extended the same approach to deal with the dynamics of change in the biological realm (see Chapter 1, "The Intellectual Standing of Charles Darwin, and the Legacy of the 'Scottish Enlightenment' in Biological Thought").

The field of Anthropology, however, was formally inaugurated by the French physician Paul Broca (1824–1880), with the establishment of the Société d'Anthropologie de Paris in 1859—ironically the same year that Charles Darwin produced the full development of his idea that the myriad forms of the biological world had all arisen and been shaped by the continuing action of the everyday forces still in operation: evolution by means of natural selection (Darwin, 1859). Broca's Société served as the model for the creation of comparable organizations subsequently in both England (1863) (Burrow, 1963) and Germany (1869 and 1870) (von Eickstedt, 1937:127). Broca specifi-cally rejected Darwin's explanation (Broca, 1860), though subsequently he reluctantly conceded that some form of evolution was impossible to deny (Broca, 1870, 1872). Darwin's explanation for evolutionary change was also rejected by Cuvier's successor in paleontology, Albert Gaudry (1827–1908), who, as it happened, was the teacher of Marcellin Boule (Gaudry, 1878; Boule, 1908).

As a consequence, the approach to dealing with human "evolution" in French biological anthropology and human paleontology was an anti-Darwinian approach, and, because of the inertia of tradition, it has largely remained so ever since (and see Chapter 3, "Tales of the Phylogenetic Woods," and Chapter 9, "The Roots of the Race Concept in American Physical Anthropology"). But if that accounts for the treatment of human evolution in France, how did that become the establishment view in the England that had given rise to the Darwinian "revolution" in the first place?

There are several components in the answer to that question, but the two main ones involve, first, the rejection by the majority of late nineteenth- and early twentieth-century biologists of Darwin's proposed mechanism for driving evolution—natural selection (and see the treatment in Bowler, 1963); and, second, the realignment of England from 200 years of Germanic ties via the House of Hanover of its monarchy to alliance with France in 1914 at the start of World War I.

A century previously, Napoleonic France was regarded as the main threat to peace in Europe. This had been the stimulus for the English and Prussian cooperation that led to the final defeat of Napoleon at Waterloo in 1815. By the beginning of the twentieth century, however, the territorial ambitions of the German Kaiser were the menace that led to the *entente cordiale* and then the military cooperation between France and England as the First World War broke out in 1914. It seems odd to reflect how national traditions and political loyalties can influence the way people think about various aspects of the world and how the habits of thought so engendered can continue for generations beyond the events that conditioned their emergence.

At least as odd are the different perspectives of those events held by the different participants. World War I has now been consigned to the history books, as those who actually experienced it have dwindled to a diminishing few, but, in America, it is an accepted item of belief that "we" went "over there" and won. To the English, it was a matter of going across the Channel to defeat the "Huns." However, the war was principally fought on French soil with the French defending their homeland against the invading "Boche" and emerging as victors with full expressions of noblesse in recognizing their obligation to British and American assistance. The Germans, on their part, never acknowledged defeat on the field of battle. Instead, they tended to point to the presumed perfidy of the financiers on the home front by whom they had been "stabbed in the back." The financial houses named were invariably "Jewish"—a scapegoating tradition that continues today in Pat Robertson's Christian Coalition (Lind, 1995)—and the stage was set for a rerun of the whole horror show as World War II and its accompanying anti-Semitic Holocaust (Kuttner, 1992; Bessel, 1993).

Whatever else it was, World War I was a Franco-Germanic war fought on French soil with France and its Anglo-American allies emerging victorious. But while America had a tradition of gratitude towards the French going back to 1776 when they provided assistance in the American Revolution, England had a history of enmity toward France that extended all the way back to the Norman Conquest of 1066. The differences in intellectual style and mutual suspicion between the English and French worlds has been one of the main reasons that it took so long for Darwinian evolution to be given a hearing in French biology (Stebbins, 1974; Boesiger, 1980; Limoges, 1980). Darwin himself, when he came to realize that no one in the French intellectual world was likely to make any attempt to take his proposals seriously, expressed his exasperation in his complaint about "horrid unbelieving Frenchmen" (quoted in F. Darwin, 1887, vol. II, p. 255).

For the English to forge a functional working alliance with France in World War I, it meant conceding to aspects of French intellectual style. While this was essential for a successful war effort, it carried over into other areas as well. A "lost generation" of Anglo-American writers epitomized by Ernest Hemingway and James Joyce lingered on after the war in the world of French café society and of salons such as that of Gertrude Stein where they indulged themselves in the display of a self-consciously avant garde literary stance. Meanwhile, the outlook of the students of human evolution also acquired a French stamp that has continued to characterize the field ever since.

During the first decade of the twentieth century, a general view of human evolution was summarized in England by William J. Sollas, an Oxford geologist, as a picture of temporal and morphological stages with earlier and more robust forms giving rise to later and less robust ones (Sollas, 1908). The same view was presented in a small first book, *Ancient Types of Man* (1911), by Arthur Keith of the Royal College of Surgeons in London, who was later knighted for his role in establishing what became the ongoing outlook of English biological anthropology. Both Sollas and Keith were expressing the view that had been first articulated by the Strassburg (or "Strasbourg" after World War I) anatomist Gustav Schwalbe (1844–1916), though this was not clearly acknowledged (see Schwalbe, 1904, 1906).

The switch in Keith's outlook came very close to coinciding with the outbreak of the war. Actually Strassburg was one of the points of contention between Germany and France. In a move designed to add to France's *gloire,* Louis XIV—"the Sun King"—had conquered Strassburg in 1681, and it remained a part of France until the Franco-Prussian war of 1870–71 when it was annexed by the victorious Germanic forces. In 1918, it returned to France as Strasbourg, and the German-speaking faculty of the university was fired and replaced by a French-speaking faculty (Hoche, 1939). The citizens of Strasbourg themselves do not speak either French or German. Their language is called a Germanic "dialect," which in fact is a completely separate language, as different from German as Dutch or English, both of which are technically Germanic languages. One of those who lost his position after the end of World War I was Schwalbe's own pupil and successor, Franz Weidenreich, later to become celebrated for his description of the Chinese *Homo erectus* specimens and a perpetuator of his mentor's view of human evolution as a series of temporal and morphological stages.

Meanwhile, Keith's conversion to the French outlook actually was initiated in 1911, just a few years before the outbreak of the war. The first installment of Marcellin Boule's celebrated monograph on the Neanderthal find at La Chapelle-aux-Saints had just appeared, and Keith and his wife made a summer pilgrimage to the famous archaeological localities of the lovely Dordogne area of Southern France where several decades of work had revealed the tools, living sites, and spectacular cave art of their Ice Age inhabitants (Keith, 1950:319 ff.). Although Keith never became comfortable in either the German or the French language and literature, his late summer visit to France in 1911 amounted to a conversion experience. From that point on, his treatment of the human fossil record was simply an English version of the outlook of Marcellin Boule. This in turn has been the model for the overwhelming majority of English-language treatments of the subject ever since.

While Keith had spent his retirement years living in a cottage on the Darwin estate in Kent, and, in the minds of many, was regarded as a kind of embodiment of the Darwinian spirit, in fact he had rejected the core of Darwin's theoretical stance. In his own words, "I could as easily believe the theory of the Trinity as one which maintains that living developing protoplasm, by mere throws of chance, brought the human eye into existence" (Keith, 1946:217). To the end of his long life, he maintained that natural selection had not been the principal driving force in organic evolution as Darwin had claimed (Keith, 1955:103), even while he paradoxically identified himself as a staunch and loyal Darwinian. Rather than attempting to deal with the dynamics of change in an ongoing organic line, he invoked invasions and exterminations and the rise of evolutionary novelty "elsewhere" for reasons unknown—all simply manifestations of the outlook exemplified in the writings of Marcellin Boule. These in turn went right back without break to the pre-Darwinian outlook of Georges Cuvier early in the nineteenth century. In 1832, Whewell had characterized this view as "catastrophism," and, that being the case, it seemed to me that its application to the interpretation of the human fossil record could legitimately be called "hominid catastrophism," and I did so in what I include here as Chapter 2, "The Fate of the 'Classic' Neanderthals." The story of the intellectual currents that have contributed to the continuing non-Darwinian nature of the currently accepted treatment of human "evolution" is told in Chapter 3, "Tales of the Phylogenetic Woods."

Biological anthropology traces its professional intellectual roots primarily back to the outlook of the founding in 1859 of the Société d'Anthropologie de Paris by Paul Broca. His main focus was on the question of "race," and, surprisingly enough, he had adopted his approach largely from the outlook of the American anatomist Samuel George Morton (1799–1851) of Philadelphia. Morton's interest had been shaped by the troublesome loom of the continuing existence of slavery in the United States. Integrally related to this was the presence of three major population segments uprooted from their diverse original areas of long-term residence—Africa, Asia, and Europe—and artificially juxtaposed in a hierarchy of social inequality established and maintained by the possession of firearms by the dominant European-derived component.

Broca, as had Morton before him, started with the unexamined assumption that "the races" exist as discrete entities that can be identified as steps in a ladder of relative worth running from inferior to superior in the fashion of the eighteenth-century *scala naturae*—the Great Chain of Being. In his views, the task of anthropology lay in its use of measurements for the purpose of classification—the determination of who gets assigned to which category—and ultimately in justifying the initial assumptions of differences in relative rank. Questions concerning how human biological differences arose were largely shrugged off as beyond our powers to answer. Ever since that time, biological anthropology has treated the study of the human fossil record and the study of contemporary human biological variation as separate compartments. This accounts for the organization of the essays in this book into an initial section on paleoanthropology (Chapters 1–7) and a subsequent section (Chapters 8–12) dealing with the biological variation currently visible in the living peoples of the world. The treatment of the latter in historical perspective is presented in Chapter 9, "The Roots of the Race Concept in American Physical Anthropology." In Chapter 12, "The Cultural Ecological Niche," I have tried to tie the key contributions in both those realms of concern into a single integrated treatment.

After I first realized that the traditional treatment of human evolution was not grounded in the outlook of evolutionary biology, it seemed to me that all that was needed was a clear demonstration that such was the case, after which the participants in the field would immediately say, "Why, yes, of course!" and then turn around and deal with the subject in straightforward and processual fashion. So I wrote what is reprinted here as Chapter 2. It had its impact, all right, but not of the sort I had hoped. If it is remembered at all, it is as an ad hominem polemic. The suggestions it offered concerning the nature of the dynamics that had produced change in the human fossil record sank like a stone without leaving even a ripple. Neither students nor the majority of professional scholars showed any support, and, after a decade of stasis, it slowly dawned on me that if there were to be any attempts to follow up on the theoretical suggestions offered, they would have to be made by me.

For reasons I expand on in Chapters 6 and 7, I started my efforts with an attempt to deal with human tooth size, past and present. Inevitably the same theoretical points are made repeatedly, and some of the same examples are used over again in several of these chapters. Although it may look redundant here, the reader must realize that this gambit has had virtually no impact on the majority of the internationally recognized exponents of paleoanthropology. Consequently I have made repeated use of the same examples that show the evolutionary continuity that is so widely ignored.

I was able to get something of a beginning in museum collections in America—Harvard's Peabody Museum, the American Museum of Natural History in New York, and the Smithsonian Institution in Washington, D.C.—where repose collections of human skeletal material representing people from many of the diverse parts of the world. The project really only got going when I had the good fortune to negotiate a visiting professorship at Auckland University in New Zealand on my sabbatical of 1973–74. It is only a jump from New Zealand to Australia, and, with the help of an ingenious travel agent, I was able to renegotiate the ticket provided by Auckland to get me to Perth at the southwestern corner of Australia. For not a lot extra, I was able to add on transportation to Brisbane, Sydney, Canberra, Melbourne, Hobart (in Tasmania), and Adelaide before reaching Perth. Then, on the way home, I scheduled Jakarta (Indonesia), Sarawak (Borneo), Singapore, Bangkok (Thailand), Hong Kong, Taipei (Taiwan), and Honolulu at no extra cost. One of the benefits of an international round-trip ticket is that you can make unlimited stops along the way so long as each leg of the trip gets you a little closer—in a great-circle sense—to your terminal destinations. What I had managed to save from my Auckland salary made all the little extra deviations possible. And at each stop I mined the material available in the local museum collections.

Meanwhile, I had applied to the National Science Foundation to cover the rest of my expenses such as food and lodging. However, just after I had arrived in Sydney, I was notified by NSF that my project did not merit funding. At the same time, I learned from newspaper reports that the federal funding watchdog, Senator William Proxmire of Wisconsin, had gotten wind of an NSF application seeking support to measure the teeth of Australian aborigines, and he was publicly incensed at this projected waste of the taxpayers' money. Proxmire had attained a measure of fame for his "golden fleece awards," his published label given to grants awarded by NSF for projects he regarded as wasteful boondoggles.

While he used this as a means of heaping public scorn on scholars who he felt were siphoning off the taxpayers' dollars to pursue projects that were trivial or irrelevant, it had become something of a badge of honor in the scientific community. One of my former colleagues had gotten her "golden fleece award" for a project that dealt with the relations between religion and social views in a part of the Islamic world. The impact of Proxmire's public ridicule of that work has been somewhat reduced since that time by the massive and expensive problems America has subsequently faced in the Middle East precisely because of the prevailing ignorance of just what that project was geared to explore. It is clear now that some of the billions of dollars America has been forced to spend just to maintain the status quo around the Persian Gulf could have been spared if we had paid a bit more attention to the findings of that modestly funded research venture.

I cannot say that research on human tooth size has such direct relevance in terms of a payoff gained from a better understanding of our current condition, but it does provide a very clear comparative case that allows us to formulate expectations concerning the nature of the circumstances and the extent of evolutionary time involved in the development of other human dimensions that are much more difficult to measure directly (and virtually impossible to assess in the remote prehistoric past). The most crucial of these is "intelligence," and the application bears on the nature of the expectations that we should be able to offer concerning the pros and cons of crucial ongoing matters such as affirmative action. But just try to explain *that* to the Proxmires of the world.

In any case, I not only did not get NSF funding, I did not even get the bragging rights that go along with the "golden fleece award." American Express, MasterCard, and Visa to the rescue. So I borrowed to the maximum. Of course, I was unable to do anything about arranging payments until I got home six months later, by which time all my credit cards had been canceled. But the teeth got measured and, in the acknowledgments at the end of the publications presenting the results, I included words to the effect that 'this research was accomplished in spite of the National Science Foundation" with various bows to American Express and the others as well as to Ann Arbor

Bank and contributions from family members. The bank, bless its soul, agreed to refinance my house loan, though at double the comfortable old mortgage with its 6.4 percent interest rate. By the time I got everything paid off nearly twenty years later, the relatively modest $3,000 or so I had borrowed to finish that trip had wound up costing me just about ten times that much. And no sooner had I gotten square than I wound up having to use my restored cards to finance another grind through collections in Jerusalem and Tel Aviv (in Israel); Verroia and Nafplio (in Greece); Rome, Florence, and Pisa (in Italy); Monaco; and Nice, Bordeaux, and Paris (in France), because, as before, NSF, after finally funding a pilot project in China, considered the follow-up at the western end of the Old World to be unwarranted. Once again, my friendly local bank came through with help. But since I had lost my house insurance in the financial crunch, I could not use my equity as collateral. However, they were happy enough to extend me an unsecured loan at 14 percent to pay off the debt run up on the restored credit cards, which had once again been canceled. At that, this was better than the 18 percent interest rates the credit card issuers had been charging.

Those research trips and other ventures in Africa, Europe, China, Japan, and Southeast Asia were also used to build up a data base of craniofacial measurements that have allowed me to compare representatives of the various populations of the world from the perspective of local and broader regional similarities and differences. Unlike the distribution of dimensions such as human tooth size, skin color, nose form, and hemoglobin variants, the picture of craniofacial variation does not respond directly to aspects of Darwinian selection—though I did not realize that when I set out to collect the information in the first place. Initially I had tended to accept the neo-Darwinian views that all discernible traits are controlled by specific selective forces even if we have not yet figured out how. It was a tendency justly satirized by Stephen Jay Gould and Richard Lewontin as "hyperselectionism"—the "Panglossian paradigm" (Gould and Lewontin, 1979).

While I have not gone close to Gould and Lewontin's extreme of denying *any* major role to natural selection, one of the things that the size of my data base has allowed me to do is to establish a means of actually testing whether a given trait is responding to the action of selective forces or simply to the inertia of the reproductive continuity of local idiosyncrasies—"family resemblance writ large" (Brace, 1996b:136; and see Chapter 10, "Reflections on the Face of Japan"). Quite simply, a trait that is under selective force control will grade without break from one region to another, responding only to the change in intensity of the selective force that controls its expression. The most obvious such instance is skin color. The skin pigment melanin is at a maximum near the equator where the ultraviolet component of sunlight is at its most intense. Melanin prevents the penetration of cancer-inducing ultraviolet rays, and it grades off to the north and south, with that reduction being in proportion to the distance away from the tropics and to the length of time the population in question has remained at the latitude where it is found today.

This gradient in a given trait is referred to as a "cline," from the Greek word for slope. In English, we still use it in the original sense in the word "incline." Human traits that are distributed as separate and independent clines clearly show the effects of the distribution of the relevant selective forces. Skin color has one pattern of distribution, hemoglobin variants display a different one, the ABO blood group system yet another one, and tooth size has a gradient that cuts across all the others. And the pattern—gestalt—made by their intersections has no meaning in and of itself.

With a major if unexpected exception, the traits that are of adaptive value to their possessors and are under selective force control show graded and independent distributions throughout the inhabited world. The converse is that the traits that *do* show regional clumping or clustering lack any particular survival value. A political entity or even a contiguous geographical region by itself never generates a coherent biological impact on its inhabitants. Consequently, if we can recognize a trait configuration as characteristic of a particular part of the world, the patterns that we see can have no adaptive value as such. These generalizations, while of basic importance for making sense out of the meaning of human biological variation, are not immediately obvious intuitively. That is why they are treated at greater length in Chapter 9, "The Roots of the Race Concept in American Physical Anthropology," and Chapter 11, "A Four-Letter Word Called 'Race'."

The only trait that is clearly of major adaptive value but which cannot be expected to show a distribution coinciding with the graded intensity of its selective force is intelligence—or "cognitive capacity," to use the currently fashionable polysyllabic euphemism. The reason we would not expect intelligence to display any difference from one human group to another, or any gradient in its current distribution, is that the circumstances—the selective forces—that controlled just how much intelligence was needed for sheer survival were essentially identical throughout the entire realm of human existence for the full duration of the genus *Homo* over the approximately 2 million years of its existence. This is the topic addressed in Chapter 12, "The Cultural Ecological Niche," written especially to serve as the conclusion of this book.

It should be clear from what is presented in this collection of essays that a full understanding of the human condition cannot be achieved by any one of the components of the field of anthropology taken by itself. Especially in the last chapter, it should be apparent that a successful effort of this nature would require input from the ethnologists and linguists, who focus on living humans, and also from archaeologists, who deal with the evidence for the nature of human existence in the past. These then have to be integrated with what we know about the human biological condition, past and present. Although the diverse components of anthropology sometimes threaten to secede and go their own way oblivious of what the other dimensions can contribute, this would produce a picture that amounts to considerably less than the sum of its parts. Even though each separate subfield sometimes exhibits a lack of sympathy for the contributions of the others, their integrated contributions have a real chance of building a whole that is very much more than the simple sum of its various separate pieces.

If neither the humanistic nor the scientific component of anthropology can legitimately claim to stand for the field as a whole, and if neither can constitute any kind of threat to the other, it is still true that the scientific portion has suffered from the de facto absence of a systematic evolutionary perspective in the treatment of its data. Not all anthropological data, either biological or cultural, can be tied to the operation of selective forces. The question is: Which can, and which cannot? What will benefit from an evolutionary perspective, and what has to be taken on its own merits? The task of sorting this out is not particularly difficult, but it has hardly been begun despite the somewhat naïvely optimistic comment of nearly a generation ago just after the Darwin centennial that "Today, cultural evolutionism seems to be reviving" (Harding et al., 1960:2). At that time, I had similar hopes for biological anthropology, and I was just as premature. Now, with the advent of the end of the millennium, we should be able to say with confidence that conditions should be ripe, even at this belated date, to initiate the effort.

For a starter, it is time that we took seriously the eighteenth-century idea that human beings—and, indeed, human societies as well—developed by a combination of chance and constraint in comprehensible fashion from predecessors of less than "modern" form. By definition, such a process can only be called evolution. Looking at the past of our field and projecting a hope for the future, I would urge that all aspects of our subject matter deserve systematic treatment from an evolutionary perspective. The idea of evolution in anthropology then really does warrant being regarded as a once and future thing. To add a suitable postscript, we can borrow from the epitaph penned by T. H. White (1958) to *The Once and Future King.* Taking advantage of the fact that "king" and "thing" rhyme in English, and that their Latin counterparts, *rex and res,* scan comfortably in the same verse scheme, a minor modification can generate a most appropriate epigram:

Hic Jacet Idea Immura,
Res Quondam, Resque Futura.

(Here lies buried an idea,
A once and future thing.)

CHAPTER 1

The Intellectual Standing of Charles Darwin, and the Legacy of the "Scottish Enlightenment" in Biological Thought
(1997)

Prologue

In the spring of 1995, I was contacted by Marshall Sahlins, chair of the Department of Anthropology at the University of Chicago, who asked me if I would be willing to prepare a presentation for one of the sessions of a year-long series that he and George W. Stocking, Jr., were organizing entitled "Anthropology, Postwar/ Premillennial: Intergenerational Conversations." Sahlins had been on the faculty of the University of Michigan when I first arrived. In fact, he was largely responsible for my being hired. He was a former student of Leslie White—famous for having written *The Evolution of Culture* (1959) among other things in a similar vein—and had long been interested in the applications of evolutionary concepts to matters anthropological (see, for example, the book that he edited with another of Leslie White's former students, Elman Service, *Evolution and Culture*, 1960). Of course, he was well aware of my own interest in evolution, and he asked me if I would prepare a presentation on evolution in anthropology to be given in January of 1996.

Naturally I was delighted by the opportunity, and, before my visit, I produced a quantity of manuscript on the matter that I entitled "Evolution in Anthropology: Or, the Once and Future Thing," and I duly presented this in Chicago on January 15, 1996. In the course of my preparations, I had generated a section on aspects of Darwin that were underappreciated in science in general and in anthropology in particular. As it happened, the total amount of material I had assembled was so great that I had to cut out whole sections to fit within the allotted time, and one of the sections that I cut out was the one on Charles Darwin.

At the end of the academic year, I found that I was left with what amounted to a respectable chapter on Darwin that I felt ought to merit submission for publication. For several decades, I have been a member of the History of Science Society, so it occurred to me that there might be some interest in the course of my argument among the readership of their flagship journal, *Isis*. Consequently, I duly polished it up in *Isis* format and sent it off. The reviewers basically agreed with everything I had written, but felt that it was inappropriate for *Isis* since the readership already accepted the nature of the gambit I had taken. Two of the reviewers suggested that it might be appropriate for an audience where Darwin was still misperceived. At that point, I thought to myself, "Well, of course!" and biological anthropology immediately came to mind. As the subsequent chapters of this book will demonstrate, the thought processes of evolutionary biology are still partially alien to those in the business of dealing with human evolution. With that in mind, then, I rewrote it in the style of the *Yearbook of Physical Anthropology,* incorporating some suggestions made by Professor Emeritus Ernst Mayr, and sent it off to the *Yearbook*'s editor, Ted Steegmann. It duly appeared in the *Yearbook of Physical Anthropology* 40:91–111 (1997a). That is the form in which it appears here.

Even as I was finishing this Prologue and after the proofs had gone off to the *Yearbook,* a further testimony to Darwin's expository skill appeared from the pen of that quintessentially urban—and urbane—film critic and writer David Denby. He seemed almost surprised to discover the balance and fluency of Darwin's literary style. "Against my will, I was beginning to admire his writing: the steady, evenhanded, respectful description.... The prose is quiet but also confident.... Fearing nothing, exaggerating nothing, Darwin reintroduced into English prose intimations of the marvellous" (Denby, 1997:56). As will be seen in the section that treats Darwin as a writer, he was not the first to arrive at that conclusion.

∽ ∽

DARWIN AND THE CONCEPT OF EVOLUTION

Despite all the qualifications and disclaimers, the outlook evoked by the word "evolution" is inextricably associated with the name of Charles Darwin. Curiously, it was a word not used in his justly acclaimed masterpiece, *On the Origin of Species by Means of Natural Selection, or, the Preservation of Favoured Races in the Struggle for Life,* to give it its full title (Darwin, 1859). An assessment of the treatment of evolution involves the appraisal of intellectual styles. The mere fact of evolution itself—"descent with modification," as Darwin phrased it in its most succinct form (Darwin, 1859:420)—is so banal and self-evident that it is simply the consequences of history perceived in the light of simple common sense. Thomas Henry Huxley exclaimed, "How extremely stupid not to have thought of that!" (Huxley, 1887:551) when he first read Darwin's exposition of the concept and the idea of natural selection in the *Origin,* and we smile in a slightly condescending fashion as we recall the incident.

Consider the Tibetan parable concerning the durability of Mount Everest: "Chomolungma is the mightiest of mountains. Once in a thousand years, an eagle flies over its peak and brushes the crest with a single beat of its wing. When by the repetition of this process the mass of Chomolungma shall have been reduced to the level of the sea, there will have passed one second of eternity." We emulate Huxley as we nod appreciatively and ponder at the various ways in which the human mind can phrase the obvious. However, we know full well that even though mountains rise and are worn away by the accumulation of natural events, the abrasion produced by the feathers of a bird's wing does not represent the principle causative mechanism.

Although Darwin had verbalized the picture of organic evolution in such a fashion that it seemed self-evident, Huxley never did come to grips with the full dynamics of Darwin's synthesis. This remains true for many right up to the present—including, curiously enough, the bulk of those who concentrate their professional efforts on the study of human evolution. In part, this is a matter of perspective. A human being is born, lives, and dies. Others go through the same cycle in unending repetition, and no two humans are exactly alike. Still, it is not clear from the vantage point of a single life, or even from the contemplation of what one knows of other lives, that there is any cumulative or permanent alteration in the nature of the cycle itself. It took a Darwin to perceive that, in the long run, not only was cumulative change the norm, but also the discernible differences between all living species had been its natural consequence and all living matter—all plants and animals—were descended from a single common form. Further, unlike the allegorical example of the actions of a hypothetical eagle feather, he worked out a plausible mechanism by which that picture of change could have been produced.

It was a breathtaking intellectual achievement, but it did not take place in a vacuum. Any number of critics have pointed to earlier formulations of the idea of evolution and then have denigrated Darwin 'or lack of originality or failure to give credit to his predecessors (Butler, 1882; Zirkle, 1941; Barzun, 1958; Darlington, 1959; Himmelfarb, 1959; Bethell, 1976; Popper, 1978; Eiseley, 1979; Barham, 1995). The denigrations, however, are almost invariantly self-serving and designed to demonstrate the supposedly superior worth of the critic by demeaning the magnitude and nature of Darwin's accomplishment.

Yes, Democritus and Epicurus in classical Greece suggested that the world operates in a mechanistic and processual fashion, as did their Roman follower, Lucretius, in the first century B.C.E. Yes, Buffon and Darwin's own grandfather Erasmus in the eighteenth century and Lamarck just before Darwin's birth linked manifestations of organic form to environmental differences, and their views were all transmitted to Darwin as part of his general educational background. But then, knowledge of water power, the wheel, and the principles of mechanics was widely distributed across the Old World. As the late Joseph Needham has so abundantly shown, all the essential pieces were available in China as far back as anywhere else and yet, for reasons that are still somewhat obscure, the Industrial Revolution and its consequences first took place in a restricted portion of Northwest Europe (Needham, 1969).

A good case can be made that Darwin represented a specific product of that same process (Browne, 1995:543). The European Enlightenment that spawned the Industrial Revolution generated the traditions that coalesced into the several manifestations of professional science, and it is certainly no accident that these were particularly vigorous in those areas most directly affected by the Protestant Reformation. One of the best illustrations of this is the resounding declaration of pious Protestant faith in Puritan New England that "*Philosophy* is no *Enemy,* but rather a mighty and wondrous *Incentive* to *Religion*" (Mather 1771:1). Others have dealt with this at greater length elsewhere (Lovejoy, 1936; Merton, 1938). The full development of that theme is beyond the scope of my current presentation. I am going to suggest, however, that the currents which coalesced in British industrialism and science were generated by the Scottish Enlightenment and that Charles Darwin was very much a product of that phenomenon.

THE OUTLOOK OF THE SCOTTISH ENLIGHTENMENT

Robert K. Merton has made an eloquent case for the impact of the Protestant Reformation on the genesis of the scientific outlook (Merton, 1938). In the sixteenth century, Martin Luther had argued that every informed individual was competent to make judgments concerning right and wrong without specific instructions and guidance from the ordained clergy (Friedenthal, 1967). The growing faith in the competence of human decision-making capacity spread with the expansion of the areas under Protestant control in northwest Europe. Further, the realm where individual competence was considered a relevant issue began to extend beyond matters of religious ethics to the secular realms of politics and technology. The very idea of popular democracy as a desirable or even viable form of government was one of the consequences. Of course, this had to contend with the previously established systems based on inherited status and wealth that gave more weight to certain individuals than to the average citizen.

One of the other consequences in this faith in the capability of the informed human mind to make valid decisions was the belief that the pursuit of knowledge was a good thing in and of itself and could be of material as well as spiritual benefit both individually and collectively. The Protestant Reformation under John Knox had introduced this Luther-derived outlook to Scotland in the sixteenth century where it took root and flourished over the next two centuries. The "union" with England in 1707 and the collapse of "The Forty-Five"—the unsuccessful rebellion by "The Young Pretender," Charles Edward Stuart or "Bonnie Prince Charlie"—made it clear to most Scots that their future welfare lay in mastering the ways of their English neighbors to the south and turning them to their own advantage.

Eighteenth-century Scotland, then, in classic Protestant fashion, embarked on a campaign of self-improvement. The first step was learning to speak English, and the second was in a focus on education that stressed the cultivation of those practical skills that constituted their own version of the Age of Reason, the Scottish Enlightenment. This took the form of what has variously been called "Scottish Realism," "Scottish Philosophy," or "The Scottish School of Common Sense" (Cousin, 1857; McCosh, 1875; Grave, 1960). Although various figures such as Francis Hutcheson (1694–1747), David Hume (1711–1776), and Adam Ferguson (1723–1816) can be regarded as manifestations of the Scottish Enlightenment, the principal embodiment was that exponent of the School of Common Sense, Thomas Reid (1710–1796), specifically in the views he expounded in *An Inquiry Into the Human Mind, on the Principles of Common Sense* of 1764 (Duggan, ed., 1970).

In good Protestant manner, Reid refused to accept knowledge that was conveyed solely on the basis of constituted authority. Similarly, he did not accept the existence of innate ideas as advocated by René Descartes (1596–1650) or Bishop George Berkeley (1685–1753) on the one hand, but, on the other, he rejected the extreme skepticism of David Hume. To Reid, the existence of a real world was a "self-evident truth," and, in good Baconian fashion, this could be known through observation and experiment (Swetlitz, 1988:78). His real, material world was a Newtonian one where there is an identifiable cause for every discernible event. That world is available through perception by the senses—induction, as Bacon used the term—after which, through analysis and abstraction—deduction, again in the Baconian sense—the knowledge of its nature is gained. This is what Reid called "common sense."

The definition was neither as simple nor as straightforward as its proponents tried to suggest. Since the self-evident is "incapable of proof, the truths of common sense have no logical antecedents" (Grave, 1960:151). Ultimately, this means that common sense in fact has to be characterized as "metaphysical belief" (ibid., p. 120). At one level, it simply reflects "good sense" as opposed to "nonsense" (Lehrer, 1989:152). Beyond that, in almost Chomskian fashion, it included the assumption of a ubiquitous aspect of human capability demonstrated by the structure of language and its universal grammatical nature (Grave, 1960:105–106). Despite the effectively a priori nature of this assumption, it was not regarded as an equivalent to one of Berkeley's preexisting ideas. As illustrated by the universal presence of language, Reid felt that the ability to reason was a common possession of all human beings whether philosophers or peasants, that is, it was a capacity that characterized the human condition. Adding complication to this was the view that truths vouched for in the knowledge shared by a community came closer to reflecting the wisdom of God than could be the case for the judgment of a single individual. Viewed in that way, the highest manifestation could be called "*communal* sense" (Wills, 1978:188). It was this latter form of the definition that was so influential in America (and see Thomas Paine's *Common Sense* of 1776; see Wills, 1978:303) and which was picked up and used by Thomas Jefferson in drafting the Declaration of Independence. In contrast, it was the version stressing the capacity to reason inherent in every individual that was stressed in practical fashion by what was to emerge when the various sciences crystallized into professional form after the end of the eighteenth century.

At a quasitheological level, the roots of the Unitarianism in the northern British Isles as well as in New England in America were clearly located in

Thomas Reid's Scottish Philosophy of Common Sense (Howe, 1970:5, 32). The Darwins of Shrewsbury were Unitarians. Charles's father, Dr. Robert Waring Darwin, gleefully quoted the words used by his own father, Dr. Erasmus Darwin, in describing Unitarianism as "merely a featherbed to catch a falling Christian" (Browne, 1995:12). Erasmus Darwin was twitting his friend Josiah Wedgwood's drift away from the orthodox church toward secularism. At the same time that Charles Darwin began studying medicine in Edinburgh in 1825, Ralph Waldo Emerson was finishing his training at a Harvard Divinity School dominated by a Unitarian outlook and dedicated to the Common Sense of Thomas Reid (Howe, 1970:5; Allen, 1981:81). Later in the nineteenth century, this became secularized in the "Pragmatism" of Charles Sanders Peirce and William James in America, in the inductive logic of John Stuart Mill in England, and in the Logical Positivism of the Vienna Circle in Europe (James, 1907; Williams, 1947:185; Buchler, 1955; Naess, 1968; Kenny, 1990; Diggins, 1994). The influence of the School of Common Sense on continuing currents of philosophy has been explicitly recognized (Woozley, 1970:91) to the extent that the twentieth-century representatives of "English Philosophy," George Edward Moore (1879–1958) and Ludwig Wittgenstein (1889–1951), have been called the "Cambridge philosophers of common sense" (Williams, 1947:188).

Its impact on shaping political traditions in America and France has also been noted (McCosh, 1875; Bryson, 1945; Wills, 1978), as has its impact on ideas concerning education (Sloan, 1971). Finally, its role in shaping the outlook of the emergence of the systematic pursuit of science, particularly physics and chemistry, has been given specific recognition (Olson, 1975). The science of geology, in addition, had been given major impetus by the nonpracticing Edinburgh physician James Hutton (1726–1797), singled out as an exemplar of "Common Sense" among eighteenth-century scientists (Olson, 1975:17). Hutton, of course, was the major influence on the thinking of the Scottish-born geologist Sir Charles Lyell (Wilson, 1972:511). Lyell, in turn, has been described as Darwin's "role model" (Browne, 1995:324). Darwin gave full credit to "Sir Charles Lyell's grand work on the Principles of Geology" (Darwin, 1859:282; and see his tribute to Lyell in F. Darwin, ed., 1887, vol. III, p. 196). He even went so far as to say that, "I always feel as if my books came half out of Lyell's brain" (quoted in Young, 1985:84). The intellectual stance of Charles Darwin, then, is a clear-cut manifestation of the continuity of the characteristic mode of thinking of the Scottish Enlightenment.

BIOLOGICAL ANTHROPOLOGY
AND TWENTIETH-CENTURY THOUGHT

While the biological sciences now largely take it for granted that Darwin's vision underlies their general approach (Dobzhansky, 1973; Alexander, 1980), there are some notable exceptions, and among these are large segments of paleontology and biological anthropology (Eldredge and Cracraft, 1980; Wiley, 1981; Groves, 1989; Rightmire, 1990; Kimbel and Martin, eds., 1993; Stringer and Gamble, 1993; Tattersall, 1994, 1997). A look at a sampling of the latter will illustrate some of the dimensions of the ambivalence involved.

In less than five years now, the calendar millennium will indeed be with us, but I am not at all sure that the biological portion of anthropology will have actually entered it in the metaphorical sense. At the end of the previous decade, the futility of the efforts "to drag paleoanthropology 'kicking and screaming into the twentieth century'" (borrowing the words that the late Adlai Stevenson had used in a political context) was given explicit recognition (Brace, 1989:444), and it looks very much as though this will not happen prior to the arrival of the twenty-first. To my dismay, the direction in which the field is going is expressed by the words "We believe that Darwinism...is... a theory that has been put to the test and found false" (Nelson and Platnick, 1984:143). What has been taking place is something I have referred to as the "great leap backwards" and the reaffirmation of an outlook that is not merely pre-Darwinian but positively Thomist (Brace, 1988:133). Accompanying that, biological anthropologists who should know better not only have demonstrated an unawareness of their own intellectual past but have actually engaged in the attempt to rewrite it. The almost certain consequence of that ignorance of our history is that we shall be condemned to repeat it.

A case in point is the recent treatment of that famous symposium on "The Origin and Evolution of Man" held at the Cold Spring Harbor Laboratory on Long Island in the summer of 1950. Rather than having been an occasion where the currents of neo-Darwinian thought were brought into the anthropological cloister, as its surviving participants remember it, it has been described as "an attempt to consolidate and institutionalize an approach to human evolution that owed more to political conviction than to science" (Shipman, 1994:191). According to this reading of events, the upshot of that symposium was that there are some aspects of human biology "that were better left unexplored" (Shipman, 1994:190). Certainly the potential for political misuse of anthropology was recognized by the participants, but the general consensus of the meeting was the diametric opposite of that charge. This can best be illustrated by quoting from the "Concluding remarks of the chairman," Curt Stern:

> The political implications of statements or conclusions regarding the origin and evolution of man have been in our minds again and again.
>
> Knowing the terrible harm which has grown out of misconceptions…there is a tendency to shy away from conceptual regions, or from terms, which might be exploited by ill-will or stupidity. I believe, that science should not yield to such derived impulses. We should look for the truth wherever it can be found. We should not assume that facts do not exist because their uncritical postulation has been detrimental (Stern, 1950:412).

In essence, this is a restatement of the credo of the defenders of "natural theology" in the Enlightenment, a position that was elegantly articulated in 1831 in the Presidential Address to the Geological Society of London by the Woodwardian Professor of Geology at Cambridge, Adam Sedgwick (Hallam, 1983:51–52).

The same author who gave that curious rendering of the 1950 Cold Spring Harbor Symposium also managed to botch the import of the Darwinian synthesis that preceded it. Experimental geneticists were said to have focused on the role of mutation as the agent of evolutionary change to the extent that selection was regarded as "irrelevant" (Shipman, 1994:151). That may have been true of De Vries over a generation earlier, but it was most definitely not the stance of those who created the synthesis.

Continuing that undocumented assertion, the further claim is made that, "Rather than pointing to natural selection as the main or only motor producing evolutionary change, the geneticists became entranced with a concept known as *genetic drift*" (Shipman, 1994:151). It is true that one of the contributors to the synthesis, Sewall Wright, did offer genetic drift as a secondary and less important mechanism (Wright, 1931, 1943, 1946), but virtually all of the figures involved, including Wright, stressed natural selection as the principal driving force (Fisher, 1930; Wright, 1931, 1932, 1980, 1988; Dobzhansky, 1937; Huxley, ed., 1940; Mayr, 1942; Simpson, 1944). One of the more important of them, Sir Ronald A. Fisher, spent the rest of his life denouncing Sewall Wright for even suggesting that genetic drift was a possibility and dogmatically maintaining that natural selection is the sole and sufficient mechanism (Fisher and Ford, 1950). The dogmatism of this stance has sometimes been attributed to the neo-Darwinian synthesis as a whole and properly criticized as "hyperselectionism" (Gould and Lewontin, 1979). For a full recounting of the history of the development of these matters, there is no better rendition than the magisterial survey by Ernst Mayr (1982). Predictably, however, biological anthropology has reacted to that treatment in characteristically pre-Darwinian fashion (Tattersall, 1984).

THE MISPERCEPTION OF CHARLES DARWIN

If this version of the evolutionary synthesis can serve to illustrate just how far off the track contemporary biological anthropology can stray, the picture it presents of the beginnings of evolutionary biology and the nature of its founder, Charles Darwin, is even more of a travesty. Consider this: "Often lionized as a great thinker, Darwin plodded along on his subject like an uncertain little man who has gotten hold of an idea too big for him" (Trinkaus and Shipman, 1992:33). Portraying him as a witless clod, the claim has been put forth that "He was simply blotting paper, soaking up life's ink" (Shipman, 1994:23). The same set of points was made over a generation ago by the literary critic, historian, and irascible curmudgeon Jacques Barzun, who declared that "Darwin was a great assembler of facts and a poor joiner of ideas" (Barzun, 1958:74 [revised from 1941]; and see the similar stance taken by Himmelfarb, 1959). These in turn fed off Darwin's own self-deprecatory comments that "I have no great quickness of apprehension or wit" (Darwin, 1887:82), and that he owed his success to "industry in observing and collecting facts" (Darwin, 1887:72).

Actually, tucked away in the midst of his apologia, Darwin in fact mounted a modest defense of his "fair share of invention as well as common sense" (Darwin, 1887:86), and supported this in his statement in the *Origin,* as in his letter to his publisher, that his whole volume constituted "one long argument" (Darwin, 1859:459; Paston, 1932:170; Mayr, 1991). As Mayr has properly cautioned in regard to Darwin's "Autobiography," it "was written with that exaggerated Victorian modesty that induced Darwin to belittle his own achievements and the value of his education" (Mayr, 1982:394). The most recent biographical treatment has referred to his "Autobiography" as "an exercise in camouflage" and "a smoke screen almost as effective as if no records had been left at all" (Browne, 1995:x–xii). In Mayr's assessment, "biographers all too readily have tended to accept his words at face value, particularly where Darwin made disparaging remarks about his own abilities, and then wondered how such an uneducated dullard could have become the architect of perhaps the greatest intellectual revolution of all time" (Mayr, 1982:394).

Even subsequent defenders of a Darwinian vision of evolution have often described him in condescending fashion. In C. D. Darlington's treatment, for example, he is depicted as "a rather quaint naturalist with an eye for detail and a mind which became confused when engaging in theory" (Darlington, 1959; Ghiselin, 1969:256; Reed, 1978). Right in line with this, the recent assessment of the origins of evolutionary thought as seen from the perspective of biological anthropology is that Darwin's ideas would never have survived if it had not been for their presentation by Thomas Henry Huxley, "the man more brilliant than Darwin" (Trinkaus and Shipman, 1992:21; and note Barzun's assessment of Huxley as having been "a far keener thinker," Barzun, 1958:74). Continuing in the same vein, another voice representing current biological anthropology has asserted that "Darwin...must have been every bit as dull in person as his prose suggests he was" (Harpending, 1996:99). On the other hand, one American visitor, writing from Down on July 12, 1872, described his pleasure in conversation with "the best brain in Europe" by declaring that "Darwin was as simple and jovial as a boy, at dinner," continuing that "I never met a more simple, happy man" (Brace, 1894:321). His most recent biographer concurs: "Clearly he was not nearly as dull as he maintained" (Browne, 1995:xi).

To add some perspective, Huxley privately commented that *The Origin of Species* was "one of the hardest books to understand thoroughly that I know of" (Huxley, 1901, vol. II, p. 190). The most recent full-scale treatment of Huxley's intellectual contribution observed that he "never fully came to terms either with Darwin's 'dynamic' attitude towards nature or his 'pragmatic' conception of the logic of science" (Di Gregorio, 1984:199). Huxley clearly had a preference for a view in which change occurred by sudden and unexaminable means in the mode of the subsequent saltationists and more recent proponents of punctuated equilibria (Eldredge and Gould, 1972; Di Gregorio, 1984:197). These trends reach their extreme in the more uncompromising promotion of "cladistic" logic (Wiley, 1981; and see the skepticism in the accounts of Brace, 1988; Kellog, 1988; and Dennett, 1995; and in the hilarious spoof by Queller, 1995). As with his intellectual progeny, Huxley evidently was more comfortable with a world of order as opposed to a world of process (Rehbock, 1985:172).

It seems more clear than ever in retrospect that Darwin would have come to be regarded as the giant that he was even had there been no Huxley. Huxley, however, could never have achieved the stature for which he is remembered if there had been no Darwin. Study after study continues to uncover further dimensions of Darwin's intellectual sophistication, and it would be to our benefit to heed the warning offered in the first full treatment of Darwin's philosophical competence: "The reader would do well to beware of a number of recent books which attempt to discredit Darwin's intellect or character" (Ghiselin, 1969:28). A still more recent assessment from the realm of professional philosophy has declared, "If I were to give an award for the single best idea anyone has ever had, I'd give it to Darwin ahead of Newton and Einstein and everyone else. In a single stroke, the idea of evolution by natural selection unified the realm of life, meaning, and purpose with the realm of space and time, cause and effect, mechanism and physical law" (Dennett, 1995:21).

Cautions against the persistent efforts at denigration, past and present, include the demonstration that "the myth seems to have been already current that Darwin was a mere naturalist and an amasser of facts—a man of limited intellect and small capacity for abstract thought" (Ghiselin, 1969:136). That "myth" stems from Darwin's own times. His publisher, John Murray, sent the manuscript of the *Life and Letters of Charles Darwin*, edited by his son Francis Darwin to the Duke of Argyll for review. The Duke, who had been one of the pallbearers at Darwin's funeral in Westminster Abbey, wrote back that while Darwin "was the greatest observer that ever lived," he was also remarkable for "the extraordinary defectiveness of his philosophical faculties" (quoted in Paston, 1932:169–170).

Although even so sophisticated a student of evolutionary biology as the late George Gaylord Simpson made the claim that "Darwin was no philosopher" (Simpson, 1964:50), the converse was stated in convincing fashion at the same time (Mayr, 1964:xix), and the subsequently published full-length treatment of his command of philosophy concluded that he was "a century ahead of his time" in that field, and that "Those who condemn Darwin as incompetent in philosophy do so either from ignorance of his ideas, or because they, personally, would prefer to reject his conclusions" (Ghiselin, 1969:159). While this nicely places the Duke of Argyll, Simpson clearly does not fit in either of those categories, and it would seem that his assessment was really more a reflection of his own lack of background in philosophy. As we shall see, Darwin's success was the result of an almost unique example of the combination of both scientific and philosophical sophistication.

In similar fashion, Darwin's expository style has been denigrated, starting with his own contemporaries and continuing right up to the present. In Huxley's words, "exposition is not Darwin's *forte* and his English is sometimes wonderful"—where "wonderful" is something "to be wondered at" (Huxley letter to Sir Michael Foster in 1888, quoted in L. Huxley, ed., 1901, vol. II, p. 203; and see Barzun, 1958:32). Darwin himself contributed to this assessment in his autobiography, saying, "I have as much difficulty as ever in expressing myself clearly and concisely" (Darwin, 1887:80). This continues to be accepted at face value in some quarters, as for example in the scornful reference to "Darwin's diffuse style of illustrating his thesis by anecdote after anecdote, one rambling natural history after another" (Shipman, 1994:92).

In addition, he is accused of exhibiting the "amateurish foible" of being "careless about footnotes and proper attributions" (Shipman, 1994:92)—this by an author who got both the page and the quote wrong for Darwin's famous line in the *Origin* that "Light will be thrown on the origin of man and his history" (Darwin, 1859:488).[1] As an example of Darwin's supposed carelessness, he is charged with having made an "interesting slip" in the 1858 letter to Lyell in which he referred to the "sketch" of his major thesis as having been written out in 1842 (Shipman, 1994:31). This is considered a "slip" because the author asserts it as fact that Darwin's "sketch" was written in 1844. Presumably his mention of the supposedly erroneous earlier date was a demonstration of his willingness to distort the facts to stake a claim to intellectual priority (Shipman, 1994:31).

Again, the carelessness is actually on the part of the accuser since the truth of the matter is that Darwin did write his "Sketch" in 1842. The "Sketch" of June 1842, running to 35 pencil-written pages, was the basis of what was expanded into the "Essay" of the summer of 1844 (F. Darwin, ed., 1887, vol. I, p. 68). At 230 pages, that "Essay" could actually count as a book, and it contained many of the phrases later used in the *Origin*. Long after his death, both the "Sketch" and the "Essay" were eventually published in the first decade of our own waning century along with a valuable "Introduction" by Darwin's son Francis (F. Darwin, ed., 1909). This was all subsequently reprinted in 1958 with the addition of the paper by Alfred Russel Wallace that had been read on his behalf at the Linnean Society of London in July of 1858. These are collected in a volume edited by Sir Gavin de Beer, who also contributed a Preface that reflected on a century of the developments in evolutionary thought set in motion by Darwin's extraordinary initial contribution (de Beer, ed., 1958).

Darwin's detractors, anthropological and other, have tended to identify several specific areas of presumed deficiency in each general aspect of treatment—for example his supposed weaknesses in scholarship, philosophy, and writing. When specialists in each of these realms have examined Darwin's

---

1 Shipman (1994:23) cites Darwin's words as having been located on page 449, and renders the quote as it had been modified for the subsequent editions where he had expanded it to read, "Much light…"

performance, it is interesting to note the extraordinarily high marks they have generally given him. These realms are not absolutely independent of each other, and a certain inevitable crossover will take place in the consideration of each. Since his performance can only be assessed in terms of what he wrote, it is reasonable to start with the assessment of Darwin as a writer.

DARWIN AS A WRITER

Consistent with the repeated grumbles he articulated about his struggles with written expression, his daughter, Henrietta Litchfield, noted that "He did not write with ease," and "He corrected a great deal" (F. Darwin, ed., 1887, vol. I, p. 130). However, her brother added another perspective when he stated that their father's writing was, "above all things, direct and clear" and "characterized by a simplicity bordering on naïveté, and in its absence of pretence" (F. Darwin, ed., 1887, vol. I, p. 131). I well remember my own reaction on first reading the *Origin* when I was in high school almost exactly fifty years ago. Instead of finding it "difficult" or abstruse, it was so transparently clear that I felt a certain sense of disappointment. I had anticipated that some sort of revelatory initiation would have been my reward after a long hard struggle. Instead, the book was simply the voice of common sense articulating in chatty and friendly fashion what seemed patently obvious, and I was at a loss then to understand what all the fuss was about. Of course, it was not obvious before he said it, and it is a measure of his genius that he was able to generalize about the complex interrelationships of the natural world in a fashion that made them seem almost self-evident to his readers.

More than one analyst has noted that "He used everyday terminology to convey precise and definite meanings with elegance and clarity" (Ghiselin, 1969:189). Even more than that, "no major works of science have ever been concerned more profoundly or in a more revolutionary way with Man and Nature than Darwin's *The Descent of Man* and *The Origin of Species*," and, "unlike almost all other major seminal works in science, they were quite accessible in language and ideas to the general lay educated public" (Leatherdale, 1983:6). As many of us have learned through painful experience, rendering the complexities and mechanisms of the natural world in written form is not an easy thing to do. Consequently it should be perfectly obvious why Darwin felt it necessary to correct a great deal and why he commented on the difficulties he had in being clear and concise. Good writing is hard work, and, since Darwin's writing is extraordinarily good, it should hardly come as a surprise to discover that he struggled to make it so.

In line with those who have chosen to portray Darwin as a narrow and limited figure who was unaware of the richness and dimensions of his cultural contemporaries, the author of the Introduction to the 1968 edition of *The Origin* opined, "Presumably he would have approved no more of the works of his contemporary, George Eliot, than she did of *The Origin*" (Burrow, 1968:12). A more recent appraisal, however, "controverts both these assumptions" (Beer, 1983:266). In contrast to the claim that he was only interested in "light" fiction where the heroine was pretty and there was a happy ending (Burrow, 1968:12), the record shows that he was fully conversant with both contemporary philosophy and literature. Early in 1859, even before he delivered the manuscript of *The Origin* to his publisher in London, Darwin had purchased Eliot's *Adam Bede* as soon as it appeared. In the book-lists of his Notebook, he gave it "the rarest of comments": "Excellent" (Beer, 1983:266).

George Eliot (Marian Evans Lewes) on her part, after some initial reservations, became similarly impressed with *The Origin*. Her husband, George Henry Lewes, had been given an advance copy to review for *Blackwood's* (the book's formal date of publication was November 24, 1859). In her journal entry for November 23, Eliot noted, "We began Darwin's work on 'The Origin of Species' tonight. It seems not to be well written: though full of interesting matter, it is not impressive for want of luminous and orderly presentation" (quoted in Haight, ed., 1954, vol. III, p. 214). Her opinion changed as she became more familiar with it. In her journal for November 24, 1859, she wrote: "A divine day. I walked out and Mrs. Congreve joined me. Then music, 'Arabian Nights,' and Darwin" (quoted in Cross, ed., 1885, vol. II, p. 105). Eventually she concluded that Darwin had contributed a "step towards brave clearness and honesty" and that *The Origin* "will have a great effect in the scientific world" (letter to Madame Bodichon, December 5, 1859, quoted in Cross, ed., 1885, vol. II, p. 108). Not only was she right in that prediction, but it went on to have an enormous impact on the literary world as well—including her own contributions, as for example in *Middlemarch* (Levine, 1986:60). Her only complaint, in direct contrast to that of the "blotting paper" school of thought, was that it was "sadly wanting in illustrative facts" (Cross, ed., 1885, vol. II, p. 108).

In fact, when Darwin had submitted his manuscript, he apologized to his publisher, John Murray, because it was "without references to authorities and without long catalogues of facts" (quoted in Paston, 1932:168), which is why he persisted in referring to a 500-page book as an "Abstract." He had intended to include the word "Abstract" in the title, but Murray objected and it was dropped, though it remained in the text (Burrow, 1968:34). Despite its dearth of extensive references and documentation, no one ever questioned the accuracy of the examples Darwin chose to cite or the fact that an enormous amount of observation lay behind the case he was presenting. His reputation as a thoroughly competent biologist had been solidly established by his exhaustive four-volume treatment of the Cirrepedia—the barnacles—of the world (Darwin, 1851a, 1851b, 1854a, 1854b). Although the claim has been made that his "proliferation of other works reeks of avoidance and self-protectiveness" (Shipman, 1994:26), both Joseph Dalton Hooker and Thomas Henry Huxley later wrote to Francis Darwin that his father's "barnacle work" was one of the wisest moves that he had made (Hyman, 1959:24). Recently, the British moral philosopher Mary Midgley has concurred by declaring that the eight years of his barnacle work was "no mere displacement activity but an admirable tactic" (Midgley, 1995:1197, agreeing with the treatment by Darwin's most recent biographer: Browne, 1995:472, 507).

Among those who have realized the effectiveness of his rhetorical skills, one appraiser, using "The methods...of modern literary criticism" (Hyman, 1959:70), has claimed that *The Origin* can be regarded as "a dramatic poem of a special sort" (ibid., p. 26). In fact, despite the denigration that Darwin took "no delight in words as such and had little feeling for literature" (Burrow, 1968:12), his reading lists for the years from the late 1830s through the 1850s show him ranging from Shakespeare and Montaigne through Sir Walter Scott and Thomas Carlyle. He acknowledged his fondness for Byron, Coleridge, Gray, Shelley, and the historical plays of Shakespeare. Among the books he kept in his cabin on the *Beagle* besides Humboldt's *Personal Narrative of Travels* and Lyell's *Principles of Geology* was Milton's blank-verse epic *Paradise Lost* (Bölsche, 1906:83; Browne, 1995:176, 211). The volume of Milton's poetry was "the one book he never left behind when he set out on his isolated land-journeys from the *Beagle*" (Beer, 1983:31–32). One can even hear Miltonian echoes in passages such as the one in which he evokes the metaphor of the "tangled bank" (Hyman, 1959), and in the sonorous last sentence of *The Origin,* which starts "There is a grandeur in this view of life..." (Darwin, 1859:490).

The writer who likened *The Origin* to poetry even went so far as to note that the language sometimes "gets quite Biblical" and could constitute "something like a sacred writing" (Hyman, 1959:34). Whether or not it warrants that apotheosis, another comparably qualified critic has declared it to be the "summa of the 'literature of fact' of the nineteenth century" (White, 1976:43). The same analyst generalized even further in concluding that *The Origin* "must rank as a classic in any list of the great monuments of literature" (ibid., p. 37). Of course, denigrations of Darwin's work date right back to his own time, and his publisher's editor, Whitwell Elwin, spoke of his works as being "full of puerilities, and the productions of an inferior, not at all of a master mind" (quoted in Paston, 1932:270).

Closer to the present, the eminent historian and irascible critic Jacques Barzun became almost choleric at the idea that some have treated *The Origin* as "a masterpiece of English literature," regarding this as "an opinion which can only come from revelation by faith and not from the experience of reading the work" (Barzun, 1958:79). He concluded that "Darwin does not belong with the great thinkers of mankind" (ibid., p. 84), and that "the *Origin of Species* was greater as an event than as a book" (ibid., p. 30). That reaction bears a striking resemblance to the way in which Darwin was treated by his French critics, starting in the latter part of the nineteenth century, and, coming from Barzun almost a century later, it is more an indication of the continuity of French intellectual traditions than of an attempt to deal with the issues themselves. Barzun, in fact, can stand as a living manifestation of the themes of French antievolutionary thought explored at length by Stebbins (1974:117–163) and Boesiger (1980:309–321).

DARWIN'S USE OF METAPHOR

Adding to its power, as many critics have remarked, is Darwin's extraordinary and skillful use of metaphor. One of these has noted that "The exuberantly metaphorical drive of the language of *The Origin* was proper to its topic" (Beer, 1983:38); and this, in the words of another, "is one of the reasons for the unusually wide and powerful effect of Darwin on general ideas and literature" (Leatherdale, 1983:4). The very use of the term "natural selection" had the effect of reifying "Nature" and has led to the skeptical rhetorical query, "does nature select?" (Young, 1985:79). Furthermore, there are metaphorical implications in his use of terms such as "struggle," "chance," "accident," and many more. It was a technique that he had adopted from Lyell, and, as Lyell had used the "metaphor of decipherment" (Beer, 1983:44) to uncover the "history of the globe" (Lyell, 1830:88), Darwin applied it in the attempt to gain insight into the history of the living forms that have been earth's denizens. Another literary commentator mined the *Poetics* for Aristotle's claim that "to be a master of metaphor...is...a sign of genius, since a good metaphor implies an intuitive perception of the similarity in dissimilars" (Hyman, 1959:33). "By this criterion," he declared, "Darwin displayed genius as morphologist and metaphorist alike" (idem), and he noted further that Darwin's

43

approach was "Perhaps not so far as it might seem from Proust's comparable venture in comprehending the duration of past time" (ibid., p. 34).

Darwin presented his case in narrative fashion, and some readers ranging from his own contemporaries right on up to the present day objected to his storytelling style (Shipman, 1994:92). "Not properly scientific" was the feeling of those who took their science rather too seriously. As our postmodern world approaches the millennium and the intent of an author or a text has been demoted to a position of lesser status than that of how it can be read (Kendrick, 1995:12), surely Charles Darwin has earned his ultimate vindication. Umberto Eco's latest *tour de force* "reminds us of the authoritarianism of narrative itself, the eternal dictator who is the story teller" (Kelly, 1995:9). In retrospect, it is abundantly clear that Darwin knew full well that "Only by telling a story can you tell if an idea is valid" (idem). Darwin told story after story, and whatever the ambiguities that emerge from attempts at deconstruction, the overarching point toward which they were all directed remains unquestioned and unrefuted.

Darwin's use of metaphor, however, was not just a matter of giving his writing the power to engage the attention of his readers, though it also had that effect. It has been argued that what impelled him to choose that form of presentation was that he had reason to think that one of his intellectual models, Sir John F. W. Herschel, would not accept the unadorned framework of his argument as constituting an acceptable manifestation of scientific logic. Herschel was an astronomer, a philosopher of science, and the author of *Preliminary Discourse on the Study of Natural Philosophy,* a work that had a profound influence on Darwin, who read it during his last year at Cambridge and again in 1838 (Herschel, 1830; Ruse, 1975:164). Since the nature of the available biological data did not lend itself to the precise form of quantification demanded by Herschel's vision of the logic of science, Darwin clothed "the bare logical skeleton of his argument...with the plausible and relevant imagery of his metaphors and analogies. This was never a question of abandoning science for mere rhetorical fiction and fancy; Darwin's metaphors did a full scientific job" (Manier, 1978:156). In Herschel's eyes, however, Darwin failed to accomplish his purpose, and that redoubtable figure is quoted as having denigrated natural selection as "the law of higgledy-piggledy" (quoted in F. Darwin, ed., 1887, vol. II, p. 241).

While Darwin suggested that it might have been possible to present his case without resorting to the use of metaphor, at least one analyst has argued that this could not have been done: "I hold a view of the scientific uses of metaphor which denies that Darwin's metaphorical expressions could have been replaced by completely literal statements setting forth the core of his theory" (Manier, 1978:169–170). At the base of this argument is the suggestion that "At least two key concepts, population and chance, were not readily express- ible and manageable within the context of that scientific discourse which was the common and uncontested possession of Darwin and his contemporaries" (ibid., p. 70). Darwin understood full well that populations were not mere aggregates but in fact were structured groups that had to be considered in the context of the coadaptation of organism and environment. In his perception of chance, he recognized the impossibility of reducing causal chains to single sources. This could be dealt with metaphorically, but could not profitably be reduced to the simple equations preferred by formal logicians, which is one reason why Herschel found Darwin's argument so vexing (idem).

Far from being a mindless "laundry-list," Darwin's seminal volume "almost shimmers with metaphysical promise" (Durant, 1983:466). The implications were clearly understood by his Christian opponents, such as Bishop Samuel Wilberforce, who was the anonymous author of the review of Darwin's *Origin* appearing in the July issue of *The Quarterly Review,* the main intellectual periodical produced by Darwin's own publisher, John Murray ([Wilberforce, 1860]; Paston, 1932:27). Darwin's former teacher at Cambridge and the person who had introduced him to geological field work in 1831 (Rudwick, 1974:113–114), the devout Biblical literalist Adam Sedgwick, had already made some of the same objections at the meetings of the Cambridge Philosophical Society and in his comments on *The Origin* in *The Spectator* in March of the same year (Sedgwick, 1860:285–286; Burkhardt, 1974:71). Nei- ther critic was characterized by the "ignorance" or "lack of understanding" with which they have often been charged, any more than are those of our contemporaries who now deny the value of Darwin's contributions. Sedgwick and Wilberforce, however, along with others such as Herschel and William Whewell, then Master of Trinity College at Cambridge and author of the three-volume *History of the Inductive Sciences* (Whewell, 1837), were seriously offended by Darwin's failure to incorporate "final causes" into his explanatory scheme—that is, his failure to depict a specific role for their Christian God.

DARWIN AND THE PHILOSOPHY OF SCIENCE

It will be instructive to consider a bit further one of Sedgwick's complaints, because that can give us a little insight into some of the assumptions concern- ing the philosophy of science that continue to hamper the appraisal of Darwin's accomplishment. Sedgwick claimed that Darwin's work had not followed proper inductive procedures and had in fact started by assuming what was to be proven (Sedgwick, 1860; Nelkin, 1977:11). There is a wondrous irony in the realization that, despite a century and more of accusations that Darwin was nothing more than a fact-gathering machine, his severest contemporary critics had in fact charged that his principal fault lay in his failure to confine his exposition to the theory-neutral compiling of data, which they held to be the appropriate manifestation of scientific behavior.

According to the generally accepted outlook of Darwin's contemporaries, the proper practice of science proceeded in an Aristotelian "inductive-deductive" fashion. This had been affirmed by Roger Bacon at Oxford in the thirteenth century and reasserted late in the sixteenth century by Sir Francis Bacon at Cambridge as the currents of the Reformation engaged English intellectual life (Losee, 1972:61 ff.). This then came to be regarded as the accepted way of doing things during the time when the practice of science took on a life of its own in the Enlightenment and subsequently. Compatible with the traditions of Enlightenment-style "natural theology," Darwin included quotes both from Sir Francis Bacon and from Whewell's Bridgewater Treatise as epigraphs facing the title page of his *Origin* (the latter being from Whewell, 1833). Later, in the "Autobiography" posthumously included in his *Life and Letters,* he asserted that he had always "worked on true Baconian principles, and without any theory collected facts on a wholesale scale" (quoted in Ghiselin, 1969:4; and in Beer, 1983:82).

Those words were right in line with what was expected for the time, but there has been a belated but growing realization that they do not constitute an accurate description of what he actually did. That "realization," however, is structured by the verbalizations of the philosophical orthodoxy of our own times, and these may well have added further aspects of confusion. For example, one reassessment of the Victorian scientific outlook has stated that "Darwin, like other scientists of his day, gave much lip service to 'induction,' and such hypocrisy has long obscured the real nature of scientific discovery" (Ghiselin, 1969:35). To label a recognition of the role of "induction" as "hypocrisy," however, implies an acceptance of the claim by the late Sir Karl Popper that "induction is a myth" and that "No 'inductive logic' exists" (Popper, 1978:148). In Popper's view, "induction was a myth which had been exploded by Hume" (ibid., p. 80), and science can only proceed through attempts at falsification or refutation of hypotheses by the application of deductive logic (ibid., p. 79).

For those who have accepted this at face value, Darwin's "long, involved inductive argument" (Hull, 1967:335) was at odds with what currently is perceived as the only proper—that is, the "hypothetico-deductive"—mode of scientific behavior (Hull, 1973:35). In contrast, however, at least one recent appraisal of Darwin's understanding of the philosophy of science has concluded that "Darwin applied, rigorously and consistently, the modern hypothetico-deductive scientific method" (Ghiselin, 1969:4). That in fact was the approach advocated by those voices of Cambridge-style "common sense" philosophy, Herschel and Whewell (Ruse, 1975:166, 180). Furthermore, in "sophisticated modernistic" fashion, his approach involved the development of "a testable hypothesis," which he then proceeded to confront "with as many potentially falsifying cases as he could" (Reed, 1978:213).

Interestingly enough, it was a lawyer who first clearly perceived the technique of presentation that Darwin had used to promote his argument. His publisher, John Murray, had taken the manuscript sight unseen at the recommendation of Sir Charles Lyell. He was completely baffled by what he read and felt that Darwin's theory was "as absurd as though one should contemplate a fruitful union of a poker and a rabbit" (quoted in Haynes, 1916:232). His chief editor, Whitwell Elwin, had gotten Lyell to suggest trimming the theory and concentrating on Darwin's own observations on pigeons. Elwin felt that this was "an admirable suggestion. Everyone is interested in pigeons" (quoted in Paston, 1932:172). To get another opinion, he asked a legal friend, George Pollock, to read it. Pollock did so and recommended that it deserved to be published, though it was "probably beyond the comprehension of any living scientist" (Haynes, 1916:232). In appreciation of the way in which Darwin developed his argument, Pollock noted that he "had brilliantly surmounted the formidable obstacles which he was honest enough to put in his own path" (quoted in idem). In essence, he had done his best at attempting falsification in full Popperian fashion. Belatedly, it has finally been realized that "his theory was necessarily hypothetical rather than traditionally inductive" (Beer, 1983:51).

While this may make the current analysts somewhat more happy with the status of Darwin's intellectual credibility, this is really more a comment on current philosophical dogma than it is on what Darwin actually did. Again, in diametric opposition to the assumptions of the "blotting paper" school, the assessment of his approach as indicated by the Notebooks that he generated between 1837 and 1839, a full 20 years before the appearance of *The Origin*, has concluded that "every factual inquiry was initiated and understood within a general theoretical framework" and that, from what they contain, it is not possible to reconstruct whether "...there was ever a point in his actual research program where he proceeded on 'pure Baconian principles'"

(Manier, 1978:116). Of course, this does not speak to his outlook over the previous five years when, as a scientific neophyte, he was circling the world on the *Beagle*. Even then, however, right from the time of his pre-*Beagle* field trip with Sedgwick in Wales, his geological work was basically involved with the testing of hypotheses (Browne, 1995:143, 186, 215). That was clearly evident during his first solo effort at geologizing on St. Jago in the Cape Verde Islands, and continued to be abundantly true for his following work in the Andes and subsequently (ibid., p. 294).

In 1860, a year after the appearance of his magnum opus, he wrote to Sir Charles Lyell that "Without the making of theories, I am convinced there would be no observations" (in F. Darwin, ed., 1887, vol. II, p. 315). Later in his "Autobiography" he reflected, "My mind seems to have become a kind of machine for grinding general laws out of large collections of facts"; and Francis, in his "Reminiscences" of his father, commented that "it was as though he were charged with theorising power ready to flow into any channel on the slightest disturbance, so that no fact, however small, could avoid releasing a stream of theory" (quoted in Beer, 1983:79). Writing to Henry Fawcett in 1861, Darwin declared, "How odd it is that anyone should not see that all observation must be for or against some view if it is to be of any service" (quoted by Gould, 1992:2).

A hypothesis can be regarded as "a provisional truth, presenting itself provisionally as fiction, and seeking ultimately to find confirmation" (Beer, 1983:80). No one realized that more acutely than Darwin, and it is this that accounts for the countless stories and scenarios that he related in *The Origin* and in his other books. The eventual perception of this aspect of Darwin's approach nearly a century after his death can be shown in the words "Darwin spent well over twenty years trying to refute his hypothesis of natural selection, and he was more immersed in the relevant problems and data than anyone before or since. The best argument for the irrefutability of his theory is his failure; indeed, it is the only argument for its irrefutability" (Reed, 1978:217).

When one takes all of this into account and adds it to the record of what he actually did, his whole outlook takes on a strikingly modern aspect (Ghiselin, 1969; Manier, 1978; Beer, 1983). I am going to go further, however, and suggest that Darwin was actually a major step ahead of where much of the philosophy of science now finds itself as the twentieth century comes to a close. The impact of the late Sir Karl Popper has been to denigrate induction and promote deduction to a position where it counts as the sole logical activity associated with the pursuit of science. Strict deductivism, however, "is a thesis of an intrinsically *frivolous* kind" since it cannot add to what is already known (Stove, 1982:99). In essence, it is tautology. The practice of strictly deductive procedures for the first millennium after the establishment of Christianity has led to this being characterized as "a period of depressing intellectual stagnation" (Mayr, 1982:308). Darwin, in his gentle nondogmatic way, declared that he was always skeptical of initial hypotheses and always ready to give one up when facts could be shown to be in opposition. He concluded, "this has naturally led me to distrust greatly deductive reasoning..." (Darwin, 1887:83).

Now that I have raised the specter of the "frivolous," I cannot resist the opportunity to quote from the oeuvre of I. Wright Drivell, that indubitably cross-cousin of I. Doolittle Wright and a fellow colleague in the Department of Homopathic Anthropopoetics at the University of Southern North Dakota at Hoople, an institution better known for the illuminating products of the current occupant of its General Electric chair, among them *The Definitive Biography of P. D. Q. Bach (1807–1742)?* (Schickele, 1976). Suitably couched in the Scottish meter of Robert Burns, Drivell's effusion is part of a longer opus that he called "Punctured Cladomania" and which first appeared in Brace (1988:133—the full verse appears at the end of Chapter 4). As the reader can easily see, it is a pretty characteristic bit of Drivell:

"Hypothetico-deductive;"
Jargon phrase that's so seductive;
Denies what might be called inductive
 For the view,
The known can never be productive
 Of the new.

But science viewed in such a way
Is nothing more than idle play;
For though the sun arose today,
 Yet to our sorrow,
Deduction cannot let us say
 'Twill rise tomorrow.

As early as his Notebooks of 1838, Darwin had declared his dedication to the "hypothetical-deductive" approach advocated by Herschel and Whewell, but first he noted that it was necessary "to establish a point as a probability by induction" and then test it deductively (F. Darwin, ed., 1887, vol. I, p. 93, vol. II, pp. 79, 286; Ghiselin, 1969:4; Manier, 1978:157). Interestingly enough, Huxley, quite in contrast to Sedgwick's appraisal, specifically lauded Darwin for precisely this approach in his review of *The Origin,* and noted that Darwin had proceeded "in exact accordance with the rule laid down by Mr. [John Stewart] Mill" ([Huxley], 1860:309). Although it was unsigned, as was the case with Wilberforce's review (1860), the identity of the author in both cases was universally known. Ironically, Darwin may never have read Mill's *System of Logic, Ratiocinative and Inductive...and the Methods of Scientific Investigation* (1843) before framing the structure of his own argument (Mill, 1843; Manier, 1978:194).

When we put Darwin's approach into the context of the history of philosophy, it is apparent that his vision of induction anticipated by the better part of a century that of the founder of Pragmatism, the American philosopher Charles Sanders Peirce, who, in contrast to Popper, started with the declaration that "All our knowledge may be said to rest upon *observed facts*" (in Buchler, ed., 1955:150). C. D. Broad once noted that although inductive reasoning may be regarded as the "scandal of Philosophy," it has "long been the glory of Science" (Broad, 1926:67). If the continuing current of Popperism still denies that induction has a legitimate role to play, it has provided no guidelines on how to acquire the information used in framing hypotheses (Brace, 1988). While some suggest that science proceeds by selection among randomly generated hypotheses, the skeptical appraiser will reply that hypotheses do not come out of "randomizers" (Midgley, 1982:126).

Although Darwin had transcended the outlook which stressed the claim that order in the world constitutes proof for the existence of a Designer, as had been defended by Archdeacon Paley (Paley, 1802; and see Darwin's rejection of this on page 87 of the edition of his "Autobiography" with the original omissions restored, published by Barlow, 1958), he had been much taken with the way in which Paley marshaled his case, and he adopted that technique to defend his "transmutation theory" (Manier, 1978:164). As has been realized, "Paley's form of argument, cumulative rather than deductive, was very much Darwin's own in *The Origin*" (Burrow, 1968:58; and see in Barlow, ed., 1958:32). Rather than confining himself to strict falsification in approved Popperian fashion, Darwin further concentrated on corroboration in the manner of his eighteenth-century Anglican predecessor, the Reverend Thomas Bayes, an approach now recognized by the designation "Bayesian statistical inference" (Iversen, 1984). Popper did allow a role for corroboration (Salmon, 1968:28), but it was based on a treatment of probability that was opposite to that commonly used in science: that is, the recommendation that one should focus on the most unlikely hypotheses because they are the easiest to refute (Popper, 1959:200, 1963:219). Darwin, however, followed in the tradition of what has been called "Bayes's Theorem" and attempted to provide "a more accurate and explicit portrayal of the interaction between assumptions, data, and conclusions than is evident in the superficially simple syllogisms of falsificationist logic" (Fisher, 1987:328).

Most practicing scientists would happily agree with the observation by the philosopher-physicist Gerald Holton that, in science, there are two meaningful types of statements: "namely, propositions concerning empirical matters of fact (which ultimately boil down to meter readings) and propositions concerning logic and mathematics (which ultimately boil down to tautologies)" (Holton, 1973:21). Whether induction is considered at the level of meter readings as Holton indicates or "the laws of probability" of John Maynard Keynes (Keynes, 1921; Broad, 1922:81), Darwin was indeed using an inductive-deductive approach quite in the manner that characterizes the best of science being done at the present time. The most recent appraisal of Darwin's standing from the point of view of current philosophy fully concurs (Dennett, 1995).

DARWIN AND THE HISTORY OF SCIENCE

The roots of that approach are indeed Baconian and right in the tradition of the Enlightenment and Natural Theology (Paley, 1802), but the course by which it was transmitted into the various branches of science as these became professionalized was fundamentally shaped by the Scottish Enlightenment. What has been referred to as "Scottish Philosophy," the Scottish "School of Common Sense," or "Scottish Realism" (McCosh, 1875) has been recognized as the source for the professionalization of the "hard sciences" (Olson, 1975). While it has not been stressed previously, an equally valid case can be made that Scottish Realism was of comparable importance for the development of professional geology via Sir Charles Lyell on the one hand and the development of professional biology on the other, and that the medium for the transmission of its outlook to the latter was none other than Charles Darwin.

Both his father and his grandfather had received their medical training in Edinburgh. Grandfather Erasmus' subsequent friendships and activities all showed a clear derivation from the outlook of the Scottish Enlightenment (Schofield, 1963), and the industrial Midlands with which their families and fortunes were associated owed more to that perception of the world than it did to the tides of Romanticism that had begun to make an increasing impact on London and the more urban southern portions of England (Rehbock, 1984). Charles Darwin himself spent the years 1825–1827 in Edinburgh, and, though much is usually made of his failure to benefit from the medical curriculum with which he was nominally associated, he had become involved in the study of natural history and, under the influence of the zoologist Dr. Robert Edmund Grant, he was an active participant in the Plinian Society, before which he made his first scientific presentation on March 27, 1827 (Gruber, 1974:80–81; Browne, 1995:82).

The stamp of Scottish Realism was evident in his outlook for the rest of his life (Manier, 1978:194). Darwin was suspicious of the extreme skepticism of David Hume and the Cartesian body-mind dualism of Dugald Stewart, and his own approach to such matters was somewhat more in line with that of the good Scottish Realist John Fleming (1785–1857), whose two-volume *Philosophy of Zoology* (1822) in his library was "exhaustively annotated" in Darwin's hand (Manier, 1978:60). It should be noted that Fleming's *"Philosophy"* comes a lot closer to what we would now call the "science" of zoology, though he did deal with issues that we now tend to regard as more characteristic of philosophy (Bryson, 1945:15). Fleming's treatment of *"Truth,"* for example, is right in line with the realist views of Thomas Reid and his successor, Dugald Stewart (Fleming, 1822, vol. I, p. 232).

In line with the tendency to use the term "philosophy" to include what is now meant by "science," Captain FitzRoy gave Darwin the nickname "Philos.," standing for "Ship's Philosopher," which was enthusiastically adopted by the crew of the *Beagle* (Browne, 1995:178, 195). The very word "scientist" was only coined by William Whewell three years after the *Beagle* left port on her literally revolution-making voyage (Sheets-Pyenson, 1984:580). Given the fundamental importance of Charles Darwin for the basic outlook of the biological sciences ever since, he should count as every bit as important for the transmission of the outlook of the Scottish Enlightenment into professional biology as Dalton was for professional chemistry and Kelvin for professional physics (Cardwell, ed., 1968; Olson, 1975).

DARWIN IN BIOLOGY

Now, while I have described Darwin's outlook as of "fundamental importance" for the biological sciences, it was not automatically so (Bowler, ed., 1968). Even during his own lifetime, while his "importance" was never in question and the concept of evolution was elevated to the status of a permanent issue in the minds of the public as well as in science, the mechanism that he had offered to account for evolution was rejected by the majority of his readers both lay and professional. By the end of the century, the only thing that Darwin's scientific readers held in common was "their rejection of creationism" (Mayr, 1991:99) and the "firm belief" not only that evolution had taken place but that it had been accomplished "by natural means" (ibid., p. 100). Few were willing to grant that those means referred to natural selection as Darwin had described it (for example, Osborn, 1894). By the time the first third of the twentieth century had elapsed, that stance had hardened to the point where Darwin's mechanism was considered to have been an interesting but unworkable intellectual gambit that warranted a footnote in the history of ideas but needed to be quietly put aside while the real mechanics were worked out (Nordenskiöld, 1928; Singer, 1931).

The retrospective discovery of Mendel's work, as the field of genetics was established during the first part of the century, did not change the way most scientists perceived the nature of Darwin's insights. The nature and reality of genetic shuffling and transmission could be tested and verified in the laboratory, but selection could not push the range of variation in a given species beyond the limits already observed (Morgan, 1916:154). All of that changed, however, when Hermann J. Muller, who was then at the University of Texas, took some of his fruit flies to a local doctor's office in 1926 and got them irradiated with X-rays (Muller, 1927; Pauly, 1987:179). In one shot, he got more mutations than had been found by all the other *Drosophila* workers together over the previous 15 years. Almost immediately, it was realized that Darwin's faith that inherited variants would constantly provide the material on which natural selection could operate to produce evolutionary change was a faith fully justified. Not long after that, J. B. S. Haldane concluded that mutations constituted exactly what Darwin had postulated as "the raw material on which selection acts" to produce organic evolution (Haldane, 1929:444).

The stage was now set, and the next decade saw the reinstitution of a fully Darwinian perspective as the "Synthetic Theory of Evolution"—sometimes called the "Neo-Darwinian Theory of Evolution." It was "synthetic" because it integrated the perspectives of genetics, field and laboratory biology, and paleontology. The contributors included Haldane, Ronald A. Fisher, Sewall Wright, Theodosius Dobzhansky, Julian Huxley, Ernst Mayr, and George Gaylord Simpson, to name them roughly in the order of the dates of their initial contributions. As the only surviving member of that extraordinary group, Mayr has told its story in splendid fashion (Mayr, 1982).

From that time on, Darwin's principal ideas have continued to remain at the core of the thinking of evolutionary biology. His own genetic theory of "pangenesis" and his flirtation with the inheritance of acquired characteristics have been quietly discarded, but, consistent with the way he phrased it at the end of the "Introduction" to all the editions of *The Origin,* "Natural Selection" continues to be regarded as "the main but not exclusive means of modification" driving the course of organic evolution (Darwin, 1859:6). Inevitably, there have been major additions and further theoretical elaborations.

The world of molecular biology has enormously expanded our horizons. Among the most significant additions it has been able to provide was the demonstration of the implications of the structure of DNA—deoxyribonucleic acid—the basic stuff of heredity (Watson and Crick, 1953). This not only has enabled us to understand how the genetic material could duplicate itself in cell division and from generation to generation, but it also has allowed us to understand the atomic and molecular mechanics of exactly how the genetic blueprint operates to construct a tangible organism—a phenotype—from its basic chemical constituents (Anfinsen, 1959). Among the changes in our perceptions that this understanding has produced is a heightened awareness of the different roles of the adaptive and nonadaptive portions of both the genotype and the phenotype (Nei, 1987).

Again, as we look back, Darwin clearly understood this where the phenotype was concerned, and expressed its significance with a clarity that has yet to be surpassed. Over the past several decades, the discovery by molecular biologists of nonadaptive parts of organic structure has led to the development of a movement that has sometimes been labeled "non-Darwinian" evolution (King and Jukes, 1969). Darwin, however, had clearly recognized the difference in significance of adaptive and nonadaptive parts of organisms. In his own words, "adaptive characters, although of the utmost importance to the welfare of the being, are almost valueless to the systematist" (Darwin, 1859:427). Conversely, he recognized that "as a general rule...the less any part of the organisation is concerned with special habits, the more important it becomes for classification" (ibid., p. 414). In these phrases, he identified the differences in the problems faced by students of adaptation and students of classification with a clarity that has seldom been equaled since that time. Since the molecular focus on the distinction between adaptive and nonadaptive features can simply be regarded as "an extension of the synthetic theory of evolution," the label non-Darwinian is "misleading" and would better be simply called the "neutralist theory" and dealt with as Darwin had outlined it in the first place (Ayala, 1974:693).

Beyond the world opened up by the techniques of molecular biology, but in part made possible by that, the wealth of biological dimensions disclosed by genetic research has forced us to take account of realms that could not have been dealt with, given what was available to Darwin. It was his insight that selection works at the level of the individual (Mayr, 1992:24), and, with that perception, he did not follow Wallace's espousal of group selection (Wallace, 1864:clvi; Gould, 1980:32). However, now that we can deal with processes at the level of the gene (the "replicator" of Dawkins, 1976)—a concept not available to Darwin—it is possible to conceptualize more than a single realm where selection can operate. To deal with the differences in selection working on the gene, the individual, or, at a more inclusive populational unit, the terms "level" and "vehicle" have been used (Wilson and Sober, 1994), though there are reasons for preferring a less restrictive term such as "domain" (Williams, 1992; Brace, 1994). Another kind of complication is added when relationships are reckoned in terms of "inclusive fitness" and "kin selection" (Hamilton, 1964; Wilson, 1975). In each instance, however, the logic applied is essentially what Darwin had used to deal with selection operating on the individual, and this is still the main focus of attention in contemporary evolutionary biology.

As most of the productive professionals in the business acknowledge, the biological sciences today derive in large measure from the outlook established by Charles Darwin starting in the middle years of the nineteenth century. Darwin, however sui generis he may seem, did not spring full-blown from an intellectual vacuum. As was true for those who can be credited with establishing the canons of professional scholarship in physics, chemistry, and geology, his intellectual style was firmly rooted in the traditions of the Scottish Enlightenment of the previous century (Merton, 1938). Those roots in turn were derived from the spreading outlook of the Protestant Reformation where it was assumed that the human mind was capable of investigating given issues, assembling the available evidence, and coming to an understanding, not just of what was right and what was not, but of how the world works in general (White, 1896; Becker, 1932; and, in narrow application, Olson, 1975). In essence, it is the outlook of professional science. It takes nothing away from the phenomenal genius of Charles Darwin to recognize him as the conduit by which this outlook was transmitted into what has become professional biology. One can only hope that, in time, this will come to be recognized in professional anthropology as well.

≈   ≈

ACKNOWLEDGMENTS

This manuscript was prepared as part of the presentation "Evolution in Anthropology: Or, the Once and Future Thing," given on January 15, 1996, as a unit in the series "Anthropology, Postwar/Premillennial: Intergenerational Conversations" at the Department of Anthropology, University of Chicago. Because the whole preparation was longer than could be given in the time allotted, the material covered in the present paper was omitted from the actual presentation. I would like to express my gratitude to Marshall D. Sahlins and George W. Stocking, Jr., for inviting me to participate in the series they generated, thus giving me the impetus for producing the present paper. My thanks and appreciation are also extended to Dr. Richard J. Kaplan of the Rand Corporation, Santa Monica, California, for his long-time support in providing valuable references and sources. I am also indebted to Stanley Garn and Ernst Mayr for critical reading and valuable suggestions.

CHAPTER 2

The Fate of the "Classic" Neanderthals: A Consideration of Hominid Catastrophism (1964)[1]

Prologue

In popular thought, few subjects are more closely identified with the interests of professional biological anthropologists than the perennial Neanderthal "problem." That Neanderthals are thought of in terms of a "problem" or a "question" is remarkably similar to the way in which Germans thought about Jews prior to World War II. In both instances, the objects of such treatment were cast in the role of a collective "other" whose differences have been assumed to indicate the extent of their failure to qualify for fully human status. The treatment of Jews in such a fashion is no longer considered defensible, but there are none left to query the pro forma denigration of Neanderthal differences as indicators of their less than human capabilities. That I should put a consideration of the Neanderthals near the beginning of this book, then, should qualify as par for the course for a biological anthropologist whose main interest is in the course and dynamics of human evolution.

When I was in graduate school four decades ago, it was accepted as a matter of general credence that nothing resembling Neanderthal form could possibly have been ancestral to living human beings. "Too crude by half," seemed to be the general feeling, though it was never really spelled out. Features of Neanderthal form such as the thickened bony arches curved above the eye sockets of the skull—the brow ridges; the lack of an indentation below the cheek bone—the "canine fossa"; the bulbous shape of the rear of the skull—the "occipital bun"; various aspects of curvature in the long bones; and a series of other "peculiarities" were all labeled "specializations" that were treated as stigmata of "inferiority" that presumably doomed the European Neanderthals to an abrupt and mysterious extinction at the same time that people of "modern" appearance suddenly replaced them.

As a general rule, the anthropologists who have presented the "facts" of this scenario have rather coyly avoided discussions concerning the mechanisms driving the posited changes, but a variety of nonanthropological writers have been much less reluctant. H. G. Wells was one of the earliest to take advantage of the possibilities in his story "The Grisly Folk" (1921), and, a generation later, William Golding

---

1 Parts of this paper were read at the 1962 meetings of the American Anthropological Association at Chicago, Illinois, November 18, 1962. I should like to express my gratitude to M. L. Brace and R. V. Humphrey for the illustrations.

dragged that theme out to book length in *The Inheritors* (1955), a tedious tale which shows that even a Nobel Prize–winning novelist cannot create gripping dialogue if his protagonists are constrained to communicate in grunts and gestures and have not quite gotten the hang of articulate speech.

Whatever the drawbacks of these efforts as examples of "literature," the anthropological world has accepted them with enthusiasm, and the structure of their assumptions has been fed back into the field as consistent with the findings of "science." This is clearly evident in the productions of Chris Stringer (*In Search of the Neanderthals,* by Stringer and Gamble, 1993) and Ian Tattersall (*The Last Neanderthal,* 1995), and in the efforts of the more serious of their camp followers such as Roger Lewin (*In the Age of Mankind,* 1989) and Jamie Shreeve (*The Neanderthal Enigma,* 1995). It goes down from there, however, and a number of journalistic opportunists have enthusiastically pandered to the legions of what Umberto Eco has called "lobotomized mass-media illiterates" (Eco, 1984:71). Most prominent among these is Jean Auel, the author of a series of steamy pot-boilers beginning with *The Clan of the Cave Bear* in 1980. The genre continues with John Darnton's *Neanderthal* (1996) and Petru Popescu's *Almost Human* (1996), and more are sure to follow.

More than 40 years ago, the late English anatomist-anthropologist Sir Wilfrid E. Le Gros Clark observed that "On purely morphological grounds (and without reference to paleontological evidence), there is no certain argument why *H. neanderthalensis* could not be ancestral to *H. sapiens*" (Clark, 1955:45). That was in fact quite a radical admission for the time, and one which has been dismissed a priori by most recent writers on the field including virtually all I have cited above. Clark followed up that intriguing comment with the conventional disclaimer, "But, in this particular instance, the fossil record shows clearly that such was not the case," (idem). Yet his treatment of that fossil record produced no such demonstration, and, I should add, no subsequent treatment of the fossils available has supported that conclusion despite what the authors have claimed. I was intrigued by his admission of the possibility of a Neanderthal ancestry for "modern" human form, and, since the actual fossil record did not refute it, I was drawn into the investigation of just why the overwhelming majority of paleoanthropologists simply dismissed the possibility out of hand. The result was the paper "The Fate of the 'Classic' Neanderthals: A Consideration of Hominid Catastrophism," published in *Current Anthropology* in February 1964.

The way *Current Anthropology* does such things is to send its feature articles to a series of specialists who prepare commentaries that are then sent back to the initial author for rebuttal. They had actually invited a group of 50 scholars to participate, and some 16 prepared critiques. I have omitted those here to spare the general reader the tedium of the technical nit-picking of academic debate. My own original presentation is reproduced here just as I originally wrote it, and, as I reread it, I cringe at the self-importance that emerges all too often from the somber scholarly prose. The reader will note that I also used the term "man" to designate the collective human phenomenon as virtually everyone did a generation ago. Recently anthropology has become sensitized—in fact, traumatized—by the charge that this has "sexist" implications. This has left us without a word to refer to ourselves as a collective entity since virtually every other possible alternative has the same problem. The French simply shrug their shoulders and continue to use *l'homme* to refer to the species as a whole, philosophically noting that all French nouns are categorized by gender but that there is no sexist implication about it. The Germans add a third gender, noting that the epitome of nubile femininity, *das Mädchen*, is designated by a neuter noun. It's a curious irony that English speakers, who do not class their nouns by gender, are the only ones who are paralyzed by the problem of trying to find a single nonsexist word to use for the species as a whole. I have not tried to fix this here and have left my manuscript as it was originally written.

Aside from those officially asked to comment by *Current Anthropology*, I had also sent a copy to my favorite uncle, John Donaldson, then Professor of Anatomy at the University of Pittsburgh Medical School. I knew he would be interested, and indeed, he wrote back that he and his wife Dorothy, my father's eldest sister, had read aloud to each other Henry Fairfield Osborn's *Men of the Old Stone Age* (1916) early in their marriage. Clearly he was fully familiar with the prevailing orthodoxy, and he predicted that the reactions of the profession at large would appear as if impelled by exhortations "shouting 'To your tents, oh Israel,' 'Man the barricades!' and 'Summoning Spirits from the vasty deep' to gather at Piltdown to the rallying cry of 'Save our Family Tree' and organising a 'Ban the Neanderthal' march on the British Museum." He went on to note that I would find myself "having the same feeling of being accepted enthusiastically that the men of the Seventh Cavalry had at the Little Big Horn." He also noted "with some trepidation…the injection of humor here and there. Just think how such a thing might undermine the science." As he continued, the defenders of "Truth" in the business, "frozen by professional pride and jealousy, would have to become human if a little humor could be injected into the approach. Just think, though, of the stigma of being one of those who got Anthropology referred to as the 'Happy Science'." John had been a devotee of the limerick, though, I should hasten to add, only of the suitably expurgated versions of that genre. His own, however, were produced long before I had discovered the versifications of the Department of Homopathic Anthropopoetics, at the University of Southern North Dakota at Hoople. Some of the latter adorn a series of the subsequent chapters in this book, and I like to think that, though John's long and happy life had ended before they were extruded into the public domain, something of his spirit lives on in them.

Although the general theoretical model first presented here is just as valid today, albeit largely ignored, there is one point on which I was clearly wrong. The Mount Carmel fossils at Skhūl and the Qafzeh fossils near Nazareth, in Israel, pre-date the "'classic'" Neanderthals of Iraq and western Europe by 50,000 years and more (and see Chris Stringer's graphic depiction of the changed status of the dating of the Israeli fossils, Stringer, 1990). On the other hand, despite the widespread assertions that they prove the existence of "modern" form while full Neanderthals were still around, it should be abundantly clear that those two supposedly "modern" groups are significantly different from each other and do not represent the same phenomenon. Their aspects of "modernity" are not the same and could only have arisen from long-term responses to different selective force regimes in different parts of the world. These issues are the subject of separate treatment in Chapters 6, 7, and 8, and in the Prologue to Chapter 12.

My principal regret about the writing of this paper is an inadvertent omission. One of the figures who was invited to submit comments (and who did not do so) was Sherwood L. Washburn, now Professor Emeritus at the University of California, Berkeley. After the paper appeared in print, Washburn wrote me in high dudgeon on March 23, 1964, beginning with "Dear Brace" and signing himself "Washburn." (Over the previous several years he had written to me as "Dear Loring" and signed himself "Sherry"—in fact, at his request, I had sent him a prepublication draft of my manuscript). In the midst of the invective in this and a subsequent letter of April 13, he had raised a very real and valid point. I had made the case that specific cultural developments such as cutting tools and the use of fire in food preparation had predictable consequences for the maintenance of particular aspects of robustness such as tooth size (and note the follow-up to this in Chapters 6 and 8). As Washburn implied in his letters and references to his own published work, my examples appeared to be a focused application of suggestions concerning the importance of tools in influencing the general course of human evolution that he had previously made in print (Washburn, 1959, 1960). He was absolutely right. I could only reply somewhat lamely that it was a shame that he had not responded in print when invited by *Current Anthropology* so that the issues could have been brought to the attention of the anthropological readership.

In fact, his general recommendations had been a part of my own graduate education, and I had incorporated them so thoroughly into my own viewpoint that I had lost track of the specific identity of their source. Sherry Washburn was one of the major figures responsible for helping biological anthropology incorporate the dynamics of evolutionary biology after World War II, and this was just one among many points where his influence played an important role in steering the field in productive directions.

All of the main points of my 1964 paper remain valid today even though the complexity of the whole picture has undergone a quantum increase. It all seemed so patently obvious to me then, and I felt that once I had laid the matters out, my readers would say, "Why, yes, of course!" and forthwith attempt to deal with the question by the simple application of an evolutionary perspective. Nothing of the sort happened, and the same willful overlooking of the data immediately before us continues as a matter of course as the current century has come to an end (and note, for example, the most recent commentary by Ian Tattersall and Jeffrey Schwartz, "Hominids and Hybrids: The Place of Neanderthals in Human Evolution," in the June 22, 1999, issue of the *Proceedings of the National Academy of Sciences*). When I wrote that paper, I also included suggestions concerning key matters in understanding the course of human evolution. These too have been universally overlooked, though I went on and developed some at considerably greater length. Those efforts are documented in the subsequent chapters in this volume. However, since the basics were all laid out in *Current Anthropology* in 1964, this is the logical place to start.

$\backsim$ $\backsim$

Were this the skeleton of the oldest man, then the oldest man was a freak, and in antediluvian times, as today, there must have been malformed human beings such as are welcomed by the adherents of the teaching of the descent of mankind from the apes... (Mayer, 1864:16).

At the time when Darwin and Huxley first claimed that man evolved from a primate similar to the anthropoids of today, little evidence substantiated by palaeontological facts was available. In the meantime, however, quite a number of fossil forms have been recovered all of which may justifiably be claimed as "missing links." Yet, strangely enough, the more such intermediate types came to light, the less was the readiness of acknowledging them as ancestors of *Homo sapiens*.[2] In many cases the skepticism apparently was the last bastion from which the final acceptance of Darwin's theory could be warded off with a certain air of scientism (Weidenreich, 1943a:44).

Interpretation of the hominid fossil record has inevitably been colored by the climate of opinion prevalent at the time of the discovery of the major pieces of evidence. What are now recognized as being the earliest known hominids were not the earliest fossil hominids to be known, which may account in large measure for the fact that their essential humanity was not recognized at the time of their discovery. When the first Australopithecine was found in 1924 (Dart, 1925:195–199) there already were candidates for all the postulated stages of human evolution, and the suggestion that this was anything more than just another fossil ape was greeted with a notable lack of enthusiasm (Bather, 1925:947; Keith, 1925c:11, 1925d:462–463; Smith, 1925:235; Woodward, 1925:235–236; Hooton, 1946:288).

At this time the earliest known hominid was *Pithecanthropus erectus* (now properly considered *Homo erectus* by Weidenreich, 1940:383, 1943b:246; Mayr, 1951:113), and even the most enthusiastic proponents of the human status of this fossil had to concede that if culture had indeed been associated with the population of which it was a member, then that culture must have been of the crudest recognizable sort (Hooton, 1946:298). Pithecanthropus was widely hailed as Haeckel's "missing link" (Haeckel, 1899b:469; Miller, 1929) and was considered to exist on the very borderline

---

2 This reaches its extreme in the writings of Boule, Osborn Keith, Hooton, and Vallois who deny human ancestral status to every substantial and well-dated fossil discovery that in any way differs from modern man (Boule, 1913, 1921, 1923, 1937; see also Schwalbe, 1913:601–603; Keith, 1915, 1925a. [1928], 1931; Osborn, 1919; Hooton, 1931:392–393; 1946:288, 298, 412–413; Boule and Vallois, 1957:92, 126, 145, 258).

of human and subhuman stages in evolution. With the bottom-most rung in the scale of human evolution presumably occupied, it took some 30 years and an abundance of evidence (Broom, 1939, 1947, 1950; Broom and Schepers, 1946; Broom and Robinson, 1947a and b, 1949a and b, 1950a, b, and c, 1952; Dart, 1948a, b, and c, 1949a, b, c, and d; Broom, Robinson, and Schepers, 1950; Robinson, 1952a and b, 1953a, b, and c, 1954, 1956; Le Gros Clark, 1955a and b; Leakey, 1959, 1960a and b) before the hominid status of the Australopithecines became generally acceptable (Bartholomew and Birdsell, 1953; Oakley, 1959; Brace, 1962a). Opinion is still far from being unanimous, and, despite the necessary relationship between Australopithecine anatomy and tool use (Keith, 1949:204; Bartholomew and Birdsell, 1953; Heberer, 1959b:418–419; Brace, 1962a and b), and the clear unbroken sequence of cultural evolution from the Oldowan to the atomic bomb (Leakey, 1936:40–56, 1954:66, 70; Cole, 1954:123, 131–138; D. Clark, 1959:121 ff.), many authorities prefer to reserve judgment (Chang, 1962:5) or to deny the Australopithecines lineal precedence to morphologically more modern hominids on geological grounds alone (Robinson, 1954:196, 197; 1956:172; Boule and Vallois, 1957:92; Piveteau, 1957:314; Kurtén, 1962:490), ignoring the fact that the geological placement of the Australopithecines is so fluid that even absolute dating techniques differ in the age assigned by more than 100 percent (Emiliani, 1955, 1956, 1958, 1961; Evernden, Curtis, and Kistler, 1957:15; Curtis, Savage, and Evernden, 1961; von Koenigswald, Gentner, and Lippolt, 1961:720–721; F. C. Howell, 1962; and Oakley, 1962:420).

If the climate of opinion prevalent at the time of discovery has had such a profound and lasting effect on the interpretation of fossil material found within the last 40 years, it should be instructive to consider the effects exerted by the mid-nineteenth century climate of opinion on the interpretation of the first hominid fossils to be discovered more than a century ago. The first publicized discovery of skeletal remains now attributable to an earlier stage in human evolution occurred in Germany in 1856 (Fuhlrott, 1857; Schaaffhausen, 1857a and b; 1858; Busk, 1861) just three years prior to the publication of Darwin's *Origin of Species* (1859). Even in England where Darwin's influence was relatively stronger than elsewhere, sympathy with an evolutionary viewpoint was far from being unanimous as is evident from the record of the conflicts (Huxley, 1860, as reported by Hardin, 1960b:25; Huxley, 1861). In Germany, where the Neanderthaler was found, evolution, despite the support of Haeckel (1897, 1899a:487), met with continued scientific opposition and was much longer in being accepted (Potonie, 1958:278). In the absence of stratigraphic evidence for antiquity, the Neanderthaler could have been found some years later and still have been given a similar reception. With no proof for its age and no morphologically similar skeletal material available for comparison, these remains, which clearly differed in form from modern man, were judged as being not normal (Mayer, 1864; Virchow, 1872). The power of this judgment was such that later, when datable remains of clearly similar morphology finally did turn up (Spy, found in 1886; La Chapelle-aux-Saints, found in 1908), the interpretation tended to remain the same though the basis changed markedly and totally different kinds of evidence were offered in its support.

The nineteenth-century view was summarized by Virchow in 1872 when he enumerated the pathological characteristics of the remains. From that point on, Neanderthal was regarded as being peculiar, and the peculiarities were at first thought to be pathological in origin. Circumstantial evidence in favor of Virchow's interpretation was offered by the fact that fossil man was already known to exist (Broca, 1868; Rivière, 1872) and his form was not radically different from that of modern man. As yet, degrees of antiquity were but dimly perceived, and, in addition, the resemblance of the so-called Old Man of Cro-Magnon to modern man had been enthusiastically stressed with greater confidence than its edentulous condition properly warranted. With a restored set of teeth occluded in characteristic Upper Palaeolithic fashion, his face would have looked far more like that of Combe Capelle and the supposed paradox of its short wide form would have been eliminated. Virchow's final denial of the antiquity of the Neanderthal find was based on the assumed age of the individual. Because of suture closure, it was assumed that he was elderly, and Virchow claimed that no one could live to such an advanced age in a nomadic or hunting-and-gathering society (Potonie, 1958:277). He must, therefore, have belonged to a sedentary group and great antiquity would not have been possible (Virchow, 1872:163).

By the end of the century, however, much more was known concerning the relative placement of the various subdivisions of prehistory (de Mortillet, 1910). At Spy, the two individuals of Neanderthal-like morphology had been found in a Mousterian layer definitely prior to the Upper Palaeolithic (Fraipont and Lohest, 1887; Twiesselmann, 1958; Bordes, 1959), and a calva had been found that differed even more from modern man and which belonged to a geological time far earlier even than Spy (Dubois, 1894). Putting these facts together, Gustav Schwalbe tried to support a view of human evolution in three stages starting with Pithecanthropus, developing through Neanderthal into modern man (Schwalbe, 1904; 1906a and b: esp. pp. 8 and 166). Schwalbe's views had the advantages of simplicity and logic, though they did run counter to the strong current of thought which was decidedly uncomfortable when suggestions were advanced that man might have evolved from something which looked less manlike than man (cf. Gregory, 1949:508).

Furthermore, for the next 20 years the most significant work on fossil man was to come from France because of the fact that relatively extensive remains of Neanderthalers were to be discovered at four different sites: e.g., Le Moustier 1908, La Chapelle-aux-Saints 1908, La Ferrassie 1909, and La Quina 1911. While the Le Moustier skeleton was the first of this group to be found (Hauser and Klaatsch, 1909; Klaatsch and Hauser, 1909), the somewhat devious activities of the discoverer, the series of unfortunate reconstructions, and the long delay before a description was published combined to deprive it of the notice that it should have received (Weinert, 1925). Because the description of the La Ferrassie skeletons was entrusted to Boule, work on them was delayed by his preoccupation with the previously discovered La Chappelle find, and, in fact, a study of the La Ferrassie remains has yet to be published though a half century has elapsed since their discovery. The discovery of the La Quina material (H. Martin, 1911) was apparently eclipsed by the simultaneous publication of the first major installment of the description of La Chapelle-aux-Saints (Boule, 1911). Thus, by chance, the find at La Chapelle became the center of attention as the most complete Neanderthal to have been discovered, and, as a result, the work that has long been regarded as definitive for the Neanderthal "type" was a product of French scholarship.

After their discovery on August 3, 1908, the Abbés A. and J. Bouyssonie and L. Bardon sought the advice of their friend and colleague Abbé Henri Breuil who suggested that they give the bones to Professor Marcellin Boule at the Muséum d'Histoire Naturelle in Paris for detailed study and description (Breuil, 1958:1). Boule with great industry and dispatch produced a series of works culminating in the tomes of 1911, 1912, and 1913 (Boule, 1908a and b, 1909a, b, and c, 1911, 1912, and 1913) in which he depicted the Neanderthals in terms that have served journalists and scholars ever since as the basis for the caricature of the cave man. Since he was not prepared to accept such a creature in the human family tree, he settled the question to the general satisfaction by declaring that the Neanderthals as well as the Pithecanthropines— the only other nonmodern hominid fossils known—became extinct without issue (Boule, 1913:242, 246–49; 1921:242, 245; 1923:244, 247).

At the time when Boule established the view that Neanderthal could not be the ancestor to subsequent forms of men, he offered two points in support of his conclusion (Boule, 1913:243; Schwalbe, 1913:601). It is instructive to look at these today since they are both accepted without much question, though the evidence involved has undergone marked changes (Vallois, 1954, 1959:134–136, 153–156).

1   Modern forms of man already existed at the time of the Neanderthalers.

2   The Mousterian was suddenly replaced by the Upper Palaeolithic and the very suddenness of the change indicated that the bearers of the Upper Palaeolithic must have been developing their cultural traditions elsewhere for a considerable period of time. As a corollary to this, it was claimed that the anatomical differences between the supposed immediately succeeding populations were so great that they precluded the possibility of evolution.

Both of these points are offered in support of his claim that modern forms of *Homo sapiens* have an antiquity which extends far back into the Pleistocene, but, even at that time, the evidence in their support was very far from being adequate. Curiously enough, both points persist in anthropological writings of recent years, and, while different evidence is offered, it is equally inadequate, as will be discussed shortly.

Boule's candidates for morphologically modern precursors or contemporaries with Neanderthalers were the Grimaldi skeletons—the so-called "Negroids" from the Grotte des Enfants at Menton (Boule, 1903b:525)— and later the Piltdown skull (Boule, 1913:246, 1921:172; 1923:174; Schwalbe, 1913:601–603). These he felt were proof of the early existence of modern forms of man though he was aware that Cartailhac (1912:231, 252, 265) had already cautioned that the Grimaldi finds were to be associated with Aurignacian cultural material overlying the Mousterian (Boule, 1913:213). The reason for Boule's acceptance of Piltdown as valid evidence is not at all clear from the literature, though it may have depended upon the personalities and friendships of the people involved. Previously Boule had examined and rejected the evidence for the antiquity of Galley Hill, Clichy, Denise, Grenelle, Ipswich, Olmo, Bury St. Edmonds, and others (Boule, 1913:210, 242; Schwalbe, 1913:596, 602), though these could be regarded as at least as reliable as Piltdown.

Boule's position on the replacement of the Mousterian (and hence, Neanderthal man) by the Upper Palaeolithic (and hence, *Homo sapiens* in the modern sense) is remarkably similar to the theory of catastrophism supported by Cuvier just a century earlier as an explanation for geological successions (Cuvier, 1834:107; Boule, 1921:9; Dehaut, 1945). This should not be surprising since Boule was trained as a palaeontologist in mid-nineteenth century France where paleontology, comparative anatomy, and geology were taught by Cuvier's disciples and immediate successors who followed in detail the teachings of their late master. Cuvier's explanation for the apparently sudden changes visible in specific stratigraphic sequences was based on his feeling that stratigraphic columns literally recorded all the events which had formerly taken place. A sudden change in faunal content indicated that a corresponding sudden change in the animal populations must have taken place at the past time indicated. The appearance of new forms of animals in succeeding superimposed strata did not necessarily signify creation de novo, but rather indicated that these animals had previously existed elsewhere in the world, and, following the catastrophe that had eliminated their predecessors in the area under examination, they swept in as an invasion and suddenly occupied the area of their extinct precursors (Dehaut, 1945; Eiseley, 1958:67).

These views have their roots in the eighteenth and early nineteenth centuries when some sort of explanation was needed for the sequences being discovered in the fossil record and when a theory of evolution was emotionally unacceptable and had not yet been worked out as an encompassing explanatory principle. Cuvier's influence was so strong that many continental scholars, when faced with the development of evolutionary thinking, tried to illustrate every possible way in which it would *not* work instead of examining it rationally and trying to understand how it *could* work. The battle fought by these people has been a defensive one emphasizing negative facets (Vallois, 1954:112), and the result has largely been a devious and unproductive delaying action.

Boule, following the tradition in which he had been trained, attempted to show that the morphological gap between Neanderthal and modern man was so large and the temporal gap was so small that the former could not have been the ancestor of the latter. The extinction of the one and the invasion of the other was postulated, and the result was the development of what could be labeled the theory of hominid catastrophism—still vigorously advocated by Boule's disciple Vallois (1946, 1949b, 1954, 1959) and echoed by many others (W. W. Howells, 1942, 1944, 1959; Heberer, 1944, 1949, 1950, 1951, 1956, 1959a and b; F. C. Howell, 1951, 1952, 1957; Breitinger, 1952, 1955; Le Gros Clark, 1955a; Patte, 1955; and Gieseler, 1959; to name a few). In his efforts to give his arguments the greatest possible effect, Boule claimed that Neanderthals exhibited many characters that subsequent unbiased research has failed to substantiate. Thus, despite Boule's claims, there is no trace of evidence that Neanderthalers had exceptionally divergent great toes or that they were forced to walk orang-like on the outer edges of their feet (Morton, 1926:314); there is no evidence that they were unable fully to extend their

knee joints (this should have been settled by the excellent work of
Manouvrier, 1888 and 1893, but was dismissed by Boule, 1912:140); there
is no evidence that their spinal columns lacked the convexities necessary for
fully erect posture (Straus and Cave, 1957); there is no evidence that the head
was slung forward on a peculiarly short and thick neck (Stewart, 1962:152);
and there is no evidence that the brain was qualitatively inferior to that of
modern man (Montagu, 1960:196; Comas, 1961:307–308).

One could logically ask, then, in what ways, if any, the Neanderthals do
differ from modern men. In general, they convey the impression of skeletal
rugosity including the wide epiphyses of the long bones, the relative thickness
of the hand and foot bones, and the relative stoutness of the ribs (see the general listing of characteristics by F. C. Howell, 1957:335–336), but primarily
their distinctiveness occurs in the size of the face (Morant, 1927:339; F. C.
Howell, 1951:387, 1952:403) involving gross tooth dimensions and supporting
architecture (cf. Brace, 1962b:349). No one of these differences is outside the
range of variation of modern man, but taken together, the face dimensions,
especially, indicate a population noticeably distinct from any populations
existing today, yet there is no good reason why such a population could not
have been ancestral to modern man (Hrdlička, 1929:620, 1930:348; Weinert,
1925:53, 1936:515, 1944b:231; Weidenreich, 1943a:46–48; 1947a:190, 196;
1949:156; Le Gros Clark, 1955a:45). In fact, given the aggregate human fossil
material from the Australopithecines through the Pithecanthropines and presumably on up, it would be most extraordinary if something like Hrdlička's
Neanderthal phase had not occurred just prior to the development of more
modern forms (Weidenreich, 1949:156).

Since the time of Boule's analysis, very few attempts have been made to
compare Neanderthals as a group with other human populations. One of these
(Morant, 1927) compares individual (mainly La Chapelle-aux-Saints) measurements with the range of modern population means, and, however correct
the conclusions may be, this remains highly dubious as a statistical procedure
(Abbie, 1952:81). Another study (Thoma, 1957:58) does not even use measurements but relies on subjective appraisal of morphological features, arbitrarily designated as single gene traits, and does not allow for any population
variability at all (see analysis by Brace, 1962c). These works, as those of Boule,
are not concerned with how the characteristics of modern man developed and
what they developed from, since their primary purpose is a negative one—to
demonstrate that Neanderthal man could not have had any descendants.

While the morphology and particularly the functional significance of
morphological differences has been left largely unstudied (for an attempt to

reverse this trend see Brace, 1962a and b), there has on the other hand been much interest in the question involving the possible contemporaneity of modern man with the Neanderthals. The idea has been that if evidence of a morphologically modern population could be found at the same time as, or earlier than, the Neanderthals, then this would serve as the logical ancestor to modern man, and we need never fear that anything so "brutish" as a Neanderthal would show up in our family tree. The popularity of this approach has been enormous in spite of the fact that over the years the candidates offered to represent this supposed population have proved to be a shadowy lot, impossible to pin down (Stewart, 1951:102–103; F. C. Howell, 1957:341–342).

Boule himself offered the Grimaldi skeletons as contemporaries of Neanderthals (1913:213, 243) though Cartailhac had already noted that they should be considered Aurignacian and hence subsequent to the Mousterian (Cartailhac, 1912:252, 265, 297). Boule also regarded Piltdown as a possible early stem from which modern man arose (Boule, 1913:246; 1921:172). The famous exposure of the Piltdown remains as fraudulent (Weiner, Oakley, and Clark, 1953) means that both of the pieces of evidence that he offered in favor of this view must be discarded. Curiously enough, Schwalbe in his extensive review of Boule's work on La Chapelle noted the Aurignacian status of Grimaldi and the questionable nature of Piltdown but still was so impressed by Boule's weighty scholarship that he partially changed his former assertion (1906a:5, 8, 25, 31) that Neanderthals had been the direct precursors to later forms of men (Schwalbe, 1913:602).

Following the capitulation of Schwalbe in 1913, the standard interpretation of the European Neanderthals was that they were a curious and peculiar group of "specialized," squat, clumsy, and unadaptable men doomed to sudden extinction following the first stadial of the Würm glaciation when faced with the invasion of a population of "noble," "handsome," "cleanlimbed," fully modern men of superior form and culture (Keith, 1915:136, 505; 1925a [1928]:198–199; 1946:141; Osborn, 1919:272; Boule, 1921:242–245; 1923:244–247; Burkitt, 1921:90; de Morgan, 1921:55; Capitan, 1922:18; MacCurdy, 1924: vol. I:209–210; Sollas, 1924:254; Hooton, 1931:357, 393; 1946:412; W. W. Howells, 1942:192–193; 1944:170, 207; 1959:205–207; Knight, 1949:156; F. C. Howell, 1951:406, 410; 1952:402; 1960:224; Mayr, 1951:113, 116; Leakey, 1953:205; Clark, 1955a:57, 63, 71, 74; Boule and Vallois, 1957:255–258; Piveteau, 1957:598; Place, 1957:80, 84, 90; Hibben, 1958:34, 39; von Koenigswald, 1958:21; Potonie, 1958:283–285; Bates, 1961:34; Lasker, 1961:101; Dobzhansky, 1962:180; and many others).

In one of the most thoughtful considerations of the mistakes commonly made when appraising human fossil material, Le Gros Clark (1955a:39–45) considers the implication of the frequent use of the term "specialized" in reference to fossil man (1955a:40), noting that on morphological grounds alone such arguments are inapplicable to Neanderthal man and his possible relations to what he distinguishes as *Homo sapiens*. Yet Clark himself subsequently uses "specialized" (p. 71) and "specialization" (p. 74) to characterize the Neanderthals and presumably to exclude them from *sapiens* ancestry—this in spite of his caution that it is not legitimate to use in this way, as arguments against ancestral relationships, characters which are not, among other things, "related to any marked degree of *functional* specialization" (1955a:41, italics Clark's). Despite his excellent advice, neither he nor any other recent author follows it, and there is no mention of the functional significance of those facets of Neanderthal morphology which serve to distinguish it from that of more recent man. (For an attempt to view these features from the point of view of changes in selective pressures, see Brace, 1962b:347–349). Properly speaking, the only real human "specialization" is culture, and, since culture is not a product of the human gene pool, arguments claiming cultural specialization as a reason for failure to survive are dubious to say the least. Any such argument claiming anatomical specialization as a reality, let alone as a significant reality, must be more carefully worked out than that offered by Vallois (1959:134) who simply follows Boule in offering a sterile repetition of the features wherein Neanderthal differs from modern man, labels them specializations, and assumes thereby that he has proven the inability of modern form to have arisen from anything called Neanderthal. The authors cited above have preferred to rely on the tentative time estimates advanced by Quaternary geologists, whose work they were unable to appraise competently, as proof that there was insufficient time for the Australopithecines, Pithecanthropines, Neanderthals, and modern men to be related in any direct sense, and in this way they have perpetuated what Gregory calls "the anachronism of demanding that the remote ancestors of any line must already possess all the habits and features of its distant descendants" (Gregory, 1949:508). For instance, not one of the well-preserved Western European Neanderthals can be given a date with a possible plus or minus variation of much less than 20,000 years, which means that there is a 40,000-year time span within which they could occur. Any statement claiming a sudden transition in the form of the inhabitants of Europe at or before 35,000 or so years ago assumes a knowledge of Neanderthal dating that we simply do not possess.

The widespread certainty that a gap in the stratigraphic sequence necessarily indicated a break in the continuity of the local population—catastrophism in the best pre-Darwinian tradition—was momentarily upset by the find of a population at Skhūl (Mount Carmel, Palestine) in 1931–1932 that was morphologically intermediate between Neanderthal and modern peoples (Keith and McCown, 1937; McCown and Keith, 1939). Thus there was great relief among the proponents of Neanderthal extinction when Mount Carmel was presumably demonstrated to have been Third Interglacial (Garrod and Bate, 1937; Garrod, 1958:183, F. C. Howell, 1958:186; 1959; 1961:10) and hence necessarily prior to the more primitive Neanderthalers. With *sapiens* occurring earlier than Neanderthal, then the likelihood was considered eliminated that Neanderthal was the ancestor to modern man, and the relief of those who were manifestly uneasy about the possibility of discovering a Neanderthal skeleton in a *sapiens* closet was apparent. But it was an uneasy relief, and the attempt to grasp at early *sapiens* straws continued (Vallois, 1949a:357–358; 1954:123; McCown, 1951:92; W. W. Howells, 1959:223; Montagu, 1960:230–250).

With the existence of fossil skeletal material from various places exhibiting a complete graduation from fully Neanderthal to fully modern morphology, former efforts to deny the Neanderthals ancestral status on the grounds that they were too "specialized" or "peculiar" or just plain "different" have lost their force, though remnants of such arguments still exist (Kälin, 1946:284; Heberer, 1949:1472; 1955a:88; Vallois, 1954:114–116; 1959:134–135). Whereas "thirty years ago it almost became a sport of a certain group of authors to search the skeletal parts of Neanderthal Man for peculiarities which could be proclaimed as 'specialization', thereby proving the deviating course this form had taken in evolution" (Weidenreich, 1943a:44), this has now been abandoned by most scholars and the case has been reduced to one of dating—for instance the primary concern exhibited by F. C. Howell for geological relationships rather than for morphological change and the factors influencing it (F. C. Howell, 1951, 1952, 1957, 1958, 1959, 1960, 1961, 1962). As Le Gros Clark says, "On purely morphological grounds (and without reference to paleontological sequence), there is no certain argument why *H. neanderthalensis* could not be ancestral to *H. sapiens*. But, in this particular instance, the fossil record shows clearly that such was not the case" (Clark, 1955a:45).

Interestingly enough, in his various works Clark himself apparently has been guilty of three "fallacies," all of which he warns against. He refers to *sapiens* skulls in Europe prior to the last major glaciation on what he calls "reasonably sound" geological evidence (Le Gros Clark, 1959:34). Since in this particular instance he refers to no specific fossil, one cannot appraise what he means by "reasonably sound," but if as he implies elsewhere his reference is to the dating of such finds as Fontéchevade (Clark, 1955a:67), Mount Carmel (Clark, 1955a:69), and Krapina (Clark, 1955a:70), then he has been guilty first of the fallacy of relying on tentative and inadequately documented dating procedures (Bordes, 1961; Higgs, 1961a:139; 1961b:153). Clark himself has recognized the "equivocal" nature of the dating of many hominid fossils (1955a:37) but this does not deter him from using such equivocal data to support his previously drawn conclusions. For instance, despite Clark's claim that the Fontéchevade remains were found in situ (1955a:67; see Movius, 1948:367), the circumstances surrounding the discovery are anything but clear. The remains were apparently discovered in a block of material in the laboratory (Vallois, 1959:7), documentation remains inadequate, no stratigraphic section remains as a check, and from the conflicting accounts it is difficult to discover just what the circumstances surrounding the discovery really were (Bordes, 1961). In this instance, Clark appears to be following the tradition established in British anthropological circles of being so anxious to prove the great antiquity of *sapiens* forms that any such indication, no matter how tenuous, will be accepted until proven false.

As far as the dating of Krapina is concerned, he states that "it is now generally agreed that the deposit belongs to the last interglacial period" (1955a:70), basing his statement on the faunal associations. Since he quotes no sources, it is not possible to discover how this general agreement is made. It should be noted, however, that Krapina was not dug stratigraphically and the exact faunal associations of the human skeletal material are still unknown (Vuković, 1959). Furthermore, *Dicerorhinus merkii* survived beyond the last interglacial in southern Europe and would be no necessary time marker for Krapina even if it were conclusively indicative of the layers in which the human remains occurred (Vallois, 1959:88) and, finally the most recent reappraisal would be inclined to place it in a Würm interstadial, the Göttweiger. (Guenther, 1959:205, 208). The recent discussion of the removal of Skhūl from the Riss-Würm interglacial needs no more comment here (Higgs, 1961:153).

Second, Clark is guilty of another fallacy to which he alludes (1959:35)— that of inferring form and taxonomic affiliation on the basis of fragmentary and inadequate evidence. Thus he offers the Fontéchevade fragments as being not demonstrably different from *Homo sapiens* (1955a:67), yet, problems of dating aside, the uncertainties surrounding the form of the major fragment

(Fontéchevade II) are clearly apparent despite the extraordinarily poor quality of the illustrations in Vallois's monograph (Vallois, 1959: p. 15, Fig. 4; p. 35, Fig. 12 and Plate XV). When tracings are made of these, enlarged to the same size, and superimposed for comparison, the differences between the form of the vault prior to restoration (see Figures 2-1 and 2-2) and that claimed following restoration (Figures 2-3 and 2-4) are so great that the only hint that the subject is the same skull is in the rough similarity in outline of the broken margin on the right. With such gross disagreement apparent in the work of the only author who has made a close study of the original, the claim that the reconstruction of the frontal width indicated a lack of brow ridge (Vallois, 1959:35–36) becomes simply a statement unsupported by any evidence. Figure 2-5 shows Figure 2-2 superimposed on Figure 2-4 and reveals width discrepancies of 20 percent, leaving the reader quite unable to see the factual basis for Vallois's conclusions.

Vallois's claims concerning the significance of the placement of the supposed trace of frontal sinus must be taken on faith since it fails to show in the poor photographs. Apparently it is in a part of the frontal devoid of the external bony table (Vallois, 1949a:348; 1954:125; 1959:60–65), and any cranial contour based on diploë alone—even in a skull that has not spent any time in the ground—is not something which can be used with much confidence. The simple presence of sinus in an otherwise undistinguished piece of frontal is not in itself evidence either for or against the existence of a brow ridge, as can be seen from Krapina frontal number 2 in which the sinus extends 27 mm. above the top of the naso-frontal suture and a good 15 mm. above the maximum swelling of a well-developed brow ridge at glabella (Figure 2-6). The top of the sinus is above any trace of the start of the brow ridge.

Furthermore, the assertion that the presence of a sinus precludes the juvenile status of Fontéchevade I implies a knowledge of the age of development of the frontal sinus in possible Neanderthal populations that we do not possess, in spite of Vallois's reference to the eight-year-old La Quina child (1954:124). When it suits their convenience, authors frequently refer to the supposed fact that distinctive Neanderthal morphology develops early in life (F. C. Howell, 1951:406; Boule and Vallois, 1957:223–224; W. W. Howells, 1959:202–203), yet when an undoubted Neanderthaler is found, such as Le Moustier, which lacks the supposedly typical brow ridge, then there is no hesitation to refer this to the relative youth of the bearer (Weinert, 1925:16), conveniently ignoring the fact that at age 16 the Le Moustier "youth" had relatively little growing left to do.

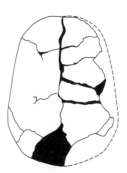

Figure 2-1 Enlarged tracing of a photograph of Fontéchevade II, *norma verticalis,* before restoration. From Vallois, 1959:15, Fig. 4.

Figure 2-2 The same tracing shown in Fig. 2-1 with the outline completed.

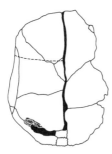

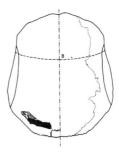

Figure 2-3 Tracing of a diagraph drawing of Fontéchevade II, *norma verticalis.* From Vallois, 1959:35, Fig. 12.

Figure 2-4 Tracing of the completed outline of Fontéchevade II, after restoration. From Vallois, 1959:36, Fig. 13.

Figure 2-5 Figure 2-4 superimposed on Figure 2-2, with the superimposed lengths set equal.

Figure 2-6 Krapina frontal number 2, *norrna frontalis.* Drawn from the original.

It appears that in accepting the Fontéchevade remains as representative of a presumed population, many recent authors, including Le Gros Clark himself, have not heeded the warning that Clark advances against utilizing individuals for comparison where size, sex, and particularly age are in doubt (Clark, 1955a:33). F. C. Howell has repeatedly urged caution in relying too heavily on such fragmentary pieces of evidence as Fontéchevade for the primary prop supporting radical theories (F. C. Howell, 1951; 1957:342; 1958:194), and despite Montagu's somewhat indignant expostulations (Montagu, 1952) it would seem that Howell's comments should have had more influence.

In connection with this same fallacy of inferring from inadequate data, Le Gros Clark (1955a:64) and many others (Hooton, 1946:333; Stewart, 1951:102; Boule and Vallois, 1957:185–186; Piveteau, 1957:533–534; W. W. Howells, 1959:217; Montagu, 1960:202) have stressed the mixture of neanthropic and primitive features in the Steinheim skull, but few such commentators (excepting W. W. Howells, 1944:171 [not repeated in 1959]; C. Howell, 1951:399–401) have even mentioned the fact stressed in the descriptive monograph that the skull had undergone a considerable amount of post-mortem deformation (Weiner, 1936:466–468). This is clearly visible in the cast as can be seen from Figure 2-7. The presence of a canine fossa claimed by Boule and Vallois (1957:185) is not conclusive in either cast or photographs, the claimed absence of prognathism could just as easily be due to the fact that the incisor-bearing part of the face is missing, and furthermore the whole facial skeleton has been badly warped postmortem. The "laterally compressed" aspect of the skull supposedly indicating *sapiens* form (Hooton, 1946:333) should be taken literally since the whole left side of the skull has been deformed toward the midline (Weinert, 1936:469) as can be seen from the fact that the width of the palate between the third molars is only 35 mm. (versus 40 mm. for the minimum mean modern figure listed in Martin, 1928:931, though Martin mentions an individual minimum of 33 mm.), and the biauricular breadth is only approximately 82 mm. (compared with the minimum modern individual dimension of 100 mm. recorded in Martin, 1928:765). (These measurements were taken from the cast.) The occipital has apparently been slightly warped underneath creating the supposedly *sapiens* "rounded back and neck region" (W. W. Howells, 1944:171). Finally, the brow ridges and the forehead, as noted in Weinert's description (1936:478, 500) and recently recognized only by Montagu (1960:202) are reminiscent of Pithecanthropus rather than Neanderthal or *sapiens* (see Figure 2-8). The presumably "neanthropic'" features of Steinheim, then, would seem to occur mainly in the reconstructions of those who would have them appear that way.

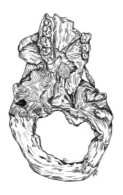

Figure 2-7 Steinheim *norma basalis.* Drawn from the cast with the aid of a camera lucida.

Figure 2-8 Steinheim *norma lateralis.* Drawn from the cast with the aid of a camera lucida.

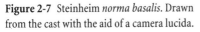

Finally, in considering inferences made from incomplcte remains, one must refer to the famous Swanscombe skull. Reference could also be made to Ehringsdorf and Quinzano where the face is likewise missing (Clark, 1955a:66–68), but since, excluding the fragmentary and dubious Fontéchevade remains, the greater part of the case for *sapiens* antiquity rests on Swanscombe, it will be considered by itself. Unlike the Fontéchevade finds, there can be no doubt concerning the late second interglacial age of the Swanscombe remains (Oakley, 1953:44; F. C. Howell, 1960:195–198). If the form of the vault were indistinguishable from modern man this would be most suggestive, though by itself not conclusive. The original detailed report found no measurements or proportions wherein the remains could be considered distinguishable from recent *Homo sapiens* (Morant, 1938:71, 95) despite the Neanderthaloid biasterionic breadth. Yet on the other hand it could not be distinguished from the warped and distorted Steinheim skull (Morant, 1938:78, 97).

In connection with the appraisal of unquantifiable characters, Clark quite properly warns against overemphasis of "primitive" features of fossil remains simply because the material is old (Le Gros Clark, 1959:35); however he neglects to warn against the overemphasis of "modern" features by authors whose desire to find clear evidence for the pre-Würm existence of morphologically modern man is so strong that some have expressed it as a "need" (McCown, 1951:92, Weckler, 1954:1022). Still, with Clark's caution against inferring from inadequate data (1955a:64) and his emphasis on the consideration of total morphological pattern (1955a:15–17), and despite his admission that further finds might show that Swanscombe was quite distinct from modern form (Le Gros Clark, 1959:35), yet he concludes that it is indeed indistinguishable from modern man (1955a:66). He feels that if the face were of a form comparable to the "extreme Neanderthal type" this would be reflected in the anatomy of the preserved vault parts. Since he indicates that this is not the case, he believes that the brow ridges could not have been more pronounced than those of the Steinheim skull (1955a:66), though, as has been indicated above, the Steinheim brow is so far from being *sapiens* in form that it is better compared with Pithecanthropus than with the Neanderthals, and yet as Morant has indicated the Steinheim vault differs less from the modern "type" than does the Swanscombe (Morant, 1938:78).

To contrast with Clark's confidence in the sapient form of Swanscombe, Weidenreich felt that attempts to classify it were doubtful until proof could be brought forward of the characters of the brow and face (Weidenreich, 1943b:273; 1947a:194; note a similar cautious view offered by Keith, 1949:264). This was a logical recognition of the fact emphasized by Morant that the greatest distinction between Neanderthals and subsequent forms of men occurs in the development of the face (Morant, 1927:339, 374–375; F. C. Howell, 1951:387; 1952:403; Brace, 1962b:349). In spite of his good morphological caution and the other solid theoretical reasons for insisting on full documentation before a fossil be accepted that would contradict most of the evidence for human evolution, Weidenreich has been criticized for possible "morphological dating" (Stewart, 1951:98) and for "preferring morphological to geological evidence in the dating of fossils" (Straus and Cave, 1957:359). In retrospect, however, his cautions were well founded. The association of Piltdown fragments, in which he refused to believe (1936:117–119), has been proven fraudulent, and, after some thoughtful skepticism regarding the morphology of the Swanscombe skull (Sergi, 1953; Breitinger, 1952:132–133; 1955:38; Drennan, 1956), one of the very people who questioned Weidenreich's motives in urging such caution has himself observed that the occipito-mastoid crest of the Swanscombe skull looks much more like that of the known Neanderthals than that of modern man (Stewart, 1960:363; 1961:210, 216). These observations, showing that the anatomical evidence for pre-Neanderthal *sapiens* is far from secure, suggest the final fallacy which weakens the case of the proponents of such views.

This fallacy might be called that of establishing broad and far-reaching theories of human evolution on poorly documented samples—in many cases single dubious specimens. This has been clearly warned against by F. C. Howell (1957:342; 1958:194), and though it has been recognized by Le Gros

Clark (1959:35), in this as in the other instances cited he has failed to follow his own very good advice.

A brief listing of the major authors and their candidates for ancient *sapiens* should show how the evidence has changed since 1908 without becoming any less nebulous.

Boule 1908	Grimaldi
Boule 1913	Grimaldi and Piltdown
Keith 1915	Galley Hill (Piltdown)
Osborn 1919	No evidence at all except sheer faith
Osborn 1922	Piltdown
Hooton 1931	Piltdown (Galley Hill)
Howells 1944	Mount Carmel
	(Galley Hill and Swanscombe)
Hooton 1946	Piltdown, Galley Hill, and Swanscombe
Keith 1949	Abandons the view
Le Gros Clark 1955	Swanscombe and Fontéchevade
Boule and Vallois 1957	Fontéchevade
Montagu 1960	Swanscombe and Fontéchevade

This should suffice to show that the evidence has undergone a complete change while the argument has remained substantially the same. The words of Samuel Butler, uttered in protest to the triumph of Darwinian views but now peculiarly appropriate in their support, complained that "no matter how much any one now moves the foundations, he cannot shake the superstructure, which has become so currently accepted as to be above the need of any support from reason" (Butler, 1878:276).

Evidently the theoretical framework has not altered since the influential works of Boule on La Chapelle-aux-Saints, and a great majority of the students of human evolution have been primarily concerned with the attempt to demonstrate that various nonmodern hominids were the contemporaries of modern forms of man. The aim was to prove thereby that these nonmodern hominids could not be the forerunners of truly modern men.

Despite this clearly antievolutionary bias, fully realized 20 years ago by an interested sociologist (Gillette, 1943), no modern work goes so far as to deny that human evolution occurred (though Boule and Vallois, 1957, would deny almost all of the fossil evidence for it). It would seem rather to be a case of "out of sight, out of mind" since the crucial events in the development of *sapiens* morphology are generally pushed back in time to a point where "the fossil record dwindles into obscurity" (Brace, 1962c:730) and people are not likely to be disturbed by the sight of a human ancestor who looks rather less than human.

The effect of Boule's work and the immediate and continuing influence which it has had (Keith, 1915, 1925a, 1928, 1931, 1946; Osborn, 1919; MacCurdy, 1924; Hooton, 1931, 1946; W. W. Howells, 1944, 1959; Montagu, 1945, 1951, 1960; Vallois, 1954, 1959; Clark, 1955a; Patte, 1955; Piveteau, 1957; Lasker, 1961) was so powerful that F. C. Howell has recently commented that he knew of no "thoughtful worker in the field in the past half century" who has advocated a view involving the evolution of men of modern form from the European Neanderthals (F. C. Howell, 1957:341). Actually he is forgetting the views of Hrdlička (1926, 1927, 1930), Weidenreich (1928, 1940, 1943a, 1946, 1947a, 1949), Weinert (1925, 1932, 1936, 1944a, 1944b, 1951, 1955) and others (see Vallois, 1954:113) who must be accounted as thoughtful workers however much one may disagree with them on some points. As far as the effect that their opposition to the picture painted by Boule has had, they might just as well have never existed.

It is interesting that the fundamentally antievolutionary, or at least non-evolutionary, tone of palaeoanthropology as represented in the writings of the majority of western European and American authors has been clearly recognized by Russian and Polish anthropologists (Roginski, 1947, 1951; Wierciński, 1956; Dambski, 1957). The willingness of eastern European students to accept the fossil record as indicative of the evolution of man may stem in part from the prestige that Hrdlička continued to enjoy in the country of his birth and neighboring areas (Dokládal and Brožek, 1961:456), though it would seem that at least part of the reason may be based on sociopolitical ideology and not on basic biology—witness the pointless pregenetic insistence on typology (Wierciński, 1962; esp. the comment by Michalski on pp. 32–35) and the continued fruitless attempts to view the issues of human biological variation as revolving around the long-dead conflict of polyphyletism with monophyletism. In the "conflict" it is claimed that "it is the Soviet students who now stand in the van" and exhibit "the correct attitude" (Dambski, 1957:179). It appears however that the "van" stalled before a concern was developed for natural selection and the mechanisms involved in heredity, and it would seem to have remained stationary ever since. This criticism, while primarily directed at the purposeless typologies of the living, can also be made of the great majority of the attempts to interpret the human fossil record. It is hoped that this paper will serve as a preliminary effort to reverse the trend.

In the desire to prove Neanderthal extinction, it would appear as though many recent authors have rejoiced in chronological indications, however

shaky, that would tend to confound a logical view of human evolution
(Le Gros Clark, 1955a:38, 45; Place, 1957:76; Hibben, 1958:27, 36–37; F. C.
Howell, 1958:187; W. W. Howells, 1959:226). Thus both Hrdlička and
Weidenreich have been taken to task for putting more reliance on the morphological developments, which they were professionally competent to evalu-
ate in their thinking about evolutionary development, than in the tentative
orderings that the very incomplete geochronological studies sought to assign
to certain fossil specimens (Stewart, 1949:15; 1951:97–98; Le Gros Clark,
1955a:72; Straus and Cave, 1957:359). Admittedly the concept of morphological dating, as applied by Hrdlička to the New World, thoroughly deserved the
criticism which it received, but condemnation was pushed beyond the specific
to the general with the implication that the morphological assessment of evolutionary development and hence possible age is never a legitimate procedure
(Stewart, 1949:16). As an indication that the criticism was carried too far,
the same source deplored the fact that by 1948 Sir Arthur Keith had finally
wavered in his former blind acceptance of the geological appraisal of the
Galley Hill skeleton (Stewart, 1949:14; 1951:97). Ironically, in a publication
which appeared at the same time as the criticism, it was finally and unassail-
ably demonstrated that the supposedly objective evidence for the antiquity of
Galley Hill was worthless (Oakley and Montagu, 1949).

  Interestingly enough, Keith's original reasons for claiming great antiquity for modern forms of man were not based primarily on geological indications of the great age of *sapiens* skeletal material, but rather were founded
on the inverted application of the principle of morphological dating itself. In
Keith's mind, anything so unique as modern morphology must have required
a great extent of time in which to develop, and, therefore, on form alone, he
judged modern man to be very ancient (Keith, 1925a [1928], vol. I:x, 265–266,
vol. II:711). This is not only "very close to morphological dating," this in
fact is morphological dating. Thus while Keith is generally credited with the
staunch defense of Galley Hill and Piltdown as proof of sapient antiquity,
in his writings he maintained proper caution by noting the morphological
problems of Piltdown and the legitimate question concerning the geological
authenticity of Galley Hill (1925a [1928], vol. II:713). His basic thought was
that "the proof that man of a modern build of body was in existence by the
close of the Pliocene period is presumptive, not positive" (Keith, 1925a
[1928], vol. II:711), and his presumption was based on his feeling that
immense time was necessary for evolution to work—time which he then
believed the Pleistocene could not offer.

This, of course, brings up the real source of Keith's troubles. In 1915 he had felt daring in offering a stretch of 400,000 years as the duration of the Pleistocene, and by 1925 he felt compelled to reduce this to 200,000 years and was unhappily contemplating the presumed necessity of further reducing it to little more than 100,000 years (Keith, 1925a [1928], vol. I:xiv–xv). It seems to have been the fate of Sir Arthur Keith to have been the victim of other people's mistakes—witness Piltdown. In 1925 he recognized the strain to which his reliance on extant geological estimates had forced him to subject the fossil evidence and compared his position to that of Huxley when Kelvin, by the "precise" methods of physics, had reduced the age of the earth to 24 million years (Chamberlain, 1901:225; Keith, 1925a [1928], vol. I:xv; Eiseley, 1958:233–a244). Although Keith said in despair, "there must be a mistake somewhere" (1925a, vol. I:xv) yet he persisted in using a date for the Pleistocene that would not allow an evolutionary explanation for the known hominid fossils (1931:34). When at last he became aware of a Pleistocene date in the neighborhood of 1 million years (1949:164, 208), he modified his former interpretations and abandoned the attempt to prove great relative antiquity for modern forms of men (Keith, 1949:265), reluctantly admitting Neanderthal man into the ancestry of "the proud Caucasian" (1949:263) though he persisted in refusing to admit that this could have taken place in Europe (1949:244).

Clarifying the doubts cast on some of Weidenreich's views, subsequent events have shown that his suspicion of the validity of Piltdown and the sapient form of Swanscombe, while certainly "very close to morphological dating" (Stewart, 1951:98), was suspicion well founded (Weiner, Oakley, and Clark, 1953; Stewart, 1960, 1961). Other facets of Weidenreich's work, such as his claim for giant hominid ancestors (1945:115), his failure to recognize the significance of the Australopithecines (1943b:268–269; 1945:121), and his approach to orthogenesis (1941:435; 1947b:407, 416) will draw few defenders now.

Whatever the weaknesses in the works of Weidenreich, Hrdlička, and Weinert, their similar approaches to the Neanderthal question deserve careful consideration, which so far has not been given them. Because Hrdlička published his views extensively before Weidenreich, he will be considered first, while Weinert, as the last major living representative of such an interpretation, will be considered after Weidenreich.

The full development of Hrdlička's ideas can be seen in his Huxley Memorial Lecture for 1927 reprinted in the Annual Report of the Smithsonian Institution for 1928 (Hrdlička, 1929:593–621) and repeated and emphasized in 1930 (Hrdlička, 1930:328–349). It is not surprising that the perspective of more than 30 years should reveal that Hrdlička cannot be substantiated in some of his ideas, but what is surprising is that these turn out to be remarkably few and do not affect his major thesis.

Thus he refused to accept geological indications for a succession of four glacial maxima in Europe during the Pleistocene (Hrdlička, 1927:271; 1929:617–618; 1930:346; cf. Keith's similar views, 1925a [1928], vol. I:x, 265–266; 1931:34–36), though, since he did recognize the evidence for the onset of peri-glacial conditions at the time of the Neanderthals, he was able to view evolutionary problems where early Würm populations are concerned from the point of view of changes in selective factors. Hrdlička's question (1930:345) concerning the motivation of a supposed *sapiens* population to invade a Europe in the grip of a most unappealing climate might be parried by the postulation that the Neanderthal-*sapiens* change took place during the Göttweiger interstadial, though both the skeletal and the geological evidence is still not even adequate to frame the question let alone answer it and hence such an answer must be in the nature of an evasion.

While Hrdlička made a conscientious effort to view the human evolutionary changes he observed in terms of changes in selective pressures, he did not have a sufficient grounding in evolutionary genetics, and, consequently, he misinterpreted the significance of the great morphological variability that his extensive familiarity with the skeletal material had led him to appreciate. Noting Neanderthal skeletal variability and postulating increasing stringency of selective pressures, he inferred that the two were connected in a cause-and-effect relationship, though he did not tackle the problem of why the ultimate change resulted in a reduction of general muscularity and a reduction in size of the facial skeleton (1929:619; 1930:347). Weidenreich, faced with similar problems in later years, likewise could see no logical rationale for such reductions and concluded by assigning them in some cryptic way to the enlargement of the brain (Weidenreich, 1941:343–435). It is interesting to note that F. C. Howell goes no further than to assign "classic Neanderthal" form to "severe selective pressures" (1951:409; 1952:403; 1957:337) but does not say how this works and makes no effort to view *sapiens* evolution from this point of view. Le Gros Clark, for his part, is simply content to quote F. C. Howell (1955a:61).

In speaking of an increase in population variability, Thoma (1957:496, 502) noted that according to sound evolutionary theory (Simpson, 1944) this should indicate a decrease in selective pressures, but since he, like the other authors cited, feels certain that Palaeolithic conditions call for strong selection, he explains the variability (for the Mount Carmel populations) as a result of hybridization. Actually, all of these authors have failed to appreciate the fact that culture, rather than climate, has been the prime factor to be reckoned with in assessing the selective pressures operating on man. If Neanderthal and Neanderthaloid (e.g., Mount Carmel) actually do show unusual variability, then it seems logical to view this as a reduction in the former adaptive significance of the traits in question. With the clear indications of the increase of special tools for special purposes beginning in the Mousterian and continuing without break through the Upper Palaeolithic in Europe and the Middle East (Bordes, 1958; Smith, 1961), the extreme rounding wear seen on the anterior teeth of earlier populations, indicative of extensive use of the dentition as a tool, gradually reduces, and it can be inferred that developing culture has reduced the adaptive significance of the huge Middle Palaeolithic dentition and its supporting facial architecture (Brace, 1962b:348–349). In conjunction with principles recently elaborated (Brace, 1963), the ultimate result of the reduction of the adaptive significance of a structure will be the reduction of the structure itself. This provides the final reason for the transformation of a Neanderthal into a *sapiens* population that Hrdlička, Weidenreich, and Weinert postulated but could not quite account for.

Aside from these weak points in Hrdlička's reasoning the rest is quite sound in spite of the fact that it has been almost completely ignored. First of all, he recognized that a view calling for Neanderthal extinction demands that there should be a demonstrable sudden replacement in Europe of one population by the other which had been developing elsewhere. While Hrdlička did not observe, as he might have done to some effect, that this in miniature was precisely the type of stratigraphic explanation which Darwin was up against nearly a century before in refuting the prevailing views of Cuvier and catastrophism, yet he did note that there are a number of problems which views involving extinctions and invasions must face.

1   Invasion and replacement presupposes a long double line of evolution, which is so unlikely as to require solid proof before it could be rendered acceptable. Furthermore, an invasion to be successful in the face of an established population presupposes a large invading force, and a large invading force presupposes a still larger mother population elsewhere. As Hrdlička noted, there is no clear evidence for any such large non-Neanderthal population in Europe, and there certainly is none in Asia or Africa. To this one might add that, despite the efforts of a whole subsequent generation of students all anxious to prove *sapiens* antiquity, there is neither cultural nor skeletal evidence for these phantom *sapiens*

populations, and the few individuals offered as such (for instance Steinheim, Swanscombe, Fontéchevade, and Kanjera) are distorted, fragmentary, of dubious date, or downright un-*sapiens*.

F. C. Howell (1951, 1952, 1957, 1959) has sought to provide a reason for a long independent period of evolution for two hominid lines by claiming the climatic isolation of Europe during the early Würm, but the marked cultural similarities between Europe and the Middle East as opposed to either one and other parts of the Old World (Africa or eastern Asia) would seem to indicate that the ecological zone stretching from Iran across the northern Mediterranean border to southwest Europe, far from being broken up into cultural isolates, was a zone in which similar cultural elements maintained circulation—i.e., a kind of Middle Palaeolithic or Mousterian culture area. Evidence for claimed isolation is going to have to come from human cultural/ physical data and not exclusively from speculations based on climatological information.

2   Differential rates of evolution for postulated different human groups, as Hrdlička noted, need to be justified. Why should one group, the European Neanderthals, cease to evolve? Hrdlička's question might be strengthened by noting that selective pressures must have been quite similar in their operation on human populations throughout the then north temperate areas of the Old World during the Pleistocene. Certainly the cultural parallels archaeologically evident between Europe, southern Russia, and the Near East are striking evidence that the cultural solution to environmental problems has been quite similar from the time of the third interglacial on up. If, as has been suggested (Brace, 1962b:343), culture is a major determiner of the selective forces operating on human populations, then there is no reason to regard the selection in Europe as having been different in nature from that to the East, and the supposed evolutionary stagnation of the European inhabitants is still unexplained.

3   If invasion and population replacement did occur, presumably due to the superiority of the invading population, Hrdlička asks:

a   Why did the invading population not prevail sooner?

b   Why did they take over the precise caves and sites formerly occupied by the Neanderthals?

c   Why did this supposedly superior population live exactly the same kind of life their predecessors had? Since evidence is accumulating to indicate that the European Upper Palaeolithic may be largely the product of cultural evolution in situ, it might be added that the superior newcomers must have arrived cultureless or have abandoned their own so-far undiscovered culture to take over that of the Neanderthalers whom they presumably displaced. This in fact comes close to being the argument used in one of the most strained explanations yet produced (Weckler, 1954:1015–1016).

d   What example can one give from contemporary and historical knowledge of the complete extinction of a whole group of humanity by the action of another one?

Of all the sound and compelling questions asked by Hrdlička, only the last facet of this one, which is relatively trivial, seems to have drawn any response. W. W. Howells (1944:208) and Vallois (1954:120) offer the American Indians as an example of the presumed extinction of a whole group of humanity, noting that they will never noticeably affect the physical type of the United States, and, for the purposes of future excavators, they might as well be extinct. This of course assumes that the future anthropologists can ignore the accumulation of evidence from the 60 million inhabitants of Mexico and the countries further south (*Encyclopaedia Britannica World Atlas,* 1960:39) where pre-Columbian genes represent a substantial proportion of the common pool. The previous requirement noted by Hrdlička, of a large invading population and an even larger parent population, would of course have been met, rendering Howells's and Vallois's example inappropriate even if it were true.

Of all the major figures still actively concerned with problems in human evolution, only Vallois still frankly champions a picture of separate human lines evolving in parallel fashion in neighboring or even the same geographical areas (1959:155). This he believes is solidly consistent with the concepts developed by vertebrate palaeontology and evolutionary theory since the beginning of the century, and he considers the supposed parallel lines to indicate hominid adaptive radiation.

Nowhere, however, does he consider what is adaptive about such presumed parallel developments, nor does he make any effort to consider the primary hominid adaptive mechanism, which is not to be seen in the lists of traits on which he relies. The mechanism, of course, is culture. One can even view the adaptive niche inhabited by man as a cultural niche. Conceived in this way, the "competitive exclusion principle" that Hardin uses to explain the existence, in the long run, of only one species in each ecological niche (Hardin, 1960a) clearly shows why only one hominid species has existed at any one time during the Pleistocene. Such an approach combined with what is known about the distribution of the Mousterian simply will not allow the long-time separate development of *sapiens* and Neanderthal lines. Symbolic of Vallois's failure to consider the relationship between human morphology and the primary adaptive factors influencing it is Vallois's statement, when describing the Fontéchevade remains, that his concern is chiefly with the "anthropology," and for that reason he leaves out the archaeology (Vallois, 1954:114). To be sure, "anthropology" in France means "physical anthropology," but perhaps one of the reasons for the consistently antievolutionary position taken by French physical anthropology is that, in relegating all concern for culture to ethnologists and archaeologists, they have eliminated human adaptation from their thinking, and without an understanding of this it is of course difficult to interpret the hominid fossil record from an evolutionary point of view.

It would seem that any view that attempts to picture the Neanderthalers as "aberrant," "extreme," "special," or "specialized," and as having been a blind end in evolution which became extinct without descendants would have to be able to answer in convincing fashion the points raised by Hrdlička, yet, though such views are practically unanimous among the students of fossil man today, none has attempted such answers.

While Hrdlička was thoroughly familiar with the early human skeletal remains prior to 1930 and had made one of the most significant attempts to interpret them, he does not seem to have been as familiar with the literature as he was with the bones. While he quoted from the published works of five of the most influential scholars of his day (Hrdlička, 1930:326–327) and remarked with what should have been devastating effect that "they give us *H. sapiens,* without showing why, or how, and where he developed his superior make-up" (Hrdlička, 1930:345; see also 1927:270), yet he apparently believed that "all these opinions can probably be traced, directly or indirectly, to the authoritative notions arrived at during the earlier years of this century, on material less ample than at present, by one of the foremost students of Neanderthal man, Gustav Schwalbe" (Hrdlička, 1927:250; 1929:594; 1930:327). He cites no reference to back up this accusation, but, in a recent though much milder version of the same view, F. C. Howell lists as sources Schwalbe's publications in 1901, 1906, and 1923 (F. C. Howell, 1957:340). A check of these and others (Schwalbe, 1897, 1899, 1901a and b, 1902, 1904, 1906a and b, 1913, 1923 [actually written in 1916 just before his death]) not only has failed to reveal any evidence for this (cf. Weidenreich, 1928:9) but has clearly shown that quite the reverse was true. Prior to this yielding to the influence of Boule in 1913, he had arranged the available fossil men as stages in a linear sequence—Pithecanthropus, Neanderthal, and modern—which he believed represented the course of human evolution (Schwalbe, 1906a:25; 1913:602). Rather than Schwalbe, whose views apparently were basically the same as Hrdlička's, the latter should properly have implicated the views of Boule and the fundamentally antievolutionary ethos of French palaeontology which, via the subsequent espousals by Keith and Osborn and others, have delayed the acceptance of the human fossil record from an avowedly evolutionary point of view from that day to this.

A proper appreciation of the position of Schwalbe is raised since it gives a clue to the background of his pupil and, later, colleague Franz Weidenreich, one of the very few scholars besides Hrdlička to have attempted to view the Neanderthals as a normal facet of human prehistoric development. Weidenreich's views, reflecting the years he spent in China, are less oriented toward the specifically European fossil record, and his attempts to interpret the position of the Neanderthals were always made from the point of view of his larger views of human evolution. As a result, his general thinking was a little more sophisticated, while his specific treatment of European Neanderthal problems is much more sketchy than the above recounted views of Hrdlička.

In general, Weidenreich maintained that no more than one species of man existed at any one time during the Pleistocene (1943b:253). While he recognized that long-standing differences in the selective factors prevalent in different geographical areas would result in local differentiations yet he believed that interpopulation contact involving inevitable genetic exchange had always been sufficient to maintain specific unity within the genus *Homo*. This view receives considerable confirmation from the Lower Palaeolithic archaeological record that shows the broad spread of similar culture traits over wide areas of the Old World (Oakley, 1950; Braidwood, 1957). Where culture traits have spread, genes must have spread also.

Yet despite Weidenreich's clear reasoning concerning prehistoric population dynamics, one recent work presents a diagram of "the Polyphyletic or Candelabra school, modified (and exaggerated)" purporting to represent Weidenreich's views of human evolution (W. W. Howells, 1959:236). In this diagram, vertical lines are used to represent evolutionary continuity in four areas of the world, but the horizontal and diagonal lines of Weidenreich's own original diagram indicating genetic interchange between adjacent populations have been eliminated (Weidenreich, 1947a:210). After decreeing that Weidenreich's areal populations must follow rigid separate grooves, Howells expresses incredulity that these four lines should converge to produce "the same kind of man everywhere" (W. W. Howells, 1959:235; see also similar sentiments expressed by Vallois, 1959:154). The scheme is then rejected as being too rigid.

This, however, has not done justice to Weidenreich's intent. To take a specific instance, Weidenreich regarded the Pekin group, with which he was most familiar, as a direct ancestor to *Homo sapiens* with a closer relationship "to certain Mongolian groups—than to any other races.... *This statement does not mean that modern Mongols derived exclusively from Sinanthropus or that Sinanthropus did not give origin to other races*" (Weidenreich, 1943b:253, italics added). Certainly the inhabitants of a given area have a larger proportion of genes derived from the previous inhabitants of that same area than of those from any other area, but there is always going to be a certain amount of genetic interchange with adjacent populations as Weidenreich has indicated, and he has regarded this interchange as sufficient to have maintained the unity of the human species at any given time level during the Pleistocene. To picture his scheme of evolution as consisting of rigid separate grooves is not to exaggerate it; it is to misrepresent it.

The views of Weidenreich, while expressed in the terms of a morphologist and human palaeontologist, correspond quite closely to those expressed by a population geneticist (Dobzhansky, 1951:1067), which should not be surprising since in fact both types of scholar are concerned with the same problem—human evolution. While they approach it from different directions, they can be expected to agree with each other as they converge.

While Weidenreich, being less familiar with the European stratigraphic and skeletal records than Hrdlička, accepted the view of the supposed stratigraphic break between the Neanderthal and *sapiens* inhabitants of Europe which the proponents of hominid catastrophism have advanced, yet he notes that this still does not deny the possibility that evolution from a Neanderthal population to a *sapiens* one did not occur in another part of the world (1943a:47). Recognizing this as a possibility, he was careful to note in relation to Neanderthal man in Europe that "in no case, however, can the capability of his advancing into *Homo sapiens* be denied" (Weidenreich, 1943a:48; cf. Le Gros Clark, 1955a:45).

Weidenreich clearly accepted Hrdlička's Neanderthal Phase of Man (Weidenreich, 1928:59; 1943a:40) noting in effect that it is much more reasonable for human palaeontologists to explain evolution in terms of the fossils already on their desks rather than to engage in the perpetual pursuit of phantom populations of supposedly sapient form (Weidenreich, 1949:153). In one of the last things he wrote, Weidenreich, like Hrdlička (1930:348), asks the question, "If Neanderthal Man, for example, was not an ancestor of modern man, who was this ancestor?" (Weidenreich, 1949:156).

With such substantial views and challenging questions offered by two of the major figures in American physical anthropology in the twentieth century, it is legitimate to wonder why they have received no serious consideration, why the views find no supporters, and why the questions remain unanswered. Certainly it cannot be due exclusively to the demonstrable discrepancies in some of the other issues supported by Hrdlička and Weidenreich, for one can cite the example of Sir Arthur Keith whose conviction of *sapiens* antiquity sails on without him (Stewart, 1951:98) despite the fact that the major issues for which he stood on race, eugenics, and Piltdown have had to be abandoned.

It would seem that at least part of the failure of the ideas of Hrdlička and Weidenreich to have their deserved impact can be assigned to the positions occupied by both men. Weidenreich, following his introductions to a similar viewpoint by Schwalbe, taught for one-third of a century as an anatomist and physiologist, but the final phase of his career, where he was specifically dealing with fossil man and human evolution and where his evolutionary thinking reached its published expression, was spent in connection with the museum world. Hrdlička's entire career was spent in a museum, and however much a museum environment may encourage research, it does not guarantee the general recognition of the knowledge thus gained.

Meanwhile, Hooton was attempting to build American physical anthropology in the image of Sir Arthur Keith, and the success that he had can be seen in the almost unanimous acceptance of Keith's general evolutionary views in spite of the demise of Galley Hill and Piltdown and in spite of the fact that Keith himself abandoned them at the end of his life. Weidenreich and Hrdlička had no students, and, as a result, their thinking is unrepresented in the current generation of anthropologists. It is an interesting commentary on the strength of academic tradition to note that these two men were among the few physical anthropologists of their generation not specifically trained in the concepts of hominid catastrophism—one having been specifically trained to view the hominid fossil record from an evolutionary viewpoint, and the other having acquired his anthropological training largely by himself and independent of any established scholar or school of thought.

No discussion of Neanderthal interpretations would be complete without some consideration of Hans Weinert, the only living anthropologist who has actively maintained that the known Neanderthals represent a previous stage in human evolution. Weinert has represented this point of view since the 1920s but has, if anything, drawn even less notice in the French- and especially the English-speaking worlds than has either Hrdlička or Weidenreich. Part of the tendency to overlook his work may be due to the language barrier, though his views have been translated into French (1944a). While he wrote the section on fossil man in the widely read compendium *Anthropology Today* (1953), it remains in German and one fears that this only serves as an exercise for graduate students boning up for their language exams.

The disruptions suffered by German anthropology as a result of two world wars and the stifling influence of the Nazi regime have meant that few German anthropologists have achieved much recognition since the 1920s. Writers on fossil man such as Breitinger, Gieseler, and Heberer accept the predominant views of the significance of the Neanderthals advocated by French (and derived English and American) anthropology (Heberer, 1955b). In this area, Weinert is the sole perpetuator of German evolutionary views dating from prior to World War I, and some of the failure of his position to receive recognition may be traceable to the general eclipse of German anthropology.

The other possible reason for his failure to attract serious consideration is his insistence, almost amounting to an obsession, that the human ancestor was a chimpanzee (1944b:204–205, 208–211, 228–229, 243–244, 263; 1953:102, 104). This, however, should have been put in its proper perspective by his clear recognition that both men and chimpanzees have been pursuing long independent courses of evolution since the Tertiary (Weinert, 1951:28, 54–55). Perhaps his acceptance of Piltdown (1944b:223), despite the suspicion of German anatomists from Schwalbe (1913:602) to Weidenreich (1936:117–119), can be traced to this early confusion. In any case, if one reads Australopithecine or even prehominid for chimpanzee wherever it occurs in his earlier writings, then his reasoning makes quite good sense.

If the Pithecanthropus-Sinanthropus skulls can be taken as morphologically intermediate between the immediate prehominids and modern man and if they do represent a stage in the prehistoric development of the genus *Homo* (denied by Boule, 1913:263; 1921:109; 1923:109; 1937:20; by Vallois, 1946:370; and implicitly denied by Boule and Vallois, 1957:145, 191, 257), then the rest of Weinert's arguments must be given serious attention.

At the outset, he noted the frequent lack of a clear correspondence between the record of archaeology and the geological time scale and the untrustworthiness of absolute time designations. Thus his position is less dependent on the accuracy of premature time estimates than is the position of those who prefer a catastrophic to an evolutionary explanation for the hominid fossil record. His major arguments run as follows:

1   Neanderthal morphological characteristics fit nicely in between those of Pithecanthropus and those of modern man, and it would be difficult

on morphological grounds alone to deny the existence of a Neanderthal stage in the line that developed into modern man (1942b:245).

2 "Everywhere we meet Middle Palaeolithic forms of men, only the Neanderthaler and nothing else is to be found" (1944b:248). If in fact the Neanderthals became extinct without issue, this would mean that "up to now we have always found in the Middle Palaeolithic only the remains of extinct side lines but never individuals of our own ancestral line" (1944b:244; also 1947:105).

3 The frequency of Neanderthaloid features visible in Upper Palaeolithic skeletal remains, particularly among those of the earliest known Upper Palaeolithic, is particularly marked in comparison with their evident descendants, the later Neolithic and modern peoples. Especially notable in this respect are the finds at Brünn, Brüx (noted in this same context by Schwalbe, 1906b), Chwalynsk, Combe Capelle, Lautsch, Mount Carmel (actually a late Mousterian population), Podbaba, Podkumok, and Předmost (Weinert, 1946:243–261; 1947:103–104, 136–138; 1951:177–191).

Not since before the last world war has any other established authority specifically recognized the morphological intermediacy of the earliest Upper Palaeolithic populations between the earlier Mousterian and more recent peoples (Coon, 1939:37), though a number of authors have apparently been aware of the possible implications since they have taken pains to explain that, in these cases, there is nothing really reminiscent of Neanderthal morphology or that for reasons of dating this could not be linked in an evolutionary series with the Neanderthals (Vallois, 1959:93, 135–137). On the other hand, the recognition of this morphological intermediacy has led a number of authors to seek some sort of explanation, and, being unwilling to concede that "pure" *Homo sapiens* did not exist in remote antiquity, they have suggested varying degrees of hybridization between a "classic" Neanderthal and one or another sort of "modern" form of man (Coon, 1939:38–44, 51; Montagu, 1940:521; Hooton, 1946:337–338; Thoma, 1957–1958; W. W. Howells, 1959:228). This, however, becomes exceedingly vague when the "modern" element in the mixture is described as "primitive sapiens" (W. W. Howells, 1944:202–203; Thoma, 1958:43), which in turn is considered as differing irrevocably from Neanderthal form by nuances in the degree of brow ridge division, of canine fossa, and relative chin development. Since the functional significance of these features is not considered, it is not at all clear why so much importance should be attached to them—particularly when it is realized that the range of variation among modern peoples greatly exceeds the difference between for instance Skhūl V and La Ferrassie I (cf. brow ridges in Australian versus Chinese, canine fossa in Negro versus Eskimo, chin in Tasmanian versus European).

There is no doubt that the available evidence is insufficient to constitute proof in the sense of "highly significant" statistical probability for any given hypothesis as was realized by Hrdlička (1930:345), though this should not be taken to indicate, as Vallois does (1945:113 ff.), that a catastrophist hypothesis is therefore more likely than an evolutionary one. Before a defense of the evolutionary point of view is undertaken, it should be briefly mentioned that two schools of hominid catastrophism exist at the present. The first is represented solely by Vallois who still maintains the position established by Boule that, if there is any relation between Neanderthal and modern forms of man, it was due to common ancestry at a time so remote that there is no fossil evidence for it. This view, entitled "Présapiens" by Vallois (1959:97 ff., 144–156), might be called the position of extreme (or "classic") catastrophism, in opposition to the modified (or "progressive") catastrophism of Sergi, Heberer, F. C. Howell, Breitinger, Le Gros Clark, and others (entitled the "Préneanderthal" theory by Vallois (1959:139–144)). This latter view has relied heavily on the third interglacial status of the Skhūl remains as an indication that a population existed prior to the European Neanderthals of the early Würm whose morphological features were closer to those of modern man. The removal of Skhūl from the third interglacial (Higgs, 1961a and b) and the discovery of early Würm Neanderthals of "classic" form in the Middle East (Solecki, 1955, 1960, 1961; Stewart, 1959, 1962) indicate that the sequence and timing of hominid developments in southwest Asia was not significantly different from the picture derived from the European record. This leaves primarily Saccopastore as support for the views of modified hominid catastrophism, and an appreciation of the expression of sexual differences in the Neanderthals (Weinert, 1947:96–98) and the great but generally ignored range of variation of the "classic" Neanderthals themselves (Brace, 1962c:731) should remove the arguments built on this basis.

Recently F. C. Howell has stated in reference to the possibility of a Neanderthal phase in human evolution that, "unfortunately, this point of view has still to be meaningfully stated in terms of modern evolutionary theory" (1957:331), though he regards such a concept as "no longer useful since there was marked variability from one such group to another" (Howell, 1957:343). This, of course, implies that Hrdlička's definition of Neanderthal was conceived in terms of physical characteristics which, in fact, it was not. Since I believe that some concept of Neanderthal Phase can prove useful, it should be worthwhile to restate it—I hope meaningfully—and see whether the "marked variability" correctly noted by Howell is indeed a fatal flaw.

While quantities of writing exist on the subject of the Neanderthals, almost no concise definition is offered. Hrdlička's definition, however, is not only concise, it is the only one offered in conjunction with clear evolutionary principles. It is worth quoting it here.

> The only workable definition of Neanderthal man and period seems, for the time being, to be, *the man and period of the Mousterian culture.* An approach to a somatological definition would be feasible but might for the present be rather prejudicial. [Hrdlička, 1930:328, differing trivially from Hrdlička, 1927:251; Hrdlička, 1929:595; italics Hrdlička's.]

Contrary to what one might have expected, Hrdlička's definition, then, was primarily a cultural definition. If culture is "the principal adaptive mechanism employed by man in his so far successful bid for survival" (Brace, 1962b:343), then it makes good sense to view the major stages of human evolution in terms of major changes that culture has undergone. Since major cultural changes have in each case altered the selective pressure operating on the human physique, then there is good reason to expect a correlation between the cultural and the physical changes in the human fossil record, and we should be able to fill in the somatological part of the definition left blank by Hrdlička.

Necessarily the sequence of stages so discovered will depend on the completeness of the information that we possess, and inevitably our information is sketchy for the earlier part. Here, again, culture shows an advantage over skeletal material alone as a guide since the archaeological record, whatever its defects, is far more complete than the record of hominid fossils. Fortunately there are just enough of the latter to make, tentatively, some of the correlations necessary in the construction of such a scheme.

Utilizing the cultural and skeletal evidence available, four stages in human evolution can usefully be postulated which simply constitute a redefinition with the addition of an Australopithecine stage, of the scheme offered by Schwalbe (1906a:8) and defended by Weinert (1932; 1951:57–59; 1955:304) and Weidenreich (1940:381; 1946:29)—realizing of course that future increases in information will show that these are really arbitrary points chosen in what is actually a continuum. The four stages are presented diagrammatically in Figure 2-9, with an indication of the cultural-biological

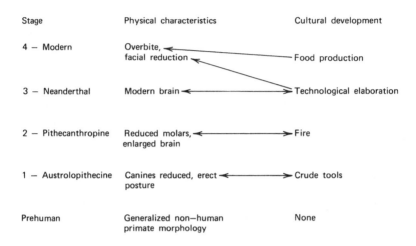

Figure 2-9 The postulated stages in human evolution with the related selective pressures indicated by the associated cultural developments.

interactions designated by the arrows. Since this paper is primarily concerned with the Neanderthal problem and since these designated relationships have been discussed elsewhere (Brace, 1962a and b), it need only be added that the biological consequences of the cultural changes indicated in stages 1 and 2 probably were delayed in much the same way that the general facial reduction of stage 4 is the consequence of the cultural elaboration of stage 3.

Specifically, reliance on tools for defense, characterizing the difference between the Prehumans and the Australopithecine stage, meant that projecting canines were no longer necessary equipment and hence free to vary. With the cumulative effect of random mutation inevitably resulting in the reduction of those structures whose adaptive significance has been reduced or suspended (Brace, 1963), the canines of the first tool users could be expected to reduce after a sufficient period of reliance on tools (and hence culture in the larger sense) as the primary means for defense. The same kind of delay can be expected before the reduction of the molars followed the regular utilization of fire (and perhaps the addition of significant and regular quantities of protein to the diet as a result of the development of effective hunting techniques; meat does not have to be chewed as much as other foods since protein digestion is primarily in the stomach and there is less requirement to be mixed with salivary enzymes).

Among the bearers of the Mousterian cultural traditions assigned to stage 3, "the post-cranial skeleton is basically modern human in over-all morphology" (F. C. Howell, 1957:335). The brain has reached its modern size and, despite the attempts of Boule to characterize its supposed "structural inferiority"' (Boule and Vallois, 1957:246; see also Boule, 1912:182–206; surviving in Patte, 1955:500), there are no indications that the brain was functionally different from that of modern man (Weidenreich, 1947b; Montagu, 1960:196). Clear differences can be seen only in the metric and morphologic characters relating to the face (Morant, 1927:333–340, 374; F. C. Howell, 1951:387; Brace, 1962b:347–349). With much of the organization of the human face concerned with the supporting role it plays in regard to the dentition, any change in selective factors affecting the teeth will ultimately have effects on total facial morphology. According to published figures, there is no evident difference between the gross tooth dimensions and little between the tooth forms of the Pithecanthropine and the Neanderthal stages shown in Figure 2-9. See Figure 2-10 (Pithecanthropine and Neanderthal tooth measurements compiled from Weinert, 1925:32, 37, 39; Weidenreich, 1937:17, 24, 29, 38, 81, 82; Dahlberg, 1960:245; and Brace, unpublished). It is evident that the greatest difference in the teeth of the Middle Palaeolithic and those of modern man occurs in the anterior part of the dental arch.

In the absence of any other reliable evidence pertaining to the facial morphology of the Pithecanthropine stage (where no complete face is preserved), it can be tentatively assumed that this was not significantly different from that of the Neanderthal stage except in the area of the brow ridge where the face is hafted onto the skull. Selective factors pertaining to the dentition, then, can be presumed to have changed little between the Pithecanthropine and the beginning of the Neanderthal stages, but following the Neanderthals, the reduction, amounting to the transformation into the modern face, is clear evidence of such a change (see comments by Keith,1925b:318–319). It has been suggested elsewhere that technological elaboration starting in the Mousterian and proceeding on through the Upper Palaeolithic introduced specialized tools to perform the variety of tasks formerly handled by the teeth—especially the front teeth (Brace, 1962b:347–349). The adaptive significance of a large dentition having been thus reduced, it is free to vary, and the probable effect of accumulating random mutations is reduction (Brace, 1963).

With such an explanation for the significance of the difference between Pithecanthropine, Neanderthal, and modern form, I suggest that a morphological corollary be added to Hrdlička's cultural definition of Neanderthal as a stage or phase of human evolution:

> *Neanderthal man is the man of the Mousterian culture prior to the reduction in form and dimension of the Middle Pleistocene face.*

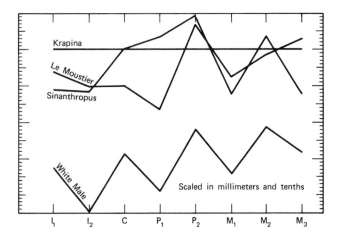

Figure 2-10 Middle Pleistocene, Neanderthal, and modern tooth-crown size (M.D. + B.L.), with Krapina taken as the line of reference. See Table 2-1 for figures.

Table 2-1 Crown Size Measurements (M.D. + B.L.)*

	Krapina	Le Moustier	Sinanthropus	White Male
I1	19.13	18.5	18.02	15.88
I2	17.53	16.5	16.53	13.10
C	19.21	18.2	19.25	16.31
PM1	19.95	18.3	20.30	16.05
PM2	18.34	19.0	19.28	16.11
M1	25.26	24.5	23.73	21.86
M2	23.45	23.3	23.63	21.32
M3	22.53	22.8	21.31	19.72

* These are the measurements from which Figure 2-10 was constructed. Adapted from Brace, unpublished; Weinert, 1925; Dahlberg, 1960; and Weidenreich, 1937, respectively.

This view of human evolution in general and of the problems represented by the interpretation of Neanderthals in particular is offered in place of the views of hominid catastrophism generally held, which apparently had their theoretical bases in the early nineteenth-century doctrines of Georges Cuvier and which have dominated anthropological thinking for the past 50 years following their application to the extensive French Neanderthal material by the palaeontologist Marcellin Boule. Such views reach their extreme with Weckler's curious formulation that pictured hypothetical populations tramping to and fro over vast distances "for reasons not as yet ascertained" (Weckler, 1954:1013), but perhaps the clearest expression of this view is in the writings of the French prehistorian Teilhard de Chardin who believed that the phases of human development "displace each other rather than pass into each other directly,...neither Peking Man,...nor Neanderthal Man have any direct offspring left today in the living world: they have been swept away by *Homo Sapiens*" (Teilhard de Chardin, 1943:25–26; also quoted by Weidenreich, 1947a:197).

To eliminate the headache concerning the origin of modern man by claiming that he sprang full blown from the mind of a troubled palaeontologist into an early Pleistocene stratum is to propose an explanation which borders on mythology. Instead, it is urged that the orientation based on standard evolutionary theory as developed by Schwalbe, Hrdlička, Weidenreich, and Weinert be reexamined and a systematic attempt be made to view the known hominid fossil record in these terms as modified by more recent theoretical advances in the thinking of genetics and ecology.

Finally, in keeping with the promise inherent in the title of this paper, I suggest that it was the fate of the Neanderthal to give rise to modern man, and, as has frequently happened to members of the older generation in this changing world, to have been perceived in caricature, rejected, and disavowed by their own offspring, *Homo sapiens.*

~ ~

Epilogue

As I noted in the Prologue, nothing has fundamentally changed the situation in the 35 years since this chapter was first written. Although many additional pieces have been added, there has been nothing that would change the picture I defended 35 years ago. As far as the fossil and archaeological evidence and interpretations are concerned, I brought these up to date in my Skomp Lecture at the University of Indiana in 1992 (Brace, 1992). Since then, there has been a successful effort to extract mitochondrial DNA from one of the bones of the original discovery in the Neanderthal, and much has been made of the fact that that sample of Neanderthal mtDNA from the first hypervariable region of the mtDNA control region—HVRI—differs from the mtDNA of living humans by 27 base pairs while living human populations differ from each other by an average of 8 pairs out of the 333 base pairs tested (Krings et al., 1997). More recently, they came to similar conclusions from testing the sequence of base pairs in the second hypervariable region—HVRII (Krings et al., 1999). My initial reaction had been that "a single mitochondrial lineage does not a population make" (Brace, 1997b:4). Subsequently, a check of mtDNA variation within and between great-ape groups has shown a picture of variation that simply dwarfs the range of human diversity. The range of variation even within single social groups of chimpanzees can be greater than the whole human spectrum, and the variation between the four chimpanzee groups tested expands that picture even more (Gagneau et al., 1999). At the same time, the range of visible physical distinctions between the human groups is an order of magnitude greater than the almost imperceptible differences between the various groups of African chimpanzees. Despite their genetic diversity, the chimpanzees, when given the opportunity, treat each other as though they were members of the same species. With this as a comparative example, it would seem that the modest mtDNA differences between the single Neanderthal tested and recent human beings would hardly warrant consigning them to separate species.

In 1992, I finished my Skomp Lecture with a few utterances from that deservedly obscure versifier, I. Doolittle Wright, in the Department of Homopathic Anthropopoetics of the University of Southern North Dakota at Hoople, and it seems appropriate to repeat them here. It is typical of his ineptitude that his title contains an unintended self-deprecation. He calls it:

Catastrophe in Rhyme

I repeat my perennial scold,
Our profession is shaped by the mold
    Of the covert view
    That the roots of the new
Are not to be found in the old.

The source of the general rule,
Transmitted by Marcellin Boule,
    That Neanderthal
    Had no offspring at all,
Is the Neocatastrophist School.

But it seems unaccountably strange
To deny that the strength of a range
    Of natural forces
    Suffice as the sources
That shape biological change.

There's something completely absurd
In the view that's been recently heard;
    The claim that stasis
    Can serve as the basis
Of all that has ever occurred.

Mechanics are never detected
In the popular view that's projected;
    Since all that works
    Is change by jerks;
And Darwin is flatly rejected.

For that's how most scholars behave,
And it's easy enough to be brave,
    When objection at most
    Is the groan of the ghost
As it turns in its Westminster grave.

But if Darwin were with us today,
Consider just what he might say;
    "Examine the strata
    Containing the data,
And use the ensuing array."

Now ponder that primitive brood,
Eating their undercooked food;
    The ones that are early
    Are rugged and burly,
With tools that are simple and crude.

Then look at what happens with time,
As a result of the technical climb:
    The reduction of stress
    Means there's more of the less,
With moderns emerging sublime.

If we stick to the fossils involved,
The problem is easily solved;
    Since Neanderthal form
    Can serve as the norm
From which our species evolved.

CHAPTER 3

Tales of the Phylogenetic Woods:
The Evolution and Significance of Phylogenetic Trees
(1981) [1]

Prologue

Eighteenth-century naturalists such as Linnaeus utilized the principles of formal logic traceable to Aristotle—"The Philosopher" to his Medieval admirers—to deduce the proximity or distance of each living form from each other. Linnaeus "took from the old logica materialis the concept of genus, species, and difference" (Hennig, 1966:79) and used this to produce his hierarchical classification. This, he felt, was the goal of scientific endeavor. As more than one historian of science has realized, for Linnaeus, "classification was no matter of mere convenience but the heart and soul of science" (Greene, 1959:182–183; and see the agreement from one of his most respected biographers, Larson, 1971:144). The hierarchy he produced, however, was a fixed and changeless manifestation of God's intent, the "Great Chain of Being." Positions in that hierarchy did not indicate actual kinship between adjacent forms. Higher or lower status on the Chain only demonstrated relative proximity to the Divine at the top, and the whole was simply an indication of relative merit as it was established by God's design.

It was the genius of Charles Darwin's to convert the tree-like relationships in Linnaeus' Great Chain into a depiction of the actual relationships between living things since their departure from a common ancestral form at some time in the past (Lovejoy, 1936; Ghiselin, 1969). Ever since Darwin, scholars have been depicting the course of evolution by constructing tree-like dendrograms. Anthropologists are no exception, and the history of anthropological ideas concerning their reading of the course of human evolution can be seen in the kinds of phylogenetic trees they have constructed.

As the American Association of Physical Anthropologists approached the 50th anniversary of its founding, the late Frank Spencer, who had become recognized as the historian of the Association, planned, with the help of Noel Boaz, a retrospective at Charlottesville, Virginia, where our organization had been born in April 1930. Spencer, who had been one of my own doctoral students at Michigan in the previous decade, graciously asked me to survey the way in which biological anthropology has viewed human evolution through the changing nature of the phylogenetic trees they have generated. Noel T. Boaz and Frank Spencer then edited the Jubilee

---

1 Delivered at the University of Virginia, Charlottesville, December 11–12, 1980

Issue of the *American Journal of Physical Anthropology,* December 1981, which included not only the papers given at Charlottesville the previous December but also the retrospective papers given earlier at the 50th meetings of the Association in Detroit in April 1981. As can be seen from the scope of history represented in my paper as it is reproduced here, the editors were extremely lenient in allowing me to cover a time span that precedes the dates that they had intended to cover by nearly a full century. I hope that my exercise of the privileges of seniority and mentorship can be seen to have been in a good cause.

Now well over 15 years later, I can see a point or two where my rendering of the history of ideas was somewhat off the mark. Specifically, my claim that Eugene Dubois, the Dutch physician and discoverer of the original *"Pithecanthropus" erectus* in Java, had been an assistant in Haeckel's Institute at Jena was not correct. I had simply taken the word for that from Hans Weinert's *Menschen der Vorzeit* (1947:33). After my paper had been published, a splendid biography of Dubois was presented by Bert Theunissen as a doctoral dissertation in the Netherlands. Subsequently this was translated into English (Theunissen, 1989). Dubois himself had not been a student of Haeckel, but his professor in Amsterdam, Max Fürbringer, had been a Haeckel student and subsequently initiated Dubois into his outlook (Theunissen, 1989:78). New information can alter our understanding of the history of ideas just as it does of the course of organic evolution.

≈   ≈

I ntellectual traditions frequently shape the way in which scientific questions are posed as well as the procedures undertaken to answer them.
When I attempted to provide a paleoanthropological illustration of this realization some 15 years ago (Brace, 1964), one of the commentators phrased
the rhetorical query, "Since when in science can one base oneself on arguments of nationality?" (Genovés, 1964:23). This objection was raised in
regard to issues relating to the phylogenetic treatment of a particular set of
human fossils, and, from the perspective of the history of science, a relatively
minor matter. The proper response, had I been adequately prepared, would
have been to note the reaction of a figure of unimpeachable stature to the various ways in which a truly major scientific synthesis was perceived. The best
example is the reaction of none other than Charles Darwin to the reception
of his theory of evolution by means of natural selection. In a letter he wrote
to the French anthropologist Armand de Quatrefages, he said, "It is curious
how nationality influences opinion; a week hardly passes without my hearing
of some naturalist in Germany who supports my views, and often puts an
exaggerated value on my works; whilst in France I have not heard of a single
zoologist, except M. Gaudry (and he only partially) who supports my views"
(in F. Darwin, ed., 1887:299).

The Comparative Reception of Darwinism (Glick, ed., 1974) admirably
documents the fact that there are indeed different national styles of thinking
when it comes to dealing with major aspects of science. If this has been true
for the treatment of the interpretation of organic evolution in general, it has
also been true for approaches to the study of human evolution in particular.
As this paper will attempt to show, this is graphically illustrated by the various forms that are offered as human phylogenetic trees.

NINETEENTH-CENTURY ENGLAND

Verbal portrayals of human descent in the form of a tree are present in the
very earliest written records and are commonly found in cultures that lack
a system of writing. Further, many cultures contain accounts of the kinship
between humans and particular members of the animal kingdom, though
these are usually expressed in symbolic and totemic form and rarely, if ever,
rendered as identifiable parts of a literal family tree (cf. treatments by Frazer,
1887; Freud, 1950; Lévi-Strauss, 1962). While there were occasional earlier
attempts to portray a more than biblical human antiquity and a putative
lineal kinship with nonhuman ancestors (see the treatments in Eiseley, 1958;

Greene, 1959; Osborn, 1894), it is clear from the record that a systematic concern for the course and forms of human ancestral development did not begin until after the publication in 1859 of that extraordinary scientific landmark *On the Origin of Species,* by Charles Darwin.

To be sure, despite popular assumptions to the contrary (Wilberforce, 1860:135; Broca, 1862:314), Darwin only alluded to the possibility that his approach could be applied toward an analysis of the human condition, barely more than two paragraphs from the end of his epoch-making work, when he wrote, "Light will be thrown on the origin of man and his history" (1859:488). In subsequent editions, this was expanded only to the extent that he said "Much light will be thrown...." (cf. 1872:504).

If this seems in retrospect to be brief to the point of being cryptic, the implications were not lost on Darwin's contemporaries despite the fact that he himself waited a dozen years before developing the theme in *The Descent of Man* (1871). While Darwin proceeded with deliberate caution, others were quicker to follow the path to which he had pointed. Nor did these accounts display signs of unseemly haste. The evidence for human antiquity presented by Sir Charles Lyell (1863) was the product of several decades of meticulous fact collecting. Likewise the demonstration of the biological affinities of human with particular nonhuman form by Thomas Henry Huxley in *Evidence as to Man's Place in Nature* (1863) was a masterful synthesis based on an enormous amount of information.

Curiously, although Huxley, Lyell, and later Darwin (1871) dealt with the prehistoric skeletal material known at that time, including the original Neanderthal remains, they all avoided the gambit of arranging them in hypothetical lineages purporting to show the course of human evolution. That they should eschew such a step seems an odd bit of caution on the part of the authors whose works embody some of the most daring innovations of the entire nineteenth century. In fact, however, in spite of their very different personalities, all three displayed an intellectual style that came relatively directly from the ethos of the Scottish Enlightenment. Lyell, as intellectual heir of Hutton and Playfair, was born and raised in Scotland (Eiseley, 1959; Wilson, ed., 1970; Wilson, 1972). Darwin's introduction to both natural science fieldwork and biological theory was in Edinburgh just before the effective end of the Scottish Enlightenment (Gruber, 1974:39, 80–81). And, for whatever historical reason, one of the most penetrating observers of the history of science has noted that "Huxley's personal creed was a kind of scientific Calvinism" (de Beer, 1970:917).

Not only did they exemplify the application of the Protestant Ethic in the realm of science (Merton, 1938, esp. pp. 415–419), but, as has been noted for their British contemporaries in the physical sciences (Olson, 1975), the particular style displayed was very much that of the Scottish Philosophy of Common Sense. If the naïve extremes of the inductive empiricism of Bacon and Locke were avoided, nonetheless there was a faith that the powers of human reason were sufficient to discover the nature of the world, whose structure was assumed to be logical. And if they recoiled from the extremes of skepticism of a David Hume, and feared the related position of "materialism," at the same time they displayed an elaborate caution when it came to considering anything that could be regarded as a possible projection of the ideals whose loci are primarily in the human mind. Given the nature of the available evidence and the tenor of the times, it is hardly surprising that the exemplars of British science in the latter part of the nineteenth century refused to speculate on the possible specifics of a human line of descent.

FRANCE

If the English were slow to suggest schemes for human phylogeny, the French were even slower. For one thing, even among the few who accepted the possibility of organic evolution, a Darwinian form of mechanism was explicitly rejected (Gaudry, 1878:250, 257; Topinard, 1888:473; Stebbins, 1974:138, 164). Furthermore, the effective founder of the field of anthropology in France, Pierre Paul Broca, was an avowed polygenist and vocally unsympathetic to a Darwinian approach (Broca, 1870, 1872; Schiller, 1979:226, 232).

By this time, of course, the whole field of vertebrate paleontology had been in existence for more than a generation following its creation by Georges Cuvier by the beginning of the century (Simpson, 1961:43, Coleman, 1964:2, 114). As the field of human paleontology developed in France late in the nineteenth and early in the twentieth centuries, it adopted an outlook that was rooted in the catastrophism that characterized its older model (Brace, 1964, 1966). Because of the quantity of physical evidence for the form of prehistoric human appearance found in France late in the last and early in the present centuries, and because of the interaction of European political and intellectual history, an essentially French viewpoint has played a very important role in shaping the enduring traditions in the field of paleoanthropology.

As a consequence of this, much of the field, especially in France, has continued to show an orientation that has been either covertly opposed to or silent regarding the depiction of schemes that try to arrange the known fossil record into an evolutionary sequence. Even when ultimate human origins are conceded to be "monophyletic," the depiction of subsequent human development is in a "polyphyletic mode" where the lines of development are viewed as proceeding separately in the form of a "bush" (Vallois, 1952:78–79; see Figure 3-1; Thoma, 1973; Gould, 1976; de Benoist, 1979). The same analogy has been used by French archaeologists to depict the course of prehistoric cultural development (Bordes, 1950). It is interesting to recall that Cuvier himself insisted that "life was a bush, not a ladder" (Eiseley, 1958:88), though in that instance he was opposing the formulations of those who were attempting to defend an integrated and hierarchical *scala naturae*.

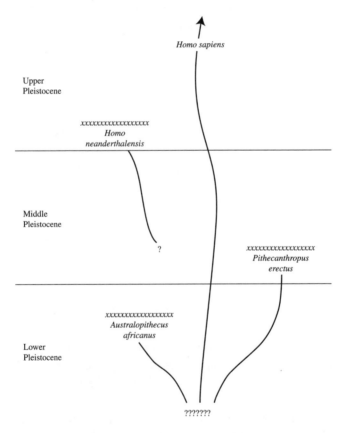

Figure 3-1 A version of the polyphyletic formulation favored by French anthropologists, adapted from Vallois (1952:77) with the addition of *Australopithecus*. All nonmodern fossil hominids are considered to have become extinct without descendants (from Brace et al., 1979:168).

Finally one must note that a kind of mystical evolutionism was promoted in a French context even though it had no positive impact on the actual study of the course of human evolution. This was initiated by Henri Bergson in his *Évolution Créatrice* (1907) and continued in Teilhard de Chardin, especially his posthumous *Le Phénomène humain* (1955). Lovejoy's appraisal of Bergson was written before Teilhard's works were published, but it could serve to characterize them as well. He noted that the central insight of such a philosophy was "a thing to be reached, not through a consecutive progress of thought guided by the ordinary logic available to every man, but through a sudden leap whereby one rises to a plane of insight different in its principles from the level of mere understanding" (Lovejoy, 1936:11–12). As Medawar observed in regard to Teilhard, this "stands square in the tradition of (German) *Naturphilosophie*" (Medawar, 1967:72), but though he regarded much of it as "nonsense," he added, "on further reflection I see it as a dotty euphoristic kind of nonsense very greatly preferable to solemn long-faced germanic nonsense" (1967:9). In any event it contributed nothing to interpretations of the hominid fossil record.

HAECKEL AND GERMAN ROMANTIC EVOLUTIONISM

The first formal phylogenetic tree purporting to depict the course of human evolution was the creation of that extraordinary scion of German *Naturphilosophie* Ernst Haeckel. The prehistoric portions of this structure, at least in its earliest manifestations, were based on hypothetical constructs. The first of these was *"Pithecanthropus,"* which he included without comment in his system of the mammals in the second volume of his *Generelle Morphologie* (1866:clx). At the same time he also suggested the possibility that the term "Erecta" could be used as a taxonomic designation for the human family. In later discussions he added the form *"alalus"* to serve for "speechless men" while he used *"Pithecanthropus"* to represent "ape-men" (1870:590, 597). By the end of the century, *"alalus"* was demoted to become the species name for this hypothetical *"Pithecanthropus"* and this in turn was considered to be ancestral to *Homo sapiens* via the further hypothetical form of *Homo "stupidus"* (1899:35; see Figure 3-2).

All of this is relatively well known and considered relevant only insofar as it contributed the name that the Dutch physician Dubois later gave to the material he found in Java between 1890 and 1892. Also well known are the different positions that Haeckel and Virchow took in regard to the interpretation of the original Neanderthal skeleton and Haeckel's gloating, after having

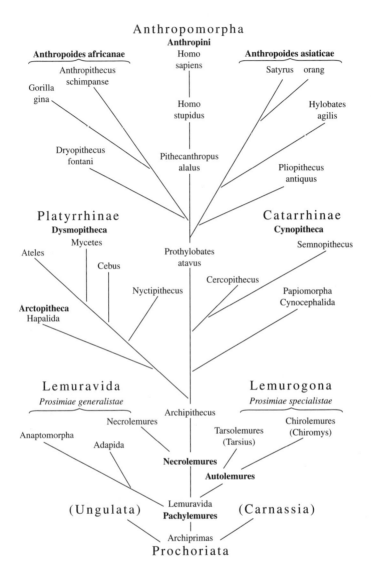

Figure 3-2 The Primate family tree according to Haeckel (1899:35).

outlived Virchow, when he felt that Dubois's discoveries and Schwalbe's interpretations proved that Virchow had been wrong (Schwalbe, 1901; Haeckel, 1906:108–109). There is more to the story, however, and the point of adding it is to demonstrate how matters of a distinctly nonscientific nature can have a bearing on scientific assessment.

Eugene Dubois received his training in Germany and in 1880 was an assistant at the institute of anatomy at Jena just at the time that Haeckel's influence was on the rise. It was there that Dubois picked up his interest in evolution and the orientation that he was later to try to apply to the material he collected in Java (Weinert, 1947:33). It is interesting to note that Dubois first referred to the famous Trinil discovery as *"Anthropopithecus"* (1891), the term Haeckel used for the chimpanzee. When he found the femur, he kept the same generic designation though he changed the species from *"troglodytes"* to *erectus* (1892). In his full published report he recognized that he had more than a chimpanzee, and it was then that he used Haeckel's generic term for "apeman" and called it *"Pithecanthropus erectus"* (1894). He presented substantially the same views at the third International Congress of Zoology at Leyden in 1895 (Dubois, 1896).

Then, as has often been noted, he remained silent on the matter for more than 20 years and refused to let visitors see his material (Spencer, 1979:415–420). Finally, when he did resume consideration of it, he had undergone a radical change of mind and regarded his *"Pithecanthropus"* not as a transition form but as a giant extinct gibbon (Dubois, 1932, 1935). Some of the accounts tend to lead the reader to suspect that Dubois had become a little "queer" (Wendt, 1956:299), but there are some other things that may have been involved. For one thing, the interpretation that regarded his fossil as a giant gibbon had in fact been offered by none other than Virchow at that Leyden Congress in 1895 (Virchow, 1895:746–747). Even though Dubois later claimed that he got the idea from the first edition of Boule's *Les Hommes Fossiles* (Boule, 1921:109; Dubois, 1935:583), it would appear that it was the influence of Virchow that was of principal importance (Ackerknecht, 1953:203).

The fact that Dubois switched from the Haeckel-oriented views of his youth to those of Virchow, Haeckel's longtime rival, brings us back to the nature of their disagreement. An older reading of the history of science suggested that the issue was where they stood in regard to Darwinian evolution. Haeckel presumably stood for an evolutionary interpretation of both Neanderthal and "Pithecanthropus," and Virchow opposed it. The real nature of the Haeckel/Virchow opposition, however, was quite different, and the buffetings suffered by anthropology, however important they may seem to us, were an unintended and relatively inconsequential byproduct of a much more important dispute (Virchow, 1877; Haeckel, 1878; Gasman, 1971).

Haeckel, in fact, in the latter part of the nineteenth century, was busily promoting an aggressive German nationalism of an anti-Semitic and anti-Christian (particularly anti-Catholic) nature that may well have been painful to Dubois's Catholic sensibilities. In any case, the movement of which Haeckel was an active part resulted in a gigantic armed conflict that swirled around the edges of Dubois's own small country. A possible index of Dubois's feelings can be seen in the fact that, after World War I was over and he returned to the arena of scholarly publications, he changed the spelling of his given name from its German form (Eugen) to its French one (Eugène) and ceased entirely to use the German language as the medium for his reports. Whatever the truth may be, it is clear that Dubois's switch from the position advocated by Haeckel to that defended by Virchow cannot be explained by a consideration of the anatomical and paleontological data available at the time.

If some thought that Haeckel simply represented Darwin written in German, the reality was quite otherwise. As Gasman has written:

> Although he considered himself to be a close follower of Darwin and...invoked Darwin's name in support of his own ideas and theories, there was, in fact, little similarity between them. Haeckel himself thought of evolution and science as the domain of religion and his work therefore assumed a character which was wholly foreign to the spirit of Darwin. Darwin's empiricism, his caution in the face of speculative theories, his general mechanical conception of the workings of nature were all in striking contrast to Haeckel's biology. For Haeckel, evolution did not only mean the process of change from one species to the next. Evolution for him was a cosmic force, a manifestation of the creative energy of nature (Gasman, 1971:11).

What Virchow, the cautious, empirical liberal really feared was not materialism or mechanistic evolutionism but the elevation of Haeckel's peculiar brand of evolutionary mysticism to the status of a state religion (Virchow, 1877). The subsequent course of German history has shown that Virchow's fears were fully justified. As the most careful appraisal has shown, Haeckel displayed "a romantic rather than a materialist approach to biology....The content of the writings of Haeckel and the ideas of his followers—their general political, philosophical, scientific, and social orientation—were proto-Nazi in character...a prelude to the doctrine of National Socialism" (Gasman, 1971:xiv).

In a major way, this had an impact on the world that has been far more momentous than French romantic evolutionism. One other minor and almost unnoticed casualty was the effort to produce a human phylogenetic tree based on real fossils. This construction was formulated by the Strassburg anatomist Gustav Schwalbe and was greeted with considerable satisfaction by Haeckel

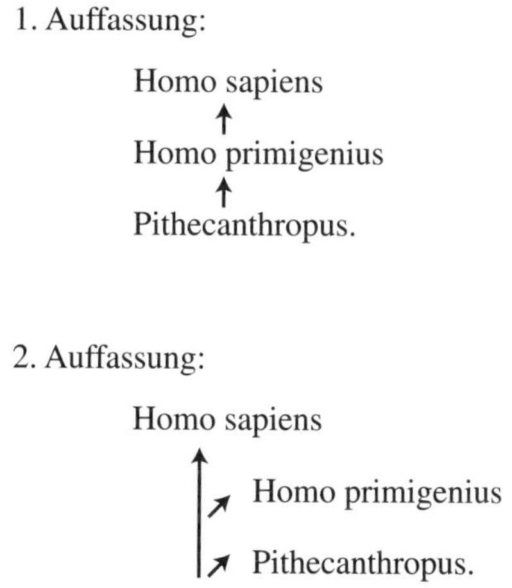

1. Auffassung:

Homo sapiens
↑
Homo primigenius
↑
Pithecanthropus.

2. Auffassung:

Homo sapiens

Homo primigenius

Pithecanthropus.

Figure 3-3 Two possible arrangements of the known hominid fossils by Gustav Schwalbe. "*Homo primigenius*" was the term he used for Neanderthal (from Schwalbe, 1906:14).

himself (1906:109). Schwalbe produced two possible arrangements of the then-known *erectus,* Neanderthal, and modern fossils (see Figure 3-3, from Schwalbe, 1906:14). One could almost be regarded as a cladogram, and the other, for which he declared his preference, was a simple phyletic line.

Initially, Schwalbe's formulation was adopted with some approval in England (Sollas, 1908; Keith, 1911a, b). By the outbreak of World War I, however, Keith had a complete change of heart (1915, 1925, 1931a, b), and for the next half-century almost no recognizable vestige of Schwalbe's well-considered formulation was to be found. Further, Hrdlička, in his splendid summary of the known human fossil record, completely misrepresented Schwalbe's position and its significance (Hrdlička, 1930:327). Hrdlička's curious treatment of Schwalbe's views, which were actually quite similar to his own, may have been due to his antipathy for things German (Spencer, 1979:15, 18, 769–770), though this can be no more than informed speculation.

The last pre–World War I phylogenetic scheme associated with German romantic evolutionism was the wondrous concoction by the Breslau anatomist Hermann Klaatsch (see Figure 3-4 from Klaatsch, 1910:567; Wegner, 1910:120). As with the phylogenetic trees of Haeckel, the organizing principle was basically hypothetical, and known fossil and modern specimens were added only after the fact. It had few defenders, and after a blast of criticism from Keith (1910, 1911b), the type of construct that it represented disappeared from serious scientific consideration.

111

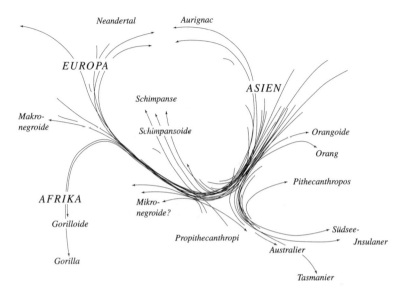

Figure 3-4 The hypothetical scheme of human, ape, fossil, and hypothetical forms suggested by Klaatsch (1910:567).

ROMANTICISM AND SIR ARTHUR KEITH

When the late Lord C. P. Snow spoke of "the two cultures," he provided evidence for the fact that the paradigm shift from the Age of Enlightenment to that of Romanticism had not been as all-encompassing as Lovejoy's treatment would lead one to believe (Snow, 1963; Lovejoy, 1936). Snow himself was at home in both a literary and a scientific milieu, though he was aware that this was not true for most intellectuals. In the middle of the nineteenth century, the gulf between the two realms, while appreciable, was not quite so unbridgeable. Charles and Emma Darwin, for example, enjoyed the company of Thomas and Jane Carlyle. Conversely, the historian of philosophy George Henry Lewes was given an advance copy of Darwin's *Origin* to review for *Blackwood's* (Barzun, 1958:34). After the "Oxford Movement" and the conversion of John Henry Newman in England (1845, see O'Connell, 1969; Weatherby, 1973) and the end of the Scottish Enlightenment (Hook, 1975), however, the gap grew to such an extent that communication between the sides dwindled to the point where some of those who attempted to provide bridges produced serious misrepresentations instead. One such was Sir Arthur Keith.

Through his numerous books and articles, Keith earned a reputation in England as one of the foremost students of human evolution. He was a self-proclaimed follower of Darwin (1950:562), and, on his retirement from the Royal College of Surgeons in London, he spent the rest of his life in a house on the grounds of the Darwin estate at Down—in the eyes of the public, supposedly a continuing symbol of the Darwinian spirit. Some years ago (1964) when I noted that Keith and the majority of the students of the human fossil record displayed a reluctance to interpret the evidence from the perspective of Darwinian evolutionary principles, it was clear that they had bowed to the influence of the non-Darwinian ethos that prevailed in France after World War I. In the case of Keith, however, I had not realized the extent to which the ground was already prepared for his defection.

Keith specifically mentioned the fact that it was the influence of French paleontology that led to the change in his views (Keith, 1946:141; 1950:318–319). The phylogenetic trees which then served as the frontispieces for his most influential work (1915, 1925) had a distinctly French cast to them as Vallois in effect noticed nearly 30 years ago (Vallois, 1952; and see Figure 3-5). With changes in dates and some other details, some of the main points of Keith's formulation continue to be apparent in the schemes of his immediate (Hooton, 1931; 1946:413; see Figure 3-6; Leakey and Goodall, 1969:108; L.S.B. Leakey, 1965, and interpreted in Cole, 1975:255; see Figure 3-7) and more remote (R. E. Leakey and Lewin, 1977:84–85; Kennedy, 1980) intellectual heirs. In his scheme building, however, Keith and his followers did not go to quite the skeptical extremes of the "évolution buissonante" formulations which the French tend to prefer (see Figure 3-1). Instead they tended to retain some of the speculative continuity that was first apparent in the diagrams of Haeckel.

It is interesting to note, in this regard, that Keith retained a warm admiration for Haeckel (Keith, 1935). Further, Keith's ideas concerning racial purity, and his enthusiasm for war and prejudice as devices for promoting racial development (1931b), are startlingly close to Haeckel's and subsequent Nazi racial policy. Like Haeckel, Keith's self-declared enthusiasm for Darwin (cf. 1950:562) masks a more basic commitment to romantic mysticism. In his autobiography (1950) he noted his youthful enthusiasm for Thomas Carlyle, and it is clear from a careful reading of his writings that Carlyle continued to remain the dominant influence in his mode of thinking (cf. Keith, 1931b:27). In Darwin's appraisal of Carlyle, he recounted on one occasion his pleasure in listening to Carlyle's discourse (Litchfield, ed., 1915:II:21), and on another that "I never met a man with a mind so ill adapted for scientific research" (F. Darwin, ed., 1887:1:64). In some respects, a bit of that judgment could be applied to Keith himself. Although Sir William Bragg, in his presidential address before the British Association for the Advancement of Science in

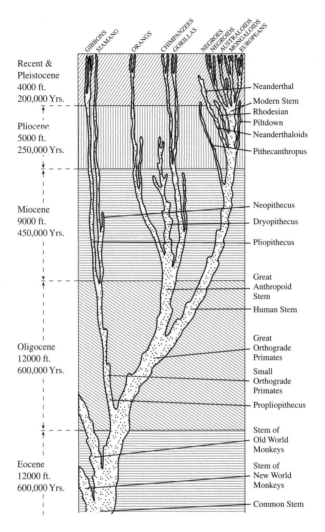

Figure 3-5 The Boule-influenced diagram prepared by Sir Arthur Keith to serve as the frontispiece of his *The Antiquity of Man* (1915, 1925).

1928, chided the outgoing president, Sir Arthur Keith, for his materialism (Spencer, 1979:74–75), Keith's "materialism" had far more in common with the vitalism of Haeckel (and for that matter Bergson) than with Darwinian mechanism. Keith rejected the role of chance in evolution in a manner quite akin to Paley's "natural theology" of more than a century earlier (Paley, 1802). "I could as easily believe the theory of the Trinity as one which maintains that living developing protoplasm, by mere throws of chance, brought the human

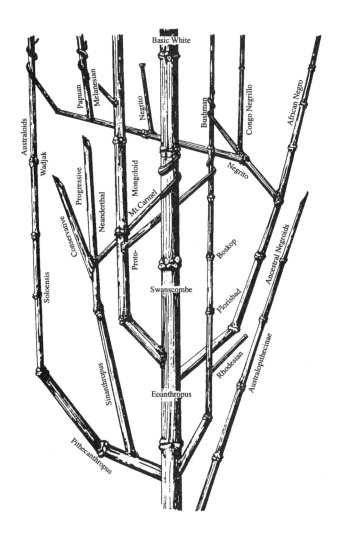

Figure 3-6 The refinement of Keith's polyphyletic diagram by Hooton (1946:413).

eye into existence. The essence of living protoplasm is its purposiveness" (Keith, 1946:217). Then in a passage that could easily have come straight from Haeckel he added, "I have just affirmed that there are evolutionary processes inherent in living things and therefore in Nature—trends of change which are akin to human purpose and human policy" (1946:218). There is little of the cautious empirical Darwin in his writings, and it is interesting how little of Darwinian mechanism is to be found in the schemes of his English and, via Hooton, his American successors.

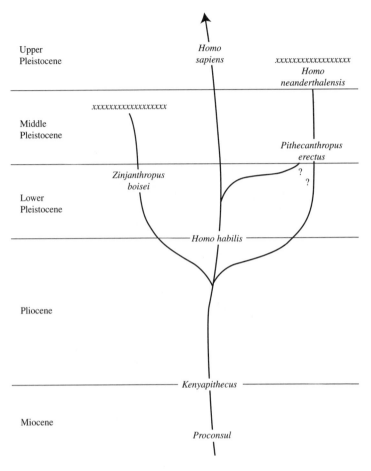

Figure 3-7 The family tree preferred by the late L. S. B. Leakey. The only hominid fossil accepted as a possible human ancestor is his own "*Homo habilis*" (adapted from Leakey, 1965:115 as depicted in Brace et al., 1979:169).

CLADISTICS

In order to avoid the manifest subjectivity of the past, and in an effort to make assessments of evolutionary relationship more objectively testable, many students of evolution have recently engaged in the practice of constructing diagrams with twigs and branches called cladograms. These are offered to depict phylogenetic relationships. Although there is more than a little difficulty in rendering time on a cladogram (Delson et al., 1977:265), and this was not even considered when Julian Huxley first proposed the term "clade" (Huxley, 1959), the sharing of "derived"—that is, modified or nonprimitive—traits, which is the basis for adjacent placement of terminal twigs, is assumed to be based on recency of descent from a common ancestor (Cain and Harrison, 1960; Mayr, 1974). According to some advocates, "trees should always be based on cladograms" and discussions of evolutionary dynamics should follow after the construction of the trees (Tattersall and Eldredge, 1977:205). Although the proponents of this approach would prefer to label it "phylogenetic systematics" (Eldredge, 1979), the term "cladistics" is a lot easier to get straight and is preferable for a number of reasons (Mayr, 1974:95).

Indeed cladograms based on shared trait states are easy to draw up, and in many instances they may constitute satisfactory depictions of evolutionary relationships (see Figure 3-8), but there are some things that they do not handle very well, and a number of scholars have issued caveats with varying degrees of stringency (Mayr, 1974; Van Valen, 1978; Gingerich, 1979). The fact that cladistics has trouble with time is even occasionally offered as a virtue of the approach as shown in the phrase that it represents "phylogeny without true time dimension" (Delson et al., 1977:265). Having eliminated a concern for time, the authors go on to decry the attempt to depict ancestor–descendant relationships which they declare to be "untestable." One must grant, of course, that the paleontologist cannot test his problems in the laboratory like a modern chemist, but there are more than a few who do not regard

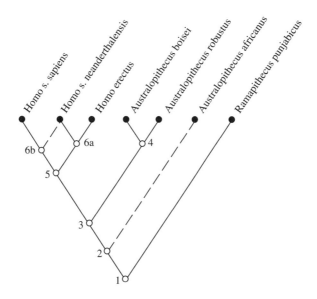

Figure 3-8 An example of a plausible hominid cladogram (Eldredge and Tattersall, 1975:235).

this as sufficient reason for declaring that paleontology ceases to be a science when it deals with matters that are unique to its domain, namely time and relationships. Even the cladist who has noted that "the probability of recognizing ancestors in a fossil sample is zero" goes on to suggest that the likelihood of studying the nature of ancestry is "quite substantial" (Vrba, 1980:77).

Aside from the problem of dealing with time, which surely is crucial for any study of evolution (Van Valen, 1978), there are two other matters that cladistics has trouble handling. One of these is the problem of differing rates and times of change for different traits within a single line or between related lines, i.e., mosaic evolution (Mayr, 1974). In the case of hominid evolution, for example, the timing of changes in brain size (Holloway, 1980a, b) and tooth size (Brace, 1979a, b, c) is quite different, with the result that there are still major questions in regard to the cladistic affinities of more than a few important early hominids.

Another problem that clouds the practice of cladistic analysis is the matter of continuing change after a given branch point. As Mayr has noted (1971:16, 17), cladistics ignores the distinction between evolutionary parallelism and evolutionary convergence, but one could go further and observe that it cannot handle phyletic divergence either (cf. Eldredge and Cracraft, 1980:73–74). It is perfectly possible for forms to diverge after a branch point and then later reconverge to produce a misleading picture of phyletic affinity. Turner's depiction of a possible connection between the Hoabinhian people of the Southeast Asian Mesolithic and the Jōmon people of Japan may well be a case in point (Turner, 1979).

Cladistic analysis in fact assumes that the main significant steps in evolution take place at branch points and that what happens subsequently is of considerably less importance. Inevitably those who favor the use of cladograms to illustrate phylogenetic relationships also prefer to regard evolution as primarily a process of fits and starts. This is embodied in the term "punctuated equilibria" to describe the course of organic change (Eldredge and Gould, 1972; Hecht et al., 1974). The promoters of this approach in fact seem to have taken one of Simpson's three major modes—quantum evolution (Simpson, 1944:198, 206; 1953:389–393)—and elevated it to a position of principal importance. As has been abundantly demonstrated (cf. Vrba, 1980), there are many instances where species appear suddenly in the fossil record and enjoy long periods of apparent stasis before vanishing. Whether or not the initial shaping was done in a small, isolated, and peripheral population is another matter entirely. In fact the extreme exponents of cladistics reject any concern for evolutionary dynamics as a matter of principle (Gaffney, 1979:88).

It is also clear from the data of paleoanthropology that gradualism does occur despite the bald but unsupported statement to the contrary by Gould and Eldredge (1977:135). Hominid brain size doubled over a span of 1.5 million years until it effectively reached its modern size some time before the onset of the last glaciation. Subsequently it evidently has displayed the expected equilibrium, but at the same time human tooth size has reduced by a full 50 percent in a broad belt running from Europe to Japan (Brace, 1979b, and in preparation). Although this dental change may seem like a sudden event in the full span of evolutionary time, it was not accompanied by speciation, it did not take place in isolation, nor was it particularly peripheral. Furthermore, the preceding expansion in brain size took place gradually over a suitably long period of evolutionary time and evidently was shared by the entire hominid population.

Those who have been principally behind developing the picture of punctuated equilibria, whether or not they are proponents of cladistics, have placed it in opposition to the models of evolutionary gradualism that they have traced to the world views and political philosophies of the initial proposers, principally Darwin, Lyell, and their English contemporaries (Gould, 1977). Others of course have noted that Darwin's views were very much a product of his background. Karl Marx, writing to Engels, observed, "It is remarkable how Darwin recognizes among beasts and plants his English society…" (Schmidt, 1962:37). Commenting on the continuing favor with which Darwinian ideas are held, Gould and Eldredge have noted, "The general preference that so many of us hold for gradualism is a metaphysical stance embedded in the history of western cultures: It is not a high-order empirical observation induced from the objective study of nature" (1977:145).

The possibility must be considered, however, that there may be just as much of social conditioning inherent in the recent enthusiasm for punctuated equilibria as opposed to gradualism. Not only are many of the supporters products of an affluent post–World War II milieu in which instant gratification was accepted as due, but as the originators of the view have noted, "it may also not be irrelevant to our personal preferences that one of us learned his Marxism literally at his daddy's knee" (Eldredge and Gould, 1977:146).

Finally, one can suggest that the origins of the paleontological traditions in the scholarship of nineteenth-century France may also be of some consequence. The current in modern paleontology that accepts the discontinuous nature of the stratigraphic record as indicative that the history of organic life has been discontinuous (Gould, 1965), the emphasis on sudden, dramatic change (Gould, 1974, 1978a, b), and the stress on speciation events in small isolated groups remote from the area of consideration followed by sweeping take-overs, all are remarkably similar to the outlook that characterized nine-teenth-century French paleontology. A century ago this contributed to the French rejection of the idea of evolution by means of natural selection. Its reemergence today in the writings of a generation of paleontologists who have not looked carefully into the traditions of the field in which they have been trained could well lead to its being designated "neocatastrophism" (Brace, 1978:983). In view of what we can suspect is the lurking French connection, it would be appropriate here to recall what the French would say in this regard: *Plus ça change, plus c'est le même chose.*

THE HOMINID PHYLETIC PICTURE

If the interpretive styles of a century ago are still with us in several guises, in addition a quantity of fossil material has been accumulated that was simply undreamed of by the empirically oriented thinkers who framed the first evo-lutionary syntheses. Given what we now possess, the possibility of building various kinds of descent "scenarios" is almost inevitable. As has already been noted, Gustav Schwalbe made the first attempt to deal with the known hominid fossils early in this century from what would now be regarded as the perspective of "evolutionary systematics" (see Figure 3-3). Although this was largely forgotten with the eclipse of German views that generally occurred fol-lowing World War I, the approach was not entirely without subsequent devel-opment. Over 40 years later and bolstered by many more fossils, Schwalbe's student and, briefly, successor at Strassburg, Franz Weidenreich, produced a sophisticated elaboration (Figure 3-9, from Weidenreich, 1947:201; and see also Weidenreich, 1946a:24). By this time, however, the paradigm that gov-erned interpretation in paleoanthropology, despite some lip-service to Dar-win, was largely that of the French tradition. As a consequence, in the few instances where Weidenreich's work has been mentioned, it has been seri-ously misrepresented. One major work, actually dedicated to Weidenreich in memoriam, stressed the long-continued geographic isolation of separate developing hominid lines (Coon, 1962). Another redrew his diagram to remove all of the connecting lines that indicated contact between geographi-cally adjacent populations and then labeled it the "Polyphyletic or Candelabra School" (Howells, 1967:241). In fact, however, the polyphyletic stress on regional isolation was more a reflection of the expectations of the readers than it was inherent in either Weidenreich's diagrams or his discussion.

In their appraisal of the dynamics of hominid evolution, both Weidenreich and Dobzhansky (1944) noted that, once the level of the genus

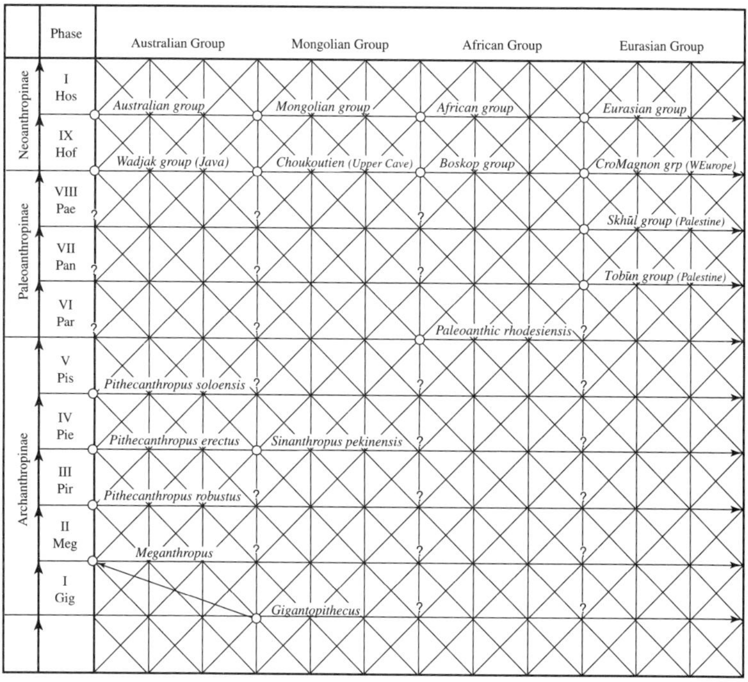

Figure 3-9 This famous diagram is more scenario than tree, and has more implications than the simple designation of "polyphyletic" would lead one to believe (Weidenreich, 1947:201).

Homo had been reached, the geographic isolation that would lead to local speciation would no longer occur (Weidenreich, 1943b:253, 1946b:414). Gene flow across population boundaries then would be sufficient so that the genus would contain a single albeit regionally differentiated species. If, as Dobzhansky noted, modern *Homo sapiens* constitutes a "single polytypic species" (Dobzhansky, 1944:265), the expectation was implicit that the same thing should have been the case for the previous history of the genus *Homo*. This was the basis for the suggestion that, prior to the appearance of what we recognize as "modern" form, the human line passed through a grade of organization (cf. Huxley, 1958) characterized by larger jaws and teeth and a skeleton displaying greater robustness and more pronounced muscle markings. The first such prehistoric skeleton to be recognized was the one discovered in the Neanderthal in 1856, and there are some scholars who felt that this was reason enough to attach that name to the stage through which human form had passed before reaching its modern configuration (Hrdlička, 1927, 1930; Weidenreich, 1928, 1943a; Brace, 1964).

This does not mean, as some have assumed, that the European Neanderthals gave rise to the modern Chinese—or Africans or Indonesians. Instead it means that one would expect to find that the local predecessors of Chinese, Africans, and Indonesians—and any other modern population where continuity in situ can be expected extending back to the last interglacial— would display a degree of robustness in teeth, jaws, skeletons, and muscle markings comparable to that observed in the European Neanderthals. The idea of a polytypic Neanderthal Stage as the antecedent to modern forms of *Homo sapiens* has been criticized for many reasons (Howells, 1974, 1976; Thoma, 1973, 1975; Santa Luca, 1978), but it still seems more useful than the alternatives available that, at best, are largely cladistic in nature. As Mayr has put it, "It results in a great deal of loss of information to ignore the adaptive component of evolution expressed by the concept of grade..." (Mayr, 1974:107).

In Europe itself, where the evidence collected is more abundant and better known than anywhere else, the most thorough recent analyses have shown that the transition of Neanderthal to modern tooth and face form occurs gradually and without any break (Brace, 1979b; Smith and Ranyard, 1980), and it is clear that there is no reason why such a transition could not be documented for the postcranial skeleton as well (Trinkaus, 1976, 1977). In Africa, the evidence is scrappier and the dating much more tentative, but there is nothing inherent in the material from Omo (Kibish) to Florisbad (Day, 1969; Rightmire, 1978) or anything in between (Robbing, 1972) that would contradict such a view. And in China, Mapa and the recently discovered Da Li skull (examined at the Institute of Vertebrate Paleontology and Paleoanthropology in Beijing, 1980, courtesy of Prof. Wu Xin-zhi) make splendid Neanderthal Stage precursors of the modern Chinese. Finally, the evidence from Indonesia also is consistent with a picture of in situ continuity from early Middle Pleistocene *erectus* to Solo and possibly via Wadjak to modern Australian form.

At the Neanderthal level the quantity of material available from widely dispersed areas creates the very real problem of whether a single term is adequate to encompass it all. In spite of the efforts of pheneticists and cladists to reduce taxonomy to a rigidly defined and presumably objective science, the element of "art," as Simpson has noted (Simpson, 1961:110, 227), will continue to remain in the practice of the proverbial "competent systematist" (Carter, 1951:118–119).

Earlier in the course of hominid evolution there is another problem that is just as difficult to deal with. This involves the question of how to designate continuous change through time. Of course, one solution is simply to deny that the hominid phyletic line gradually evolved from one species into another, which is precisely the tack taken by one recent survey (Stanley, 1979:80–82). Otherwise, if full cladistic logic were followed (Eldredge and Cracraft, 1980:114, 244), we would still belong to *Australopithecus africanus* if indeed the last splitting event in hominid evolution occurred when *africanus* and *boisei* differentiated.

Most paleoanthropologists, however, accept an in situ transition from *Australopithecus* to *Homo* at the generic level and then from *erectus* to *sapiens* at the specific level. The problem, then, is the classic one of successive species—where to draw the lines, and what to call the lineage and when. When we only had a few points in time represented, it was easy enough to give them names without regard to whether the entities named were discrete events or points on a continuum—the "piers" of Sollas's "ruined bridge which once continuously connected the kingdom of man with the rest of the animal world" (Sollas, 1908:337). While the gaps remained, they provided either room for the presence of a presumed "God" or justification for the specific essentialism preferred by the cladists.

Now, however, the accumulation of recent discoveries has confirmed Sollas's assumptions. While this is gratifying to those with Darwinian expectations, it has created the terminological problems alluded to above. At the earliest level, *"afarensis"* has been proposed as specifically distinct from *africanus* because of its possession of a series of features that are clearly more primitive (Johanson and White, 1979)—"plesiomorphic" in the cladistic lexicon. But the differences in these traits are no greater than those by which modern human "races" are distinguished, and they indicate at most that *africanus* had simply been pursuing the same adaptive strategy for a longer period of time. If the same logic were rigorously applied to the recent hominid fossil record, then the Neanderthals would once again warrant a separate specific designation from *sapiens*. Even the Skhūl specimens and possibly such early Upper Paleolithic groups as Předmost would have to be consigned to separate species. All of this remains unresolved even though there can be little doubt concerning the probable status of the Hadar and Laetoli specimens as representing the condition ancestral to all subsequent hominids.

At a slightly more recent level of time, the same sorts of problems (and more) becloud the status of what has been called *"habilis."* Using the most numerous data available, namely, tooth measurements, a kind of "stratophenetic" (cf. Gingerich, 1976, 1979) arrangement has been made that then is used to defend a tree in which *"habilis"* is regarded as the direct descendant of *"afarensis"* and the immediate precursor of *erectus* (Johanson and White, 1979:327–328). A similar scheme has been defended using multivariate distance measures (McHenry and Corruccini, 1980:1104).

While this may very well be correct, it does not tell us when to change the generic or even the specific names. Further, it is just possible that the legitimate *H. erectus* and *A. africanus* specimens may have been lumped from different sites and time periods to make up the *"habilis"* group in the first place (Brace et al., 1973). Part of the difficulty has been caused by the prolonged delay in the proper comparative treatment of the original material on which the proposed taxon was based.

Even Holloway's recent suggestion that the braincase of the type specimen, OH 7, warrants the designation *Homo* can be challenged on solid quantitative grounds (Holloway, 1980b:273; Wolpoff, in press). His further comment that final taxonomic placement will have to await the appraisal of the dentition raises another major problem, even though the one comparative and quantitative treatment of the dentition published has shown that the teeth of the type specimen cannot be distinguished from *Australopithecus africanus* (Brace et al., 1973).

But the problem is that the brain and the teeth may very well be following separate evolutionary courses. This certainly was true late in the Pleistocene where brain size did not change at all but the dentition reduced by up to 50 percent (Brace, 1979a, b, c). Mosaic evolution is not only difficult for cladists to handle, it is difficult for the evolutionary systematist to represent in the form of a tree. At this point we are back to the "art" in Simpson's taxonomic practice. Even the complex schemes offered (cf. Figure 3-9; Brace, 1979c:105) are cluttered and difficult. One solution is to indicate the core of the tree by points based on the data from one evolving dimension and then subjectively depict a trunk that is wide enough to include a number of the detailed schemata that have been proposed. This is done in Figure 3-10 (from Brace et al., 1979:173). Whether this can accommodate the resolution of the brain size issue and the data from other dimensions that will eventually be considered is impossible to predict at the present time. At least it provides a framework for the various contending hypotheses that are currently being considered.

It is evident from the variations that are produced by the use of the different measures or their combinations that such simple quantitative procedures do not give us a single Platonic truth. Even the summed use of metrics representing the considerable amount of teeth available to us—however satisfying some of us may think this to be—only gives us a picture of evolution in one dimension. If we were to have similar quantities of information for other traits, many would present pictures that are quite different. Both schematic simplicity (Figure 3-10) and indications of considerable complexity (Figure 3-9) have their utility. No one has a monopoly on "truth." Although it

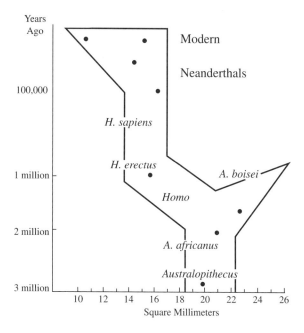

Figure 3-10 The dots within this tree are based on actual data points, sums of mean cross-sectional areas for the teeth in the dental arches of the populations named. The lowest dot is based on the material from Hadar and Laetoli. The dot between *africanus* and *boisei* is from the material at Swartkrans and Kromdraai. The earliest dot in the *sapiens* section is from the Krapina Neanderthals. The classic Neanderthals of western Europe are just above that, and the two dots at the top display the range between Australian aborigines and modern Europeans. (From Brace et al., 1979:173, based on data recorded in Brace, 1979a, b.)

is legitimate to feel that many have helped increase our understanding of the dynamics by which humanity emerged, it is just because we can never know the whole of that "truth" that a multiplicity of schemes will continue to be constructed and will continue to be of value.

In the past, I have often closed my comments with a bit of doggerel from the pen of that irascible versifier, I. Doolittle Wright, of the Department of Homopathic Anthropopoetics at the University of Southern North Dakota at Hoople. His efforts, however, have been limited to the use of the limerick form, and given the serious nature of the present occasion, it occurs to me that a more appropriate mode of expression would be preferable. Since I started the current paper with observations concerning the debt of Darwin and his contemporaries to the ethos of the Scottish Enlightenment, it seemed only fitting to record my own levels of skepticism in suitable Scottish form.

Although, as the name shows, he is not a proper Scot, nevertheless Wright's cousin I. Wright Drivell, a fellow faculty member in the Department of Homopathic Anthropopoetics, has dabbled in the use of the favorite stanza of Robert Burns. In response to Wright's simple certainties, Drivell, acting the veritable killjoy, replied to his cousin crossly with his:

Owed to Trees

As we survey the path we've trod
Of knowledge gained by labored plod,
Now each aspiring learned clod
Will try to see
How he can be a bit like God
And make a tree.

The record shows that those who strived
Produced results that look contrived;
Are twigs then based on traits derived,
To make a clade?
Do branches show the route arrived,
To reach a grade?

However much they try to please,
The schemes expand by twos and threes;
The viewer then who thinks he sees
Can only fail
To tell the forest from the trees
—To no avail.

~ CHAPTER 4 ~

Punctuationism, Cladistics, and the Legacy of Medieval Neoplatonism
(1988)

Prologue

After I had written the essay reprinted here as Chapter 2, I was bemused by the fact that it had made so little difference in the thinking of the majority of the students of human evolution. It slowly dawned on me that, while they all exhibit a fascination for the anatomical details of long-defunct hominids, few had any interest in the processes by which evolutionary change had taken place. The intellectual revolution initiated by Charles Darwin evidently had not yet had its impact on the outlook of the students of the evidence from which we deduce the course of the human past. For a variety of reasons, paleoanthropologists and a good many paleontologists have remained loyal to a pre-Darwinian outlook.

In the introductory notes preceding Chapter 3, I noted that Linnaeus had felt that the exercise of classification was the main activity associated with science. The principles of arranging things by names—"taxonomy"—are basic to dealings with the world of living things, and classifying is and will always remain an essential part of the biological sciences. Before he wrote his epoch-making synthesis *On the Origin of Species*, Charles Darwin spent eight years mastering the classification of the barnacles of the world (and see the magisterial treatment by Browne, 1995). Only then did he turn to the task of dealing with the mechanics by which biological change occurs.

Over the past generation, classification has been enormously aided by our ability to encode digitized data and treat them by computerized means. The actual intellectual processes involved are exactly the same as they were in Linnaeus's day in the eighteenth century, but the quantity of material that can be dealt with is orders of magnitude larger. The approach now generally used goes by the name of "cladistics," though its practitioners prefer the polysyllabic rendition, "phylogenetic systematics" (for example, Wiley, 1981). The celebrated natural history essayist Stephen Jay Gould has succinctly defined things this way: "A clade is a branch on an evolutionary tree, and cladistics attempts to establish the temporal order of branching for a set of related species" (Gould, 1981:6).

Strictly as a methodology, cladistics has much to recommend it. Given our computerized capabilities, it is quick and easy and allows us to handle enormous amounts of information all at the same time. Some of its practitioners, however, have brought a quantity of dogma along with the methodology, and this should give

127

pause to the potential user. The assumption that species are all absolutely equivalent entities may be methodologically convenient, but it is not always biologically justified. The assumptions that species remain unchanged between branching points and that change can only occur suddenly (for unknowable reasons), at the point of splitting at which time the parent species ceases to exist and two new sister species begin their existence, are also simply dogmatic assertions unsupported by the study of real events.

At least as troublesome is the application of cladistic methods to dealing with the human fossil record when there is very real reason to suspect that low but persistent levels of gene flow continued to maintain a single but widely dispersed and morphologically differentiated species. If the same techniques were used to assess living human populations, we would discover that there are at least half a dozen different species of *Homo sapiens* alive in the world today.

These thoughts and worries about the dogmatism and lack of concern for evolutionary processes evident among what are sometimes called "born-again cladists" led me to generate the following essay. I sent a copy to Michael Ruse, the philosopher of biology at the University of Guelph, Ontario, to get his reactions. He wrote back with the comment that he thought I was "spot on," and asked me to submit it to the journal he was just in the course of founding—*Biology and Philosophy*—which I did. His reviewers did not like it, however, so it remained an orphan for a while. The Harvard zoologist, Ernst Mayr, suggested further changes, which I duly made, and then sent it to Brunetto Chiarelli, founding editor of *Human Evolution*, who published it as it stands.

ᕗ   ᕗ

The current dominant orthodoxy in paleoanthropology has adopted the stance of cladistics and/or punctuationism and abandoned any concern for the mechanics by which selection has operated to control the course of human evolution. Rather than being a "new" intellectual development, this is simply the most recent manifestation of a tradition of thinking that goes back via Linnaeus to medieval scholasticism where reality was assumed to consist of discrete entities that can be dealt with solely by the exercise of deductive logic. While the construction of cladograms serves the useful function of proposing testable hypotheses, the promotion of cladistic logic as the only valid approach represents a great leap backwards into medieval intellectual stagnation. If an inductive component is not restored to paleoanthropology, it will cease to maintain its credibility as a productive science.

THE PUNCTOGRADUAL CONTROVERSY

Even at the time of the first full and formal exposition of organic evolution as the expectable norm in the biological world, there was a disagreement among the protagonists of such an expectation concerning just how the changes of which evolution consisted came about. To Darwin, the observations he had accumulated indicated that the processes of change would normally occur by gradual means (1859:471; and see Hull, 1974:51; and Herbert, 1986:119), but, almost on the very day of publication of his magnum opus, and even while offering his "claws and beak" in defense of Darwin's synthesis, Thomas Henry Huxley chided Darwin with the words "you have loaded yourself with an unnecessary difficulty in adopting *Natura non facit saltum* so unreservedly" (letter of November 23, 1859, in L. Huxley, ed., 1900 I:189). This was a view he repeated in his second unsigned review of the *Origin* in *The Westminster Review* the following spring. In this he noted that Darwin had "embarrassed himself" by his gradualist stance, and he declared his own belief that a recognition of the fact "that nature does make jumps now and then…is of no small importance" in making a solid case for "the doctrine of transmutation" (T. H. Huxley, 1860:310).

What Huxley was articulating was a theme that had arisen with the birth of the science of paleontology under Cuvier's aegis a generation earlier (Coleman, 1964:2, 114; Rudwick, 1972:117), when it was realized that living forms at the several periods of the remote past were different in a major sense from the ones that prevail at present. Although Cuvier and his successors provided abundant evidence for the fact that organic succession was regularly characterized by change, they shied away from a treatment of the mechanics involved (Gaudry, 1878:257; Topinard, 1888:473; Coleman, 1964:135).

Much the same was true for his immediate disciples and successors, for example Agassiz in America (Lurie, 1960), Owen in England (MacLeod, 1965; Rudwick, 1972:214), and Gaudry in France (Gaudry, 1878). Not only did they avoid the discussion of mechanism, but they were specifically opposed to the mechanism that Darwin offered. It is one of the wry ironies of the history of science that the field which has provided the most direct and abundant evidence in support of Darwin's theory of evolution should also be the last to accept the implications of a Darwinian outlook. Part of this is due to the fact that paleontology started as a French intellectual endeavor, and French biological sciences have remained resolutely anti-Darwinian until very recently (Stebbins, 1974; Boesiger, 1980), and the other part of it has to do with the discontinuous nature of the vast majority of the stratigraphic record. And if this has been true for paleontology in general, it has been even more true for paleoanthropology in particular where French dominance is especially evident (Brace, 1964, 1981).

Cuvier perceived the record of the past as a series of fits and starts, marked by extinctions followed by repopulatings either by preexisting forms from some peripheral area or perhaps by creation de novo. It is interesting to note that even the non-Darwinian attempt to characterize and regularize Cuvier's outlook was not done in France but in England where it was given the name of "catastrophism" (Whewell, 1832:126). Today, a century and a half later, the same stance has again been formally proposed as the expectable norm under the label of "punctuated equilibria" (Eldredge and Gould, 1972). More than one observer has realized that it could just as well be called "neocatastrophism" (Brace, 1978:983; Godfrey, 1981:9). Another has somewhat dramatically promoted it as the "Lizzie Borden Syndrome," presumably because the new fossil record replaces the old in a fashion that is "sudden, sweeping and violent" (Bakker, 1985:2).

Although "the theory of punctuated equilibrium" has recently been said to be "as dead as a doornail" (Levinton, 1986), it is in fact alive and well and has achieved the status of what could be regarded as the dominant orthodoxy in paleoanthropology (Eldredge and Tattersall, 1982). It pervaded the invited presentations at the recently concluded Ancestors Exhibition at the American Museum of Natural History in New York where it coexisted in comfortable compatibility with the cladistic outlook that nurtured it (Delson, ed., 1985).

While not all adherents of punctuated equilibria are cladists—and Stephen Jay Gould is a prominent example who has articulated his reservations (Webster, 1982; Gould, 1986:68)—the great majority share many if not all of the tenets of cladistics. To quote one recent appraisal, "the emphasis on the speciation event is one reason so many adherents of punctuated equilibria are also cladists—the strict dichotomous branching of lineages also emphasizes speciation and not adaptation as the central focus of evolutionary studies" (Cachel, 1986:453). The suspicion voiced concerning adaptation by punctuationists (Lewontin and Gould, 1979) and its complete absence in treatments of cladistics (for example, Wiley, 1981) would support that assessment, but there is an aspect of the use of cladistic logic that has great appeal to those who favor a punctuationist approach, and it is to the consideration of this that the remainder of this paper is dedicated.

Before continuing, however, I should at least state my position on the punctogradualist issue. While I am among those who put a gradualist interpretation on parts of the hominid fossil record (Brace, 1964, 1988) where others do not (Eldredge and Tattersall, 1982), it is not the invariant steady-rate kind of gradualism that has been set up as a "straw man" by the promoters of punctuated equilibria (Lewontin, 1986). In fact, I have repeatedly noted that the hominid fossil record, which is my own particular area of concern, is sometimes characterized by stasis and at other times by rapid change (Brace, 1979; Brace, Rosenberg, and Hunt, 1987), and, if different anatomical features are examined, one of these may have been going through a period of change while another remained static, whereas at another time it may have been vice versa, presenting a classic picture of mosaic evolution (Mayr, 1963:596, 637). I am in fact suspicious of any expectations a priori, whether they be for stasis or for change, though the regularities of change in the noncoding sections of DNA appear to justify many of the claims of the "neutralist" position (Nei, 1983; Nei, Stephens, and Saitou, 1985; Nei and Tajimo, 1985). And since the hominid fossil record displays a classic picture of the gradual emergence of one taxon out of another, I am particularly suspicious of statements which conclude that it is "self-evident" that "no single evolutionary lineage may be subdivided into a series of ancestral and descendant species" (Wiley, 1981:34). It is this, rather than an expectation of Darwinian gradualism, that has all the aspects of a dogma.

HISTORY

In the oft-quoted words of the late philosopher George Santayana, "those who cannot remember the past are condemned to repeat it" (Santayana, 1906:284). I suspect that no one who reads this will be unfamiliar with that phrase, and that there are many who would regard it as a truism that is so well-known as to have become trite. Since most of us pride ourselves on being steeped in the traditions and lore of our chosen fields, I further suspect that there are few if any who feel that they might just exemplify Santayana's warning.

And yet, I fear that many of us are ignorant of important dimensions in our intellectual heritage, and that some of the ongoing controversies and discussions are indeed a repetition in modern dress of those of an earlier age. The aim of the present paper is to examine several of these dimensions in both their ancient and modern manifestations and to see how temporal continuity has been maintained. The history of ideas may not resemble geology to the extent that we can take it as axiomatic that "the present is the key to the past," but certainly in both fields it is impossible to understand the present without knowledge of the past (and note the nearly identical expression in Tolstoy, 1985).

THE CATEGORICAL QUANDARY

To sharpen the matter a bit, one could note the application of Santayana's sentiment in the postscript to the recent literary success *The Name of the Rose*, wherein the author, that extraordinary linguist, medievalist, and writer Umberto Eco, observes that "the Middle Ages are our infancy, to which we must always return for anamnesis" (Eco, 1983b:74).

Many of you, I am sure, may feel that an author's commentary on a recently written mystery story is of questionable relevance to the study of biological evolution, but I am going one step further and offering for your consideration the possibility that this in fact points to what should be an important concern for those who would build cladograms and taxonomies, or otherwise dabble in the practice of constructing "scenarios." Here again, and in explicit detail, the matter is expounded by the same author, Umberto Eco, this time in his *Semiotics and the Philosophy of Language* (1984). "Outrageous!" I hear you cry, "how can a linguist, and, worse yet a philosopher of language, tell us anything about the nature of biological change in the past?"

You are right, of course, he cannot. Yet when a new hominid species is proposed, when the characteristics of this or that fossil are examined and its affiliations proclaimed, or when serological and morphological traits are analyzed to assess population distances and relationships, the result is a verbalized construct that purports to represent objective reality. Formulations of such verbalized constructs, however, follow the canons of hierarchical logic that are part of the fabric of Western civilization, and it is more than legitimate to inquire whether they actually display the nature of the real world as much as they reflect human linguistic behavior and the traditions of verbalization for its own sake.

This in turn is a reflection of that dualism in outlook which, since its explicit development in the writings of Plato, has permeated the thinking of the Western world, whether it be the this-world/other-world outlook of medieval Christianity or the efforts to delineate the essence of specific identity by Linnaeus and his predecessors or Willi Hennig and his followers (Lovejoy, 1936:52, 147; Hennig, 1966:154, 157, 165, 215; Larson, 1971:143; Losee, 1972:26; Eldredge and Cracraft, 1980:67; Wiley, 1981:1–2, 148–153, 287–290; Vrba, 1984:118, 130). This would seem to exemplify the remark credited to Alfred North Whitehead that "the safest characterization of the European philosophical tradition is that it consists in a series of footnotes to Plato" (Lovejoy, 1936:24). That Platonic strain which Sir Karl Popper has called "essentialism" (Popper, 1947:I:15, 28, II:8–20; Mayr, 1972:83) has been shown to underlie the typological thinking that was such an important theme in pre-Darwinian biology (Mayr, 1982:38). As the late George Gaylord Simpson reminded us, it is "pre-evolutionary and non-evolutionary." He went on to note that "[i]t still underlies a great deal of taxonomic practice but is now seldom favored in theory" (Simpson, 1951:286).

Actually Simpson wrote this before the resurgence of essentialism-in-the-guise-of cladistics had taken place. Recently it would seem that there is a growing movement (for example, Webster, 1984, and references) to restore the theoretical favor that Simpson and others (e.g. Mayr, 1957, 1959, 1963, 1972, 1982; Hull, 1965a, b) had felt lacked credibility. The punctuationist motto, "stasis is data" (Gould, 1982:85), exemplifies this change of heart even if the "logic" underlying the stance would appear to be as flawed as the grammar of the expression.

To give an unusual but thought-provoking perspective to the dangers inherent in typological thinking, consider the warning penned in that most unlikely of places *The Supper of the Lamb*—a cookbook written by an Anglican priest—in a passage that reflects both aspects of the author's identity: "But if man's attention is repaid…his inattention costs him dearly. Every time he diagrams something instead of looking at it, every time he regards not what a thing is but what it can be made to mean—every time he substitutes a conceit for a fact—he gets grease all over the kitchen of the world. Reality slips away from him and he is left with nothing but the oldest monstrosity in the world: an idol…. Idolatry has two faults. It is not only a slur on the true God; it is also an insult to true things" (Capon, 1970:17–18).

Categorical thinking is perhaps inevitable, and there have been those who have felt that human thought as we know it would be impossible without the use of those discrete mental symbols we use as a shorthand analogue of the real world (Ritchie, 1936:279; Langer, 1942:21–28; Whorf, 1956). One could argue that, even more than the "gradualism" for which the following phrase was offered, it is categorical thinking that is a "metaphysical stance embedded in the history of [human] cultures" (Eldredge and Gould, 1977:145). If then we confront the typology inherent in our very words and thoughts, we must also guard against the intellectual and practical paralysis to which the extremes of philosophical skepticism can lead. But more of that later.

THE LOGICAL QUANDARY

The flaws of typological thinking have been treated in thoughtful detail by many authors. Less well-treated, however, has been the matter of the transmission and nature of the philosophical and logical tradition mentioned by Simpson, though the case can be made that it is equally important.

It is well-known that the practice of taxonomy in modern biology differs little from that codified by the eighteenth century Swedish naturalist Carl von Linné, whom we know better by the Latinized version of his name, Linnaeus (Simpson, 1961). Ever since Darwin, most taxonomies, at least implicitly and often explicitly, reflect evolutionary and phylogenetic assumptions (Darwin, 1859:486; Simpson, 1961:36–52, 66, 221; Mayr, 1982:209).

Recently, proponents of cladistics, or what they would like to call "phylogenetic systematics," have abandoned a Darwinian concern for forebears, denigrating this as "ancestor worship" (Delson, Eldredge, and Tattersall, 1977:265, 276; Eldredge, 1979:166), and have regarded the information to be gained from fossils as "worthless" (Hennig, 1966:140–145, 165). As has been noted, evolutionary trees specify ancestors, but cladograms, like Linnean classifications, do not (Eldredge and Cracraft, 1980:239; Nelson and Platnick, 1984:153–154).

In addition, cladists have also abandoned a concern for stratigraphy (Delson, Eldredge, and Tattersall, 1977:265) and have regarded it as a virtue that the product of their analysis is "phylogeny without true time dimension" (Delson, Eldredge, and Tattersall, 1977:266). This gives us the curious paradox of scholars identified as being in the discipline of paleontology—"a science dealing with the life of past geological periods as known from fossil remains" (*Webster's Ninth New Collegiate Dictionary*, 1983:848)—who deny the utility of studying both past geological periods and fossil remains, and it has led at least one biologist to wonder whether this foretells the extinction of the field of paleontology itself (Thomson, 1985).

What is more, a concern for the forces of selection or any other evolutionary mechanism is also abandoned in favor of an avowed if unexamined faith in the hypothetico-deductive approach of Sir Karl Popper (Gaffney, 1979:86, 88, 100), the principal source and major modern representative of what has been called "irrationalist" philosophy (Stove, 1982:viii, 48, 50, 86, 102). In common with that eminent Victorian opponent of Darwin Sir Richard Owen, they display a "relative lack of interest in the causal mechanism by which organic diversity (is) produced" and a "reliance on an idealistic metaphysics" (Rudwick, 1972:214; also noted in Hull, 1983:63 and ff.).

What we see, then, is a retreat "into the security of Linnaean systematics with its concern for the elucidation of the two-dimensional, time-lacking design of the organic world"—a phrase that was used to describe the position of another troubled Victorian, St. George Mivart, who tried to reconcile himself to Darwinian evolution on the one hand and orthodox Catholicism on the other and failed on both accounts (Gruber, 1960:35).

The most direct clue to the intellectual legacy of the cladistic approach comes from the recognition that, in their use of "nested sets," cladograms have the same structure as Linnaean hierarchies (Eldredge and Cracraft, 1980:239). As many have noted, Linnaean hierarchies on their part bear a striking similarity to the nominal trees constructed *"per genus et differentiam specificam"* by medieval logicians, even though it has been claimed that Linnaeus himself never confused natural and logical forms (Larson, 1971:137, 144, 149). In the words of his most thoughtful assessor, "while logic is used as the instrument of scientific method, reality is not reduced to logic" (Larson, 1971:22, and note the confirmation by Lindroth, 1983:4).

Although this latter may have been true for Linnaeus, it most certainly was not true for his predecessors whose work is described as being characterized by "the Aristotelian method" (Larson, 1971:5). Actually, in his biological work, as Ernst Mayr has noted, Aristotle himself displayed "an empirical, almost pragmatic approach rather than that of deductive logic" (Mayr, 1982:152, and note similar assessments by Larson, 1971:23, and Preus, 1975:184; note also, however, that philosophers of science, rather than working scientists, can look at Aristotle's "science" in quite a different way as does Grene, 1963:238, 240, 251). Mayr (1982:307) would concur with those who award to "The Philosopher" a key position in the founding of the biological sciences (Thompson, 1913:30; Dampier, 1942:23, 95; Preus, 1975:250), observing that "[n]o one prior to Darwin has made a greater contribution to our understanding of the living world" (Mayr, 1982:87). In fact he goes still further and regards Aristotle as "unquestionably the father of scientific methodology" (1982:25), a kudos that must rank with his recognition as "the first Philosopher of science" (Losee, 1972:6).

But if Aristotle dealt with his perceptions of the natural world in one set of works (Thompson, trans., 1910) and logical methodology in another (McKeon, ed., 1941)—predication, entailment, *determinatio, abstractio,* and so forth (Larson, 1971:21, 22)—he shied away from tying the two together in a single coherent enterprise. Such, however, was not so for his followers, and a good case can be made for regarding this as the source of the difficulties encountered by biological systematizers from Caesalpino to Linnaeus to Hennig and their followers.

The figure principally responsible for taking the themes of Aristotelian logic and welding them together in a systematic format—a hierarchical tree—was Porphyry, the third-century student of and successor to Plotinus, the founder of the Neoplatonist school in Rome (Warren, 1975:9–10). It was Porphyry who was principally responsible for introducing and ensuring the importance of Aristotle in the intellectual traditions of the Western world (Walzer, 1966:289). But it was not the "pragmatic" and "empirical" Aristotle of the *Historia Animalium* where reality was first determined by observations from which generalizations are then drawn—induction, to use Aristotle's own preference. Rather it was the "logical" Aristotle of the Organon, but with the priorities altered. It was in the *Isogoge* that Porphyry reversed Aristotle's order and insisted that his modes of signification could be understood only in the light of the analysis of the ways in which one term can be related to another by predication (Moody, 1935:67; Warren, ed., 1975). The effect of this was to restore the status of Plato's views to which Aristotle had been opposed. A world of essences was assumed a priori, and verbal dialectic—deductive logic—was enthroned as the means of dealing with it (Moody, 1935:67; Balme, 1980:6–10).

At this juncture we can return to the implications of the analysis by Umberto Eco as, in the words of one appraiser, he "lays his axe joyously to the ancient logical tree of the followers of Aristotle and its modern offshoots, which hopes to make sense of meaning by reducing it to a sequence of branching alternatives" (Sturrock, 1984:17). As Eco has noted, Porphyry, in developing Aristotle's ideas in the *Isogoge,* "only suggests verbally the idea of tree but the medieval tradition has definitely built it up" (Eco, 1984:61). Eco eloquently documents the growth of the Porphyrian tree in the medieval Christian world. It is also perfectly apparent that Linnaeus simply represents the link by which this tradition is projected into modern biological thought.

Medieval Christianity, however, was not the only heir to Porphyry. Both the Islamic and Jewish scholarly milieus incorporated the Neoplatonic manifestation of Aristotle via the writings of the twelfth century Spanish-born contemporaries Averroes and Maimonides (Minkin, 1957:121). Both wrote predominantly in Arabic even though Maimonides was Jewish. With the incursion of Islamic zealots from North Africa in the middle of the century, the latter fled Spain and, somewhat ironically, settled next to Cairo where he became the physician of Saladin (Minkin, 1957; Schweitzer, 1971:65). Both were also translated into Latin and Hebrew in the subsequent century, and neither had much effect on what could be regarded as science in either the Islamic or Jewish worlds. Both were read and studied by scholars in the Middle Ages (Minkin, 1957:107; Schweitzer, 1971:66) when their influence joined the mainstream of Christian scholasticism with the consequences that Santayana, Popper, Eco, and a great many others have described in detail. Both, however, were also read and studied in the scattered manifestations of the medieval Jewish community where the Porphyrian refinements of Aristotelian logic were sharpened still further.

In Eastern Europe, which, for various reasons, had become the "numerical center" for the Jewish Diaspora by the "early modern era" (Schweitzer, 1971:56–57), the narrowing traditions of medieval scholarship produced "a kind of learning that was increasingly divorced from the life of the people, given over as it frequently was to intellectual games like *pilpul*—the clever yet arid and sterile resolution of seeming paradoxes in the Talmud" (Schweitzer, 1971:149). At the same time that Western European Christian theologians were engaged in the kind of disputation which some have apocryphally compared to attempts at deducing the number of angels that could stand on the head of a pin (Adler, 1982:19), their Jewish counterparts in Germany and Poland were engaged in the "hair-splitting dialectics" of *pilpul* that many rabbinical authorities uneasily felt gave a false perspective on reality and degenerated into useless sophistry (Adler et al., eds., 1905, vol. 10, pp. 39–43; Roth, ed., 1958:1508–1509). Even so, the training produced by engaging in such mental gymnastics was recognized to be of value and has remained a part of the Jewish intellectual tradition.

The point of this excursion is to demonstrate the continuity and strength of the Neoplatonic faith in the power of deductive logic as the principal tool for dealing with the world (Russell, 1940a:19; Moore, 1961:12). The dialectical outlook, whether manifest in the political stance learned at one's "daddy's knee" (Gould and Eldredge, 1977:146), or the "critical rationalism" that scientists credit to the legacy of Sir Francis Bacon's *Novum Organon* of 1620 (Morison, 1965; Feyerabend, 1978:175), has two inherent flaws that require the attention of all who would use it in the service of science.

The first of these problems is the unanswerable one that involves the relation between logical predication and actual entailment. The Porphyrian tree assumes rigid predication, but Aristotle himself was the first to criticize the Platonic approach to reality as a valid logical operation (Larson, 1971:23; Mayr, 1982:88). Whereas Plato claimed a primacy for dialectic, Aristotle denied it (Moody, 1935:67). Logic, as Aristotle noted, can neither refute a statement, nor draw a conclusion about an accident or property of a thing, or about its genus (Larson, 1971:23). In a hierarchy where each step is determined by *presence* or *absence* of characters, *absence* of a trait does not lead to further distinctions because "there can be no specific forms of negation" (Larson, 1971:23), but *presence* does not ensure entailment. If a logical species entails a difference, "the difference *does not* entail the species: 'mortal' has a wider extension than 'animal rational and mortal'" (Eco, 1984:64, italics Eco's; a view which is essentially the same as that expounded in Hull, 1974:47). Since *differentiae* do not contain each other, the classic Porphyrian tree not only is no longer ordered and hierarchical, there is no guarantee that it is even finite (Eco, 1984:66).

If this is the logical critique of attempts at deductive structuring, many of us can cite the pragmatic example of the frustrations that ensue when we tinker with exclusion/inclusion criteria in our attempts to use any of the many available cluster analysis programs to analyze real data (cf. Brace, Mahler, and Rosen, 1971:59–63; and note the problems of numerical taxonomy discussed by Ruse, 1973, especially in Chapter 8). Umberto Eco, speaking of the problem of using the Porphyrian tree in linguistics, comes to a conclusion that is equally appropriate for biology: "The tree of genera and species, the tree of substances, blows up in a dust of differentiae in a turmoil of infinite accidents, in a nonhierarchical network of *qualia*" (Eco, 1984:68). And in a more and possibly overly pessimistic general expression, Eco has his protagonist, William of Baskerville, lament, "I behaved stubbornly, pursuing a semblance of order, when I should have known that there is no order in the universe" (Eco, 1983a:492).

Finally, the inherent limitations of logic per se were set forth in stark clarity by the doyen of Logical Positivism himself, the late Rudolf Carnap: "Logical statements are true under all conceivable circumstances; thus their truth is independent of the contingent facts of the world. On the other hand, it follows that these statements do not say anything about the world and thus have no factual content" (Carnap, 1963:25).

THE MEDIEVAL LEGACY

The Neoplatonic legacy is still very much with us, creating tension, dispute, and obfuscation, differing little in basic nature though much in technical and computerized elaboration from both its medieval Jewish and Christian ancestors. This would evidently justify Popper's critique "that every discipline which still uses the [Neoplatonic] method of definition has remained arrested in a state of empty verbiage and barren scholasticism, and that the degree to which the various sciences have been able to make any progress depends on the degree to which they have been able to get rid of this essentialist method" (Popper, 1947:II:8). Of course, since Popper's insistence on the exclusive use of deductive logic (Stove, 1973:75, 79) is a classic example of the continuity of that tradition, it too is open to characterization as "empty verbiage and barren scholasticism." And perhaps also, our preference for an analytical framework constructed of categorical certainties is given added impetus by our dependence on the power and convenience of digital computers whose mechanics dictate that everything be treated in binary either/or fashion.

Cladistics and its "derived" offshoot, punctuationism, represent the most recent manifestations of this ancient tradition. In classic Platonic fashion, "a concept of discrete species is critical" to these views (Wake, 1980:1240). Gradual species change through time is labeled "inadmissable" (*sic*) (Eldredge and Cracraft, 1980:114; and see Wiley, 1981:34). New species arise instantaneously in effect (Cracraft, 1979:26; Gould, 1982:83) by a process of splitting (Nelson, 1979:3) so that "any newly arising species has another species as its 'sister group'" (Hennig, 1966:159). Such "sister groups" by definition are "coordinate" and have "the same absolute rank" (Hennig, 1966:155). These are all assumptions a priori that have the same status as Plato's essences.

This is in fundamental opposition to Darwin's recognition that "we shall have to treat species in the same manner as those naturalists treat genera, who admit that genera are merely artificial combinations made for convenience" (Darwin, 1859:485). In our own century, Simpson has reiterated Darwin's view with admirable clarity when he declared that "the concept of a taxon, the thing really present in the classifier's mind and named and referred to by him, is invariably subjective, whether for a species or any other category" (Simpson, 1961:114). He concluded that "[a]ny taxonomic approach that presupposes a simple, natural arrangement that can be found out by either strictly a priori or strictly empirical means is doomed to failure by the nature of the materials to be classified" (Simpson, 1961:227).

The Hennigian view further specifies that the study of evolution "must be regarded as predominantly deductive" (Hennig, 1966:199). However, as has already been noted, deductive logic can tell us nothing not inherent in the premises, and it cannot lead to questions concerning the validity or even the existence of the givens (Williams, 1947:26; Salmon, 1968:27). If stasis and the equivalence of sister species are accepted as data a priori, then no amount of deduction can constitute a test. This is the reason why strict deductivism has been described as "a thesis of an intrinsically frivolous kind" (Stove, 1982:99, 102), and those who restrict themselves to deductivism condemn themselves "not just to irrationalism, but to unseriousness about science" (Stove, 1982:90). Historically "the attempts to establish truth by legalistic, deductive arguments," have led Mayr to characterize the Middle Ages as "a period of depressing intellectual stagnation" (Mayr, 1982:308). To the extent that strict deductivism is still the approved approach, we continue to preserve that tradition of "depressing intellectual stagnation."

At the methodological level, Popper and his followers have attempted to avoid the problem of "infinite regress" (first noted by Aristotle in his Posterior Analytics, *cf.* in McKeon, ed., 1941:114; Moody, 1935:70; Popper, 1947:II:9; Lakatos, 1978:3; Hofstadter, 1979:19) by restricting recommended activity to efforts at falsification (Magee, 1973:36–37). This led to the view that "falsifiability...constitutes...the scientific character of a theory" (Popper, 1952:II:260). The message of negativism in this celebrated "critical attitude" has had the effect of fortifying "millions of ignorant graduates and undergraduates in the belief...that the adversary posture is all" (Stove, 1982: 99). Furthermore this even "succeeded in persuading some of the sadder Popperian scientists that to be refuted was actually the goal of all their endeavours" (Stove, 1982:16; possibly a reference to Sir John Eccles's almost masochistic recommendation that a scientist "should even rejoice in the falsification" of a "cherished...brain-child" (Eccles, 1970:107). The ultimate consequence of this "naive falsificationism" (Lakatos, 1969:151; Woodfield, 1984:1197) would, if taken seriously, prevent anything that we recognize as science from ever having taken place (Feyerabend, 1978:176). It has been pointed out by Lakatos that Newtonian physics, when defined as the conjunction of his laws of motion and the inverse square law of gravitational attraction, is "evidently a scientific theory" even though it is unfalsifiable (Stove, 1982:91), an observation that has been considered a refutation of Popper's thesis concerning falsifiability as a necessary condition of the scientific status of a theory (Stove, 1982:93; and note the same stance taken toward the main tenets of modern evolutionary biology by Ruse, 1973:117; 1983:398).

THE "SCANDAL" OF INDUCTION

If the basis for Popper's insistence on the strict limitation of scientific activity to the realm of the deductive has properly been labeled "a frivolous species of irrationality" (Stove, 1982:101), then what happens when we turn to the induction on which Aristotle insisted as an essential part in the pursuit of knowledge (Losee, 1972:6)? As a recommended mode of procedure, induction has had its ups and downs. In the postmedieval world, Francis Bacon advocated the view that "deductive arguments are of scientific value only if their premises have proper inductive support" (Losee, 1972:63), a stance quite similar to Aristotle's original intent (and it is interesting to note that this approach, in Huxley's admiring judgment, was precisely what Darwin had taken in producing his epoch-making synthesis (Huxley, 1860:309). The subsequent efflorescence of science powered by the application of inductive reasoning, particularly in the areas of Protestant influence (Merton, 1938, 1973, especially Chapters 7 and 11), was paralleled in the Roman Catholic domain by an insistence on faith in canon law and, following Aquinas, the strict use of deductive reasoning (Lukas and Lukas, 1977:29).

Even though the extent to which induction could be held responsible for the triumphs of scientific progress was the subject of the debate between those nineteenth century giants William Whewell and John Stuart Mill (Losee, 1972:124, 152), neither doubted its crucial role (Whewell, 1840, 1847, 1849; Mill, 1843), and induction continued to be celebrated well into the twentieth century (Pearson, 1892; Carnap, 1952; Hempel, 1965). Despite the continuing accomplishments in the realm of science, professional philosophers have increasingly come to worry about the nature and status of the concept. In the words of C. D. Broad, though "Inductive Reasoning has long been the glory of Science," it is "the scandal of Philosophy" (Broad, 1926:67). Ever since Bertrand Russell, the "scandal of induction" has been at the center of a continuing controversy in philosophical writings (Broad, 1918, 1919; Whitehead, 1926:35; Russell, 1944b:683; Williams, 1947:15; Lerner, 1959 [1971]:73; Lakatos, 1968:367; Nagel, 1979:118).

One extreme of this controversy is represented by Sir Karl Popper who, consistent with his long-time negativism, maintains the view that "induction is a myth" and "[n]o 'inductive logic' exists" (Popper, 1978:148). Popper in fact embodies the modern voice of the eighteenth century Scottish skeptic David Hume (Stove, 1973:65–66), who noted that "a change in the course of nature...is not absolutely impossible" (Hume, 1739 [1888]:89). Popper extolled "Hume's formulation and treatment of the *logical problem of induction*...as a flawless gem" (Popper, 1972:88, italics Popper's). According to this, it follows that argument cannot proceed with certainty "from the observed to the unobserved," which is the traditional philosophical phrase describing induction (Stove, 1982:56) even though the term was used only once by Hume himself (*pace* Popper, 1972:88), and that was in the Appendix of his Treatise (Hume, 1739 [1888]:628). There is a similarity in this argument to the medieval theological rejection of the immutability of the laws of nature. If such a state existed, then God would be a prisoner of those laws, but faith in God's freedom from such control led to the view that, if He wanted, "with a single act of His will He could make the world different" (William of Baskerville in Eco, 1983a:207). The other consequence of this, as Adso of Melk pointed out, is that it implies that the laws and substance of being are "totally polluted with the possible," which is to say indistinguishable from "primigenial chaos," and this is not only "tantamount to demonstrating that God does not exist" (Eco, 1983a:493) but is also tantamount to denying that knowledge itself can exist.

The final problem concerning the scientific application of Popper's anti-inductive approach is in his use of probabilities. While most practicing scientists, even those who proclaim themselves most specifically devoted to Popperian principles, use probability as a measure of the reliability of the information contained in their results, yet Popper himself uses probability in quite the opposite way—i.e., as a measure of lack of information approaching tautology, in fact noting that "testability...is converse to...logical probability" (Popper, 1963b:219–220; Stove, 1982:47). Such was the challenge that Popper offered to the empiricism or positivism of Wittgenstein, Carnap, Hempel, and others (Lakatos, 1968:353; Popper, 1978:97). This is what led Popper to advocate choosing the most improbable hypothesis (Popper, 1959:419, 1963a:218) and to maintain his stance that corroboration varies inversely with probability. The practicing scientist can take some comfort from the fact that at least one philosopher has labeled Popper's assertions "absurd" (Lakatos, 1968:354). In the final analysis, if one accepts Popper's denial of induction, then one is restricted by default to a rigidly deductive approach (Stove, 1973:75, 79; Ruse, 1981:66) that can never get beyond tautology in the first place. And ultimately, a reliance on deduction also requires an acceptance of the very same assumption that Popper, following Hume, regarded as fatal to the status of induction: namely, that the laws of nature are fixed and that "its course of events will not change" (Bhaskar, 1978:218).

On a more positive note, Holton defends "the meaningfulness of two
types of statements, namely, propositions concerning matters of fact (which
ultimately boil down to meter readings) and propositions concerning logic and
mathematics (which ultimately boil down to tautologies)" (Holton, 1973:21).
Furthermore, the generation of hypotheses for testing, rather than being
beyond the realm of science as Popper would have it (Popper, 1947:II:14;
Gaffney, 1979:81), is not just a random process (Midgley, 1982:126) but
would fulfill the criteria for a definition of induction as proposed by Peirce
(in Buchler, ed., 1940:152) and Williams (1947:112–113) and of strong inference as proposed by Platt (1964:347). Peirce spells this out with these words:
"The operation of testing a hypothesis by experiment, which consists in
remarking that, if it is true, observations made under certain conditions ought
to have certain results, and then causing those conditions to be fulfilled, and
noting the results, and, if they are favourable, extending a certain confidence
to the hypothesis, I call induction" (Peirce in Buchler, ed., 1940:152).

The "confidence" Peirce mentions is a probabilistic notion and it follows
that "induction cannot hope to arrive at anything more than probable conclusions, and that therefore the logical principles of induction must be the laws
of probability" (Broad, 1922:81 speaking approvingly of Keynes, 1921; and
note the agreement by Hempel, 1965:385). Popper's equation of the highest
degree of probability with tautology, however, applies only for a probability
of 1.0. This is an example of a situation where initial conditions are defined
and would constitute "proof" in logic or mathematics. But "proof" is limited
to logical, not empirical, knowledge systems" (Schafersman, 1983:225).
Varying degrees of probability less than 1.0, generated as a result of comparing observed instances, can sustain proportional levels of confidence that we
are dealing with the same or different phenomena depending on how the tests
are set up. The credibility involved has been described as "analogous to strict
entailment although of lesser degree" (Williams, 1947:20, a view that is quite
similar to the treatment of the relation between Darwin's evidence and his
conclusions noted initially by Huxley, 1860:309, and later by Keynes, 1921:5).

This would seem to be far more compatible with what successful scientists actually do (cf. Hempel, 1965) than the denials of Popper, based on
"a few experiments" in a psychological laboratory early in his career and a
subsequent lifetime of deductive commentary (Popper, 1978:6). To reject
attempts to argue from the observed to the unobserved merely because it is
possible that the laws of nature might change is to be "hypersensitive to possibilities, but at the same time…insensitive to all differences of magnitude
between probabilities," a stance that has been called indicative of "a deeply

confused mental state" (Stove, 1982:104). Hume observed that "a change in the course of nature…is not absolutely impossible" (Hume, 1739 [1888]:89), but, as one recent philosopher has noted, "to demand, just on this account, that I should lower my degree of belief in the hotness of tomorrow's flames, is mere frivolity" (Stove, 1982:101). While Popper denies the validity of proof or even confirmation in science, he does allow a notion of "corroboration" that is tied to his idea of testability (Popper, 1963a:219). As has been noted, "[e]ither corroboration has an inductive aspect, or there is no logic of prediction. If there is no logic of prediction it is hard to see how any choice would be 'rational'" (Salmon, 1968:97).

CONCLUSIONS

Although we can never be completely sure of what happened in the remote past or what will happen in the future—and in fact, "absolute certainty…can never be attained by mortals" (Peirce in Buchler, ed., 1940:177)—this is no reason to declare that our efforts to understand both the future and the past are irrational and illogical and therefore should be abandoned. Farmers, airline schedulers, budget makers, curriculum planners, and others operate with the reasonable expectation that tomorrow and next year will arrive in fully predictable fashion. Geologists, paleontologists, and archaeologists have a similar confidence that tree rings, sedimentary deposition, rates of radioactive decay, and the other things they study behaved the same way in the past as they do today.

It is also perfectly reasonable that there should be varying degrees of confidence about different past and future phenomena. We can feel sure that it will be cold again next winter, but we can be less sure about whether it will be colder or warmer than it was last winter. Similarly we can feel reasonably confident that prehistoric rodents ensured species survival by producing many offspring during the course of each year, but we are less certain about estimates of gestation length and litter size.

Science deals with matters such as these and many others by assessing the probability that this or that is true. Repeated observations of similar phenomena raise the probability that generalizations made from an initially limited number of instances are true. The probability will increase as the number of compatible observations accumulates, but, by definition, "certainty" cannot ever occur short of an infinite number of such observations which, from a human point of view, is not only not probable but simply not possible.

The purpose of science is to increase understanding, that is, to go from what we now know to more comprehension about what was previously unknown, despite those who claim that this cannot be done. Just as literature is not created by critics, science is not produced by falsifiers alone, especially if the hypotheses that are the targets for their efforts are the most improbable that can be proposed. The generation of probable hypotheses, then, is a positive activity which involves a process that fulfills what had classically been called induction.

The proposing of cladograms is among the ways of generating hypotheses concerning the question of evolutionary relationships. These cladograms, however, are neither created nor tested by deduction alone. Where cladistics is pursued as a practical gambit rather than an ideological stance, this can be of real utility. And I would agree with Gould that for cladistics to fulfill its promise it should be rescued from the hands of its "own most vociferous champions" (Gould, 1986:68). Cladograms, then, can serve as provisional summaries of our current knowledge rather than representations of essential reality (see for instance the recent work by Sibley and Ahlquist, 1984), though they are neither more nor less desirable than trees. On the other hand, if there is no inductive component spelled out in their construction, the results can range from the whimsical to the bizarre (cf. Kluge, 1983; Schwartz, 1984:504).

So far there has been little of a productive nature to be gained from turning to philosophy for guidance in the practice of science (Mayr, 1982:131). To the philosopher who posed the rhetorical question, "[d]oes philosophy consist mainly in photographing the rear end of advancing science?" (Woodfield, 1984:1197), one is tempted to suggest that the answer so far seems to be an unqualified affirmative.[1] To the extent that cladistics assumes the essential reality and comparability of species, it represents the abandonment of Darwin (Nelson and Platnick, 1984:143, 145) and a leap backward into the Middle Ages. The issues remain the same as those that formed the basis for the struggles between the medieval plant morphologists and herbalists whose prolonged disputes have been called "one of the comedies of the human intellect" (Larson, 1971:32). There may indeed be some ironic amusement in the portrayal of the medieval fear of Aristotle's use of comedy to convey his mechanistic message (exemplified in the confrontation between Jorge of Burgos and William of Baskerville, Eco, 1983a:472–473), yet the medieval comedy

---

1   One long-time philosophy-watcher has observed, however, that this is perhaps an overly harsh judgment that would also apply to the contents of the present essay since the latter would qualify as philosophy even though they are not the product of a professional philosopher (K. Williams, personal communication).

continues in singularly unhumorous fashion. Given the perennial resurgence of essentialist and deductivist faith, evidently it will be a long time before we shall be able to say, with Pagliacci, *"La commedia è finita."*

EPILOGUE

I append herewith an idle bit of verse from that deservedly obscure wordsmith I. Wright Drivell. It is part of the collection entitled *Inverse,* which has yet to appear in print because its editor, A. Nonny Mussleigh, has been unable to convince the publishing world that the contents have any merit. This effusion of Drivell's is typical of the level of quality of the collection, and the reader can easily see why the volume as a whole has been judged unpublishable. The reason for including it here is that it succinctly mirrors some of the themes dealt with in the preceding text, even if it is far less sanguine about the justification and uses of cladograms.

Punctured Cladomania

"Hypothetico-deductive,"
Jargon phrase that's so seductive,
Denies what might be called inductive
For the view
The known can never be productive
Of the new.

But science viewed in such a way
Is nothing more than idle play;
For though the sun arose today,
Yet to our sorrow
Deduction cannot let us say,
'Twill rise tomorrow.

Gradualism is opposed
By fiat; fits and starts supposed;
But no mechanics is disclosed
Of how it works
To drive the process so proposed
Of change by jerks.[2]

---

2   With the transatlantic implications, whether vulgar or not, so perceptively portrayed by Turner (1983:131–132, 152–155, 162–163).

To get the right Platonic name,
Where sister species rank the same;
Synapomorphies rule the game
By which one gets
A branching ranked dendritic frame
Of nested sets.

Thus each new cladistic tree
Disguises with sadistic glee
The quintessential mystic plea
That's no excuse
For such a casuistic spree
Of little use.

ACKNOWLEDGMENTS

The following have offered comments, criticism, and information on previous drafts of this paper, though it scarcely needs repeating that the evident flaws remaining in spite of their assistance are mine alone. Thanks go to: G. Brace, Institut Français du Pétrole, Rueil, Malmaison, France; Prof. Paul A. Erickson, Department of Anthropology, St. Mary's University, Halifax, Nova Scotia; Profs. Daniel C. Fisher and Philip D. Gingerich, Museum of Paleontology, University of Michigan, Ann Arbor; Prof. Stanley M. Garn, Center for Human Growth and Development, University of Michigan, Ann Arbor; Prof. David L. Hull, Department of Philosophy, Northwestern University, Evanston, Illinois; Prof. Karl L. Hutterer, Museum of Anthropology, University of Michigan, Ann Arbor; Dr. Richard J. Kaplan, The Rand Corporation, Santa Monica, California, Prof. Bruce Mannheim, Department of Anthropology, University of Michigan, Ann Arbor; Prof. Ernst Mayr, Museum of Comparative Zoology, Harvard University, Cambridge; Prof. Roy A. Rappaport, Department of Anthropology, University of Michigan, Ann Arbor; Prof. Michael Ruse, Department of History and Philosophy, University of Guelph, Ontario; Prof. B. Holly Smith, Department of Anthropology, Arizona State University, Tempe; and Katherine Williams, Fallbrook, California. An abridged version of this paper was read at the 54th annual meeting of the American Association of Physical Anthropologists, Knoxville, Tennessee, April 12, 1985 (Brace, 1985).

Postscript

Here it had been my original intent to reprint another essay on classification that, after having been rejected by the reviewers after Russell Tuttle, editor of the *International Journal of Primatology*, had asked me to submit it, was also published by Brunetto Chiarelli in *Human Evolution* 8(3):151–166 (1993) as "The Creation of Specific Hominid Names: *Gloria in Excelsis Deo?* Or Praxis? or Ego?" The philosophical basis of that essay has been largely established in Chapter 4, so I am not going to repeat it here. What I shall do, however, is mine selected segments of that essay to illustrate the persistence of what I have called "nominophilia"—clearly a demonstration that typological thinking is alive and well and flourishing as what the late Thomas Kuhn would have called "normal science" in the world of paleoanthropology at the present time. In the April 1997, issue of *Natural History,* Stephen Jay Gould used his monthly column, "This View of Life," to take issue with my longtime resistance to what I refer to as the message of the "parable of droves of species," that is, the multiplication of fossil hominid names in the absence of any definitive descriptions or compelling reasons. Gould entitled his column "Unusual Unity" and used it to denounce what he called my "cardinal error of linearization" (1997:21). I wrote up my reply in a manuscript called "The Cultural Ecological Niche and the Reasons for Unity in the Human Species, Or: All That Glitters Is Not Gould." I sent this to *Natural History,* which replied somewhat stiffly that slots for their commissioned articles were allocated two years in advance. They did edit a segment of my manuscript as a "long letter," which they ran in their September 1997 issue as "One Human Line, Two Million Years." I have expanded on that essay for what is presented here as my concluding Chapter 12.

In his essay, Gould has defended the idea that we should expect all kinds of different human species to have been in existence simultaneously throughout the Pleistocene, and one of those he pictures is identified as *Homo "ergaster."* The specimen illustrated is a fine and relatively complete skeleton of a youth discovered in 1984 southwest of Lake Turkana in Northwest Kenya. It is 1.6 million years old, and its discoverers and describers identified it as *Homo erectus* after detailed and exemplary study and analysis (Walker and Leakey, eds., 1993). Of course, one can say that Gould's own special area of expertise is Caribbean land snails, and one could hardly expect a mollusc specialist to be up on the details of anthropological terminology.

Yet the very next month, in the May 1997 issue of the *Scientific American,* the chair of the Anthropology Department at the American Museum of Natural History in New York, Dr. Ian Tattersall, depicted the same specimen using the same designation with no reference to the definitive treatment by the discoverers and their colleagues. Tattersall certainly qualifies as an anthropologist, but, though he has indeed written about human evolution in general and Neanderthals in particular, his own real area of first-hand expertise is in the lemurs of Madagascar.

Now, if neither one knows the material about which they are generalizing from first-hand experience, the whole 20-year history of the creation and promotion of *Homo "ergaster"* puts them in the category of me-too-ers. It all stems back to a mandible discovered at Ileret east of Lake Turkana in northern Kenya in 1971. This was duly catalogued as specimen KNMER-992 in the collections of the Kenya National Museum and published with a full set of measurements and photographs by Richard Leakey and Bernard Wood in 1973. Measurement by measurement, it is an almost diagnostic representative of the jaws and dentition of the *Homo erectus* material from Zhoukoudian in China that Franz Weidenreich, the eminent anatomist, anthropologist, and refugee from Hitler's Germany, had published nearly two generations earlier (Weidenreich, 1937).

Just two years after its noncontroversial description, the gorilla dentition expert Colin Groves and a Czech colleague compared it to a sampling of African hominid specimens and declared that they considered that it should be regarded as the type specimen of a new species to be designated *Homo "ergaster"* (Groves and Mazák, 1975). Then they suggested that this could be used to include a series of other specimens including a number of skulls without jaws. This they did without ever making any effort to compare it with the well-known Pleistocene taxon *Homo erectus*. In fact, *Homo erectus* was not even mentioned in their article, nor was the fact that many of the people in the business already realized that the ER-992 mandible could count as a pretty average representative of that now well-known and widely distributed species. The taxon *"ergaster,"* then, has no more scientific justification than the pet names of "Mrs. Ples" applied by Raymond Dart to the specimen Sts. 5 from Sterkfontein in South Africa or "Dear Boy" given by Louis and Mary Leakey to OH 5, the "Zinj" skull from Olduvai Gorge in Tanzania.

No matter, once a name captures the fancy of paleoanthropologists, it takes on a life of its own. Within the last two years, Russell L. Ciochon, a paleoanthropologist at the University of Iowa, has identified a mandibular fragment with a couple of teeth and an upper incisor from a 1.8 million-year-old site in the Yangtze Valley of eastern Szechuan, China, as *Homo "ergaster"* rather than *Homo erectus* on the basis of the nuances of shape of the three worn teeth in spite of the fact that no formal comparison of those two supposed species has ever been made (Ciochon, 1995; Larick and Ciochon, 1996). Using the same standards, if one were to compare worn specimens of the same teeth in living Chinese and East Africans, one would have to conclude that they were separate species. And if we were to compare European, Australian, and Mexican versions of the same teeth, we would get three more species. This is not purely idle speculation. I have worked on the teeth of populations of all the areas mentioned, and I well know their differences. One could even draw individuals at random from the same population and find differences of the magnitude that are now regularly being offered as indicative of this or that species distinction.

At least Russ Ciochon was comparing the same portions of the body in making his specific pronouncements. Just this past year, Philip Rightmire, a paleoanthropologist at the State University of New York at Binghamton, has promoted the comparably ancient Bodo skull from the Middle Awash region south of Hadar of Ethiopia as a representative of *Homo "heidelbergensis"* (Rightmire, 1996). The original species name *"heidelbergensis"* was based on a single specimen, the Mauer jaw, found in a gravel pit near Heidelberg in Germany in 1907. This in turn is not demonstrably different, tooth by tooth and dimension by dimension, from specimens that qualify for inclusion in the species *erectus* that was first proposed in 1894. Taking an invalidly specified European jaw, attributing it to an edentulous African head that is three times as ancient, and calling it all a separate species is such an egregious example of "nominophilia" that it stimulated the following bit of doggerel:

> Double, double, toil and trouble,
> Mix the fragments from the rubble;
> A bit of this, a piece of that,
> Jaw that's chinless, skull that's flat,
> Scrap of femur, rib that's broken,
> Orphan molar as a token,
> Some from here, some from there,
> Another chunk from God knows where;
> Assembled in a dreamer's bubble,
> Named a species: Endless trouble.
> (adapted from Brace, 1995:171)

Not many years ago, Ian Tattersall complained about "the triumph of the lumping ethic" and felt that the field would be better served by "recognizing too many rather than too few species" (Lewin, 1986; Tattersall, 1986b). His plea has been answered in abundance by Colin Groves (1989), who has catalogued "all of the inane designations that have ever been imposed upon the helpless fragments of long-dead hominids…" (Brace, 1990:1069). I have referred to this as an exercise in "nominophilia," and it includes genera such as *Africanthropus, Anthropus, Archanthropus, Cyphanthropus, Europanthropus, Maueranthropus, Metanthropus, Palaeanthropus, Praeanthropus,* and *Pseudohomo;* plus species such as *habilis, heidelbergensis, helmei, leakeyi, modjokertensis, primigenius, rudolfensis, trinilis,* and, of course, his favorite, the one Groves created himself, *Homo ergaster* (Groves and Mazak, 1975; Groves, 1989).

With this arcane volume now being hailed as "a seminal piece of work" that may rank as a "landmark" (Paterson, 1990:452), it would appear that what I referred to as "the great leap backwards" (Brace, 1988:133, 1989:444) has been completed and biological anthropology now displays all the scientific sophistication of the thirteenth century. *Oh tempora, oh mores,* or, perhaps, more suitably, *Oy Vey!* As a recent manifestation, only this past April, the new Henry R. Luce Professor of Human Origins at George Washington University, Bernard Wood, published with Mark Collard a Review in the flagship journal of American scientific scholarship, *Science,* entitled "The Human Genus" (April 2). In this they declared that, "Because there are both theoretical and practical reasons for erring on the side of too many rather than too few taxa, we have adopted the latter, more speciose, taxonomy for this review" (Wood and Collard, 1999:65). They never say what those "theoretical and practical reasons" might be, though Saint Thomas would have understood. On April 9, I wrote to *Science* that because "the assumptions of cladistics simply do not work when there is reason to believe that one is dealing with regional variants of a single species that is undergoing mosaic evolution...there is good reason to conclude that their 'speciose taxonomy' within the genus *Homo* is a specious taxonomy." I sent a copy of my letter to Bernard Wood, and he replied that *Science* had done so as well, but, bowing to the power of the current speciose paradigm, they did not see fit to print it.

Stephen Jay Gould is fond of using baseball anecdotes to enliven his various presentations, and, in appraising his role as a public commentator on human evolution along with the other examples I have mentioned above, I am reminded of the bemused query attributed to Casey Stengel, manager of the hapless New York Mets during their inept 1962 season, "Can't anybody here play this game?" (recounted in Creamer, 1984:299). Actually, from the fact that a mollusc specialist and a lemur expert are accepted by the reading public as embodiments of scientific thinking about human evolution, it is clear that just about anybody *can* play the game, even if there are some of us in it who feel that they just do not play it very well. Somewhat over 20 years ago, I used the concepts associated with the idea of an ecological refuge area to suggest that biological anthropology might be thought of as an academic refuge area in which poorly adapted intellectual forms can survive because the competition is not very strong. At the time, I was envisioning the emergence of a new generation of better trained and more competitively competent scholars who would bring the field up to a level where it could merit serious attention from the ranks of the older and more mature sciences (Brace, 1976). As the above examples and the other ones recounted in my paper "The Creation of Specific Names" (1993) illustrate, however, my optimism was quite premature. That new generation has duly taken its place and has now become the establishment, and it has given us *Homo* *"aethiopicus," "rudolfensis," "heidelbergensis,"* and *"ergaster"* and much, much more in the full spirit of pre-Darwinian typological essentialism.

Once again, that indefatigable observer of the paleoanthropological scene, I. Doolittle Wright, has recorded his musings on the lumper–splitter clash and its effects on the field in the following doggerel. He had considered calling it "Writhes and Splimpers: To Bleep, Perchance to Scream," but he finally settled on:

Nominophilia

Consider the volatile splitter,
Excited and all of a twitter
At the fun in the game
Of adding a name
For each little variant critter.

If you make up a different name
For forms that just might be the same,
You can use the confusion
To support the illusion
That the effort will add to your fame.

Combining a fragment of face,
With a jaw from a far-off place,
They say they are able
To warrant a label,
Creating a whole new race.

But it's not always praxis that leads
To the multiplication of breeds,
Nor the glory of God,
But conceit of the clod
With his ego-aggrandizing needs.

Now a lumper's a different kind;
He thinks the world is designed
Of similar bits
That won't addle the wits
In the limited scope of his mind.

"Specify!" somebody flutters;
"Simplify!" one of them mutters;
The lumpers and splitters
Will never be quitters,
So the field is a patchwork of splutters.

As names blossom forth anew,
There's much to be said for the view
That puts its store
In "less is more"
And errs on the side of the few.

CHAPTER 5

Structural Reduction in Evolution[1]
(1963)

Prologue

At the end of the Introduction to his *Origin of Species,* Charles Darwin had written "I am convinced that Natural Selection has been the main but not exclusive means of modification" (1859:6). Those words remained through all six editions of his book, and his defense of that mechanism was one of the most important aspects of the legacy he contributed to evolutionary biology. On the other hand, Darwin repeatedly examined instances where selection had been reduced or removed. In all such instances, he noted that traits that had formerly been of adaptive value became reduced as a consequence of the relaxation of the forces of selection that had formerly maintained them. He cited many examples, but the most dramatic and convincing were the instances of the loss of pigment and functional eyes in long-term cave residents about which he stated, "I attribute their loss wholly to disuse" (1859:138). Later on he repeated this conclusion, writing, "I believe that disuse has been the main agency" (ibid., p. 454).

Such examples represent some of the minority of instances where evolutionary change occurred in the absence of selection and are more in the nature of oddments in the total picture of organic evolution. In orthodox Darwinian fashion, the positive developments that constitute the main evolutionary record have all been the result of the positive action of selection, and it is this that has drawn the interest of most evolutionary biologists. Of course there have been specialists who have focused on the study of cave dwellers (Culver, 1982) and various kinds of subterranean creatures (Hendriks et al., 1987), but there has been a general feeling among many biologists that these represent special cases that do not make major contributions to our general understanding of the course of organic evolution. However, they do show us what happens when specific aspects of selection are relaxed and what the consequences are likely to be. While this may not be applicable to our understanding of the course of evolution for many widely studied organisms, none other than Charles Darwin himself realized that the cultural traditions associated with "civilized men"

---

1 This paper is a revised version of one read at the meetings of the Southwestern Anthropological Association in Berkeley, California, on April 20, 1962. I wish to thank Professor Garrett Hardin of the Division of Biological Sciences at the University of California–Santa Barbara for his valuable comments and suggestions. He does not, however, completely agree with some of the ideas expressed, and therefore the responsibility for their statement is solely my own.

reduced the intensity of the action of natural selection on human populations (1871:I:161–162). His warning about the consequences was more on the lines of the eugenic arguments of his cousin Francis Galton, but he clearly did understand the role that culture could play in reducing the impact of specific aspects of natural selection.

Of course, Charles Darwin knew nothing about genes, mutations, and the molecular mechanics of how heredity and genetic change works. His extensive experience with living populations and their reproduction meant that the knowledge and instincts he had about the likely nature of changes were right on the mark. As the molecular nature of genetics finally became known in detail in the decade after the end of World War II, it was possible to add the nuts-and-bolts details to the general insights Darwin had correctly articulated a full century earlier. That, and the realization of the extent to which culture in the anthropological sense has increasingly interposed a barrier between the human physique and many specific selective forces, was what led me to propose a general mechanism that allows disuse to lead to the reductions Darwin observed, and how this has played a major role in producing the emergence of "modern" form in the course of human evolution.

Among the things involved is the realization that the concept of the "gene" that is widely used in such matters as the calculation of "fitness" values is vastly oversimplified. If the minimum inherited difference between one individual and another is taken to indicate a single-gene difference, then the gene gets itself reduced to a single base-pair out of the more than 3 billion in the human genome. Many balk at such a minimalist definition, but that does not change the fact that we have to look to this level to understand the nature of the most probable genetic change, i.e., the most probable mutation. If selection has been suspended, then we have to deal with the nature of the change produced by the most probable mutation. This is what I referred to as the "Probable Mutation Effect" (the PME) in the paper reprinted here from the *American Naturalist* in 1963. This even drew a reaction from that giant of American science the geneticist Sewall Wright (1964), but it is clear that he was still thinking of the gene in a black-box fashion and not from the perspective of molecular mechanism.

Anthropologists have been less than enthusiastic about it and a number of partial critiques have been written. I have dealt with the most pointed of these in my application of the PME to account for the picture of human dental reduction, especially in Chapter 6, "What Big Teeth You Had, Grandma! Human Tooth Size, Past and Present." The mechanism is comfortably compatible with the outlook of many in the world of molecular genetics, as I noted in the original paper, and this has just been reinforced as that world has become more sophisticated (cf. Nei, 1975; Ohta and Aoki, eds., 1985; Gillespie, 1997; Crow, 1999; Eyre-Walker and Keightley, 1999). In fact, that mechanism is central to the explanations in many of the following chapters. So far, there has been no plausible alternative explanation proposed to account for why so many aspects of the human physique have undergone reduction immediately after specific tools and procedures had been devised that reduced the amount of sheer brute force that had formerly been necessary for human survival. My case is laid out here as it had originally been presented in the pallidly pedantic style considered appropriate by the powers that be of the scientific establishment. The principle is applied and defended in many of the chapters that follow.

S ince the concern of this paper is with reductions in structures for which the selective importance has changed, it should be stated at the outset that this is not a return to the views of Lamarck (Osborn, 1924), or to those of any proponent of orthogenesis (Carter, 1951; Simpson, 1953). On the other hand, since the influential publication of Fisher in 1930 emphasizing the positive action of natural selection, there has been a tendency to ignore the fate of phenotypic characters that, for reasons of environmental or other changes, have ceased to confer survival benefits upon the possessing organisms.

Immediately following the epochal publication of *The Origin of Species* by Darwin (1859), the reading public became aware of the importance of the operation of natural forces in producing the organic diversity evident in the world of nature (Brace, 1863). After the first flush of excitement over the implications of evolution by means of natural selection, there was a general waning of enthusiasm when the complexities of the ramifications of such a view were brought into consideration (Eiseley, 1958). From the biological point of view, Darwin's ideas had some of the aspects of a facile explanation that did not have sufficient basis in detailed mechanics to be finally convincing. The same obstacles lay in the way of serious consideration of the work of Gregor Mendel, since his major contribution was in the statistical analysis of natural phenomena and did not really explain how heredity worked. Studies relating to process in organic systems continued to be pursued but with increasing isolation, so that during the second decade of the twentieth century it seemed to some people that Mendelian genetics was not compatible with the kind of organic change required by the thesis of evolution (Pearson, 1930).

The identification of mutations (Muller, 1927; Ingram, 1957) and the realization that they could provide the morphological variation needed for natural selection to operate (Haldane and Huxley, 1927; Fisher, 1930; Wright, 1931, 1951) brought back a frame of reference quite similar to that proposed in the first edition of Darwin's work (1859). This time it was underlain by a sufficient body of controlled observation and experiment relating to the mechanics of organic perpetuation so that a view of evolution by means of natural selection was no longer *merely* one possible hypothesis.

While natural selection was regarded as the most important factor in accounting for the direction which evolution has taken, there was evidently some feeling that there also existed a good deal of naturally occurring variation which did not have any obvious selective advantage and may not have been the product of natural selection. Random genetic drift has been proposed as a mechanism for the production of such variants, but, while examples have been cited (Glass, 1956; Dobzhansky and Spassky, 1962), there has been considerable disagreement over the role which it has played in influencing the direction of evolution, and most authorities do not consider it to have decisive significance (Wright, 1951; Fisher and Ford, 1950).

PROBABLE MUTATION EFFECT

More recent developments in the basic mechanisms of heredity (Beadle, 1945a; Watson and Crick, 1953; Crick, Barnett, Brenner, and Watts-Tobin, 1961) provide the basis for the possibility that the process whereby variation is produced may also determine the direction of the variation when selective factors are inoperative. Without the benefit of subsequent advances in the field of biochemical genetics, Sewall Wright (1929) clearly perceived the nature of such a process, which he termed "mutation pressure." Wright (1931, 1929) recognized that "Random changes in a complex organism are more likely to injure than to improve it," and proposed "mutation pressure" to describe the fact that most observed mutations "tend to reduce development of parts" and tend to be "in the direction of inactivation." Consistent with the recognition that most mutations are recessive, he (Wright, 1929) noted that "...for physiological reasons inactivation should generally behave as recessive."

Whether because the biochemistry of mutations was not more than speculation or because the inclusion of the term "pressure" in the label provided different connotations, the process that Wright originally described has been ignored or distorted. Recent discussions have assumed that mutation pressure refers to the rate of mutations (Boyd, 1950; Dempster, 1955; Moody, 1962), and since it is generally felt that known mutation rates are adequate as a source for the variability needed for natural selection to work (Simpson, 1953), differences in such rates are regarded as of only minor importance in current concerns with problems in evolutionary mechanics. This confusion seems to be an extension of the tendency discussed by Hardin (1960) where ideas or principles remain in obscurity because they have not been given concise labels. In this case, however, the label has been concise, but it has also been misleading. Perhaps the title "probable mutation effect" would be preferable.

More serious as an obstacle to the utility of the principle has been the tendency to project from the realization that mutations involve random changes in the character of genes (Neel and Schull, 1954) to an expectation that the phenotypic characters which the genes control will likewise vary in random fashion. Part of the trouble may be due to the fact that the word "mutation" is often used to designate inherited differences in phenotypic characters as well as changes in gene structure. At the level of the gene, it seems likely that mutations are truly random changes in the identity or number of the constituent units (Neel and Schull, 1954; compare Crick et al., 1961). On the other hand, the effects of random heritable change on the observable phenotype are universally recognized as being deleterious with a high degree of probability (Wright, 1929; Fisher, 1930; Dobzhansky, 1955a). Despite the recent contention of Wright (1951) that "mutations merely furnish random raw material for evolution and rarely, if ever, determine the course of the process," this paper will attempt to show that current developments in biochemistry (Perutz, 1958; Anfinsen, 1959; Crick et al., 1961; and Sutton, 1961) tend to support the earlier insight of Wright (1929) that, in the absence of selective factors, random mutation will produce progressive reduction of the corresponding phenotypic features. Although mutation is random, the probable effect is directional, that is, nonrandom.

DEVELOPMENT OF THE CONCEPT

Structural development has always been a focus for consideration by students of evolution. The development of such features as powerful canine teeth, laminated molars, horns, antlers, claws, hooves, prehensile appendages, long limbs, and great body size (to name just a few) are obviously the result of natural selection and have been of survival value to their possessors as can be inferred from the picture of their emergence in the fossil record (Gregory, 1951; Simpson, 1953).

On the other hand, there are features which differ between related species in ways that appear so unimportant that selection is not likely to have been the mechanism which produced the differentiation. Variations in inherited features such as the numbers of incisors, premolars, and segments of the tail, or length–width proportions of the brain cavity, or the many details of coloring may have no adaptive significance. Where separate but related populations exhibit differences in such features, the mechanism of production is frequently cited as being "genetic drift," though no serious scholars grant it a very important role in evolution (Fisher and Ford, 1950; Simpson, 1953). Genetic drift, as it was originally conceived (Wright, 1931), was primarily concerned with the probabilities of sampling (Glass, 1956), and it was assumed to be effective in accounting for differences in adaptively unimportant features in small populations only. The accidental separation of members of a breeding population or chance failure of a given factor to reproduce in a small group must still be regarded in the light of the original conception of genetic drift, but the chance rise of differing mutations in isolated groups which had formerly been genetically identical (that is, 'identical' for purposes of the model) must be reconsidered utilizing recent increases in knowledge about the nature of the basic genetic material and its proposed mode of action (Watson and Crick, 1953; Crick, 1958; Hoagland, 1959).

Whether what has been regarded as a single gene turns out to be a single molecule of DNA, or a segment of a DNA molecule, or is in fact a statistical abstraction which loses meaning when pursued to such a level, remains to be determined (Anfinsen, 1959). In any event, it appears that changes in single submolecular units (nucleotides) may produce what have been called mutations (Hoagland, 1959; Crick et al., 1961; Lengyel et al., 1962; Matthaei et al., 1962; Nirenberg et al., 1962; Speyer et al., 1962a and b).

At present it appears that the primary function of the basic genetic material is to serve as a blueprint for protein production (Crick, 1958; Anfinsen, 1959). Furthermore, the simplest form of modification of the basic genetic material accounts for single unit (amino acid) modifications in the corresponding protein (Ingram, 1956, 1957, 1959; Lehmann and Ager, 1960). Genetic units, then, only correspond directly with simple observable phenotypes where these latter are specific proteins (Crick, 1958; compare Harris, 1959). For example, the phenotypic phenomenon of sickle cell anemia is the product of the substitution of a single amino acid residue in the protein hemoglobin (Ingram, 1957).

To say that most facets of phenotypic morphology are determined by a multiplicity of genes is true (Boyd, 1950), but it does not adequately point out the fact that observable morphology is the end product of a process of growth and development influenced by the activity of a great many enzymes over a considerable period of time (Garn, 1957; Macy and Kelly, 1957). At any point in such an enzyme chain, development depends on the presence and activity of preceding enzymes, and a single modification in any of these is likely to prevent the completion of the enzyme chain or to allow a reduced version of the chain to continue (Stanbury, Wyngaarden, and Frederickson, 1960; Sutton, 1961).

Enzymes are proteins and many are under direct genetic control (Beadle, 1945a and b; Crick, 1958). The effect of mutations relating to specific enzymes is to delete or substitute an amino acid (Ingram, 1957; Perutz, 1958) with the probable result that the enzyme will become a less efficient (if indeed operable) member of the chain to which it should belong. The chain in turn is likely to be terminated or to continue in altered form with reduced effectiveness.

As a result of these probable changes, the morphological end product of growth and development will probably be altered in the direction of reduction and simplification, if not of failure to occur (Beadle, 1945b; Anfinsen, 1959). This, of course, is just a more complete expression of the long-standing observation that the great majority of mutations will be disadvantageous (Wright, 1929; Fisher, 1930). The effect of most mutations, then, will be in the reduction if not the elimination of the structures to which they pertain, which is precisely what Sewall Wright described when he proposed the perhaps inappropriate term "mutation pressure" (Wright, 1929).

Under most circumstances, however, the reduction or elimination of organic structures will be detrimental to the survival potential of the organism involved. If, however, the circumstances under which a structure had evolved should suddenly (or even gradually) cease to exist, then the structure in question would be free to vary without having any influence on the survival chances of the possessor. Subsequent variation will be at the mercy of random mutation, and, because of the probable mutation effect, reduction of the structure in question will be the inevitable result.

To illustrate with a hypothetical example that is extreme for purposes of emphasis, imagine the following situation. On a large island, a population of pigs is plagued by the depredations of a pack of dogs. In the course of time, the pigs develop a fairly effective form of dental defense—tusks. This of course occurs through the normal slow processes of mutation and selection with the dogs doing the negative part of the selecting. The populations remain in balance for a period of time until disaster in the form of a viral infection completely wipes out the canine population. The pigs continue and eventually achieve a new population balance maintained by seasonal availability of food supply, water, breeding territories, and other factors. Their tusks, however, serve them no useful purpose and are free to vary without having any effect on their survival. Since random variations are mostly detrimental to the structures involved for the reasons already cited, the tusks can be expected to reduce during the course of 50 to 100 thousand years.

Applying these findings to the evolutionary picture, one can see how directional changes can occur without the operation of natural selection and without being confined to small breeding populations. Furthermore, the changes will be in a less random manner than those postulated by genetic drift. This does not contradict the fact that the great majority of the changes that have occurred during evolution have been the direct result of the aggregate of forces called natural selection operating on naturally occurring variation. If for any reason the selective advantage conferred by the possession of a given morphological character would have as much likelihood of surviving as the original form of the feature in question, in the course of time, the mutations would occur, and, following the argument developed above, reduction of the structure that they determine would take place. Since change of environment has been a major problem with which organic continuity has had to contend, the reduction of selective advantage formerly conferred by particular characters must have been a continually recurring process in organic evolution.

The picture of vertebrate evolution abounds with examples of structural reduction. While it might be argued that in the early stages of digital reduction among the ungulates there was selective pressure favoring such a development, yet the reduction continued far beyond the point at which nonfunctional digits had become adaptively unimportant (Gregory, 1951; Simpson, 1951). Snakes and Cetaceans (Gregory, 1951) show reductions in limb structure that have proceeded beyond the point where natural selection would play an obvious role. Many other less dramatic examples occur (canine teeth in bovids, tails in anthropoid apes, jaws in termites [Emerson, 1961], and so on), where the progress of reduction has been too consistent to be explained by genetic drift and where natural selection has apparently been unimportant.

POSSIBLE ROLE IN HUMAN EVOLUTION

To turn to anthropological matters, it should be possible to discover changes in the selective pressures that coincide with changes which have taken place in observable morphology. The relation of brain size increase in the human fossil record to cultural developments noted in the archaeological record has been cited as a probable example of natural selection (Tappen, 1953), and points to biological change coinciding with changes in major selective factors. This is a recognizable case of the operation of natural selection, and is not an example of structural reduction. The best illustration of structural reduction in man is in the face. Human dental and consequently facial size can also be linked to cultural development, but in a negative way (Brace, 1962a). As technology increasingly took over tasks formerly performed by the dentition, the adaptive advantage formerly inherent in the possession of large teeth decreased, and mutations affecting the face could occur without disadvantage to the possessors. Since the majority of such mutations will result in structural reduction (compare Garn and Lewis, 1962), it is no surprise to find that the human face has become smaller as human culture has become a more complete means for adaptation.

The reduction of robustness in skeleton and musculature may be another instance of change following the suspension of formerly selective factors, and the reduction of skin color among certain populations may be yet another example. Pigmentation gives no benefits to organisms that live in total darkness, hence mutations are allowed to accumulate in the enzyme chain which results in melanin. Accumulated changes eventually result in the reduction of or the failure to produce melanin (for details of melanin synthesis, see Fitzpatrick, 1960; Lerner, 1961). It is possible that a similar trend of development has started to occur in certain human populations.

With the appearance of extensive evidence for the use of fire and evident stone tool elaboration visible in the archaeological record (Movius, 1953; Clark, 1959), it is reasonable to regard the populating of the more northerly latitudes at the beginning of the Würm glaciation as a result of cultural-technological advances. If the Neanderthal peoples inhabiting Western Europe, the Middle East, and Southern Russia at the beginning of the Würm glaciation were culturally (Bordes, 1958) and physically (Brace, 1962a and b) the ancestors to much of the present-day populations there, then we may be able to trace the relative depigmentation of many of these people in these areas back to changes in selective factors dating from that time.

Evidence of Neanderthal tooth wear indicates that they used their front teeth for far more activities than simple eating (Stewart, 1959; Brace, 1962a). Professor Coon (1961) has suggested that the extraordinary rounding wear is due to their use in leather working, and it is reasonable to suppose that the Neanderthals tanned hides for use as clothing, which they certainly must have had in order to survive in such periglacial areas.

Although the exact adaptive significance of skin color is still a matter for debate (Baker, 1958a and b; Cowles, 1958, 1959; Garn, 1961), there is general agreement that dark pigmentation is valuable if the skin is subjected to excessive solar radiation in regions of high temperatures. A population which, by the act of clothing itself, had suspended the adaptive advantage conferred by dermal melanin could be expected to have descendants among whom the enzyme chain resulting in melanin had been so modified by the accumulation of chance mutations that little melanin was produced. If one can accept the onset of the last glaciation as having occurred on the order of 70,000 B.P. (Gross, 1961) and if one used the rough figure of five generations per century, then the selective advantage conferred by the possession of melanin has been suspended in the north temperate parts of the Old World for some 3,500 generations and perhaps much longer. The relatively pigmentless peoples of European origin may owe their present appearance to such a background.

One thing all this points up is the necessity of assessing the adaptive significances of outstanding morphological characteristics when the evolution of a particular organism is being considered. These of course will change with changes in the major relevant selective factors. Obviously, then, consideration of the morphology of an organism taken out of context will at best lead to an inadequate appraisal and will frequently lead to misinterpretation. However valuable the theoretical and mathematical models of evolutionary systems may be (Dobzhansky, 1955b), there is always the danger that the models will acquire more importance than the reality which they are supposed to portray. While increased sophistication in mathematical genetics may be a good thing, it is urged that such improvements be made with an eye toward the organic systems being described and not from the point of view of refinements in probability statistics alone.

CHAPTER 6

What Big Teeth You Had, Grandma! Human Tooth Size, Past and Present
(1991)

Prologue

Teeth are the most durable parts of the human skeleton, and, not surprisingly, there are more teeth illustrating the presence of humans in the past than there are of any other tangible vestiges. The form and the size of a tooth is more directly representative of the instructions contained in the human genes than is true for any other part of the human skeleton since the crown of each tooth is entirely formed within the socket beneath the gums before it is erupted and then subject to the various influences that the environment can provide. All the other parts of the human body achieve their final form as a result of a kind of compromise between the carrying out of genetic intent and the effects of environmental influence during the process of growth. A tooth crown, however, has achieved its final form before it emerges, and the only thing that can happen to it subsequently is the degradation of that form by abrasion and decay. Not surprisingly, then, those interested in the course of vertebrate evolution have devoted what might seem to be an inordinate amount of time to the study of teeth, both of fossils and of living creatures.

As one might expect, odontology has played a large role in the careers of those who have focused on deciphering the course of human evolution. I fit right into that characterization, and it should be no surprise to realize that I was one of the founding members and am a past president of the Dental Anthropology Association. I began my odontometric career as a graduate student. I was recruited by an anthropologically oriented dentist, the late E. Leon Schuman, to measure the teeth in a collection of Liberian chimpanzees in Harvard's Peabody Museum, and this led to my being included as coauthor in the resulting publication (Schuman and Brace, 1954). I have been measuring teeth ever since, though, being interested in the course of specifically human evolution, most of the teeth I have measured have been human ones.

One of the benefits of being at a research university is that there are always graduate students in the same position in which I had found myself in the early 1950s, and my papers over the years have frequently included student coauthors. While it gets publications into the students' records, it has probably been of even greater benefit to me. Tooth measurements are very straightforward, and the statistics needed to analyze them are pretty basic, but, as the quantities increase, things soon get beyond the adding-machine or desk (now pocket) calculator stage. Computerized treatment is inevitable—and wonderful—but my problem is one of obsolescence. No sooner do I finally learn how to handle one computer system than it is labeled "out-of-date" and the University refuses to support it anymore. A newer and better system is then installed, leaving me computer-illiterate once again.

Enter the graduate student. Most of them already know how to handle our latest toys even before they enter our program. In any case, they learn the ins and outs far faster than I am able to do, and my data get analyzed in jig time. The work gets done, and the results get published, and everybody wins. The example I have selected here (Brace, Smith, and Hunt, 1991) was done with the collaboration of Shelley L. Smith and Kevin D. Hunt, who are now launched on successful anthropological careers as faculty members at the University of Texas at Arlington and at Indiana University in Bloomington where they, in turn, are involving graduate students in their own work.

I actually wrote this paper at the specific request of Clark Spencer Larsen, who is another Michigan product now on the faculty of the University of North Carolina and currently President of the American Association of Physical Anthropologists. Larsen was the principal organizing force behind the volume *Advances in Dental Anthropology* in which this paper and a series of other pioneering works appeared. I was up to my eyeballs in manuscript preparations that year and reluctant to take on another, but I am eternally grateful to Clark for gently putting the pressure on me to generate this contribution.

When I began looking at the record of human tooth-size change well over three decades ago, I realized that no systematic picture of tooth size variation had been assembled for the living human populations of the world, let alone their fossil predecessors. So I began to collect measurements on representative samples from all the quarters of the world. There are large areas that are still poorly documented in the data files I have managed to accumulate, but at least we are now in the position to make rough comparisons and generalizations. When handling so many different samples in a single treatment, it is impossible to make tooth-by-tooth and dimension-by-dimension comparisons. That is why the "summary tooth-size" figure (TS) was introduced (Brace, 1980). Some have grumbled that it lumps an awful lot of separate elements together, but the answer to that is: so does stature. All those separate leg and pelvis components are under independent genetic control, and then there are the more than 20 separate vertebrae of the spinal column plus the components of the skull itself which have separate genetic contributions and are influenced by different aspects of the environment. Despite all that, students of human biology have continued to make productive use of stature in comparing living and prehistoric populations. It is my contention that we are at least as justified in using a measure of effective tooth size. With the help of my coauthors, Shelley L. Smith and Kevin D. Hunt, this chapter shows how that can be done.

∽   ∽

INTRODUCTION

More than 20 years ago, the complaint was voiced that systematically collected information on the nature and extent of variation in human biological dimensions was in woefully short supply, and that we did not even have a coherent body of data on such an obvious and easily treated matter as the basic sizes of human teeth, past and present (Brace, 1967). Australian aborigines, ever the subject when the focus of concern is on what used to be called "primitive man," had indeed been studied in exemplary fashion, but, even in that case, Australia was treated as though it were a single typological entity and as though one local group of aborigines would give us all the information we needed to understand the continent as a whole (Campbell, 1925).

Other living groups with a comparable claim to "exotic" status in the eyes of Occidental investigators have received similar attention. Thus it was that, among others, both South African Bantus (Jacobson, 1982) and Bushmen (Drennan, 1929), Japanese (Miyabara, 1916; Yamada, 1932), East Greenland Eskimos (Pedersen, 1949), and Aleuts (Moorrees, 1957) have all received treatment. Recently, John Lukacs has been adding to our knowledge concerning dental metrics on the Indian subcontinent (Lukacs, 1984, 1985). To date, however, nothing fully comparable exists for such major geographic blocs as Europe, Russia, China, Mexico, or any part of South America. There seems to be some sort of tacit feeling that these all constitute that curious abstraction, "anatomically modern" *Homo sapiens,* which presumably is such a known and invariant commodity that further study would be redundant.

If this is true where the issue is the comparison of dental dimensions of the various living human populations, then it has classically been even more the case where the populations concerned are distributed in terms of temporal as opposed to geographical separation. So it is that the Neanderthal dentition has received its full share of attention (Patte, 1962), but, with a few notable exceptions (Brabant, 1970; Frayer, 1978), there has been no comparable interest in treating the dentition of Upper Paleolithic and succeeding human populations in any given area. The general feeling was well expressed a few years ago in a presentation in Ann Arbor by the celebrated commentator on matters of evolutionary biology Stephen Jay Gould (October 30, 1986). He had just declared that the late Pleistocene human fossil sequence is a fine demonstration of his favorite generalization concerning the course of organic evolution—punctuated equilibrium. And, in response to my question concerning the aspects of Upper Paleolithic anatomy that are intermediate between Neanderthal and modern size and shape, he expostulated: "But the Upper Paleolithic is represented by the Cro-Magnons, and they are us" (and see also in Gleick, 1983:64). By analogy, again, further consideration presumably would be redundant.

But, are Cro-Magnons really "us," and, if so, how did they get to be that way? What were the forces that shaped the emergence of that form? Where in fact did "we" come from? Does the prehistoric record in Europe where they are found give us any answers to these questions? And of what relevance is this to the evolution of the "modern" human condition wherever we find it in the world today? This chapter focuses on what can be regarded as a single adaptive trait—human tooth size—and considers the circumstances that have influenced its maintenance and change in an attempt to gain a perspective on the larger issues that lie behind the questions raised above.

IMMACULATE CONCEPTION IN THE GARDEN OF EDEN

The answers that are currently accepted as the view of "normal science" in the Kuhnian sense (Kuhn, 1962) bear a startling similarity to those offered a generation before the publication of Darwin's *Origin* to account for the picture of organic succession provided in broad terms by an examination of the geological record (Cuvier, 1826). Specifically, some postulated catastrophe had presumably overwhelmed the previous inhabitants of the area in question, and their successors, who had been thriving elsewhere beyond the scope of scrutiny, moved in as replacements. The processes by which these successors had been shaped could not be assessed, since these had occurred in a region remote from the area under observation. Such matters, then, were considered beyond the scope of proper "science" and ultimately knowable only to *l'auteur du monde* (Topinard, 1888:473).

Even before Darwin developed his vision of evolution in the organic world produced by the operation of discoverable natural forces (Darwin, 1859), the assumption that such changes were spastic in nature and produced by forces that were essentially unknowable was labeled "catastrophism" (Whewell, 1832:126). The reemergence of this as a general paradigm in "modern" paleontology has been recognized by some as deserving of the appellation "neocatastrophism" (Brace, 1978:983; Godfrey, 1981:6), and its application to the human fossil record had been referred to previously as "hominid catastrophism" (Brace, 1964).

As was true a generation ago, research on human origins is almost exclusively concerned with the discovery and naming of categorical distinctions, and the consequent proliferation of specific names based on trivial differences has recently been presented as a virtue rather than a vice (Tattersall, 1986).

168

A concern for the study of the mechanics of evolutionary process has been explicitly rejected (Gaffney, 1979:88) in favor of a faith in the unexaminable "speciation event" by which "equivalent" taxa emerge, as it were, by "special creation" (Hennig, 1966; Gish, 1979). Truly, as Tuttle has warned, a new age of taxonomic splitting is upon us (Tuttle, 1987, 1988:397).

Thus the possibility that the Middle Pleistocene fossils of Java and China and the Neanderthals of Europe and the Middle East could have been the ancestors of the modern inhabitants of each of these areas is summarily dismissed (Stringer, 1974, 1984, 1985, 1989; Stringer and Andrews, 1988; Stringer et al., 1984; Rightmire, 1983; Bräuer, 1984a and b, 1989; Cann et al., 1987; Diamond, 1989; Mellars, 1989). Instead, modern human form is presumed to have arisen somewhere in sub-Saharan Africa.

No reason is suggested for why this should have occurred in Africa and nowhere else in the world. No process has been suggested that would have generated modern form. No archaeological evidence has been advanced to indicate the subsistence strategy of the emergent "modern" population. When nonmodern candidates have been identified as potential ancestors, they are done so by being redefined as *"sapiens"* even when they lack the one trait essential for that designation, namely a modern-sized brain. And finally, there is no unequivocal evidence even for the existence of these presumed early "moderns."

In regard to the last point, among the most prominent sites mentioned is Border Cave in Natal (Beaumont, 1973, 1980; Beaumont et al., 1978; Butzer, 1978). Although the material is extremely scrappy, it is clearly "modern" in form (de Villiers, 1973, 1976), and most closely related to the current inhabitants of southern Africa (Rightmire, 1979). However, there is no certainty that the human skeletal elements are actually contemporary with the strata in which they were found, and so far there has been no convincing response to Klein's expostulation that "Those Border Cave remains didn't come out of excavations. They came out of dumps" (Rensberger, 1980:7; Klein, 1983:34). The two Omo Kibish skulls are also referred to though, again, the casual manner of their discovery (Leakey, 1984:91) and the questions concerning their dating and affinities make them dubious props for such a wide-ranging hypothesis (Klein, 1983:35).

Finally, the material from just east of Klasies River Mouth on the southern coast of South Africa is cited as support for the idea that humans of modern form were living there more than 100,000 years ago (Singer and Wymer, 1982; Stringer et al., 1989). Similarly, the morphology is clearly "modern," but once again there is a problem with assessments of antiquity. The principal direct dating of the site (Bada and Deems, 1975) was by the same technique that had been used to proclaim an antiquity of perhaps 70,000 years for modern human form in California (Bada and Helfman, 1975). The latter, as has subsequently been shown, is post-Pleistocene (Taylor et al., 1983, 1985). Other aspects of confusion concerning the stratigraphy and relationships have also been voiced (Deacon and Geleijnse, 1988).

The most widely cited evidence for the "out-of Africa" hypothesis, however, is not even from Africa itself but from Israel, namely the discoveries made over the last half century at Qafzeh near Nazareth (Köppel, 1935; Vandermeersch, 1966, 1981; Stringer and Andrews, 1988; Mellars, 1989). Presumably, Qafzeh represents the first step of the spread beyond the assumed African cradle of origin en route to the establishment of "modern" human form in the rest of the Old World.

No serious challenge has been raised yet concerning the antiquity of Qafzeh, which has been dated from 90,000 to 115,000 years on the basis of two different techniques (Schwarcz et al., 1988; Valladas et al., 1988), but some other very real problems remain. First, the Mousterian industry with which they are associated is the same as that later found with undoubted Neanderthals all the way from Iraq to southern Russia and western Europe (Garrod and Bate, 1937; Blanc, 1958; Rust, 1958; Ullrich, 1958; Solecki, 1963; Bordes, 1977). The people at Qafzeh, then, practiced the same kind of subsistence strategy as did the "classic" Neanderthals 50,000 years later. In fact, their life ways were identical since, if we can trust the archaeological evidence, it would appear that they shared the same culture.

Second, from an odontometric point of view, there is nothing "modern" about the dentition of Qafzeh. Summary tooth size (TS) for Qafzeh is 1,494 mm^2 (calculated from Vandermeersch, 1981:176–177), while that for the "classic" Neanderthals of western Europe is 1,415 mm^2 (Brace, 1979b:537). The difference in these figures is derived solely from the fact that the post-canine teeth in Qafzeh are even larger than those found in the Neanderthals (Figure 6-1). In the latter, the anterior teeth contribute 27 percent of the cross-sectional area, whereas the anterior tooth size contribution in Qafzeh is 26 percent of TS. In modern human populations (Africans, Amerindians, Asians, Australians, Eskimos, Europeans, India, Oceania), our data show that the anterior teeth in each case make up 24 percent of TS.

Finally, a metric assessment of the Qafzeh 6 craniofacial skeleton using multiple discriminant function assessment of 15 craniofacial measurements shows that it is significantly different ($p \leq 0.01$) from modern human craniofacial form in six of the eight major geographic clusters tested (Brace, in press;

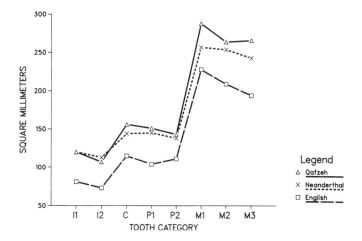

Figure 6-1 Tooth size profiles comparing Qafzeh, European "classic" Neanderthals and modern western Europeans (English). Each point represents the mean cross-sectional (MD × BL) area of the tooth listed on the horizontal axis where that figure is the sum of the maxillary and mandibular tooth category mentioned. The points for Qafzeh are from Vandermeersch (1981), and the ones for Neanderthals and for modern English are from Brace (1979b).

Brace et al., in press b). The only modern human populations from which it could not be excluded were from sub-Saharan Africa (Dahomey, Gabon, and the Haya of Tanzania, $p = 0.663$), and Australia–Melanesia ($p = 0.317$). If Qafzeh represents a form that can be ancestral to anything, it must represent the appearance of the precursors of modern sub-Saharan Africans, less likely the Australo-Melanesians, but no one else. The same can also be said for the material from Border Cave and Klasies River Mouth after a general assessment of their morphological affinities.

The continued enthusiasm for finding an identifiable sub-Saharan African cradle for the origin of all "modern" human form, then, owes more to the Judaeo-Christian faith in the traditions of a Garden of Eden than it does to anything that can be called science (Brace, 1979b:539, 1986, 1989; Brace et al., in press b). There is virtually no unequivocal evidence to support that faith, and no processes or dynamics are considered by which such an origin could have occurred. As it is generally presented (Cann et al., 1987; Stringer and Andrews, 1988), this model of human origins has more in common with the "special creation" in the "scientific" creationist approach of Christian fundamentalism (Morris, 1974:104, 133) than with anything resembling the expectations of evolutionary biology. Finally, the invocation of support from

171

mtDNA work relies on evidence that is passed on via the female line without male input and suggests a genesis that must have been the result of what could only be referred to as a form of immaculate conception.

What we are seeing is a reversion to the typological essentialism of Medieval scholasticism (Brace, 1988a), a "great leap backwards" as it has been called (Brace, 1989:444). The same "logic" by which such specimens as Kabwe, Petralona, and Steinheim are removed from *Homo erectus* works just as well to deny that modern Asians or Australians can be called *Homo sapiens*. Although the possible consequences are almost certainly unintended, there is a very real chance that this movement could be used to strengthen the racist advocacy evident in the works of Arthur Jensen (Jensen, 1969; 1980; Neary, 1970), and, more recently, J. Philippe Rushton (Rushton and Bogaert, 1987, 1988).

It is not our purpose to use the present occasion to frame a definitive rebuttal. What we hope to do, however, is to add a bit more perspective to the use of dental data, and to suggest that, if other aspects of past and present human biology were treated in similar fashion, this might just point the way to a more productive approach to the study of human evolution. Specifically, we shall argue that differences in tooth size between living human populations are strictly in proportion to the length of time that specific food preparation techniques have been a part of the cultural repertoire of each particular population in question, and that this can be tested by the use of both skeletal and archaeological data.

THE STUDY OF HUMAN TOOTH SIZE

Previous work has clearly shown that there are major differences in tooth size between the living populations of the world (Brace, 1980; Brace and Ryan, 1980; Brace and Hinton, 1981). Furthermore, it is apparent that human tooth size underwent a clear-cut reduction during the Late Pleistocene and, even more rapidly, in the Holocene (Brace, 1967, 1979b; Brace and Mahler, 1971; Brace et al., 1987). In addition, this picture of recent reduction is valid in all of the major geographic regions so far studied (Brace and Mahler, 1971; Brace, 1979b, 1980; Hinton et al., 1980; Brace and Nagai, 1982; Brace et al., 1984; Brace and Vitzthum, 1984; Lukacs, 1984, 1985; Calcagno, 1986).

Sexual Dimorphism

Although the larger picture provided by this research is beyond challenge, there are a host of problems that remain concerning the details and the interpretations. We would like to mention some of the more prominent of these here. First, there is the question of sexual identification. Specification of sex is especially important in populations where sexual dimorphism is great or even unknown. Of course, as Oxnard has pointed out, teeth "do not bear recognizable gonads" (Oxnard, 1987:65). Consequently it is virtually impossible to separate loose teeth by sex. The result is that our assessment of tooth size in populations at the level of antiquity of the Neanderthals and earlier can be made only on the basis of pooled samples of males and females, and we have to hope that both sexes are well enough represented to make our picture generally appropriate for the group in question. Whenever possible, however, we have used the mid-sex mean for the various metric dimensions treated, that is:

$$(\Sigma \bar{X}M + \bar{X}F)/2$$

(Brace et al., 1987; Brace and Hunt, 1990). All the between-population comparisons presented here use data that have been compiled in this fashion (see Table 6-2 on p. 177 and Table 6-4 on p. 183).

Tooth Size in Relationship to Body Size

It is widely accepted that there is a low but positive correlation between tooth size and body size within any given human population (Garn et al., 1966, 1968; Brace et al., 1987). Consequently, it is legitimate to ask whether the change in tooth size through time is simply a reflection of a change in body size. It is also legitimate to consider the related question of whether the differences in tooth size between the various living human groups can be accounted for by differences in body size.

Most of our data on tooth size in both recently living and prehistoric populations come from specimens that lack associated postcranial elements. On the other hand, particularly where it is a matter of data on recently living human groups, most of the teeth we have been able to measure are still implanted in the facial skeletons in which they had grown. It is on the basis of these craniofacial remains that we have been able to make our assessments of sex.

Furthermore, we can also use cranial dimensions to give us some idea of the size of the individuals involved. Although cranial size does not have a one-to-one correspondence to body size, we can argue that the main differences in brain size between the individuals and populations of the world are almost entirely the allometric expression of differences in body bulk. The measurements of the portion of the cranium that houses the brain should therefore give us the most readily acquired access to an assessment of brain size, and we would suggest that this in turn can provide us with the only indication of body size that we are ever likely to have (Martin, 1983; B. H. Smith, 1989).

In the past, Karl Pearson and his disciples produced various formulae designed to give estimates of actual cranial capacity (Pearson, 1926; Hooke, 1926). Measurements of maximum cranial length, width, and height were used in conjunction with carefully worked out constants where the results were checked against the figures derived from direct measurements of volume. The approximation of true capacity from the use of only three measurements made on the exterior of the cranial vault is most impressive, but the use of a constant can add nothing to our understanding of variation in cranial size. This can be gained only by the treatment of the actual measurements used. For this reason, we have avoided the use of the various formulae previously suggested and have treated the three measurements as though they were the axes of an ellipsoid. We suggest that this amounts to treating the individuals and populations of the world in fair and equivalent fashion.

To represent tooth size, we have used a product of the mesial-distal and buccal-lingual dimensions of the tooth crowns. These have been referred to as "cross-sectional areas," and the issues surrounding their uses have been discussed previously (Brace, 1980; Brace et al., 1987). A great deal of information on tooth size is available as has been noted, and, while there is also a great deal of information available for cranial dimensions (see, for example, Howells, 1973), it is much less easy to assemble information on the covariation of tooth size and cranial size from data gathered on the same individuals in a series of populations. And, if we were to attempt a comparison of individuals where we had metric representations of each tooth plus the cranial variables, then our sample sizes for each group would be too small to allow us to get any reliable results.

For these reasons, we have restricted our within-population tooth-size/body-size appraisal to a consideration of the cross-sectional areas of M^1 and M^2 and the three principal cranial dimensions. Since this amounts to comparing areas with volumes, we have converted our data into comparable units by using the square roots of the former and the cube roots of the latter.

The within-population correlation between tooth size (TS) and the brain size indicator of body size (BS) is positive, but it ranges from low (0.12) to moderate (0.60) (Brace et al., 1987). When calculated across a series of 21 groups ranging from Japan to Australia, the correlation is clearly negative

(−0.384) (Brace and Hunt, 1990). And when we calculate the coefficient using 23 representatives of the 8 major geographic clusters of human populations (Brace et al., in press b, and see Tables 6-1 and 6-2), the correlation is nearly 0 (0.034) and it is not significant ($p = 0.879$). In any case, where the issue is modern *Homo sapiens* as a species, it is obvious that tooth size has become decoupled from body size during the recent evolutionary past (Brace et al., 1987).

Variance

Mean BS figures were calculated from individuals with all three measurements present. Standard deviations were produced for the mean of each. For our population comparisons, we used mid-sex means, but there is no acceptable way to produce standard deviations for these. A figure produced by adding the male and female standard deviations and dividing by two would not be legitimate, but it is little better to merge the male and female data to produce a single estimate of variance. The larger male dimensions have a weighting effect that cannot be corrected. This is the reason we have left the separate male and female standard deviations as columns in Table 6-1.

The problem with generating something of an equivalent to variance for TS is even greater, since the N figure for each tooth category in most of our groups is different as we have indicated in Table 6-3, on p. 181. In the few instances in which enough complete dentitions were available so that a σ could be produced for a single group, the figure ranged from 79 for Hong Kong Chinese to 141 for South Australian Aborigines (Brace, 1980:144). The Australian data produced the largest coefficients of variation for modern human odontometrics, either by individual tooth or TS.

Oddly, the smallest σ and the smallest coefficient of variation we have encountered is from a series of isolated teeth collected at the clinic in the University of Michigan Dental School. These were arbitrarily grouped into 50 "pseudo-individual" dentitions possessing a tooth in each category. Since the teeth all came from different real individuals of unknown sex and represented an uncontrolled sampling of European, Asian, and African ancestry, those pseudo-individuals cannot reflect any real population in the world. Yet, with a TS of 1,153 and a σ of 32, this curious group has a lower coefficient of variation than any real population for which we have data.

To be on the safe side, we suggest that the variance figures derived from the South Australian data are least likely to overestimate real differences. On

Table 6-1 Names, Ns, and Collection Location for Samples Used in Constructing Figure 6-2.

Population	F	M	Total
Ainu[a,b]	46	59	105
N. Australia[c]	6	12	18
S. Australia[c]	12	10	22
Breton[d]	10	21	31
S. Afr. Bushman[e]	41	49	90
N. California[f]	15	9	24
Chengdu[g]	40	46	86
N. China[a]	1	42	43
Dahomey[d]	16	17	33
England[h,i]	12	25	37
France[d]	18	21	39
Gabon[d]	19	19	38
Germany[j]	10	30	40
Hong Kong[k]	36	78	114
India, Bengali[j]	10	18	28
Italy[l]	16	26	42
Japan[a,b]	71	126	197
Michigan[m]	27	34	61
Norway[n]	18	26	44
Peru[f]	11	7	18
Shanghai[o]	61	86	147
Tanzania[i]	18	18	36

[a] University Museum, University of Tokyo.
[b] Department of Anatomy II, Sapporo Medical College.
[c] Department of Anatomy, School of Medicine, Edinburgh University.
[d] Musée de l'Homme, Paris.
[e] Howells, 1973.
[f] Lowie Museum, University of California–Berkeley.
[g] Department of Anatomy, Chengdu College of Traditional Chinese Medicine, Chengdu, Sichuan, People's Republic of China.
[h] British Museum (Natural History), London.
[i] Duckworth Laboratory, Cambridge University.
[j] American Museum of Natural History, New York.
[k] Prince Philip Dental Hospital, University of Hong Kong.
[l] Peabody Museum, Harvard University.
[m] Museum of Anthropology, University of Michigan.
[n] Anatomical Institute, University of Oslo.
[o] Fudan University, Shanghai, People's Republic of China.

Table 6-2 Mean TS and BS Figures Plus Male and Female BS Standard Deviation Values for the Samples Displayed in Figures 6-2 and 6-3.

Population	TS	BS	δM	δF
Ainu	1,141	1,812	140.1	145.6
N. Australia	1,272	1,532	175.4	136.4
S. Australia	1,429	1,682	153.3	176.9
Breton	1,126	1,633	119.5	125.5
S. Afr. Bushman[a]	1,139	1,453	—	—
N. California	1,238	1,789	131.2	136.5
Chengdu	1,203	1,662	183.1	143.7
N. China[b]	1,261	1,715	137.6	—
Dahomey	1,274	1,656	115.1	121.5
England	1,120	1,672	116.2	134.3
Eskimo	1,280	1,761	137.2	103.2
France	1,130	1,663	93.7	97.5
Gabon	1,335	1,623	123.8	119.6
Germany	1,141	1,666	168.1	103.6
Hong Kong	1,154	1,714	121.7	111.9
India, Bengal	1,144	1,522	159.9	137.8
Italy	1,149	1,675	147.4	134.9
Japan	1,222	1,712	141.9	130.5
Michigan	1,260	1,705	168.5	114.6
Norway	1,103	1,712	136.7	119.9
Peru	1,297	1,638	201.0	122.2
Shanghai	1,197	1,708	145.0	114.4
Tanzania	1,362	1,633	119.5	125.5

[a] Howells (1973) prints male and female σ figures for individual dimensions, but no variance figures can be calculated for their products.
[b] A female N of I does not permit calculation of a variance.

the basis of these data, it has been shown that a TS difference of 50 mm^2 has a probable significance of 0.05>0.02 when N is >60, and >0.01 when N is > 135. When TS differs by 100 mm^2, the p value is 0.001 when N is >60. This is the basis for the suggestion that a TS difference of 50 mm^2 is probably significant, and that a difference of 100 mm^2 "almost certainly has some basic biological meaning" (Brace, 1980:144).

GEOGRAPHIC DISTRIBUTION OF TOOTH SIZE

On the basis of Euclidean Distance analysis using 18 craniofacial variables (Brace et al., 1989) from samples representing all the major geographic and ethnic human populations of the world, we can show that the biological spectrum of modern *Homo sapiens* is reasonably well represented by eight relatively distinct population clusters: African, Amerindian, Australo-Melanesian, Eskimo, European, Indian, Jōmon-Pacific, and Mainland Asian (Brace et al., in press a and b). These clusters emerged from the comparative analysis of more than 2,000 individual crania, and they are even more clearly delimited when the measurement battery was expanded first to 21 and then to 24 variables (Brace and Hunt, 1990).

We realized somewhat belatedly that our clusters would be even more clearly separated if our measurement battery had concentrated more on trivial rather than adaptively important dimensions, but this did not occur to us until after the analysis of data that had taken several years to collect (Brace, in press; Brace and Hunt, 1990). The clusters are consistent, however, and we use representatives of them here to display the relative tooth-size/body-size proportions found in the spectrum of living human groups.

When the simple means of tooth size and brain size for representatives of each of eight major clusters of modern human populations are plotted, it is interesting to note that Europeans fall right in the middle of the modern human range of variation when the ordering is ranked according to brain size as in Figure 6-2. When the ordering is ranked by decreasing amounts of tooth size as in Figure 6-3, Europeans are at the bottom of the modern human range of variation.

When the ordering is by relative tooth size as in Figure 6-4, Europeans are once again near the lower end of the range of variation along with the Hong Kong Chinese. Only the Ainu from the Jōmon-Pacific cluster show relatively even smaller teeth. Members of the latter cluster, interestingly enough, have among the largest cranial dimensions and presumably are the bulkiest of the groups represented. At the opposite end of the scale, some of the members of the Australo-Melanesian cluster have the largest teeth—both absolutely and relatively—of all the peoples of the world, followed in both regards by the representatives of sub-Saharan Africa.

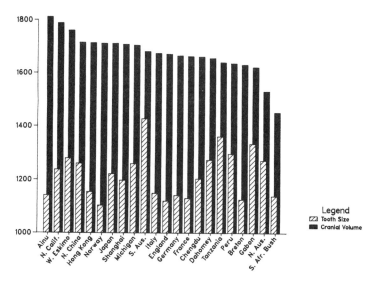

Figure 6-2 Mean cranial volume in cm³ (BS) and mean total tooth size in mm² (TS) figures plotted for 23 groups representing the eight major regional clusters of modern human populations. The order from left to right is determined by decreasing cranial volume. The collections from which these data were derived are recorded in Table 6-1, and the data used are recorded in Table 6-2.

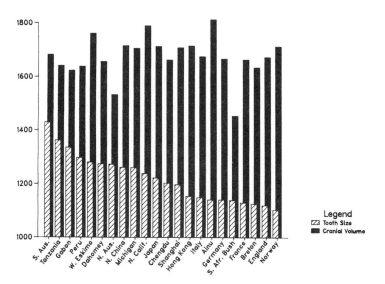

Figure 6-3 Mean total tooth size in mm² (TS) and mean cranial volume in cm³ (BS) figures for representative samples of the eight major regional clusters of modern human populations. The order from left to right is determined by decreasing tooth size.

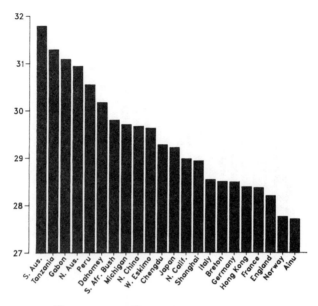

Figure 6-4 Tooth Size$^{1/2}$/Cranial volume$^{1/3}$. Relative tooth size for representatives of the eight major regional clusters of modern human populations used in Figure 6-2. Tooth-size to brain-size proportions are determined by dividing the square root of TS by the cube root of BS. For purposes of plotting, the proportion was multiplied by 10.

TOOTH SIZE REDUCTION AND TIME

If one looks at tooth size through time, it is clear that there has been a major reduction since the beginning of the Late Pleistocene. Figure 6-5 shows that both tooth size and body size have decreased in Europe over the last 50,000 years. We have added data from the modern Ainu, Chinese, and southern Australian aborigines to the right-hand end of the graph. Whereas the Ainu and the Chinese show the same kinds of dental reduction visible in Europe, the Australians clearly do not (Table 6-4).

When tooth size is considered in proportion to the figure we have taken to represent body size, as is shown in Figure 6-6, it is apparent that the reduction in the dentition is more dramatic than that in bodily bulk. Australian aborigines have not followed an identical path, however, for even though Australian tooth size has been decreasing since the late Pleistocene, it has remained larger in proportion to body size than was true even for the "classic" Neanderthals of western Europe.

It is clear that relative tooth sizes change dramatically during the Late Pleistocene in the northern portions of the Old World. These changes

Table 6-3. Average and Range of N for the TS/BS (Cranial Volume) Index

Population	BS N	TS N Range	TS N Average
Neanderthal[a]	6	5–20	13
Late U.P.[b,c]	2	12–33	25
Mesolithic[c,d]	10	46–116	80
Neolithic[d,f,g]	49	17–57	39
Modern Europe[e,g–l]	291	86–271	187
Ainu[m,n]	106	91–196	137
China[o]	227	25–234	108
S. Australia[p,q]	21	164–338	209

[a] Cranial Measurements: La Chapelle-aux-Saints (Boule, 1913); La Ferrassie (Heim, 1976); Shanidar (Trinkaus, 1983); Monte Circeo (Sergi, 1939); Amud (Suzuki, 1970); Tabun (McCown and Keith, 1939); Dental Measurements: Brace, 1979.

[b] Cranial Measurements: Obercassel (Verworn, Bonnet, and Steinmann, 1919).

[c] Dental Measurements: Frayer, 1978.

[d] Institut de Paléontologie Humaine, Paris.

[e] Modern Europe consists of Anglo-Irish, Cornish, Denmark, England, Finland, France, Germany, Ireland, Italy, Lapp, Norway, Scotland, and Sweden.

[f] British Museum of Natural History.

[g] Duckworth Laboratory, Cambridge University.

[h] Musée de l'Homme, Paris.

[i] American Museum of Natural History, New York.

[j] Panum Institute, Copenhagen.

[k] Peabody Museum, Harvard.

[l] Anatomical Institute, University of Oslo.

[m] University Museum, University of Tokyo.

[n] Department of Anatomy II, Sapporo Medical College.

[o] Fudan University, Shanghai.

[p] Department of Anatomy, School of Medicine, Edinburgh University.

[q] Murray Black Collection, School of Medicine, University of Melbourne.

evidently produced the major north–south differences now obvious in the living populations of *Homo sapiens*. If, then, tooth size relative to body size was maintained at a constant level by the forces of selection throughout much of the duration of the genus *Homo*, then the relative differences that can be seen between the various modern human populations should be proportional to the differences in the time at which the onset of change began to influence those formerly given levels of selection. Finally, the agencies that produced the Late Pleistocene reductions must have had something to do with survival in the northern areas inhabited by the human species during that time.

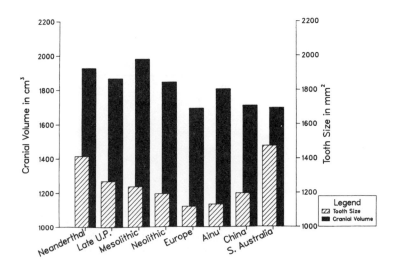

Figure 6-5 Tooth size (mm^2) and body size (indicated by cranial volume in cm^3) changes in Europe over the last 50,000 years compared with tooth size and body size in China, among the Ainu, and in southern Australia. Neanderthal, 50,000; Upper Paleolithic, 20,000; Mesolithic, 10,000; Neolithic, 5,000; the rest are all "modern." Sources and Ns are indicated in Table 6-2, and the figures used are listed in Table 6-4.

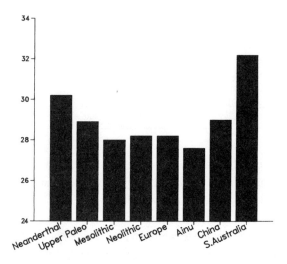

Figure 6-6 Tooth Size$^{1/2}$/Cranial volume$^{1/3}$. BS/TS proportions plotted over the last 50,000 years in Europe plus for representatives of three of the regional clusters from Asia and Oceania. The data used are from Table 6-4.

Table 6-4 Total Tooth Size (TS) and Cranial Volume (BS) for a Time Series of European Samples and Representations of the Three Main Asian and Pacific Clusters Identified in This and Previous Studies[a]

Population	TS	BS
Neanderthal	1415.0	1926.1
Late Upper Paleolithic	1267.0	1865.7
Mesolithic	1237.0	1979.9
Neolithic	1196.0	1845.9
Modern Europe	1127.0	1691.9
Ainu	1132.3	1805.4
China	1197.3	1708.3
South Australia	1429.8	1694.2

[a] See Table 6-2.

REDUCTION RATIONALES

Selection Scenarios

Whereas there can be no doubt that tooth size in the various living populations of *Homo sapiens* is smaller, though by differing amounts, than it had been in their Pleistocene ancestors, there is no agreement on the process by which reduction was accomplished. The conventional wisdom deriving from the neo-Darwinian synthesis is to regard all change as the result, by definition, of natural selection (Fisher, 1930). The obvious sticking point in this instance is to discover just what advantage there would be in having smaller, weaker, and more friable teeth.

Where dental reduction is manifest in a simplification of crown fissure patterns, as it is in many documented instances (Turner, 1976, 1979, 1986, 1989), the argument can be put forward that the greater resistance to caries offered by small and simple tooth crowns would have significant survival value (Calcagno and Gibson, 1988). We could offer the objection that 90 percent of the reduction and crown simplification had already occurred before caries achieved a level that could count as a selective force, but data simply do not exist in sufficient quantities to settle the matter in either direction. These questions relate to dental morphology, however, and, though they are not completely unrelated to the issues, we have followed the strategy of confining our work to the simple metric matter of tooth size.

One of the selectionist arguments offered is that dental reduction is simply a consequence of facial reduction (Sofaer, 1973; Sofaer et al., 1971).

The disadvantage caused by the crowding of unreduced teeth in small mandibles and maxillae would presumably lead to a selective advantage in the possession of smaller teeth. Of course, this just puts the real problem off yet another step by introducing the question of what advantage there would be in having smaller faces in the first place. Furthermore, it reverses the usual view that the forces of selection act directly on the teeth themselves (cf. Eckhardt, 1971), and that the supporting facial skeleton develops secondarily to accommodate the size of the teeth thus determined. Also, as with the caries argument, the evident effects of tooth crowding did not become apparent until after the end of the Pleistocene by which time 90 percent of tooth size reduction had already taken place.

Another selectionist argument that has been invoked to account for tooth size reduction is the "somatic budget effect" (Jolly, 1970). In this scenario, the energy saved by growing smaller teeth would increase the survival potential of their possessors. In reply to this, we are skeptical that the minuscule amount of energy saved would be enough to represent any kind of competitive edge. Between the end of the Pleistocene and the present in France, TS reduced by a total of 107 mm^2 (Brace, 1979b). If one considers that there have been approximately 500 generations in that time, then the average amount of reduction per generation is 0.21 mm^2. We doubt that the energy required to grow two-tenths of a millimeter of tooth area could amount to a discernible nutritional differential.

After looking at the various presentations, we doubt that a selectionist argument can suffice to account for the evidence we present that human tooth size has undergone differing but in some instances substantial reduction in the recent past. We are led instead to consider what has erroneously been called a "non-Darwinian" alternative. Darwin himself recognized that reduction follows when selective forces no longer require the use of a particular trait (Darwin, 1859:134, 454), though he was not in a position to discuss in detail the mechanism by which this was accomplished.

The Probable Mutation Effect

To date, the somewhat tortured attempts to use selectionist arguments to account for the observable reductions in tooth size would appear to be examples of the hyperselectionist views characterized as the "Panglossian paradigm" (Gould and Lewontin, 1979), that "favourite parlour game" in which the attempt is made to explain "everything in terms of largely hypothetical selective advantages" (Ruse, 1982:134). This is based on the assumption that everything in the biological world owes its particular manifestation exclusively to natural selection even if we are unable to see how this could be. The parallel has been noted to the "scientific vision of the myth of natural harmony—all structures well designed for a definite purpose. It is, indeed, the vision of the foolish Dr. Pangloss so vividly satirized by Voltaire in Candide" (Gould, 1980:40) where "all is for the best in this the best of all possible worlds." If we are unable to understand how that can be so, presumably it is because our finite intellects cannot comprehend the workings of a Divinely created world. Traditional Christianity would constrain us to believe even though we cannot understand. So too would those who insist that selection is the only agency that can produce evolutionary change.

The view to which Gould and Lewontin were referring was a late nineteenth century view, and perhaps it was as succinctly stated by Alfred Russel Wallace as it was by anyone: "The assertion of 'inutility' in the case of any organ…is not, and can never be, the statement of a fact, but merely an expression of our ignorance of its purpose or origin" (Gould, 1980:32). This in essence was the stance taken by one of the creators of the neo-Darwinian synthesis, R. A. Fisher (Fisher, 1930; Fisher and Ford, 1950), and it has become a part of the ruling dogma of the synthetic theory of evolution.

As molecular biology has matured, however, it has become increasingly difficult to maintain the blanket credibility of that stance, particularly since it is now evident that more than 90 percent of the molecular stuff of heredity itself, DNA, is not transcribed (Ohno, 1970, 1972; Britten, 1986; Loomis and Gilpin, 1987). In a series of chemical, behavioral, and morphological features, it can be shown that reductions are proportional to the time elapsed since they were last needed for survival. In fruit flies where reproduction is limited to parthenogenesis, female mating behavior disappears over the course of a couple of decades (Carson et al., 1982). In ground squirrels in the Lake Tahoe basin in Nevada and adjacent California, "the coordinated system of behavioral and physiological defenses against rattlesnakes is lost…after prolonged (i.e., about 60,000 years) absence of predation" (Coss and Owings, 1989:34). And in Mexican fishes of the genus *Astyanax,* and in other cave-dwelling organisms, the reduction of structures related to the perception of and the protection from light is directly proportional to the length of time that the species in question has inhabited a particular cave system (Wilkens, 1971, 1973). Even better, the structure of the protein α-crystallin in the lens of the blind mole rat, *Spalax ehrenbergi,* which has been subterranean for some 25 million years, shows an amino acid replacement rate more than four times that of the normal mammalian rate of change in the αA chain. Furthermore, when compared with six other rodents where normal vision has been maintained, that particular polypeptide chain shows nine amino acid replacements in *Spalax* as opposed to none in the other rodents (Hendriks et al., 1987:5321).

In each of these cases, the changes documented are just those predicted by the logic inherent in the Probable Mutation Effect (PME) (Brace, 1963). According to this, the most likely result of the most likely mutation will be a reduction in the phenotypic manifestation of the trait under the control of that particular locus. If the trait is subject to the forces of natural selection, most mutations affecting it by chance will be weeded out. However, if selection is reduced or suspended in reference to that particular trait, then selection will not weed out the recurrent chance mutations. Since most of these tend to interfere with the development of the trait to its full original manifestation, the trait will undergo a reduction in proportion to the length of time that selection influencing its maintenance has been reduced or suspended.

At its most basic, it is a matter of entropy which can be described by the phrase, "if anything can go wrong, it will." At least one physicist has referred to it as the 4th law of thermodynamics, though it is probably better known as "Murphy's Law" (Roe, 1952:46). One of its corollaries that applies specifically to the molecular workings of the PME is that, "left to themselves, things always go from bad to worse," though that is putting a selectionist interpretation on the results. Where selection is suspended, the structure simply deteriorates to a lesser version of its original condition, but this is neither bad nor worse—nor, for that matter, good.

A simple quantitative model was published five years ago (McKee, 1984) demonstrating that the PME would be quite sufficient to explain the picture of human dental evolution for which we have provided evidence. This has recently been questioned on several grounds (Calcagno and Gibson, 1988). The critique, however, did not take into account some of the basic aspects of molecular and developmental biology that underlie the logic of the PME, and we use this opportunity to consider some of these.

First, it was noted that there would have to be more than 25 loci relating to tooth size before McKee's explanation would work, and the opinion was expressed that the actual number of loci is only a fraction of that required (Calcagno and Gibson, 1988:506). Our reply is that the actual number is probably greater by a factor of at least 100. This does not deny the reality of the small number of major loci for which specific evidence is adduced (Lombardi, 1975, 1978; Potter et al., 1976). Instead, we suggest that these are more likely to produce the kind of changes once referred to as "sports," and that, as Darwin recognized, changes of this nature are not the normal means by which evolution occurs—whether that change is either a decrease, as in our present consideration, or an increase in size.

In contrast, we would argue that the process by which a tooth develops is along the lines of what is described in the "morphoregulator hypothesis" (Edelman, 1988). From this point of view, a tooth is an epigenetic phenomenon that emerges as the result of a substantial morphogenetic process not unlike the process by which feathers, also structures of epidermal origin, differentiate in the skin of the developing chick (Edelman et al., 1985:213–216). At the very least, such a process is controlled by more than one enzyme and at least one polypeptide cell-adhesion molecule. Each regulator enzyme in turn is made up of some hundreds of amino acid residues and each, as is also true for the amino acid residues in the cell-adhesion molecules, is specified by the three nucleotides of a codon, any one of which can be regarded as a single gene. The number of genes controlling a single enzyme then can be as much as three times the number of its constituent amino acid residues. Where the development of a single morphological entity such as a tooth is regulated by a number of enzymes and other molecules during the course of its development, the number of relevant genes runs into the thousands. The probable influence of any one, however, is far smaller than the phenomena noted by Calcagno and Gibson (1988) as the results of single gene changes. Nor is the likelihood of increase anywhere near so great as the likelihood of decrease in any of the processes mediated by a random change in the vast majority of the individual nucleotides involved. If the average mutation produces a random change of a single amino acid residue in an enzyme, the average consequence is that the enzyme will not work as well as previously if indeed it works at all. In the matter of morphogenesis, the most likely result of such a random change is that the aspect mediated by the molecule in question will be inhibited to a greater or lesser extent. A randomly occurring change, then, will have distinctly nonrandom consequences.

Finally, the complaint has also been voiced that the PME is untestable (Calcagno and Gibson, 1988:514). As the number of examples mentioned above will indicate, this is simply not true. On the other hand, this is not a matter to be dismissed lightly, and the challenge to produce credible tests must be kept clearly in mind. At the same time, the demonstration of how selection operates to produce the changes observed faces similar problems. As Ernst Mayr has cogently reminded us, "it is methodologically very difficult to prove the selective value of many characters" (Mayr, 1982:172). With all of this in mind, we suggest that, from the perspective of molecular and developmental biology, there is no reason a priori why the PME should not work under conditions of relaxed selection. This should have been obvious from an appraisal of the initial efforts to view evolutionary dynamics from the perspective of molecular biology (Anfinsen, 1959; and see the more recent work that has built on this perspective, e.g. Ohta, 1974, 1980; Nei, 1975, 1987; Kimura, 1983), and this should be even more apparent when ongoing work in morphogenesis is taken into account (Edelman et al., 1985; Edelman, 1988).

TECHNOLOGY AND TOOTH SIZE CHANGE

The conditions that result in the relaxation of those selective forces which previously maintained tooth size have been discussed repeatedly over the past several years (Brace, 1977, 1980, 1988b; Brace and Nagai, 1982; Brace et al., 1984, 1987; Brace and Vitzthum, 1984) and do not need to be repeated here. Instead, we present a brief summary.

Although the use of the anterior teeth as ancillary tools may have led to the increase of incisor size in some human populations at the end of the Middle Pleistocene and the beginning of the last glaciation (Brace, 1962, 1988b:119–120), the principal function of the dentition has always remained the processing of food (Hrdlička, 1911; Brace, 1977, 1979a; Brace and Hinton, 1981; Brace et al., 1987). As one earnest commentator has expressed it, "But primarily, teeth are for feeding with" (Hillson, 1986:5). Contrary to the usual expectations that aspects of diet should be the focus of our concern, however, we repeat the observation that "The important thing to look to is not so much the food itself but what was done to it before it was eaten" (Brace, 1977:199). If that can be accepted, it should follow that the introduction of nondental food processing techniques should lead to changes in the forces of selection that had previously maintained the dentition. At that point, we should expect the probable mutation effect would begin to demonstrate its consequences. This leads to the prediction that the Late Pleistocene and post-Pleistocene dental reductions we document should follow immediately after the introduction of specific elements of food processing technology.

Earth Ovens and the Use of Frozen Foods

Throughout most of the Pleistocene, hominids could make only intermittent use of the north temperate zone. Although we have recorded our skepticism about a recent African origin for "anatomically modern" *Homo sapiens,* there is no debate about the fact that hominid beginnings were ultimately both African and tropical. Until the latter part of the Middle Pleistocene, occupation of the more northerly portions of the Old World was only intermittent. To this day, humans retain the physiological characteristics of tropical mammals and cannot survive in the north without altering, by cultural means, the impact of environmentally imposed selective forces. The use of clothing, artificial shelter, and fire were prerequisites for permanent habitation in the north, and it is no surprise to find that all of these cultural features first make their documented appearance in the cultural complex associated with the first permanent occupation of the area extending from the Middle East to western Europe and including southern Russia. This is the cultural complex called the Mousterian.

The control of fire during the Mousterian played a crucial role in more than one respect. The possibility that fire was used earlier cannot be ruled out, though there has been much discussion and debate (Perles, 1975; Gowlett et al., 1981; Binford and Ho, 1985), but there can be no doubt that it is consistently associated with occupation sites beginning with the Mousterian, as early as Riss II well over 200,000 years ago, and continuing without break from that point on (Bordes, 1953, 1955, 1961, 1968, 1977; Mellars, 1965, 1986; de Lumley, 1976; Straus, 1989). Not only can we assume that it was used for warmth to fend off the chill as the last glaciation began to assert its influence, but we can see evidence to the effect that it was used for the purposes of cooking food for the first time. Mousterian "hearths" consistently contain fragments of burned bone, and these are not demonstrable from earlier time levels.

The Mousterian "hearth," however, is not the residue of the kind of open-air camp fire that typically comes to mind when that term is used. Instead, it characteristically retains a substantial depth even after the passage of more than 50,000 years. When seen in the vertical face of an archaeological trench, it often presents the kind of pattern that one sees in the photograph of a nebula in an astronomy book. There is the swirl of traces of charcoal apparent in the trench wall, accompanied by fist-sized fire-blackened rocks and fragments of burnt animal bone. For those who have participated in or attended the preparation of a Polynesian luau where a pig is baked in an earth oven, the pattern presented by the "hearths" visible in the wall of a trench in a Mousterian site displays a very familiar configuration. In fact, the pattern is essentially identical—a nebula-like swirl of charcoal, fire-blackened fist-sized rocks, and occasional pieces of charred animal bone, pig in the case of the residues of a luau.

It seems abundantly clear that the Neanderthals of the Mousterian were cooking their food in the same way that the Polynesians still do (Graebner, 1913; Brace, 1977, 1979a and b, 1988b; Brace et al., 1987; Green, 1979; Straus, 1989). We can suggest that the Neanderthals did this for reasons of basic practical necessity and efficiency. One of the recurrent problems faced by those pursuing a hunting and gathering way of life in an area that was becoming increasingly influenced by the onset of glacial conditions was the simple manner of dealing with food that had become frozen. Whether the Neanderthals were regularly preying on things the size of a mammoth or a woolly rhinoceros, even an animal such as a pig or a deer cannot always be entirely consumed at a single sitting. A day later, it would be frozen solid during the winter months in a periglacial setting. The technique of making a fire in an excavated pit and heating a quantity of rocks to be raked over the packet of food after the fuel is exhausted, the whole being then sealed in with dirt, was standard for earth-oven cookery in many parts of the world right up to the present time.

In the tropics, earth ovens can be used to counter the effects of the onset of spoilage of meat acquired by hunting a day or so earlier (McArthur, 1960:112; Moore, 1973). In the case of the Neanderthals, the efficient use of fuel for the purposes of thawing is an obvious impetus for the development of earth-oven cooking techniques. Large animals can be butchered into packets appropriate for thawing later in the earth oven. Small animals can be stored frozen for later use and then thawed whole.

Although we can suggest that the appearance of the earth oven during the Mousterian was probably associated with the advantages of being able to thaw meat that had become frozen, it also had an unintended consequence. Meat cooked in such a fashion can become quite tender indeed, and in such condition it requires less chewing to render it swallowable than would be the case if it remained uncooked. In turn, this should represent the relaxation of selection for maintaining teeth at the size level that can be seen throughout the Middle Pleistocene. The appearance of the earth oven in the archaeological record, then, should mark the time at which the dental reduction manifest in the Late Pleistocene had its beginning.

From this point on, individuals should have been able to survive despite the loss of a significant number though not all of their teeth. The fact that the famous Neanderthal from La Chapelle-aux-Saints had survived for years after the loss of his molars has been cited as evidence of the reduction of selection for maintaining Middle Pleistocene levels of chewing capacity that followed the development of earth-oven cookery (Brace, 1977, 1979a and b, 1988b). The subsequent picture of tooth-size reduction proceeding at the rate of 1 percent every 2,000 years has been offered as the ongoing consequence of that reduction of selection for maintaining tooth size. That rate by itself was sufficient to convert a Neanderthal-sized dentition into one of "anatomically modern" size and form by the end of the Pleistocene, and we can suggest that the reduction in the supporting facial architecture that followed the reduction of the dentition itself was what accounted for the emergence of modern human face form from a Neanderthal ancestral condition (Brace, 1979; Brace et al., 1987). Not all heated-stone cookery was of the earth-oven variety. The argument has been offered that, while earth ovens are plausible in the Mousterian, the distribution of fire-cracked rock in the subsequent Perigordian and even more recent Magdalenian was more consistent with their use in stone boiling (Movius, 1966:320–322; Leroi-Gourhan and Brezillon, 1966; Frayer, 1976:43). In any case, the consequences for the human dentition are the same.

Pottery and the Increase in the Rate of Dental Reduction

Obviously, if the development of the earth oven produced a reduction in the forces of selection that influence the maintenance of tooth size, the technological innovation represented by the invention of pottery must have had an even greater effect. Once a population has acquired the use of pottery, it possesses the capability to convert its food into drinkable consistency that would drastically decrease the necessity of having teeth at all. The point of time coinciding with the adoption of pottery should mark the onset of an even more rapid rate of dental reduction, and, as we shall show, this indeed seems to be the case.

Long after the development of the earth oven, but well before the invention of pottery, there was another development in the realm of food processing technology that also has to be considered. This is the discovery of pounding and grinding techniques and tools to assist in these practices. While these made possible the use of food items such as pulses and grains that had previously been unavailable, it did not in and of itself reduce the amount of mandatory mastication. Flat breads and cakes, incorporating both the powdered grinding stone from the flour-making process and the grit of the ashes in which they were cooked, may even have increased the amount of wear normally encountered. Certainly, there was an obvious change in the angles of wear on the occlusal planes of the molar teeth of the beneficiaries (B. H. Smith, 1984). In addition, there is some suggestion that molar wear did increase with the increase in the use of grain as a source of food (P. Smith, 1977, 1982; P. Smith et al., 1984).

With the addition of pottery to the food-processing armamentarium of the Neolithic approximately 9,000 years ago in the Middle East and at similar levels of antiquity in East Asia going back to several thousand years earlier in Japan (Chang, 1987; Nissen, 1988; Pearson, 1986), a major relaxation of the selective forces maintaining tooth substance had taken place. Thenceforth, the "beneficiaries" could survive in the complete absence of any teeth at all.

There are essentially no pre-Neolithic burials of individuals who had been completely edentulous at the time of death, but, from the Neolithic on, the presence of edentulous skeletons in cemeteries is not unusual. In many cases, the extensive record of alveolar resorption in such individuals attests to the fact that they had lived for many years in a state of complete toothlessness.

In all of the parts of the world where the use of pottery has been continuous for at least 7,000 years—namely Europe, the Middle East, China, Japan, and Southeast Asia—the rate of dental reduction is effectively the same (Brace et al., 1987). Furthermore, it is effectively double the rate where it can be tested for the Late Pleistocene. This post-Pleistocene rate amounts to approximately 1 percent per thousand years.

Genesis of Modern Differences in Tooth Size

From the available skeletal and archaeological evidence, it is evident that the hominids of the Middle Pleistocene pursued the same survival strategy virtually throughout their entire range of occupation. The generally accepted view is that this entailed a mixture of hunting and gathering, though some doubts have been expressed concerning just how much large animal hunting was actually involved (Binford, 1987). Whatever they were doing, it required a level of physical exertion that maintained a degree of muscularity and skeletal robustness that was well beyond what we would describe as "anatomically modern," and which characterized the appearance of *Homo erectus* wherever that hominid is found.

Since brain size in *Homo erectus* had not reached modern levels, it cannot be used as an index for body size in the same fashion that we have done for the representatives of *Homo sapiens*. We can only argue by analogy that the selective forces imposed by their hunting and gathering mode of subsistence produced a degree of robustness and bulk comparable to that found in the earliest representatives of *Homo sapiens,* the "classic"' Neanderthals.

The robustness of the jaws and teeth appears to have been the same both throughout the areal extent of *Homo erectus* and also through time, though the quantity of information on which that claim is based is so small that this view must be regarded as tentative at best. In general, however, it would appear that similar hunting and gathering activities led to the use of food stuffs that put the same pressures on the jaws and teeth of all Middle Pleistocene hominids. Certainly there is no evidence or reason to suspect that there was a spectrum of jaw and tooth size differences that was in any way comparable to what we can see in the representatives of *Homo sapiens* alive in the world today. A basic summary of the changes in hominid tooth size through time and the spectrum visible today can be seen in Figure 6-7.

Although the >1,600 mm^2 TS in *Homo erectus* was smaller than the 2,000 mm^2 TS found in the preceding Australopithecines (Brace et al., 1973), it was larger on the average than it is in any living human population where the spectrum runs from a maximum of just under 1,500 mm^2 down to ~1,100 mm^2 (Brace, 1979a and b). The emergence of "modern" human form was uniformly associated with dental reduction. The differences in tooth size that can be seen between the various living human populations, then, were the consequences of different amounts of reduction from the Middle Pleistocene condition. These in turn can be associated with the differing lengths of time that the forces of selection maintaining tooth size have been modified in the different parts of the world inhabited by "modern" *Homo sapiens*.

We should note that the right-to-left scale in Figure 6-7 is more "logarithmic" than literal, which means that the spread at the right-hand end is really far more sudden and dramatic than it would appear from the uncorrected nature of the plot. Because of the nature of the scaling, a certain degree of compression is inevitably represented. For example, the slight change in the line that leads from the Neanderthals of 100,000 years ago to the modern

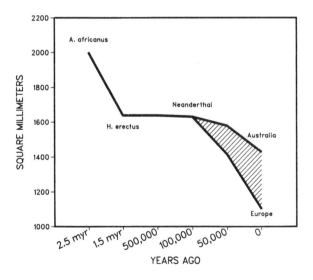

Figure 6-7 Hominid tooth size from the Australopithecines to the spectrum visible in the living populations of *Homo sapiens*. The Australopithecine (*A. africanus*) and *erectus* data are from Brace et al. (1973), the Neanderthal (Krapina, 100,000 years ago, and late Neanderthal, 50,000 years ago) data are from Brace (1979b), and the modern spectrum is recorded here in Table 6-2.

193

European condition that occurs at 50,000 is represented by the "classic" Neanderthals with a TS of 1,415 mm^2, but the change in direction of the line that leads from "Neanderthal" to "Australia" also is located at 50,000 years ago. The point in question is represented by the Kow Swamp material from the Murray River Basin with a TS of at least 1,581 mm^2 (Brace, 1980:147). The date, however, is less than 20,000 years (A. Thorne, personal communication) rather than the 50,000 years of the Neanderthal-to-Europe line, but this does not change the fact that similar dynamics are represented in both cases.

The most important of these modifications are reductions caused by specific cultural developments. The first of these, as we have noted above, is the development of earth-oven cookery. While this had become a universal cultural feature by the dawn of written history, it had an antiquity in the area occupied by the Mousterian cultural tradition that predates its appearance elsewhere. Recently, Mousterian dates of between 80,000 and 115,000 years ago have been produced for sites in Israel (Schwarcz et al., 1988; Valladas et al., 1988; Stringer et al., 1989). Although these dates seem awkwardly early when compared with the dates of sites with typologically similar Mousterian tools elsewhere (O. Bar-Yosef, personal communication), the Mousterian cultural tradition with which the earliest earth ovens are associated goes back more than 200,000 years (Straus, 1989) and clearly predates any other cultural tradition with which they can be associated. Earth ovens, we have argued, represent a cultural adaptation to survival in the north temperate zone back at the beginning of the Late Pleistocene. In line with the argument developed above, we suggest that the onset of those dentofacial reductions by which "modern" face form was produced began earliest in the areas in which the Mousterian culture originally flourished. The cultural adaptation that made survival possible at comparable latitudes in Asia appears to have been considerably later (Jia and Huang, 1985), and, presumably, the path toward dental reduction therefore did not begin quite so early in Asia as it did throughout the northwestern extent of Late Pleistocene human occupation.

In any case, modern populations that can trace their ancestry to the north temperate zone should exhibit the effects of having begun to undergo dental reduction earlier than is true for those whose Late Pleistocene forebears were located in latitudes that are farther south. The earth oven reached Australia some 30,000 years ago (Bowler et al., 1970; Mulvaney, 1975:152), and we would predict that the Australian aborigines were the last to begin the Late Pleistocene trajectory of dental reduction.

Whereas the different time level associated with the adoption of the earth oven marks the difference in the time of the onset of dental reduction, the picture is complicated slightly by the adoption of pottery at different times in different parts of the world. Pottery never did reach aboriginal Australia, and, with the late adoption of the earth oven there, we would predict that the Australian aborigines should have the largest—that is, the most unreduced—teeth of the living populations of the world today, and of course they do.

Dental reduction in sub-Saharan Africa has proceeded somewhat farther than is evident in Australia. So far, there is no archaeological evidence showing that earth ovens were ever used in Africa, but this could just be because the question has never been investigated. The extent to which tooth size reduction has occurred in sub-Saharan Africa may then be the result of the spread of pottery use without an earth-oven precursor. We know altogether too little about the antiquity of cooking in Africa, and it remains a question that deserves systematic investigation. The sporadic occurrence of pottery predates agriculture (Robbins, 1972), but its wholesale usage clearly accompanies the agricultural extension into West Africa in the second millennium B.C. (Coursey and Alexander, 1968). The subsequent postpottery rate of reduction applied over the next four thousand years may have been sufficient to produce the difference in relative tooth size in Africa as opposed to Australia.

The similar relative sizes of teeth in India, eastern Asia, and the Americas may reflect the fact that, though the postpottery trajectory had roughly the same time of onset and effect that it did in Europe, previously there had been a shorter earth-oven–associated period of reduction. On the other hand, the earliest pottery tradition in the world, the pottery of Japan, could be the reason why the groups that constitute the Jōmon–Pacific cluster, the probable descendants of the makers of the Jōmon pottery, display the greatest amount of dental reduction of any of the populations in the world today.

If our Middle Pleistocene ancestress, that putative African "Eve," was decidedly macrodont by the standards of today, it was not a dietary change that led to the reductions that produced the modern condition. Instead, it was the development of the first culinary technology that reduced the burdens of food processing that had formerly been performed by the teeth alone. It is ironic to think that, in the cultivation of the culinary arts, our gain has also led to our loss. The very traditions that culminate in the delights savored by the gourmet have led to the reductions in those parts of our anatomy that have allowed us to enjoy masticating the products of that emergent cuisine.

EPITAPH

As has happened so often in the past, we find that our hard-won insights have been anticipated by some rather unlikely people. For example, the importance of both earth ovens and pottery and the contexts within which they developed were clearly appreciated by that ethnogastronomic enthusiast Earl E. Eaton in his most celebrated work, *The Quick and Dirty Cookbook*. Remarkably, he extolled these events in verse, though it is obvious that the crudeness so apparent in his culinary accounts also pervades his efforts at so-called "poetry." He has called this offering:

Archaeogastronomy

Mammoth was tough on the jaw,
And could easily stick in the craw,
    Unless chewed enough,
    Which was hard when the stuff
Was eaten all bloody and raw.
Then after one had one's fill
Of a late autumn mammoth kill,
    It froze in a block
    That was hard as a rock,
'Til next spring put an end to the chill.

So fuel for a fire was lit
Over rocks in a shallow pit,
    And the heat from the stones
    Thawed the meat on the bones
Interred in the ashes and grit.

We suspect that this primeval scene,
And the taste that emerged from between
    The rocks in the ground
    And the food heaped around,
Gave rise to the first true cuisine.

This manifestation of gain
Didn't lead to the usage of grain,
    Which, swallowed whole,
    Just takes it toll
As gastrointestinal pain.

Whether put in a kettle and stewed
Or merely fermented and brewed,
    The invention of crockery
    Improved upon rockery
For what could be counted as food.

Sherds can serve as a clue
That a graminiferous brew;
    Prepared in a pot,
    Fermented or not,
Could be drunk without having to chew.

Commentators on matters gastronomical rarely consider the consequences that the subject of their enthusiasms might have had on human physical form. The latter task has been left to those more directly concerned, and
one of these, the unfrocked orthodontist Carey S. Moeller, had produced just
such a reflection, which he originally intended as a part of his "Orthodonto-
phobia" (printed in Brace, 1977:204). I had originally wanted to include the
whole paper in which they were first printed, "Occlusion to the Anthropological Eye," as a separate chapter here, but there simply was not enough space.

We're living on time that we borrow;
For the sweets that we love, to our sorrow;
    Produce the decay
    That will hasten the day
Of the toothless jaws of tomorrow.

Somehow it seems inevitable that the last word on dental reduction was
the one gloomily penned by that inept producer of doggerel I. Doolittle Wright
(quoted in part by Brace, 1979b:548). It seems most fitting to use the full original version to close our discussion:

We used to use teeth as a tool;
And before the invention of gruel,
    The audible crunch
    Of the things they would munch
Made abrasion the general rule.

Now dental reduction is fast,
And Man shall be toothless at last;
    He eschews his chews
    And will choose to lose
The teeth that he had in the past.

Our grip gets progressively limper,
Our defiance of Fate but a whimper;
    Bald, blind, and toothless,
    Our end shall be ruthless;
And not with a fang, but a simper.

Sic transit gloria oris.

CHAPTER 7

Cro-Magnon and Qafza—Vive la Différence
(1996)

Prologue

The background of the outlook of paleoanthropology is tied to the traditions of scholarship of nineteenth-century France as has been explained in Chapters 2 and 3. From the beginning, this has been firmly in opposition to a Darwinian view of evolution. The first human fossil to be recognized as such was found in 1856 in the Neanderthal, a valley just east of the Rhine in the western part of Germany. Thal (now Tal) is the old German spelling for the word meaning "valley," the archaic rendition being most appropriate, and the specter of that ancient relic has served as a bogeyman for the field ever since. To this very day, the suggestion that there just might be a Neanderthal skeleton in a "modern" closet is guaranteed to produce a slightly haunted look on the face of the overwhelming majority of biological anthropologists.

A decade after the discovery of that first Germanic Neanderthal, further certifiable human fossil remains were unearthed in southwestern France in 1868 at the site of Cro-Magnon in the village of Les Eyzies. This time, though the most complete of the individuals was strongly built, it did not display that degree of transhuman robusticity that has earned the Neanderthals their stigma of bestiality. Almost instantly, Cro-Magnon was adopted as an ancestral icon and invested with the attributes of a veritable Prince Charming—tall, straight-limbed, intelligent, enterprising, artistic, and possibly fair-haired and blue-eyed, though the caution was added that we have no way of deducing eye or skin color from bones alone. However, if the leg bones are used to calculate stature, the Cro-Magnon individual usually illustrated measures out to be between 5'7" and 5'8" in height.

Just as the physical attributes of Cro-Magnon were extolled in contrast to the denigrated Neanderthals, the Upper Paleolithic culture with which he was associated was portrayed in glowing terms as opposed to the "crude," "monotonous," and "unimaginative" Mousterian that had preceded it. In both the cultural and the biological realms, the very possibility that the earlier could have become transformed into the latter by normal means—by (gasp) *"evolution"*—was rejected out of hand as an insulting insinuation.

But if the earlier inhabitants of Europe, the Neanderthals, were not the ancestors of their Cro-Magnon successors, where had these latter people come from? Since Europe is the westernmost edge of the Old World, the only possible answer had to be "the East"—*ex oriente lux*. This, of course, fit nicely with the entire traditional picture of what is known of European cultural history prior to the Industrial Revolution.

It was Darwin (1871) who realized not only that humans were physiologically tropical mammals but also that our most abundant and most closely allied relatives lived in Africa, and he predicted that it was in Africa that we would eventually find the evidence for ultimate human origins. While he was pooh-poohed for that idea for over a generation after his death, subsequently and in spectacular fashion he has been shown to have been absolutely right. The trail of human ancestry in Africa now goes back more than 5 million years, and the prehominid antecedents of those earliest forms go back yet another 30 million years.

The questions still remain: Did Cro-Magnon actually migrate out of Africa? And why couldn't Cro-Magnon simply be a pared-down Neanderthal? Except for myself and one or two tentative others, that last possibility is simply dismissed without treatment. The first question, however, has drawn quite a bit more consideration. The architect of the consensus view of the Neanderthals as "nasty, brutish, and short" and an extinct side line with no living descendants was the French paleontologist Marcellin Boule (1861–1942). He and his anthropological contemporary René Verneau (1852–1938) both claimed to see African attributes in the jaws and teeth of the earliest "moderns" in the western European Upper Paleolithic (Boule, 1913, 1921; Verneau, 1906). To his credit, Verneau offered the possibility that these were not simply indications of African ancestry but merely aspects of the primitive—manifestations of plesiomophy, to use the current polysyllabic buzz-word—and possibly derived from Neanderthal ancestors (Verneau, 1924).

Since most of the profession has followed Boule's lead, there has been a continued interest in trying to identify the evidence for that assumed relatively recent African connection. French archaeological work in Israel at the site of Qafza (variously spelled as Kafzeh or Qafzeh which inevitably leads to mispronunciation, especially in French) starting in 1934 and resumed in 1965 produced a series of individuals of "modern" form but now known to date back more than 90,000 years (Vandermeersch, 1981; Valladas and Valladas, 1991). These have been lumped together with material from an even older site in Israel, Skhūl, and promoted as "Proto-Cro-Magnons" and the possible link between Africa and Europe (Stringer, 1988). This is the source of the paleoanthropological school of thought identified as the "Out-of-Africa" view (Bräuer, 1984; Stringer and McKie, 1997a and b; Tattersall, 1997; Tattersall and Schwartz, 1999) that is held by the great majority of the practitioners in the field.

But the equation of Cro-Magnon and Qafza has been made without the benefit of any metric comparisons either of the skull or of the dentition. In August 1992, I attended the Third International Congress on Human Paleontology in Jerusalem where I presented just such a quantitative treatment. I polished that presentation up in the form reprinted here (except for the spelling of Qafzeh) from the *Dental Anthropology Newsletter* (Brace, 1996a). While I was in Jerusalem for that meeting, I was able to measure the other relatively complete Qafza specimen, the female Qafza 9 housed in the collections of the Rockefeller Museum there. This was complete enough for me to get the better part of my set of measurements on it. Subsequently I ran it through the same discriminant function procedure that I used for the male, Qafza 6, which I had previously measured at the Institut de Paléontologie Humaine in Paris. As is shown in the Prologue to Chapter 12, the African posterior probability figure for Qafza 9 is .995, which ranks it as even more African than the overwhelmingly African male individual. The various European probability figures were all .000, and the Asian figure was .002. The teeth tell a different story, but that is the subject of the treatment that follows.

There remains the puzzle of why, if Skhūl dental size is the result of the relaxation of selective forces because of long-term association with Mousterian food-preparation traditions, the subsequent fully Neanderthal representatives all have teeth that are an order of magnitude larger. Bernard Vandermeersch, one of my long-time opponents in the interpretation of this material, also has recently expressed similar kinds of worry about the incongruity of the placement of the Skhūl specimens (Vandermeersch, 1997). At the moment, neither of our camps has even the beginnings of a plausible answer to this question.

~   ~

INTRODUCTION

Over the past decade or so, much attention has been paid to the question of the emergence of "modern" human form. The approach generally taken has been a plunge into the fossil record to consider nuances in the form and matters concerning the dating of this, that, or the other specimen to suggest its relevance or irrelevance for contributing to our understanding of the origins of "modern" morphology. One of the things that has been curiously neglected in this approach is any systematic attempt to come to grips with just what constitutes that "modern" condition so taken for granted by the majority of the profession that focuses on the course of human evolution as its particular subject for study. Instead, there is a wondrously Eurocentric set of assumptions that is based more on the course of post-Renaissance political history than on anything remotely like actual morphological analysis. This has been linked together with the traditions of rejecting the principles of evolutionary biology by those who purport to be students of human evolution (for a critical assessment of these traditions, see Brace, 1981, 1982, 1988, 1992, 1995).

For more than a century, the archetype of early modern human form has been assumed to be embodied in the specimens found in 1868 at Cro-Magnon in southwestern France (Broca, 1868). According to the accepted folklore of the field, Cro-Magnon illustrated the earliest manifestation of modern human appearance. This dated from the Aurignacian maybe more than 30,000 years ago in western Europe (Mellars et al., 1987, p. 130; White, 1989, p. 385), though new techniques have pushed that date back another ten-thousand years in Bulgaria and northern Spain (Bischoff et al., 1989; Cabrera Valdez and Bischoff, 1989). Starting at that time, human evolution presumably came to a halt and there has been no further change in human form. In the words of Stephen Jay Gould, "The Cro-Magnons, why, they are us!" No predecessors are contemplated, and all subsequent change is assumed to have been in the realm of culture (public presentation in Ann Arbor, Michigan, October 30, 1982; and see Gleick, 1983, p. 64; also Diamond, 1989, 1990, p. 26; Klein, 1992, p. 12).

The claim that there has been no subsequent anatomical change is manifestly untrue. A quick look at the most abundant evidence available—the teeth—shows that gross dimensions alone in the early Upper Paleolithic were closer to "classic" Neanderthal figures than to living Europeans (Brace et al., 1987; Brace, 1994, 1995). (See Figure 7-1.) The stance represented in the words of Gould can be taken for the feelings of the vast majority of those who write about the emergence of "modern" human form, and it is rooted more in transcendental faith than in anything approaching science. Rarely if ever is it supported by anything approaching statistically testable collections of data. And, who is this "us" that the Cro-Magnon specimens presumably exemplify?

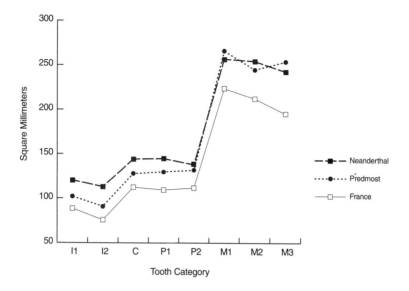

Figure 7-1 Profiles of cross-sectional areas of the summed maxillary and mandibular tooth categories of European Neanderthal, Early Upper Paleolithic, and living French samples. The data used are recorded in Table 1 of Brace (1994). The Neanderthal dental dimensions are from Wolpoff (1971, pages 176–185); the Předmost figures are from Matiegka (1934, pages 142–143); and the recent French measurements were made on specimens in the Musée de l'Homme, courtesy of Dr. J-L Heim. Data are given in Table 7-2.

PROTO-CRO-MAGNON?

We have been told that Qafza is a proto-Cro-Magnon specimen (Howell, 1959; Valladas et al., 1988; Vandermeersch, 1989). Clearly Qafza does not display archaic cranial features even if it has an archaic dentition (Brace et al., 1991, p. 35). At nearly 100,000 years (Valladas et al., 1988), it is one of the oldest representatives of "modern" human cranial form, but, once again, that specter of what constitutes the "modern" condition comes back to haunt us. Given the various "modern" manifestations present in the half-dozen or more regional clusters that can be identified (Brace and Hunt, 1990; Brace, in press b), which "us" does Qafza represent? And can it really stand for the ancestors of the population to which Cro-Magnon belonged?

I have collected craniofacial measurements on representative samples of all the major modern human clusters, and it is an easy enough thing to use discriminant function statistics to test the placement of individual specimens such as Qafza and Cro-Magnon against them (Brace, 1991a; and see Table 7-1). It is in the nature of the statistic that you cannot determine the

Table 7-1 Probability Levels by Fisher's Linear Discriminant Function That Qafza 6 and Cro-Magnon 1 Can Be Excluded from Membership in the Group Named in the Row Heading.[1]

	N	Qafza 6[2]	Cro-Magnon 1[3]
Africa	118	**0.986**	0.000
Amerind	487	0.009	0.002
Asia	763	0.004	0.000
Australo-Melanesia	237	0.007	0.000
European Continent	142	0.000	0.041
Europe NW Edge	98	0.000	**0.955**
Eskimo	155	0.000	0.000
South Asia	96	0.000	0.002
Jōmon-Pacific	448	0.000	0.002

[1] Extracted from Table 2 of Brace (in press c).
[2] Measured at the Institut de Paléontologie Humaine in Paris; courtesy of Prof. H. de Lumley.
[3] Measured at the Musée de l'Homme in Paris; courtesy of Dr. J-L Heim.

population to which an individual specimen belongs, but it is an easy enough matter to determine the groups from which it is excluded. The pattern of features found in Qafza 6, for example—the only specimen with enough variables to be treated in this fashion—can be excluded from all modern human samples except those from sub-Saharan Africa, most particularly West Africa. It would appear that the sub-Saharan craniofacial configuration has retained a statistical coherence for nearly 100,000 years.

Cro-Magnon, on its part, is clearly excluded from every "modern" human craniofacial configuration except that characteristic of Europe. And if the European configuration is broken down into its constituents, Cro-Magnon could not occur within those groups that run from eastern Europe to the Atlantic coast, though it cannot be excluded from England, the Faeroe Islands, and Norway. It is a curious little irony to contemplate the thought that the most famous fossil "modern" in France could not be ancestral to the "modern" French, but cannot be excluded from the ancestry of the recent English.

There is another curious irony in all of this. In 1839, it was the American anatomist and anthropologist Samuel George Morton who realized that the difference between the craniofacial configurations of Africans and Europeans was so marked that it could not have come about by natural means in the time he assumed was available, a time calculated since Noah's ark was presumed to have landed on Mount Ararat in the western Caucasus—Turkish Armenia—

at the end of the biblical flood. Morton's views were subsequently adopted by Paul Broca as the basis for an outlook that still prevails in French anthropology (Brace, 1982). The irony now is that the French point of view, which has never been comfortable with the perspective of Darwinian mechanism, evidently feels that 100,000 years is quite enough time to convert an African into a European, while the constituency that I represent—thoroughly Darwinian in its outlook—is quite happy in seeing a European "classic" Neanderthal become transformed by gradual means into a modern European but yet has trouble seeing how the transformation of an African craniofacial pattern into a European one could take place within the same period of time.

At issue once again is the difference between the changes in these features that simply represent continuity of the local characteristics—the consequences of hereditary inertia—and those that are the result of the shaping forces of natural selection. Tooth size, following changes in the intensity of the selective forces to which they respond, underwent a gradual reduction of nearly 50 percent during the last 100,000 years (Brace, 1979, 1994, in press c; Brace et al., 1987, 1991). One percent every 2,000 years is consistent with the Late Pleistocene rates of tooth size change plotted in other mammalian groups (Kurtén, 1954, 1959, 1967; Gingerich, 1974, 1980, 1983). If that rate of change is projected onto the tooth-bearing portions of the facial skeleton, it is a very simple matter to produce a modern western European out of a "classic" European Neanderthal.

CRANIOFACIAL FORM FROM THE PERSPECTIVE OF EVOLUTIONARY BIOLOGY

The efforts at assessing the date and the form of such specimens as Qafza and Skhūl, for example, are certainly to be applauded (Vandermeersch, 1981; Valladas et al., 1988; Stringer et al., 1989). In spite of the fact that there is nothing "modern" about the Qafza dentition (Brace et al., 1991, p. 35), the cranial morphology has been correctly identified as being more "modern" than archaic (Vandermeersch, 1981). Skhūl for its part is completely intermediate in both cranial morphology and tooth size (Brace, 1979, p. 541, in press a). (See Figure 7-2.) This does bring up the issue that none of the practitioners in the field at the present time have made any effort to assess the differences in the significance of the role played by those aspects that are under direct selective force control and those that owe their characteristic form to the inheritance of an essentially nonadaptive configuration (Brace and Hunt, 1990; Brace, in press b).

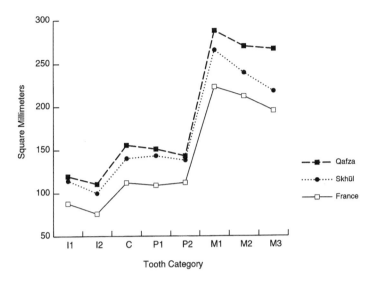

Figure 7-2 Tooth-size profiles of the Mousterian-level human fossils from Qafza and Skhūl compared with the profile of a recent French sample. The Qafza measurements are from Vandermeersch (1981, pages 176–177), and the Skhūl measurements are from McCown and Keith (1939, pages 212–213). The French tooth measurements were made on specimens in the Musée de l'Homme, courtesy of Dr. J-L Heim. Data are given in Table 7-2.

Tooth size is indeed under selective force constraints, and it should be evident that those subsistence activities that required the possession of a functional dentition large enough to last throughout an expectable life span had to have been essentially the same for Qafza as they were for the "classic" Neanderthals since there is little difference between the average gross dental dimensions of both samples (Figure 7-3). A quick check of the archaeological record will show that there was no visible difference in the cultural assemblages associated with those two samples in Israel (Clark, 1992).

Now if the single aspect of craniofacial form most directly related to the selective forces imposed by a particular mode of subsistence—the dentition—is not functionally distinguishable when Qafza and the "classic" Neanderthals are compared, what about the other aspects of craniofacial form? Even to the untutored eye, it is clear that Qafza craniofacial morphology could never be confused with that of the "classic" Neanderthals of western Europe.

Leaving the dentition aside, the question of the meaning of variation in craniofacial form has to be dealt with. In spite of prolonged efforts to view brow ridge form as a direct response to selective force applications (Russell, 1985), no one has ever been able to demonstrate that the absence of brow

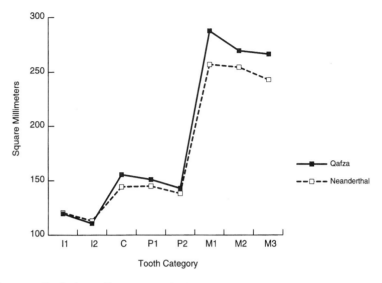

Figure 7-3 Tooth-size profiles comparing the dental dimensions of Qafza and the European "classic" Neanderthals. The sources are reported in the legends accompanying Figures 7-1 and 7-2. Data are given in Table 7-2.

ridges led to a shortened life span. For example, there is no single instance in the prehistoric or modern evidence available of an individual who had met his demise due to a collapse of the facial skeleton under the pressures of mastication. To date, we have no plausible reason to believe that variation in brow ridge form by itself is related in any way to life span or reproductive success (Brace, 1992, p. 13).

The same thing is also true for differences in the details of occipital morphology. What possible adaptive value can be read into the presence or absence of a "bun-shaped" occiput? Major differences in the size and shape of the mastoid processes have never been convincingly associated with different functional capabilities. Even the size of the area of neck muscle attachments has no clear relationship with the size and strength of those muscles themselves. The total surface area to which the neck muscles of a cow or a horse are attached is no greater than that allotted to the neck muscles of a human being, and yet, in the bovine and equine examples, the vastly heavier head is not balanced on top of the spinal column but held throughout life thrust forward in a nearly horizontal position by the continuous tension of a muscle mass that absolutely dwarfs the human condition.

On the other hand, in the course of 50,000 years of human evolution, occipital morphology has undergone far less alteration. Everything from the details of mastoid process form and nuchal muscle attachments to fully "bun-shaped" occiputs demonstrates a continuity from Neanderthal morphology to that visible in the inhabitants of the fringes of western Europe today in Norway, the Faeroe Islands, and England (Brace, 1991a, 1995, in press c). Given those aspects of occipital morphology in living northwest Europeans, one would have to predict fossil ancestors with a similar configuration. Fossil predecessors exist with the right occipital characteristics (Hublin, 1978), and they are called Neanderthals.

There are only three nondental aspects of craniofacial form that are clearly associated with the forces of selection: the relative size of the brain box itself; the thickness of its walls; and the size of the nasal skeleton. The first of these, the relative size of the portion of the cranium devoted to enclosing the brain, does not differ between representatives of contemporary hominids over the span of the last one-and-one-half million years. The same thing is also true for the second of those three key cranial features, the thickness of the skull bones themselves (Kennedy, 1991). However, both relative brain size and the thickness of the cranial vault walls have changed significantly over time, but they have never displayed significant regional differences at any given point. For more than 80 percent of the time that the genus *Homo* has been in existence, there is also no evidence for discernible differences in the size of the nasal skeleton between contemporary hominids.

In a manner similar to the emergence of tooth size distinctions, regionally recognizable differences in nasal size have only arisen within the last 200,000 years (Franciscus and Trinkaus, 1988a and b; Franciscus and Long, 1991). The contrast in the manifestation of that feature is vividly displayed when Qafza is compared with the "classic" Neanderthals. That degree of adaptively related nasal difference, however, is scarcely sufficient reason to warrant separate specific recognition. When matters are considered using this perspective, there is no more reason to separate Qafza and the "classic" Neanderthals at the specific level than there is to grant specific distinction to the difference in nasofacial features displayed when living sub-Saharan Africans are compared with northwest Europeans—or at least some northwest Europeans.

From the perspective of evolutionary biology, this simply portrays the same stance as the one articulated by Franz Weidenreich nearly half a century ago, namely, that, since the beginning of the genus *Homo*, there has been only one human species in existence at any one time (Weidenreich, 1943a, b, 1946, 1947, 1949), but it was the addition of an adaptive perspective to

Weidenreich's conception of gene flow that suggested how the mechanics could work that would both maintain specific unity at any given point in time and also produce the kind of coordinated change by which "modern" form emerged simultaneously over the whole range inhabited by the genus *Homo* (Brace, 1964, 1967, 1979, 1991b, 1992, 1995, and in press a and c).

The mechanics of the model I offered nearly 30 years ago have been alluded to piecemeal (e.g. Brose and Wolpoff, 1971; Wolpoff, 1980; Wolpoff et al., 1984), but the model as a whole has never been given any consideration at all. The measure of the extent to which it has been overlooked can be seen in the off-hand claim that simultaneous evolutionary change toward a modern configuration from various regional Neanderthal manifestations "can hardly be considered likely" (Bräuer, 1984:332). Even the recent formulations most obviously derived from it, the so-called "*multi*regional" continuity model— said to have been "first outlined in a broad theoretical context by Wolpoff et al. in 1984" (Smith et al., 1989:38)—only added the two-syllable "multi" to the original version of regional continuity and removed a consideration of the mechanism by which the whole process is driven (Brace, 1992, pp. 18–19, 1995, in press a). This being the case, it is time that the essential parts of that model were recapitulated in summary form.

CONCLUSIONS

"Modern" human form is a typological abstraction uneasily grafted onto the fact that all living human beings belong to the same species despite manifest differences in appearance. The emergence of "modern" human morphology would appear to have been produced in somewhat different fashion in different parts of the world. The essential precursor was the world-wide achievement of the intellectual and linguistic capacities that we now recognize as being uniquely human. This was the consequence of responding to the selective pressures engendered by survival within the milieu of the Cultural Ecological Niche (and see Brace, 1995, Chapter 12). The only anatomical evidence we have for this is the achievement of proportionately modern levels of brain size somewhere between 200,000 and 100,000 years ago in people who otherwise had the skeletal and dental robustness of Middle Pleistocene *Homo erectus*.

What led to the appearance of "modern" form was the reduction in that *erectus* level of robustness that followed when those sapient intellectual capabilities interposed barriers between the forces of selection and specific aspects of the human physique. These barriers were developed at different times in

209

different places, and the result was that "modern" human form emerged in mosaic fashion (and see Brace, 1995, Chapter 8). The early appearance of obligatory cooking in the north led to the beginnings of dental reduction and the subsequent shrinking of the associated parts of the face. To this day, the people in the north temperate zone have the smallest teeth in the world.

At the same time, the use of projectiles for hunting purposes in Africa (Yellen et al., 1995) relaxed the selective pressures that elsewhere had maintained those aspects of robustness characteristic of post-cranial human form throughout the Middle Pleistocene. The consequence was that the gracilization which we think of as being "modern" developed first in the south long before there was any hint of the "modern" state of dental reduction (Shea, 1989, p. 448). Eventually, projectiles spread out of Africa via Israel and were adopted elsewhere (Shea, 1992), and the process of gracilization was the predictable consequence (Brace, 1995, pp. 224–225). In similar fashion, cooking eventually spread south (Brace, in press a and c). It was not needed to thaw food, but it was eventually discovered that cooking could retard spoilage and thus prolong the period over which foodstuffs could be used. Again, the subsequent reduction in tooth size was the predictable result (Brace, 1995, pp. 225–229).

Reduction in tooth size between Qafza and modern West Africans is 17 percent, which is exactly the same as the percentage reduction between "classic" Neanderthal tooth size and the Late Upper Paleolithic in Europe (Brace, 1994). Furthermore, the pattern of larger molar-to-incisor proportions of Qafza vis-à-vis Neanderthal is preserved when modern sub-Saharan Africans are compared with modern Europeans (see Figure 7-4). A striking similarity to the African-European comparison emerges when Qafza and Skhūl are plotted on the same graph (see Figure 7-5). When the pattern of dental reduction is shown from Qafza to the modern Africans from whom they cannot be distinguished on craniometric features, the profiles of cross-sectional areas reduce in perfectly parallel fashion (see Figure 7-6), just as the tooth-size profiles of the Neanderthals and the modern French show a comparably parallel pattern (see Figure 7-7). This is treated in greater detail elsewhere (Brace, 1994).

In both the details of its dental and craniofacial size and form, Qafza is an unlikely proto-Cro-Magnon, but it makes a fine model for the ancestors of modern sub-Saharan Africans. Along with the microfauna at the Qafza site (Tchernov, 1988, 1991, 1992), the human remains are best regarded as evidence for a temporary intrusion of African elements into the Middle East that had no direct long-term consequences. Indirectly, however, the adoption of projectiles by their Neanderthal contemporaries—whether at that

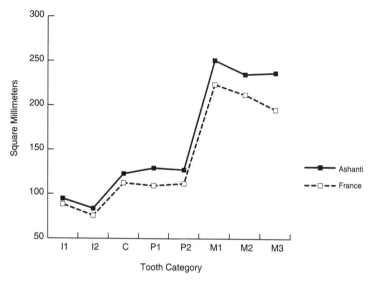

Figure 7-4 Tooth-size profiles comparing recent French dental dimensions with those of recent West Africans. The latter were from an Ashanti sample measured in the American Museum of Natural History courtesy of Dr. I. Tattersall. Data are given in Table 7-2.

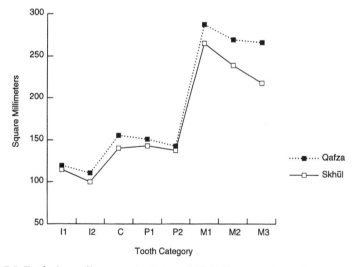

Figure 7-5 Tooth-size profiles comparing Qafza and Skhūl. The pattern is exactly the same as that shown when West Africans and French are compared—just shifted up a bit. Data are given in Table 7-2.

211

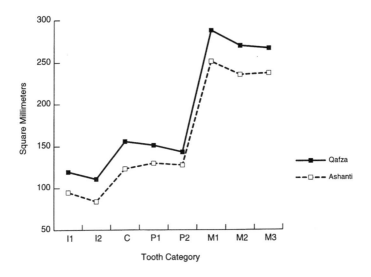

Figure 7-6 Tooth-size profiles comparing the dental dimensions of Qafza and a recent West African sample, the Ashanti mentioned in the legend for Figure 7-4. Data are given in Table 7-2.

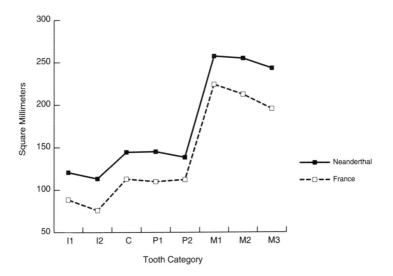

Figure 7-7 Tooth-size profiles comparing European "classic" Neanderthals with recent French. The sources are reported in the legend accompanying Figure 7-1. Data are given in Table 7-2.

Table 7-2 Cross-sectional tooth size figures for the summed maxillary and mandibular teeth in the named categories for each of the populations indicated.

Pop.	Numbers	I1	I2	C	P1	P2	M1	M2	M3
Neand.	13(5–20)	120.5	113.0	144.3	144.9	138.2	257.0	254.5	242.8
Qafza	5(3–9)	119.5	110.6	155.5	151.0	142.9	287.5	269.5	266.4
Skhūl	4(3–7)	114.6	99.9	140.3	143.1	137.9	265.4	239.2	217.9
Před.	7(4–10)	101.6	91.2	127.7	130.1	132.2	266.2	245.7	254.5
Ashan.	20(10–31)	94.8	83.7	123.0	129.5	124.4	251.0	235.2	236.9
France	45(14–81)	88.5	75.8	112.5	109.5	111.9	223.9	212.2	195.3

Data are abstracted from Table 1 in Brace (1995c). Neanderthal data are from Wolpoff (1971:171–185), Qafza from Vandermeersch (1981:176–177), Skhūl from McCown and Keith (1939:212-213), and Předmost from Matiegka (1934:142–143). Ashanti were studied at the American Museum of Natural History in New York. Specimens labeled "France" are from Brittany and Nièvre and curated at the Musée de l'Homme, Paris. Cross-sectional tooth size figures are the sum of the mesio-distal times the bucco-lingual measurements for the means of the right and left maxillary and mandibular I1...M3.

time, or earlier—led to those selective force changes that produced the transformation of Neanderthal to "modern" postcranial form. After another 50,000 years, Cro-Magnon was just what one would expect to see, but as the result of a transformation from a Neanderthal ancestor and not one that looked like Qafza.

Qafza and Cro-Magnon, then, represent earlier manifestations of African and European configurations respectively. Those patterns are alive and well in Europe and Africa today. Neither one is better nor worse than the other, they are simply different. On this note, we can celebrate that fact with the words "vive la différence!"

ACKNOWLEDGMENTS

This manuscript is based in part on the presentation given at the Third International Congress on Human Paleontology, Jerusalem, Israel, August 25, 1992. Attendance was made possible in part by the Irene Levi Sala CARE Archaeological Foundation.

CHAPTER 8

Deriving the Quick from the Dead: Bio-Cultural Interaction and the Mechanism of Mosaic Evolution in the Emergence of "Modern" Morphology
(1995)

Prologue

The issue of the origin of "modern" human form has attracted the attention of biological anthropologists and many other kinds of scholars and writers who flitter around the subject almost like moths attracted to a light-source. Like those moths, however, almost none of them ever do anything with the object of their interest. In the burgeoning literature on the emergence of "modern" morphology, there is almost no mention of the dynamics of how and why it appeared. Vague references are repeatedly made to the effect of "selective forces" and "directional selection," but what those forces are and how that selection works in specific instances is completely missing (for example, see the roster of papers in Clark and Willermet, eds., 1997). Some of my own focused efforts to deal with specific aspects, especially those documented by the dental evidence, are presented in Chapters 6 and 7, as well as here. I have also dealt with some of this at greater length in *The Stages of Human Evolution*, fifth edition (1995c; and also see Brace, 1996a).

At the same time those efforts were in preparation, I also worked up a general summary of that approach that I hoped would appeal to a broader anthropological readership. I sent this to the *American Anthropologist* with the title "Deriving the Quick from the Dead," and, in proper fashion, they sent it out to a selection of people in the business for evaluation.

Most of the commentators were either noncommittal or favorable, but one seethed with so much hostility that it bordered on the incoherent. This review started with the statement that "This manuscript is a self-promoting, accusatory, out-of-date, and inaccurate attempt by the Brace to 'straighten out' the record of modern human origins. There are many serious errors, whether in the author's delusory interpretation of the recent history of paleoanthropology (and his place in it) or in his presentation of data." In regard to one of the matters I had phrased, my choleric critic declared, "It is nothing more of Brace's hyperbole intended to insult his intellectual opponents." In the final paragraph of the review, my effort was adjudged to be "an abrasive, uninformed, and self-serving essay" that could only count as "mean-spirited drivel." The conclusion was that, "There is nothing worth publishing here."

In recounting this, I have omitted the long and convoluted portions of the harangue that the editor conceded were "intemperate," and also the points of supposed factual inaccuracy raised in the critique. These latter were easy enough to counter since, in addition to being so ineptly expressed, they were essentially without substance. The reason I have quoted from this review, however, is to illustrate an aspect of the mind-set among paleoanthropologists (and its author claimed identity as one) that has made it so hard to introduce processual thinking into the field. Not all paleoanthropologists are quite such textbook examples of foot-in-mouth disease, and most of my professional opponents have been able to express their disagreements in civil and sometimes even elegant prose. The *American Anthropologist* published the full manuscript with a shortened title and minor revisions (Brace, 1995a), and that is the version reprinted here with the title restored to its original form. As for the identity of my verbally challenged critic, it was not hard for me to guess. However, since the correspondence of the editorial office of the *American Anthropologist* is to be made part of the permanent files at the Smithsonian Institution, that is something that will become public knowledge in the near future.

Over the past two years, the *American Anthropologist* has provided a forum for discussions focusing on the origin of "modern" human form.[1] Although these discussions have not mentioned it, there has been essentially no change in the theoretical base since these matters were placed on the pages of the *American Anthropologist* for consideration a full third of a century ago (Brace, 1962), in spite of a quantum increase in the number of fossils involved and in the techniques of dating and metric analysis.

Even more striking is that not one of these published presentations has made more than passing reference to what might have produced the "modern" configuration that eventually emerged. It would appear that the absence of a concern for evolutionary dynamics noted in the *American Anthropologist* seven years ago (G. Clark, 1988; Brace, 1989) has continued to characterize the practitioners of paleoanthropology. With that in mind, it would seem appropriate to try to inject into the discussion a strain of processual thinking previously offered but generally ignored.[2]

The term *modern* properly refers to present times, but it has come to be associated with the idea of progress to such an extent that the present state of affairs has been suffused with implications of superiority over what was current in the past. If we had a usable equivalent for the French term *l'homme actuel* it would be a great blessing, allowing us to resuscitate the only English word—*man*—that has traditionally designated the collective nature of the living people of the world. If we refer to "present people," the residual implications of group distinction override the attempt to indicate a common heritage; and when we refer to "persons," as if pluralizing the discrete "person" constituted a shared humanity, all vestiges of communal identity disappear.

These purely verbal problems should, however, alert us to the pitfalls of presuming to judge the quick and the dead as collective entities. As we contemplate the phenomenon of the living, the question arises, Is there indeed something shared by all of humankind as a consequence of being alive now in contrast to what was shared by all living humans at some time in the past— 250,000 years ago, for instance? I suggest that there is, but that it is not discernible by the procedures paleoanthropologists characteristically use to determine whether the designation of *Homo sapiens* is warranted. The perspective of evolutionary biology occasionally takes a back seat to the literature

---

1 Aiello, 1993; Frayer et al., 1993, 1994a, 1994b; Krantz, 1994; Lieberman and Shea, 1994; Stringer and Bräuer, 1994.

2 Brace, 1964, 1967, 1979a; Brace et al., 1987, 1991.

of paleoanthropology.[3] Advances in computer capabilities have promoted a major resuscitation of the enthusiasm for compiling lists of anatomical minutiae in the fashion of the typological essentialism of the past, while the concept of adaptation has almost entirely disappeared from consideration. It was Darwin himself who noted that adaptive traits are almost useless for the purposes of studying relatedness, so the focus on morphological trivia can play an important role in that regard (Darwin, 1859:427). However, the changes from *Australopithecus* to *Homo* or from *erectus* to *sapiens* are adaptive changes, and these simply cannot be determined by limiting one's attention to traits of unknown adaptive significance, even when those are accumulated in mind-boggling numbers (cf. Kimbel and Martin, 1993).

All that talk about bun-shaped occiput, supra-iniac fossa, angular torus, post-glenoid eminence, and paramastoid elevation can tell us absolutely nothing about the evolutionary status of the specimens concerned, particularly when the paleoanthropologist has little familiarity with the various manifestations of those anatomical features in current human populations. For example, an appraisal of a sampling of those curiosities has led to a resurgence of the enthusiasm that the European Neanderthals warrant separate specific recognition.[4] But those who have favored this position have completely overlooked the fact that the living populations of the northwest fringes of Europe are distinguishable from the rest of the living populations of the world by the possession of precisely those self-same features (Brace, 1991a).

In spite of visible differences in such things as skin color, cheekbone shape, and tooth size, all living human populations possess to an equivalent extent the mental capacity necessary to learn a language. There are no "primitive" languages (Hymes, 1964:104; Swadesh, 1971:1). No language is easier or harder to learn than any other language. Human children the world around learn their languages at the same age, and their progress toward acquiring adult-level skills follows an identical track. This is the single most profound distinction between the human and the nonhuman, and it is shared by all living human groups. This quality alone substantiates the term *sapiens,* and, whatever their morphological differences, by this criterion all living people are equally sapient.

Unfortunately, beyond sheer relative brain size, there are no skeletal markers that can be associated with the presence or absence of language. Brain size, however, cannot be ignored. The slow increase in the size of the

---

3 Brace, 1964, 1981, 1988a, 1988b, 1992.

4 Tattersall, 1986:171, 174; Stringer, 1990:103; Rak, 1993.

brain starting with the transformation of the genus *Australopithecus* into the genus *Homo* in the lower Pleistocene came to a halt just before the beginning of the Late Pleistocene, just when the tangible manifestations of human cultural capacity began their exponential increase. A generation ago, I noted that brain size ceases to increase when "the dullest member of a group benefits from the innovations of the brightest to an equal extent" (Brace, 1967:81–82). A case can be made that the coincidence of these occurrences may be the best evidence we shall ever have for the beginnings of language as we know it.[5] It is at this time also that the codistribution of purely stylistic elements in the archaeological record presents a pattern on the map that, for the first time, shows striking similarities to the kind of picture we see when language distributions are plotted (see Figure 8-1).

I do not want to leave the impression that the beginning of language was a sudden event like the "flick of a switch," as the current paleoanthropological orthodoxy has suggested (Stringer and Gamble, 1993:204). After all, it took

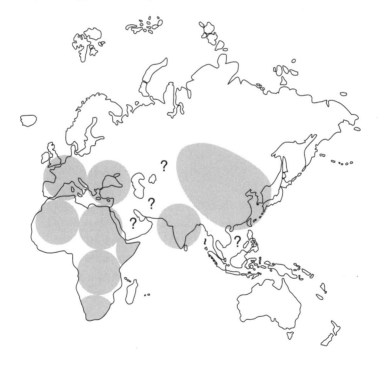

Figure 8-1 Approximate area of distribution of shared stylistic elements during the Mousterian, from Brace, 1995b:220.

5 Brace, 1988b:117–118, 1991b:150–151, 1995b:176–177, 219.

more than a million years from the first signs of brain enlargement and the first evidence for the differentiation of Broca's speech area in the left frontal lobe (Falk, 1992:11–12) before brain size ceased to increase and technological proliferation took on a life of its own. A long and slow process led to the change in the locus of vocal control from the limbic system to the cortex (Hockett, 1978:255; Jerison, 1991:82). The reorganization of the circuitry that led to the almost instinctive appreciation of syntax and the easy acceptance of symbolic attribution that is now the heritage of all human children must also have taken an extended period (Chomsky, 1975; Pinker, 1994).

It seems reasonable to suggest that when the relative brain size expansion ceased and cumulative technological elaboration began, the rudiments of language were in place; thus our hominid predecessors merit the designation *sapiens*. However, at that point, 200,000 years ago, nothing else about those ancestral hominids would strike us as "modern" in appearance. Human fossils of that degree of antiquity consistently display "modern" levels of brain size on essentially Middle Pleistocene bodies. That combination is what I have used to define the Neanderthal stage in human evolution where *stage* is a grade concept defined by Julian Huxley, though as I have used it, *stage* comes closer to Huxley's *subgrade*.[6] The term stage is preferable for its clearer anagenetic connotations, and because, in the most recent or "modern" manifestation, there is nothing even faintly adaptive about it.

THE GENESIS OF "MODERN" HUMAN FORM

From an appraisal of skeletal morphology, it is clear that relative brain size has not undergone any discernible change over the last 200,000 years or so. Everything else in the skeleton has changed, and without exception the changes have been reductions from the state of robustness characteristic of the Middle Pleistocene (Hrdlička, 1930:347). Not all aspects of the skeleton have changed at the same rate, and those various rates have different trajectories in different parts of the world. A good 30 years ago, I suggested that the key to understanding the changes by which "modern" form emerged was to be found in the cultural realm, and that this was what should have produced in situ continuity from archaic to "modern" form in each of the continuously inhabited regions of the world.[7] To be more specific, we could predict that the

---

6 Brace, 1964:17–18, 1967:89, 1991a:179, 1991b:148–150, 1995b:211; Huxley, 1958:27–28, 38; Mayr, 1974:107.

7 Brace, 1962, 1964, 1967, 1979a, 1988b, 1991b, 1992, 1995b, in press; Brace and Montagu, 1965:240, 1977:324.

root causes of "modern" emergence should be located in the Mousterian itself (Brace, 1992, in press).

When Milford Wolpoff added two more syllables to the designation of this perspective and it was reborn as the "multiregional" continuity view, an aspect of the focus on culture that was a part of the original was retained, but only as an indication of the presence of gene flow.[8] In its current manifestation, gene flow is identified as the major source of the changes that emerge to produce "modern" human form (Frayer et al., 1994a:153, 1994b:426). However, gene flow is never the source of genetic novelty in and of itself. It can serve only to distribute what is already there. The mechanism that I had put into the 1964 model has been left out of the latest incarnation. This, the "multiregional" continuity view, has made no effort to explain why the new aspects of form emerged where they did or what advantages they conveyed that should have led them to prevail in the areas to which they are supposed to have spread by means of gene flow—an integral part of my first presentation of the concept.

My first proposal that culture be considered in efforts to understand the recent course of human evolution also implied that the spread of cultural elements should be accompanied by the spread of genes. As I saw it, however, the principal role played by the spread of genes was the maintenance of specific unity since the beginning of the genus *Homo*. This was implied in the earlier version of this interpretive position presented by Weidenreich and Dobzhansky half a century ago.[9] That has been reemphasized in the most sophisticated recent assessment of the mtDNA evidence (Templeton, 1993:65, 1994:143). To be sure, gene flow would also have accomplished the spread of advantageous traits throughout the whole species in the course of time; perhaps the species-wide linguistic capabilities that we see today were distributed by just those means.

However, the principal morphological changes that distinguish living humans from their Middle Pleistocene ancestors represent no discernible advantages for their possessors. To claim that there is some sort of value in teeth that wear out more quickly, shoulders that dislocate more readily, skulls and limbs that are more prone to fracture, or joints that are more susceptible to sprains is to adopt the "Panglossian paradigm" that all change is driven by natural selection for the good of the organism (Gould and Lewontin, 1979).

---

8 Wolpoff et al., 1984; Thorne and Wolpoff, 1992; Frayer et al., 1993:17.

9 Weidenreich, 1939:85, 1943:46–48, 1946:30, 1947:201; Dobzhansky, 1944:254.

Gene flow alone cannot tell us why "modern" traits emerged where and when they did, or why they should have prevailed. These reasons were outlined in my first attempt to suggest the dynamics by which Neanderthal changed into "modern" human form (Brace, 1964:18) and are now developed sufficiently to warrant a synopsis.

CULTURE AND MORPHOLOGICAL REDUCTION

In considering the nature of the selective forces that have impinged on human chances for survival, it is useful to regard humans as inhabitants of a "cultural ecological niche"[10] (and see Chapter 12). The pressures generated by the entry into that niche profoundly influenced the shaping of human intellectual capabilities as well as the linguistic dimension. However, the cultural ecological niche as a whole has had no other specific effects on the shaping of human biological form.

The most demonstrable impact of the cultural ecological niche has been in the emergence of specific innovations that have improved human chances for survival. The archaeological record of their spread can indeed indicate the paths of gene flow. More importantly, specific aspects of culture can produce significant changes in the nature of the specific selective forces. The consequences have almost never been an intensification of a particular aspect of selective force but rather its reduction. Ever since cultural innovations began their exponential accumulation toward the end of the Middle Pleistocene, human ingenuity has devised ever more effective ways of interposing barriers between the forces of selection and the human physique.

When selection is relaxed or suspended, those traits that had once been essential for survival are free to vary with impunity. Randomly occurring mutations will not be selected against and will remain in the gene pool. But though the occurrence of a mutation is a random event, the consequences of the average mutation are very clearly directional, and the direction is one of reduction. This is a process that I called the probable mutation effect (Brace, 1963), suggesting it is the main reason why "modern" human form is a reduced version of its Pleistocene antecedents in specific instances where cultural ingenuity has reduced the necessity of having once-mandatory degrees of robustness.

---

10   Brace, 1964:14, 1967:53, 1979a:287, 1988b:72, 1991b:85, 1995b: ch. 9.

OBLIGATORY COOKING AND DENTAL REDUCTION

The best single example of the probable mutation effect is the relation between the adoption of specific aspects of technology and the ensuing dento-facial reduction. Survival in the north temperate zone during the winter and especially during periods of glacial intensification has required that food be cooked if for no other reason than simply to thaw it to the point where it can be eaten (Brace, 1979b).[11] This "obligatory cooking" (Brace, 1995b, in press) had the unintended but significant consequence of reducing the amount of chewing that had previously been mandatory.

Obligatory cooking was initially associated with the northwestern quadrant of human occupation (see Figure 8-2). As is demonstrated by the accumulation of the evidence for hearths ranging from Pech de l'Azé in the west (Straus, 1989:489–490) to Tabun in the east (Bar-Yosef, 1993:136), this dates back to the penultimate glaciation and made survival there possible on a

Figure 8-2 The shading represents the area where "obligatory cooking" made continued habitation dating from the penultimate glaciation possible. Arrows and dates indicate the subsequent spread of the idea.

---

11 Brace, 1967, 1979b, 1988b, 1991b, 1992, 1995b, in press.

continuous basis from that time to this. It also had the consequence of relaxing the forces of selection maintaining tooth size and morphological complexity. The descendants of the first people whose survival was dependent on obligatory cooking should have been undergoing dental reduction for the longest period of time among the world's populations, and should now be the ones with the smallest teeth. This is indeed the case (see Figure 8-3). Indeed, the fossil record shows a degree of dental reduction strictly proportional to the length of time that the ancestors of the sample examined had been dependent upon cooked food for their survival.[12] The tooth-size profiles from the Neanderthals through the Upper Paleolithic to Neolithic and living samples all from western Europe show just the kind of progressive reduction in tooth size predicted by that model. For the same reasons, the picture of morphological simplification has proceeded in parallel fashion.

Eventually cooking techniques spread south to areas where they had not been absolutely mandatory for survival. Again, the degree of dental reduction should be proportional to the time that cooking has been a significant part of the lifeways of the peoples in question. If we look at the evidence for tooth size in the living populations ranging from mainland eastern Asia out, via Indonesia to Australia, the record of a decrease from Pleistocene tooth-size

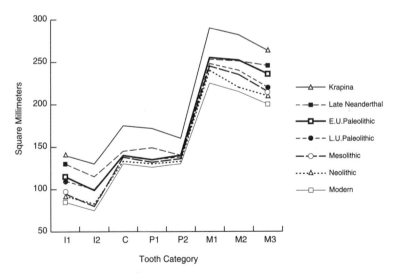

Figure 8-3 Tooth size profiles demonstrating the record of dental reduction in Europe over the last 100,000 years, from data in Brace, 1979b, and (for Late Upper Paleolithic and Mesolithic) Frayer, 1978.

---

12 Brace, 1979b, 1992, 1995b, in press; Brace et al., 1987, 1991.

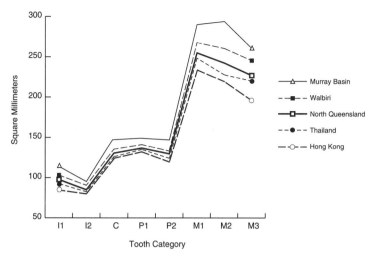

Figure 8-4 Tooth size profiles demonstrating the lessening degree of dental reduction in a contemporary transect running from the Asia mainland to southern Australia, from data in Brace, 1978, 1980, and Brace et al., 1984.

levels is almost an exact duplicate of the picture of size change through time from the Neanderthals to the living in western Europe (see Figure 8-4). In our Far Eastern example, however, we can suggest that this depicts a measure of how long it has taken food-preparation techniques to spread from the north where survival itself had required their presence back in the Pleistocene.

PROJECTILES AND POSTCRANIAL GRACILIZATION

If the trend toward departure from Middle Pleistocene levels of tooth size was a consequence of the adoption of cultural practices that began in the northwest quadrant of human occupation, the factors that led to the reduction in robustness from the neck on down appear to have had their origin in the southwestern quadrant—specifically Africa. Postcranial skeleto-muscular robustness was clearly mandatory for hunters who had to grapple by hand with their prey. It was these circumstances and not ill-coordinated, random, hyperactive flailing across "the landscape" (Trinkaus, 1987:123; Trinkaus and Shipman, 1992:368) that maintained Middle Pleistocene levels of skeletal reinforcement.

Reductions in that level of robustness should have been the consequences of a change in the techniques of predation that eliminated the requirement of direct contact between the hunters and their prey. The use of projectiles is one of the most obvious means by which this is accomplished. If Klasies River Mouth and Border Cave are to be trusted, gracilization first appears in the hominid record during the African Middle Stone Age. That should have alerted us to the possibility that hunting was being assisted by the use of projectiles for the first time. Indeed, it now appears that not only were barbed bone points manufactured by Middle Stone Age hunters (see Figure 8-5), but Levallois flakes were hefted and used as projectile points.[13]

Figure 8-5 An African Middle Stone Age bone point from the excavations of Alison Brooks and John Yellen at Katanda in Zaire near the Ugandan border. Drawn from Shreeve, 1992.

13   Brooks, 1988:347; Shea, 1988:448; Lieberman and Shea, 1994:315.

The Middle Stone Age goes back nearly 200,000 years (J. D. Clark, 1988:239, 291), and that would have allowed plenty of time for the probable mutation effect to have produced the kinds of reductions displayed in the skeletal material available for our appraisal (Rightmire, 1979, 1983).

Eventually such techniques should have spread north via the only available route out of Africa—Israel—so it is no surprise to find evidence for hafted Levallois projectile points at Qafza 95,000 years ago (Shea, 1988, 1992; Bar Yosef and Vandermeersch, 1993). It should also come as no surprise that the nonadaptive aspects of craniofacial morphology visible in the Qafza skeletons have a distinctly African cast (Brace, 1991a:189–191, 1995b:250, in press). The African source for Qafza is emphasized by the presence of two species of African mice (Tchernov, 1991:79). If the temporary extension of an African fauna up to the eastern shores of the Mediterranean can be illustrated by sub-Saharan mice, surely the presence of African-appearing people and tools should not be unexpected (see Figure 8-6).

Figure 8-6 The shaded area denotes the African Middle Stone Age where projectile-assisted hunting first developed. The solid arrow suggests the use of projectiles was brought to Israel by African immigrants at least 95,000 years ago. The broken arrows indicate the diffusion of projectile use to the rest of the inhabited world.

SKHŪL, QAFZA, AND THE IMPACT OF SELECTIVE FORCE TIME-DEPTH DIFFERENCE IN THE SHAPING OF SPECIFIC MORPHOLOGICAL TRAITS

The gracilization visible in the Qafza postcranial skeletons clearly bespeaks the effect of a longtime use of projectile-assisted hunting techniques, but the retention of teeth that approach Middle Pleistocene size levels (TS = 1494 mm²; Vandermeersch, 1981: 176–177) indicates that heat-assisted food preparation techniques had not been used prior to arrival in Israel. As befits its putative tropical source, the Qafza facial skeleton lacks the elevation and elongation of the nose that is so prominent in groups such as Skhūl (McCown and Keith, 1939:273) and other long-term residents of the north where warming and moistening of inspired air is essential for survival. Although Qafza retains Middle Pleistocene dental dimensions, the reduction in cranial reinforcements and neck muscle attachments, reflecting the reductions in postcranial muscularity and robustness, gives the cranium its rounded and relatively "modern" appearance.

Skhūl, on the other hand, displays a dentition that has already undergone sufficient reduction (TS = 1352 mm²) so that it is the same size as that visible in the late Neanderthals such as Hortus (TS = 1338 mm²) or the identically sized Aurignacians of Europe (Předmost = 1349 mm²; for instance, Brace, in press). Partial reduction in the postcranial skeleton has also begun. The scapulae, for example, display a bisulcate configuration that is halfway between the Neanderthal and the "modern" condition.[14]

The trajectories producing aspects of "modern" form at Qafza and Skhūl have evidently followed very different courses. In any case, the sample at each site retains a different aspect of archaic morphology that is conveniently ignored by those who uncritically use them as evidence for the appearance of fully "modern" human form (see critique by Brace, 1991a; Corruccini, 1992). The professional tradition of lumping the two sites together as though they were a single population shaped by the same evolutionary dynamics prevents us from being able to understand the dynamics by which "modern" form has come into being.[15]

---

14 McCown and Keith, 1939:135; Frayer, 1992:37; Trinkaus, 1992:282.

15 Howell, 1959; Stringer, 1978, 1990; Vandermeersch, 1989, 1992; Sohn and Wolpoff, 1993:341; Waddle, 1994:453.

CONCLUSIONS

There is no one general configuration that will suffice as an illustration of the "modern" condition. All living human populations possess equivalent intellectual endowments as illustrated by their linguistic capabilities. The only skeletal indication of this is the fact that cranial capacity relative to body size is the same for all of the peoples of the world.

When compared with the common ancestral condition in the Middle Pleistocene, the morphology exhibited in the rest of the body displays varying degrees of reduction in robustness conditioned by particular cultural innovations. These arose initially at different places and spread as a result of population contacts and comparative advantages of particular new cultural elements. The biological consequences form a classic picture of mosaic evolution: morphological response occurred first in those areas where innovation arose; similar morphological responses occurred elsewhere as the innovation was adopted, whether or not the genetic response in the area of origin spread along with it. Given the unlikelihood of major population displacements by small bands at approximately the same levels of technological sophistication (Krantz, 1976), individual advantageous cultural innovations can be expected to have spread much more rapidly than the genetic characteristics of the groups within which they first arose.

The adaptive key to human survival has been in the advantages conveyed by reliance on culture. The selective pressures generated by entry into the cultural ecological niche produced a level of intellect that is essentially the same everywhere. Other traits show reductions in proportion to the length of time that human ingenuity has erected culturally mediated barriers between what had formerly been specific, environmentally imposed selective forces and those aspects of the physique once maintained to cope with them. The origin and spread of those specifically identifiable cultural innovations can be demonstrated only by an examination of the archaeological record. The distribution of the elements that alter the intensity of selective forces for particular traits will produce graded responses in the form of clines leading to a nonracial picture of the nature of human biological variation (Brace, 1995a). This then leads to an appraisal of the particular manifestations of reduction in the physique of regional human groups and suggests a prehistoric course of events that can be archaeologically tested—and vice versa.

From the perspective of biological anthropology, it is clear that we can make no sense of the mosaic nature of human evolution in the latter part of the Pleistocene without specific information on the regional manifestations of the archaeological record. For this we are completely dependent on the work of archaeology. We may also be able to suggest something of the converse; that is, aspects of change in human form lead to the prediction that particular events must have occurred in the past to have produced them. Only by this archaeological testing can we pursue the study of human evolution as a meaningful scientific inquiry.

In any case, it is clear that an understanding of the emergence of "modern" human morphology can occur only as the result of a coordination between the efforts of biological and archaeological anthropologists to a greater degree than in the past. This should encourage the practitioners in each subfield to keep an eye on the work being done in the other as we approach the dawn of a new century.

CHAPTER 9

The Roots of the Race Concept in American Physical Anthropology
(1982)

Prologue

The impetus for the development of the field of biological anthropology actually stemmed from the perceptions of the visible distinctions between the peoples of the world that impinged on the consciousness of post-Renaissance travelers who returned to write about their experiences. Initially this was mainly a matter of general intellectual curiosity and remained a part of the growing realm of the natural sciences that accompanied the emergence of the Renaissance outlook. With the establishment of European colonies in various parts of the world, questions concerning the meaning of human biological and behavioral differences took on an added level of importance. Because the Europeans who had put themselves into the position of pondering these matters had done so by the act of leaving home and settling far from their own area of origin, the differences that they perceived were categorical rather than that of a natural and unbroken gradation of one population into another.

Not only that, by far the largest enterprise of European colonization was in the Western Hemisphere—the "New World." There, the categorical distinction between Europeans and "Native Americans" was reinforced by the general perception that the "Natives" were essentially variants of the same thing wherever they were encountered. What was not realized was that the "Natives" themselves were relative newcomers to the Western Hemisphere from Northeast Asia who had not had time to differentiate in the fashion universally visible among the long-time inhabitants of the "Old World."

The European-derived colonizers then imported quantities of enslaved West Africans so that there were then three populations originally from three quite separate and restricted portions of the Old World who faced each other on a day-to-day basis in positions of manifest and enforced inequality. It was this situation that gave rise to the very concept of "race" in the first place (Smedley, 1993) and, ultimately, to professional anthropology. It is no accident, then, that an anthropology primarily devoted to studying the matter of "race" arose as a serious entity in America as soon as it became a recognizable phenomenon anywhere else in the world (Brace, 1982, 1996b).

Once again, it was Frank Spencer who gave me the opportunity to look into the American focus on "race" for his volume *A History of American Physical Anthropology 1930–1980.* And once again, Frank let me stretch things back to include a major nineteenth century segment that was not part of his original intent (he did complain in his letters to me, but he let me get away with it in any case). And this is the result.

≈   ≈

Institutions are largely, but certainly not entirely, the shadows of their founders.
—E. D. Baltzell, 1979

Amerian physical anthropology, the largest such entity in the world at the moment, was mainly created by two preeminent individuals, Earnest Albert Hooton and Aleš Hrdlička, during the first half of the twentieth century. Hooton, in his four decades of teaching at Harvard, launched the careers of most of the generation of physical anthropologists who went on to establish physical anthropology curricula in the universities and colleges where the discipline presently thrives. Hrdlička was chiefly responsible for creating the *American Journal of Physical Anthropology*—the journal in which these anthropologists published their principal contributions—and the American Association of Physical Anthropologists—the society that served as the principal basis on which they could establish a professional identity and a research orientation.

Occasionally, the feeling is expressed that anything done 5 or 10 years ago is of no particular importance and what really matters is only the most recent of research publications. This viewpoint was evident 15 years ago when it was announced that "physical anthropology has now come of age [Lasker, 1964:iii]." It is perfectly true that in a rapidly developing field, research methods and results are often superseded in very short order. However, there is more than a little reason to suspect the maturity of any scholarly realm that is ignorant of the work of the previous generation, or even that of more distant predecessors. Current research cannot be pursued effectively, and future efforts cannot be planned, until our present status is clear. And we cannot really know where we are unless we have some understanding of our past.

Now that the American Association of Physical Anthropologists can look back on a half century of existence, we should have obtained enough perspective on our current position to begin to exhibit some of that maturity we have so rashly claimed for ourselves in years gone by. Some effort has been made to view the practices of paleoanthropology from a historical perspective (Brace, 1964b), but with occasional exceptions (e.g., Montagu, 1942, 1952, 1965; Erickson, 1974a and b) this has not been the case for the rest of the physical anthropology our founders bequeathed us.

If paleoanthropology, the study of the fossil evidence for human evolution, is one of the two realms that physical anthropology can claim as uniquely its own province, the other is the study of contemporary human variation subsumed by convention under that single, four-letter word *race*. Although there have been many studies reflecting on the use of the concept of race in historical and sociopolitical contexts (Benedict, 1945; Chase, 1977;

Gossett, 1963; Haller, 1970, 1971; Stanton, 1960; Stocking, 1968), they have not been the works of physical anthropologists.

Curiously, the one piece of research that attempted to put the concept of race in the perspective of intellectual history, written by a historian (Barzun, 1937), appears to have had little if any impact on anthropological thinking. Hrdlička, in fact, greeted its (unspecified) "errors" and "misconceptions" with a vigorous denunciation, suggesting that Barzun had "gone astray" to the extent that "he would lead anthropology to a crucifixion [Hrdlička, 1937:227]." The strength of Hrdlička's response suggests that Barzun had touched a raw nerve. It should be recalled that this took place before the "Synthetic Theory of Evolution" had its major impact on biological science in general (Huxley, 1940; Olson, 1960; Mayr and Provine, 1980) and on anthropology in particular (for example the *Cold Spring Harbor Symposium in Quantitative Biology* in 1950). Although paleoanthropology shows signs of the systematic incorporation of evolutionary theory in its approach (Wolpoff, 1980), the assumption that contemporary human variation can be understood in terms of "racial" variation, despite some pointed critiques (Brace, 1964a; Livingstone, 1962), sails on without any substantial change from the time when Hrdlička and Hooton were shaping the field into its subsequently recognizable form. The factors that influenced their shaping, then, stem from an earlier era. Consequently, we should take a closer look at the factors that conditioned the outlook of our "founding fathers."

EARNEST ALBERT HOOTON

Aside from the gratitude he expressed toward his teachers in England, Hooton showed little interest in examining the roots of the field that grew in America under his benevolent nurturing. Much the same can be said for the majority of the students he produced at Harvard. Most of Hooton's formal education, including his Ph.D. at Wisconsin in 1911, was in the classics. His training in anthropology at Oxford began just after the establishment of the Diploma in Anthropology, which distinction was awarded to him in 1912 (Howells, 1954). That program included study both in science and the humanities, something that is still unusual in an English higher education and that was then quite a novelty (Marett, 1937). At a time when C. P. Snow's "two cultures" had just about stopped communicating with each other (Snow, 1963), this was a laudable effort to keep the rift from becoming a chasm. Even so, the most significant figure in his training was Robert Ranulph Marett, Reader in Social Anthropology, Rector of Exeter College, and himself a classical scholar of note.

The other major influence on Hooton was Sir Arthur Keith. Although Keith, like Arthur Thomson, Hooton's other mentor at Oxford, was an anatomist and presumably represented the scientific training in his background, he was very far from being the cautious empirical worker that we associate with those scientific traditions stemming from the world of the Enlightenment.

Keith gained his medical training at Aberdeen in the 1880s at a time when medicine owed far more to the traditions of the healing arts than to those of science. Furthermore, in his autobiography, Keith spoke of his admiration for "the personality of Thomas Carlyle, who made so strong an appeal in my youthful years [Keith, 1943, 1950:562]." By contrast, he then mentioned "the personality of Charles Darwin, who engaged the wholehearted admiration of my later years [1950:562]." In his mid-60s, however, Keith was still quoting from Carlyle's *Sartor Resartus* (1931:27) to justify the conclusion of his rectorial address to the students of the Aberdeen University that "race prejudice...works for the ultimate good of mankind and must be given a recognized place in all our efforts to obtain natural justice for the world [1931:48]."

The Scottish Enlightenment, which had played such an important role in shaping the intellectual styles of Darwin and Lyell, had long since given way to the Romanticism exemplified by Carlyle (Brace, 1981; Hook, 1975; Olson, 1975; Rosenberg, 1974). In that same unfortunate rectorial address—as in his no more admirable Robert Boyle lecture given at Balliol College, Oxford, a decade earlier (Keith, 1919)—Keith opined to his student audience,

> If...universal deracialization ever comes before you...as the sole way of establishing peace and good will in all parts of our world, I feel certain both head and heart will rise against it. There will well up within you an overmastering antipathy against peace at such a price. This antipathy or race prejudice Nature has implanted within you for her own ends—the improvement of Mankind through race differentiation [Keith, 1931:48].

In this and in other passages, Keith embodies the essence of the romantic movement as contrasted with the characteristics of the preceding Age of Reason. The distinction has been characterized as "the rebellion of feeling against reason, of instinct against intellect, of sentiment against judgment,...of subjectivism against objectivity,...of religion against science [Durant and Durant, 1967:887]." Another passage from Keith's essay on prejudice displays this as clearly as possible:

> The human heart, with its prejudices, its instinctive tendencies, its likes and dislikes, its passions and desires, its spiritual aspirations and its idealism, is an

essential part of the great scheme of human evolution.... Prejudices, I believe, have their purpose. Man has become what he is, not by virtue of his head, but because of his heart [Keith, 1931:26].

Keith spent the last quarter of his long and influential life in a house on the Darwin estate at Downe, considered by many to represent the continuity and embodiment of Darwinian tradition. Yet, though he was thoroughly familiar with Darwin's life and work, he rejected Darwin's basic tenet that natural selection was the principal mechanism by which evolution occurred. In reference to the resistance that Darwin encountered, he observed that "the vast majority of naturalists held (correctly, in my opinion) that natural selection did not account, as Darwin believed it did, for the wonderful contrivances which Archdeacon Paley had so extolled in his Natural Theology [Keith, 1955:103]."

Although he stated unequivocally "I believe in Darwin and Darwinism [Keith, 1955:289]," his de facto rejection of the basis of the Darwinian view preserves the essentials of Paley's position even if it is more Presbyterian than High Church Anglican: "I could as easily believe the theory of the Trinity as one which maintains that living developing protoplasm, by mere throws of chance, brought the human eye into existence [Keith, 1946:217]." Keith in fact was a romantic evolutionist in the mold of Henri Bergson, Teilhard de Chardin, and especially Ernst Haeckel (Brace, 1981). When he declared "the essence of living protoplasm is its purposiveness," and "there are evolutionary processes in living things and therefore in Nature—trends of change which are akin to human purpose and human policy [Keith, 1946:217-218]," he was declaring his faith in a Bergsonian élan vital, which in fact was no different from Haeckel's *Monism*—a manifestation of romantic mysticism that is the very antithesis of Darwinism (Gasman, 1971; Brace, 1981).

Now, though some of the analysts of Romanticism have championed its "flexible and humane pragmatism," as opposed to the perceived evils of "materialistic mechanism" (Barzun, 1958:16), or claimed that some of its manifestations pose no threat to the present and "are in the end quite harmless [Hook, 1975:126]," one could suggest that the victims of two world wars and various manifestations of European colonialism would argue to the contrary. Carlyle himself displayed sentiments that were considerably less than enlightened in his "Discourse on the Nigger Question [1853]," and Keith added his own affirmation: "Like most of my fellows, I was a sober imperialist...Rudyard Kipling sang our creed [1950:228]"; "races were assorted in my mind into superior and inferior; I of course was of the superior race [1950:119]."

There is a remarkable similarity between these views and the proto-Nazi sentiments of the German romantic evolutionist Ernst Haeckel (Gasman, 1971; Brace, 1981), whom Keith uncritically admired (Keith, 1935). Such views also characterized the anthropology of Paul Broca in late-nineteenth-century France (Barzun, 1965:125), and it may well have been the unflattering nature of the exposé that aroused the ire of the Francophile Hrdlička.

With this as his background in "science," it is no wonder that the anthropology of Earnest Albert Hooton was tinged with more than a little biological determinism ("the primary cause of crime is biological inferiority [Hooton, 1939:130]") and racism ("we are fairly safe in assuming that the Australian is far less intelligent than is the Englishman [Hooton, 1946:158]"). Some of these "racist overtones" survived in the works of Hooton's prominent pupil, the late Carleton Coon (1962, 1965). Here the influences of French "polyphyletism" (Vallois, 1952) and Keith's similar model are both quite clear, though Coon gratuitously attributed this to Weidenreich, to whom he dedicated his work of 1962. In his last pronouncement on the subject, Keith articulated the theme that Coon was later to elaborate, without attribution, as the controversial core of his book:

> It still seems to me a very surprising thing that the modern races of mankind which we count to be members of a single species—*Homo sapiens*—should be descendants of ancestors which are regarded as being different species. If my theory is true, then the races of mankind must have converged, not diverged as time went on [Keith, 1950:631].

ALEŠ HRDLIČKA

If Hooton and his students were less than fully conscious of the strains of romantic racism that constituted a major part of their background, Hrdlička was very much aware and made a conscious effort to look at the historical antecedents of the organizational framework he sought to give to American physical anthropology, in America, which was a prominent part of three of the first four issues of the *American Journal of Physical Anthropology* (*AJPA*) (Hrdlička, 1918, revised for separate publication in 1919). This thorough and conscientious survey provides valuable perspective and information, beginning with the development of the field and continuing through its tentative beginnings in the United States.

Although they may be of no great moment, there are some interesting aspects of emphasis that may reveal how he chose to treat his subject. This in turn may help to explain the perpetuation of certain traditions of perspective in physical anthropology that Hrdlička helped to transmit but which, curiously, were not central to his own way of thinking. For example, the conventional view for over a century has been to give credit to Johann Friedrich Blumenbach for being the "father" of physical anthropology (Bendyshe, 1863–1864, 1865; Radl, 1930:167; Brace and Montagu, 1977:22). In his survey, Hrdlička does mention Blumenbach's name, but only as one among a group of "naturalists and anatomists" that included Daubenton, Camper, Lamarck, Soemmering Lacépède, and a number of others (Hrdlička, 1918:5). In Hrdlička's view, France was identified as "the mother-country of physical anthropology [1919:5]," and its "principal founder" was Paul Broca (Hrdlička, 1918:4).

This is not just a quibble over priorities and credits, for it reveals an aspect of Hrdlička's outlook that has created something of a legacy for the field as a whole, even if the result was not quite what Hrdlička may have intended. Just from the nature of Hrdlička's treatment of certain issues (the Neanderthal question, for example), it is possible to suspect that he had a bias against things German (Brace, 1964b:14, 1981). When his complex and interesting background is examined carefully, this supposition is easily documented (Spencer, 1979:15, 18, 123, 769–770). His prejudice is understandable, given his origins in a Bohemia still under the thumb of Austrian domination, even when one considers that his maternal family was of Bavarian origin, and that German as well as Czech was spoken in his home.

This same eastern European background also evidently predisposed him to admire things French, even before he knew their substance. Paris, the "City of Light," has long held place as the symbol of enlightenment for eastern European intellectuals, and for the rest of his life, Hrdlička abstained from criticizing the products of French scholarship, even when they differed radically from the conclusions that emerged from his own work (Spencer, 1979). When others, such as Barzun, pointed to the culturally ingrained bigotry so prominent in French physical anthropology—and did so with a mastery of the French context that only one who had grown up with all the dimensions of a French education could display—Hrdlička would continue to denounce the criticism, if only from a position of offended loyalty.

The intensity of Hrdlička's Francophilia, despite the brevity and occasional squalor of his crucial stay in Paris in 1896, is clearly evident in his letters to his wife-to-be in New York (Spencer, 1979: Chapters 2 and 4). During Hrdlička's three months of study in Paris, his principal contact was with Léonce Manouvrier, who was to remain a friend and confidant until his death. Manouvrier, Broca's pupil and director of the Laboratoire d'Anthropologie at the École pratique des Hautes-Études from 1903 until his death in 1927 (Vallois, 1940), held views that were in marked contrast to those of his own mentor. Although his work did not completely reflect an evolutionary point of view, his perspective on functional anatomy recognized a major component of environmental influence, and he deplored the racism of the anthropology that developed under Broca and that was used to justify French colonial enterprises (Barzun, 1965:125; Schiller, 1979:138; Spencer, 1979:116–119).

Despite the fact that the anthropology that Hrdlička subsequently put into practice took its orientation more from Manouvrier than from the predominant ethos of his French contemporaries, nonetheless, it was Hrdlička's continuing dream to found in America something equivalent to what Broca had established in France (Spencer, 1979: Chapters 7, 12, and 13, 1981:358–360). Although he never did succeed in getting a laboratory of physical anthropology institutionalized as an entity on its own, he did manage to launch a journal and a society, based on the French model, at a time when France and her allies had triumphed over German attempts at military annexation. French influence rose to new heights in the English-speaking world as a partial consequence. In physical anthropology, that influence did not focus on the mechanism stressed by Manouvrier. Instead, one finds the a priori and Platonic essentialism of Paul Broca. Insofar as evolution was contemplated in this ethos, it was the romantic evolutionism of Haeckel, Keith, and Bergson, all of whom specifically rejected the basic aspects of Darwinian mechanism (Brace, 1981). It is not surprising, then, that works actually attempting to deal with the processes of evolution are so notably scarce in the pages of the AJPA.

SAMUEL GEORGE MORTON

Whereas French influence on American physical anthropology in the twentieth century is reasonably well recognized, the nineteenth-century background to it is not only less obvious, but indeed, has been largely overlooked. In his historical review, Hrdlička did observe with considerable insight that "Physical Anthropology is a comparatively recent branch of science" and, further, "it is interesting to know that one of its main incentives was the discovery of America with its new race of people, no mention of which occurred in any of the old accounts or traditions [1918:5]." The circumstances were even more compelling, for it was due to "the characteristic American situation of three races in uneasy conjunction [Stanton, 1960:193]" that the assessment of race had immediate and major application in law, economics, politics, and all aspects of national life. The impetus for the development of physical anthropology had a drive in America, as shown for example in the career of Samuel Stanhope Smith (Jordan, 1965; Brace, 1974), which exceeded that present in the older intellectual European contexts, even where the latter had the stimulus of colonial involvement.

In his conscientious assessment of the individuals who responded to this impetus, Hrdlička gave full and proper recognition to the remarkable and original works of the Philadelphia physician and scientist Samuel George Morton. As Hrdlička notes, "Physical Anthropology in the United States speaking strictly, begins with Samuel G. Morton, in Philadelphia, in 1830 [1918:137]." Hrdlička went on to describe Morton's methodological innovations and their application to the comparative assessment of native American (Morton, 1839) and Egyptian (Morton, 1844) crania. Yet the fact that Morton's name rarely appears in English language sources after the American Civil War is not surprising for as Hrdlička concluded:

> [I]t is plain that Morton may be justly and with pride termed the father of American anthropology; yet it must be noted with regret that, like others later on, he was a father who left many friends to the science and even followers, but no real progeny, no disciples who would continue his work as their special or life vocation [1918:146].

In this assessment, however, it would seem that Hrdlička, despite his uncritical loyalty to French anthropology, seems to have missed an important aspect of the background of that phenomenon. It is true that Morton had no true American continuity. Although the failure of Philadelphia to nurture leadership (Baltzell, 1979) and the appendage of a phrenological essay to his principal work may have played some role, certainly a major reason for this lack of following is because those who claimed to be his disciples, after his early death in 1851, used his name and his work to try to justify the institution of slavery in the American South (Gibbes, 1851; Nott and Gliddon, 1854). The publication of Darwin's *Origin of Species* (1859) and Lyell's *Antiquity of Man* (1863) deprived the so-called disciples' use of Morton's work of any intellectual justification, and the defeat of the South in the American Civil War removed their social base of support. The result was the effective eclipse of interest in Morton's work in America.

In continental Europe, however, where Darwin was slow in being accepted and where the American social context was so remote that it did not influence judgment, Morton's pioneering work took root and flourished. During his life, he had been lauded by Alexander von Humboldt (Meigs, 1851:48). He had received similar praise from Anders Retzius (Patterson, 1855:xxxiii;

Retzius, 1860:264). But the person who really should be regarded as the one who continued Morton's work as his own special vocation was none other than Paul Broca. Some recognition has been granted to the fact that Broca was "heir to both the French and the American traditions of Polygenism [Stocking, 1968:40]," but the extent to which he literally represented the continuation of Morton's initiatory efforts has never been pointed out.

Broca's contribution, of course, involved a great deal more than simply carrying on Morton's work. His neurological research is viewed as having been original and fundamentally important (Schiller, 1979), and there can be no denying the energy and leadership he displayed in institutionalizing physical anthropology in France. His actual anthropological work, though showing the same levels of energetic application, was somewhat less original. The first major anthropological work for which he is known was his essay "Des phénomènes d'hybridité dans le genre humain," which was the conclusion to his "Mémoire sur l'hybridité en général, sur la distinction des éspèces animales et sur les métis obtenus par le croisement du lièvre et du lapin," which he began in 1858 (Broca, 1859–1860b). On close inspection, it is remarkably similar to Chapter 12 of *Types of Mankind*, "Hybridity of Animals Viewed in Connection with the Natural History of Mankind," which was written by Morton's self-declared disciple Josiah Clark Nott (Nott and Gliddon, 1854). The latter in turn took the more respectable parts of its orientation from the essay on hybridity by Morton himself (1847).

To be sure, these arguments over whether the production of viable fertile offspring was an adequate test of the specific identity of the parents go back to the time of John Ray in the seventeenth century and were discussed by Linnaeus and Buffon in the eighteenth century, as Broca, Morton, Nott, Prichard, and others writing on the subject were well aware. Furthermore, Morton's orientation in applying the arguments to the human condition was essentially the same as that of the French polygenist Bory de Saint-Vincent (1827 [vol. I]:69), whose influence, among others, Morton was careful to acknowledge. Broca's use of the hybridity argument, then, clearly has both French and American antecedents, but because the approach of the American Civil War was bringing such matters into the arena of public debate, the impact of its American manifestation was especially strong on like-minded readers elsewhere, as is clearly apparent in Broca's essay.

The other particular influence that Morton may have exerted on Broca has to do with the use of anthropometric techniques. Morton's remarkable volume of 1839 was the first comparative and metric treatment of prehistoric human skeletal material. As Hrdlička noted, 6 of Morton's 10 cranial measures were taken in the same way and from the same landmarks as those formalized at the Monaco agreement in 1906 "though Morton was not remembered at that convention [Hrdlička, 1918:139]." Morton's pioneering efforts may have been forgotten by that time, but an earlier generation had been aware of them. When American anthropology, though then principally an exercise in applied bigotry by Nott and Gliddon, was the subject of discussion at the July meetings of the Société d'Anthropologie de Paris in 1862, the "German Francophile" (Schiller, 1979:141) Franz Ignaz Pruner-Bey sought to sustain the view that polygenism was a doctrine that was "completely and eminently French, and the Americans referred to could only count as a pale copy (Pruner-Bay, 1862:420–421)." He was gently put in his place by Broca himself, who noted that, "If Germany has had her Blumenbach, and England her Prichard, America has had her Morton; so far French anthropology has had no name that can be put on a level with them [Broca, 1862a:423]."

Pruner-Bey went on to complain that Morton was being regarded "as if he had founded a science." He concluded that "he has founded nothing at all" and belittled what Morton had actually accomplished (Pruner-Bay, 1862:431). Broca never produced a coordinated work to represent the accomplishments of his school, but his most eminent pupil and successor, Paul Topinard, did just that in his model text *L'Anthropologie*. In this he recognized Morton's contribution, saying "only with Morton, however, did craniometry really take off [Topinard, 1876:234]." Topinard had been in school in Philadelphia when Morton was at the height of his career, but there is no record of whether there was any direct influence or, if so, whether this played any role in his outlook after he returned to France following the revolution of 1848 (Hodge, 1912).

If the florescence of anthropometry was largely the result of the energy and application of Broca (see the collected papers in Broca [1871, 1875]), the foundation on which Broca built had been solidly laid by Morton, even though Morton has never been given the credit he is due. The techniques that Broca elaborated from Morton's beginnings were adopted in England following the translation of Topinard's book (Turner, 1884:3), and, later, Hrdlička and Hooton saw to it that these returned to American anthropology as it grew in the twentieth century. Broca did in fact become the manifestation of what he had observed to Pruner-Bey to have been previously lacking in France, and he did so with such resounding success that the impact of the racial situation in the New World and of the work of Morton in shaping this branch of anthropology has been almost entirely forgotten.

THE ETHOS OF BROCA'S SOCIÉTÉ

Broca founded the Société d'Anthropologie de Paris in 1859, the same year that Charles Darwin published the *Origin of Species*. However, the date represents the only point of similarity when the implications of the ethos created by the two are considered. Broca's Société was founded for the specific purpose of promoting the "doctrine" of polygenism, which was regarded as based in "science," as opposed to the position of monogenism, which was considered to owe its formulation to a primary loyalty to Christian orthodoxy (Broca, 1860a:662; Pouchet, 1864:3).

In this regard, Broca and his associates continued in the same vein as their French precursors (Bory de Saint-Vincent, 1827; Désmoulins, 1826; Virey, 1801). Even more obviously, their defense of polygenism and their attack on monogenism used the same examples, the same analogies, and even the same rhetoric as had previously been used in America by Nott, that "prototypical Southern racist [Brace, 1974:516]," in his altercation with that equally bigoted monogenist John Bachman of Charleston, South Carolina (Bachman, 1850, 1854; Nott, 1849; Nott and Gliddon, 1854). The main difference between Broca and the "American School" was his feeling that the polygenism to which he subscribed did not justify the institution of slavery:

> One could say that the polygenist doctrine assigns a more honorable place to the inferior races of humanity than does the opposing doctrine. To be inferior to another man, be it in intelligence, vigor or beauty, is not a humiliating condition. One might blush on the other hand to have undergone a physical or moral degradation, to have descended the scale of beings, and to have lost one's rank in creation [Broca, 1860a:439, 1860b:664].

In this sense, he felt that polygenism was ethically as well as scientifically preferable to Bachman's monogenism (Broca, 1860a:438, 1860b:663).

Along with his commitment to the idea that "the great and typical differences that separate human groups are primordial [Broca, 1862b:283]," Broca initially declared his faith in the fixity of species:

> To place in doubt the permanence of species would be to attack respected traditions and at the same time to undermine the foundations of natural history, that is to say in its classifications; which by consequence would be to upset the whole world [Broca, 1860a:435].

No sooner had he said this, however, than he had to contend with the phenomenon of Charles Darwin.

His first reaction to Darwin was from a position of lofty, if not very well-informed sarcasm. "When Mr. Darwin speaks to me about my trilobite ancestors, I do not feel humility, but I tell him: what do you know of it? You were not there. And those who refute it know more about it than he [Broca, 1862b:314]." Furthermore, he articulated a theme that has echoed through French biology right up to the present day (Ruse, 1981). "Is Mr. Darwin wrong or right? I know nothing of that, I do not even want to know [Broca, 1862b:314]." The same tack was taken later by Albert Gaudry, widely credited with convincing French scientists of the value of "the evolutionist theory" (Vallois, 1966:206). Gaudry recognized that evolutionary mechanics was "well worthy of the attention of naturalists. But on that subject I avow my ignorance [Gaudry, 1878:257]." Perhaps the most extreme statement of such a position was by the physiologist Claude Bernard, a pre-Bergsonian champion of *force vitale,* who declared, "I support ignorance. That is my philosophy. I have the tranquillity of ignorance and faith in science [Cotard, 1898:53]." When Rudolf Virchow, the German physician-anthropologist and admirer of Broca and his ethos (Virchow, 1880, 1882), used the same tack in a debate with Haeckel and preened himself on the knowledge of his own ignorance (Virchow, 1877:14), Haeckel in some glee twitted him for not knowing how ignorant he was (Haeckel, 1878:27).

In a later and much more considered treatment of Darwin, Broca was forced to admit that "it is very probable that species are variable and subject to evolution [1870:238]." He then sounded a rather typical French note, echoed by his student and follower Topinard (1876:547), of giving Lamarck the credit for developing the theory of evolution and denying that Darwin's mechanism of natural selection was more than a "shining mirage" (Broca, 1870:171, 238). He concluded with the suggestion that the concept appeared first with Buffon and that it ought to be called "transformisme polygenique [1870:191]," but that its causes "are still unknown [1870:238]." The legacy that this established has remained a guide to physical anthropology ever since, and until very recently, there was little on the course of human evolution and less on the mechanisms involved that appeared in the major journals presumably devoted to that subject on either side of the Atlantic Ocean.

THE ROMANTIC CONCEPTION OF RACE

More recent treatments of race in American physical anthropology have principally been the works of the students of Hooton (Coon, 1962, 1965; Coon et al., 1950; Garn, 1965). To an increasing extent, these have focused on the testable aspects of human biology, but in the end, they generally conclude with a named list of human "races" assigned to various geographic and local regions. The connection between the biology discussed and the races named at the end is never clearly spelled out, and in fact the attentive reader cannot discover, from the information presented, just how the racial classification was constructed—other than the fact that this just seems to be the way anthropologists have always done things.

In an earlier work, however, Coon (1939) had suggested that the work of Joseph Deniker "has had a greater influence upon subsequent classifications of race than any of his nineteenth century contemporaries [1900:280]." He then labeled Deniker "the most important classifier" (Coon, 1939:280). Deniker, who became the librarian at the Muséum d'Histoire Naturelle, settled into the surroundings of Parisian anthropology in the mid-1870s and faithfully reflected the ethos of Broca's Société (Deniker, 1880, 1892, 1897).

The race classification that Deniker used was an elaboration of that favored by Broca and Topinard. The basis of the scheme was the recognition of five "families of races" or "souches" (stocks), labeled according to geographic rather than descriptive terms (Broca, 1860a:605). This in turn was essentially the same as the approach taken by Buffon, and especially by Blumenbach, and adopted by Morton with full credits to his predecessors (Morton, 1839:iv). Morton labeled his five geographic divisions "races." It is interesting to note, however, that the elaboration that he then produced by dividing these into 22 "families" (1839:4–95) is clearly a first version of what Deniker was to do over a generation later. Morton's list (1839:5–7) is almost exactly the same as that produced more than a century later as the accepted views of American physical anthropology (Coon et al., 1950:115–140). Once again, it would seem, the influence of Morton lives on, even if it is unacknowledged.

Where it is a matter of concept, however, Morton acknowledged the priority of early-nineteenth-century French authorities, such as Virey (1801) and Bory de Saint-Vincent (1827). These and their intellectual descendants in Broca's school in late-nineteenth-century Paris would all conform to the generalization offered to explain why natural selection has never been accepted in France: "The French mentality happens to be peculiarly typological [Pasteur, 1971:751]." From Cuvier to Broca to Topinard (1885:189), and on into the twentieth century, the a priori nature of race was taken as a given. As noted for Cuvier, all of them exhibited "a particular kind of typological thinking, an attitude of mind that also reflected an a priori conceptualization about the natural world [Lurie, 1960:61]."

Late in the nineteenth and early in the twentieth centuries, the categorical and hierarchical way of looking at the rest of the world was recast and tied to aspirations of "becoming" to produce the romantic evolutionism of Ernst Haeckel, Henri Bergson, and Sir Arthur Keith. This in turn was transmitted by Hrdlička, whatever his real intent, and Hooton to American physical anthropology, and has remained a poorly acknowledged theme within the field ever since.

Coon's book of 1939 hinted at the French source of the classification used, even if it missed Morton's part in shaping that source. But what is at least as important is the fact that it assured the continuity of the romantic conception of race, even though the definition was no longer verbalized. Coon's work was commissioned by the publisher to update the very popular book of the same title written by William Z. Ripley at the turn of the century (Coon, 1939; Ripley, 1899).

Ripley's work, in turn, based on his Lowell Institute Lectures of 1896, was an effort to simplify the complexities of Deniker's presentation and appeal to a general readership. Indeed, it first appeared in a series of installments in Appleton's *Popular Science Magazine* (Ripley, 1897a and b, 1898). As Stocking has pointed out, "it was primarily through his [Ripley's] work that the residual polygenism of European physical anthropology had its American impact [Stocking, 1968:61]," though, as should be obvious from the previous discussion, the polygenism mentioned was a good deal more than residual. Ripley, a lecturer in both sociology and "anthropogeography" at Columbia and Harvard (Hrdlička, 1918:274), was a protégé of the immigration restriction enthusiast and president of M.I.T., General Francis Amasa Walker (Chase, 1977:108). His book enjoyed considerable success and provided the basis for other more inflammatory works that led to the immigration restriction quotas being signed into law by President Calvin Coolidge in 1924 (Chase, 1977:270, 274, 344; Stocking, 1968:68).

Aside from the applied consequences of the genteel racism of Ripley and his followers, the most important thing about his book was the nature of the race concept articulated within it. Ripley attributed his definition to Topinard, and though the latter never put it in quite that way in all the various times he tried to express what he meant (cf. Topinard, 1879), it captured the essence of Topinard's intent so well that the spokesman for French anthropology over half a century later continued to quote it as Ripley had phrased it (Vallois, 1953:151):

Race in the present state of things is an abstract conception, a notion of continuity in discontinuity, of unity in diversity. It is rehabilitation of a real but directly unattainable thing [Ripley, 1899:111–112].

Surely this would qualify as an example of what the historian of ideas A. O. Lovejoy labeled "the pathos of the esoteric. How exciting and how welcome is the sense of initiation into hidden mysteries [1936:11]." It could even qualify for Lovejoy's "metaphysical pathos"—"the pathos of sheer obscurity, the loveliness of the incomprehensible [1936:11]." In his assessment, Lovejoy was appraising the change in views, particularly as represented in Bergson (1907) and others, which marked the rise of romanticism at the expense of the preceding age of Enlightenment. The description fits the ethos of American physical anthropology as it grew in the first half of the twentieth century. Even that choleric anti-Darwinian and latter-day defender of romanticism Jacques Barzun would have to admit that his lament that "the Romantic order of diversity in unity had merely been wished for and had not come to pass [Barzun, 1958:332]" would not apply to physical anthropology.

WHAT NOW?

The reader may well be driven to inquire, "Are things really all that bad?" The answer, of course, is "No, they are not." The average practicing physical anthropologist today is not primarily motivated by a desire to study human races. In teaching, the discussion of race is often saved until the end of the course and then mentioned with an awkward and slightly embarrassed bow to the traditions of the field. Others deal comfortably with real data from reference populations, whether these are given geographically or sociologically determined labels. Of course, those who focus on remote prehistoric populations are absolved from some of the embarrassment of the specific traditions mentioned previously, though they have been hampered by other traditions derived from the same source (Brace, 1964b, 1981).

Historical assessment does no good if it simply turns into an exercise of self-flagellation. As we look down and behold our feet exposed in historical perspective, if we are concerned about the quantity of clay apparent in their composition, we can actually do something about providing a sturdier underpinning for the future yet to come. To exorcise the demons of our past, the first thing we must do is to realize that the race concept that we inherited was partially the result of Hrdlička's failure to confront the racism in the ethos of the French anthropology that he admired so uncritically. At the same time, we must recognize the "white-man's burden" strain of elitism promoted by the Harvard of Hooton's era, enhanced by a "Proper Boston, rooted in Anglophilia [Baltzell, 1958:230]."

When we have confronted all this, we can abandon the race concept as a device for dealing with the biological nature of the humanity that is the object of study in our discipline. Instead, we can make an explicit virtue out of what in fact is a practical reality. Gene frequencies are figured as percentages of populations sampled, and the populations need only be identified as coming from a known area. In time, we can acquire gene frequency and trait manifestation data for the whole world. This we can do in relation to the intensity and duration of known or projected selective forces. In this way, we can take major steps toward dealing with the evolution of recent human populations.

What we have before us, then, is the prospect of applying to *Homo sapiens* the systematic perspective of Darwinian biology. It may seem curiously late in the history of science to be making a beginning at such an effort—a full century after Darwin's death—but the opportunity has yet to be exploited in systematic fashion, and it allows us the chance of dealing with major aspects of human variation with the excitement and enthusiasm that has tended to disappear from the well-ploughed fields of nonhuman zoology. The opportunity is ours, and if we don't seize it, others will.

CHAPTER 10

Reflections on the Face of Japan: A Multivariate Craniofacial and Odontometric Perspective (1989)

Prologue

The work on which this chapter and other related projects was based was undertaken in a deliberate effort to provide an indication of one of the possible tacks to be taken in an answer to the "What now?" query I raised at the end of Chapter 9, "The Roots of the Race Concept in American Physical Anthropology." The reason I turned my attention to the Far East in the first place was to seek a separate test case for the idea that human teeth have been reducing at a predictable rate ever since the adoption of cooking relaxed the intensity of the selection that had been maintaining them at a relatively constant size throughout much of the Pleistocene. My first efforts at investigating this question were focused on the European record since it was abundant and accessible (Brace, 1967). Not only did that general view need to be tested elsewhere in the world, so did the idea that the rate of reduction had doubled following the adoption of pottery (Brace and Mahler, 1971). The obvious thing to do was to turn to other parts of the world where pottery had a sufficient antiquity for the consequences of selective force relaxation to have become manifest. Pottery in East Asia goes back just as far in time as it does in the Middle East, and I had gotten some data from Singapore, Sarawak, Bangkok, Hong Kong, and Taiwan in 1974 that had allowed me to show that the history of tooth size change in Asia was similar to that in the West (Brace, 1976[1978]). By following up on a bit of lucky timing, I was able to get support for work in China in the summer of 1980.

The luck and timing came about like this. I had visited family on the New England coast in the summer of 1979, and, before returning to Michigan, I stopped off at Harvard's Peabody Museum on the way to pick up a few more measurements from specimens in their collections. While I was there, I looked in on my old friend K. C. Chang. We had been in graduate school together, and, late in our student phase 20 years back, we had both been in the trenches working on Hal Movius's Upper Paleolithic site, Abri Pataud, at Les Eyzies in Southern France. In our chat, I spoke of my regrets about being unable to get funding to work in China. K. C.'s reply was, "Money is not the problem. The real difficulty is in getting permission."

At that point, I was able to answer him by saying that I had already been given an invitation by Wu Rukang, the head of the anthropology section of the Institute for Vertebrate Paleontology and Paleoanthropology in Beijing. Wu Rukang (Woo Ju-Kang in the older spelling) had received his doctorate at Washington

University in St. Louis in the late 1940s just before the communist takeover in China, and he was one of the first senior Chinese scholars to visit the United States after the beginning of the diplomatic thaw in the middle of the 1970s. Earlier in that same summer of 1979, my Michigan protégé Milford Wolpoff had brought him up to Ann Arbor from Toledo where Wu was attending an anatomical conference, and my wife generated a garden party for him. We also included the head of our Center for Chinese Studies and the Dean of the Graduate School, among other appropriate figures. It was during that pleasant gathering that he invited both my wife and me to visit the Institute in Beijing.

K. C., though he has lived in America since the 1950s, had been born in Beijing. He was part of the first group of scholars from America and China to exchange visits starting in 1976, so he knew Wu Rukang and his Institute at first hand. K. C. also had been elected to membership in the National Academy of Sciences, the most prestigious scientific body in America. With that background, he was one of the figures behind organizing a program to be run through the National Academy of Sciences, with National Science Foundation (NSF) funding, promoting cooperation with the comparable scientific organization in Beijing. As K. C. told me, the program was initiated by the Committee on Scholarly Communication with the People's Republic of China, and, though it had not been formally announced yet, the deadline for receiving proposals was only two weeks off.

To put a little perspective on this, normally a scholar applying for a research grant from a funding institution spends a matter of months writing up a proposal. This can run up to six months or even a year, and then your effort is put into the hopper with all the rest, with something like one chance in ten that it will be successful. I had previously applied to NSF for support to work in Japan and had been turned down. I had also tried the National Institutes of Dental Health and been turned down there as well. One reviewer had said the model for dental reduction that I was proposing to test was so absurdly unlikely that money should not be wasted on it. Another said that it was so self-evident and well-known that it would be a waste of money to do it all over again. And a third reviewer said that the work had already been done by Christy Turner and Milford Wolpoff. It was of no avail to point out that my old friend Christy Turner, though a splendid dental anthropologist with extensive experience in Asia, had never measured a single tooth in Japan (he records dental morphology and not tooth size), and that Milford Wolpoff had never even been to Japan.

But here was K. C. telling me of a new program that had not even been announced yet and with which he himself was involved in the planning and organizing. So I charged back to Ann Arbor and plunged into two frantic weeks of proposal writing to get the thing in by the deadline. I did, typos and all, and since there were almost no competing proposals, it got me the support I needed. When I applied for follow-up support five years later, the program had achieved a high degree of visibility, and I was one of well over 200 applicants for the 6 spots funded. It got me to China, and I was able to get the measurements I needed and confirm my suspicions that, yes indeed, the trajectory of tooth-size change in Asia is comparable to that elsewhere in the world (Brace, Shao, and Zhang, 1984; Brace and Vitzthum, 1984).

While I was there, I was able to use the stop-overs allowed on international air flights to make visits to collections in Fukuoka, Kyoto, and Tokyo in Japan, and I managed to wheedle enough support out of our graduate school resources to cover subsistence when I was there. That was how I was able to get a handle on the Japanese data (Brace and Nagai, 1982), but it also plunged me into another set of problems that I had steered clear of in previous work. As I was working on the first collection of Japanese specimens in the Department of Anatomy in the Kyushu University Medical School in Fukuoka, I kept seeing nuances in the Japanese facial features that were different from the Chinese specimens I had worked on in Shanghai, Nanjing, and Beijing. When I went to Kyoto, I was helped by Hiroshi Kanaseki, an archaeologist on the faculty of Tenri University in Nara, who was the brother of one of my hosts in Fukuoka. The Kanaseki brothers were the sons of the then-retired professor of anatomy from Kyushu Takeo Kanaseki, who had established the collection on which I had worked in Fukuoka. Since the boxes in the collection in the Laboratory of Physical Anthropology at Kyoto University were labeled in Japanese characters and I had not yet learned to read them, Hiroshi Kanaseki went over the piles I was going to try to work on, and put initials on them in "the Roman alphabet"—"*romaji,*" as the Japanese call it—so that I would know what I was getting. One of my objects was to compile information on the preagricultural populations of Japan, the Jōmon.

Since I had never seen a Jōmon specimen before, I asked him if he could find me a box with a good example in it. He did, and when I opened it and looked at what it contained, there before my eyes was a full-blown manifestation of all those traits of which I had seen nuances in the Fukuoka Japanese specimens that made them look slightly different from the Chinese I had been dealing with throughout the months of July on into October. It was immediately obvious to me that the living population of Japan represents, in large part, a replacement of the people who had originally inhabited the islands by people coming from the mainland.

Yes, there were enough hints of the characteristics of the original inhabitants preserved in the living Japanese to indicate that the incoming rice farmers had absorbed rather than completely exterminated the aborigines. In the Kyoto collections, there were a few representatives of the Ainu of the northernmost island of Hokkaido, and they clearly represent the relatively unmodified survivors of the original inhabitants of the entire Japanese archipelago. The bulk of the features of the Japanese, however, ally them with the Koreans and the Chinese on the Asian mainland. As it happens, this was exactly what the senior Kanaseki had proposed as a result of his own studies on the material in the collections in Fukuoka (Kanaseki, Nagai, and Sano, 1960), but it was not the dominant view held by the main anthropological community in Japan (cf. Hanihara, 1986).

It did no good to try to tell my feelings to Japanese friends and colleagues since all I had to go on were the subjective results of eyeball appraisal. One senior Japanese anthropologist, who has been very gracious and cooperative toward me over the years, looked at me a bit dubiously and said, "Oh, I hope you're wrong." Tooth measurements alone are of no value in solving such questions. I realized that I was going to have to return to Japan another time (or times) and collect the kinds of craniofacial measurements that can be used in assessing population relationships.

I did have enough in the way of dental metrics to be able to address the problems that had sent me to Asia in the first place, and I worked these up in satis-factory fashion after I returned home (Brace and Nagai, 1982; Brace, Shao, and Zhang, 1984). It had become clear to me, however, that to argue that something as basic as the evidence for the change in tooth size through time as a result of changes in food preparation practices could only be documented if one had assurances that it was the same continuing group that was being assessed as one period gave way to the next. In the case of Japan, for example, the incoming rice farmers had measur-ably bigger teeth than the people who had been there for the previous 10,000 years and more. The characteristics of the invaders then could not have been related to the effects of long-term residence in Japan.

What I needed was a set of measurements that would allow me to be able to demonstrate whether I was dealing with the same group through time or a sequence of replacing populations. My own former mentor, W. W. Howells, had pioneered the use of craniofacial measurements in the assessment of population relationships in very successful fashion (Howells, 1973), but his measurement battery is a formida-ble roster and its application is tedious and time-consuming. I hoped that I could select a simplified version of his list with a few variables added that would work to separate the prehistoric and the modern Japanese.

The variables I added focused on the nose because my subjective assess-ment told me that this was an area where I would get usable distinctions. Not only that, I thought that those nose differences may have been the results of long-term differences in selection. I was still hoping that differences in other craniofacial mea-surements could be related to differences in local living conditions. I subsequently returned to collections in both China and Japan and collected craniofacial dimen-sions of specimens from which I had only gotten tooth measurements the first time around. It has been a kind of trial-and-error learning experience.

What I discovered was that the craniofacial measurements have almost nothing whatsoever to do with differences in life-way. Even the nasal measurements are poor in delineating what we know to be adaptive differences in nasal shape. There are several ways a long, high-bridged nose can be constructed, and the sepa-rate components that contribute to its shape are only weakly related to the very obvi-ous shape differences. But I did discover that the more measurements I used, the better I was able to tell who was related to whom, and who was not. A measurement battery of 15 variables is pretty minimal. It works, but 18 is better. Better still is a full two dozen. When one gets up to around 50 measurements in the test battery, as my gracious mentor, W. W. Howells, had done in the first place, one can get very good indications of population relationships and distinctions. The drawback is the amount of time needed to get a handle on the samples one needs for group comparisons. With my two dozen measurements, one can collect about three to four specimens an hour. By sticking to business, one can get a usable set of measurements on. say, 40 to 50 individuals in a day's work. By plugging away each year for over a decade, and now by using graduate student help, I have measurement sets on over 8,000 individuals, and it means we can test any random specimen against all of the major regional samples of the world. What is described in this chapter is the technique used to make the generalizations on clusters summarized subsequently in Chapter 11, "A Four-Letter Word Called 'Race.'"

But, I started out just to try to sort the components of Japan (Brace et al., 1989), even though the work I report on in this chapter was done before I had settled on the full complement of two dozen variables. It worked so well that I was able to generalize on the points discussed above and offer it as a simplified approximation of Howells's approach for dealing with the relationships of all the populations of the world (Brace and Hunt, 1990), helped in this instance by the invaluable contributions of my coauthors, Mary Louise Brace and William R. Leonard. It is gratifying to see that the most recent effort to deal with the relationships of the Japanese from the perspective of comparing genes and their frequencies in well-documented genetic systems comes to conclusions that are essentially the same as those that we have gotten from craniometric analysis (Omoto and Saitou, 1997).

〜　　　〜

According to legend, the Japanese are of divine origin (cf. the *Nihongi,* Aston, 1896 [1956], translator), with the rulers claiming the Sun goddess, Amaterasu, as a progenitor and others claiming descent from her younger brother, Susano-o (Lu, 1974). When myths and folk tales are subjected to critical analysis, many interpreters have detected hints of a southerly origin for many things Japanese, though whether that "south" was the southwestern island of Kyushu (Sansom, 1958) or something considerably farther afield (Vivien de Saint-Martin, 1872; Morse, 1878; Sternberg, 1929; Koganei, 1937; Ohno, 1970) remains a matter for debate. Although our own attempt to deal with the problem of Japanese origins and relations concentrates on the information to be gained from an assessment of craniofacial form, we cannot deny that a full anthropological appraisal has to take a series of nonbiological aspects into account. A summary of the views generated by the work done in those relevant aspects is presented below.

THE LINGUISTIC PERSPECTIVE

Linguists also have debated about the nature of the origins of the Japanese language. Many have noted the phonological, morphological, and semantic features that tie Japanese and Korean to Uralic and Altaic (Ohno, 1970; Miller, 1971, 1974, 1980; Chew, 1978). In the opinion of one authority (Miller, 1986:110), this shows that Japanese can trace its lineage back to a "relatively undifferentiated proto-Altaic linguistic unity," presumably in the region of the Heilongjiang (Amur River) drainage area on the Sino-Russian border. Others have identified what they believe to be an Austronesian ("Malayo-Polynesian") element in Japanese (Vivien de Saint-Martin, 1872; Sternberg, 1929; Ohno, 1970; Befu, 1971; Murayama, 1972, 1976) but they differ on whether there was an Austronesian language spoken in Jōmon Japan, which was subsequently obliterated to a large extent by the intrusive Altaic languages (Ohno, 1970; Befu, 1971), or whether the original languages were Altaic and the Austronesian elements were introduced by small groups of intruders who subsequently became absorbed (Miller, 1980; Aikens and Higuchi, 1982). Although interest in the possibility of an Austronesian "substrate" in Japanese has now waned to the extent that it is not even mentioned in the most recent treatment of the linguistic evidence for Japanese origins (Miller, 1986), we think that, in the light of the conclusions we reach in this paper, it is a matter that should be systematically reexamined.

THE ARCHAEOLOGICAL PERSPECTIVE

Since the crucial events that contributed to the populating of Japan all occurred before the dawn of recorded history, there is more than a small element of extrapolation and conjecture in the attempts of students of folklore and linguistics to clarify matters. There are a couple of other realms of investigation that can provide more direct evidence concerning those prehistoric events. One of these involves the work of the archaeologists who have studied the actual cultural remains that have survived from prehistoric Japan. Even though many conflicting interpretations remain in contention, archaeology has provided solid data and holds out the promise that a firm framework for understanding the events of Japanese prehistory is close to being achieved.

In broad terms, two main periods can be identified. The first of these, the Jōmon, extends from more than 12,000 years ago until 300 B.C. (Ikawa-Smith, 1980, 1982; Pearson, 1986). Although the Jōmon people are generally regarded as "affluent hunter-gatherers" engaged in the "intensive collection of a wide variety of wild foods" (Akazawa, 1982a:57), it would appear that they also may have practiced some form of slash-and-burn agriculture more than 6,000 years ago (Tsukada, 1986) and may have adopted irrigated rice in the northern Kyushu area before the advent of the next period (Akazawa, 1982b).

The Jōmon period was succeeded by the Yayoi period, which has traditionally been associated with the introduction to Japan of intensive rice agriculture, table-turned pottery, weaving, and the use of metals (Ohno, 1970; Befu, 1971; Bowles, 1977; Ikawa-Smith, 1980; Aikens and Higuchi, 1982). The Yayoi lasted from 300 B.C. to A.D. 300 (Akazawa, 1982b), though an excellent case has been made that the succeeding Kofun (tomb) period (A.D. 300–600) (Ikawa-Smith, 1980) is simply a continuation of the Yayoi right up to the point where the written record begins with the Nara state in the seventh century (Barnes, 1986; H. Kanaseki, 1986). While these broad outlines are generally agreed on, there are also major areas of disagreement. Specifically, what was the relation between the Jōmon and the succeeding Yayoi? Was it a case of a new population with a different subsistence technology invading from the mainland (Befu, 1971; Kagawa, 1973), or was it a case of the adoption of new techniques by the in situ Jōmon people, who simply continued and expanded in the lands where they had been shaped (Aoki and Omoto, 1980; Akazawa, 1982a and b, 1986; H. Kanaseki, 1986)? From an appraisal of the archaeological evidence currently available, this question cannot be resolved, but from an appraisal of the surviving tangible remains from prehistoric Japan—namely, the skeletons of the people themselves—we are going to suggest a choice indicated by the results of our analysis.

THE AINU QUESTION

Obviously we have to use a consideration of the modern inhabitants of Japan as our main point of reference in assessing the genesis of modern Japanese facial form. Consequently our analysis will utilize samples of modern Japanese from the northeastern, the central, and the southwestern parts of the archipelago. Complicating the matter is the fact that not all of the native inhabitants of the Japanese realm are traditionally regarded as "Japanese." Specifically, the inhabitants of the northern island of Hokkaido, the Ainu, have long been regarded as "racially" different from the rest of the people of Japan (Busk, 1867; Koganei, 1894; von Baelz, 1901, 1911; Chamberlain, 1912; S. Watanabe, 1938, 1981). Currently there are very few unmixed Ainu left due to interbreeding with the incoming Japanese during the last hundred years (Omoto, 1970, 1972). But Hokkaido did not become a part of the territory of Japan until the Meiji restoration in 1868 (H. Watanabe, 1986), at which time the Ainu constituted the recognized population of the island. Although they have traditionally been looked down on as "primitive," and stigmatized as "mere" hunter-gatherers, they evidently engaged in the same kind of ingenious and intensive exploitation of the available natural resources that had characterized the preceding Jōmon throughout Japan (H. Watanabe, 1986). Furthermore, they and their predecessors planted and harvested a variety of millets and perhaps other crops as well, so they should more correctly be viewed as having pursued a mixed subsistence economy rather than as having been hunter-gatherers in the strict sense (Crawford and Yoshizaki, 1987).

According to legendary, historical, and linguistic testimony regarding the Japanese, however, "All their traditions point to their coming from the south, and equally sure are we that when they landed they found a race of hairy men to contest their occupation" (Morse, 1878). Subsequently, somewhere between the fifth and the eighth century when the semilegendary Japanese emperor Jimmu Tenno led his forces from the southwestern island of Kyushu to conquer the Yamato plain (the Yamato district now includes modern Nara and Osaka in central Japan), he was apparently opposed by "a population of Aino race" (Astor, 1896 [1956]:109, fn. 1). As late as the twelfth century, Japan's "Wild East" was the Kanto plain, the location of the modern city of Tokyo, where the indigenous Ainu continued to block the northeastward spread of the power of the Japanese state right up to "feudal" times (Storry, 1978).

Further, the use of place names in the northeastern end of the main island of Honshu (Ohno, 1970) "shows that eastern Japan used languages related to Ainu in late Jōmon and Yayoi times" (Chew, 1978:200). In fact, "the names of very many places all over Japan, which are purely Ainu"—and this includes southern Japan as well—prompted the assertion that "enough have been brought forward to show clearly strong grounds for the belief that the Ainu once inhabited the whole of the Japanese empire" (Batchelor, 1892:284, 292, 295).

In the past, it was also observed that there were distinct traces of Ainu features to be seen toward the northern end of Honshu (and also in the southern corner of Kyushu and in the Ryukyus) (von Baelz, 1911). As Chamberlain (1912:181) remarked, "The 'Ainu type' among the Japanese is most marked in the north, where these pre-Japanese aborigines continued longest." Dermatoglyphic (Mitsuhashi, 1967) and serological (Harvey et al., 1978; Mourant, 1980) data from the modern Japanese also sustain such a view.

Who the Ainu are and where they came from has engaged the imagination of observers of Japan for over a century. In contrast to the other peoples of Asia, they are famous for their display of hirsutism, male beards and body hair being its particular manifestation. From the time of La Pérouse at the end of the eighteenth century on up to the present, the opinion has frequently been offered that they represent a far-eastern outlier of European or "Caucasoid" form (Busk [reflecting the opinion of Huxley], 1867; Bickmore, 1868; von Baelz, 1901, 1911; Koganei, 1927; Hooton, 1946). Other suggestions concerning their source range from the Tower of Babel (Kaempfer, 1906) and nonserious reflections about a "lost tribe of Israel" (Batchelor, 1892), to considering them as a northward extension of Polynesian (Vivien de Saint-Martin, 1872; Sternberg, 1929) or Southeast Asian groups (Levin, 1961; Turner and Hanihara, 1977; Turner, 1986), to looking at them as just another form of "Mongoloid" (Hanihara, 1970, 1977; Omoto, 1970; Omoto and Harada, 1975), and finally to regarding them as a northern representation of Australian aboriginal form (Hooton, 1946; Birdsell, 1951, 1967—noting that both considered "Australoid" to be a "primitive" kind of "Caucasoid" form). The last of these claims has been definitively refuted on craniometric (Yamaguchi, 1967), serological (Omoto and Misawa, 1976), and odontometric (Hanihara, 1976, 1977) grounds. These same studies also show the unlikelihood of a European connection, but there are also dental and cranial studies that equally call into question the suggestion that they are "just another Mongoloid" population (Turner, 1976, 1979, 1983; Howells, 1986; Brace et al., in press). The Polynesian matter cannot be so easily dismissed, as has previously been noted (Yamaguchi, 1967; Brace and Nagai, 1982; Brace et al., in press), and as we shall develop at greater length later in this paper.

Here we record the groups we have used and the addresses of the collections in which they are located. In each instance, we include the number of individuals with enough complete dimensions to be used in our multivariate treatment of craniofacial form. Odontometrics were collected from the same samples, but because we could get tooth measurements from many individuals who were otherwise incomplete, the numbers involved tend to be considerably larger than those associated with a relatively complete set of craniofacial data. The exception is the Mongols, where the sample was so small that we could not get a measurement for each category of tooth, so no TS figure could be calculated.

The following list includes the sample identity and number of the specimens used to assess the relations of craniofacial form in Asia and the Pacific. *Japanese:* 271 specimens; Kyushu (Southwest), 27 specimens, Department of Anatomy, Nagasaki University School of Medicine, Nagasaki; Tokyo (East Central), 113 specimens, University Museum, University of Tokyo, Hongo, Bunkyo-ku, Tokyo; Chiba (East Central), 74 specimens, Department of Anatomy II, Sapporo Medical College, Sapporo; Tohoku (Northeast), 57 specimens, Department of Anatomy, School of Medicine, Tohoku University, Sendai; *Medieval Samurai:* 17 specimens (Kamakura, A.D. 1333), University Museum, University of Tokyo; *Ainu:* 55 specimens, University Museum, University of Tokyo and Department of Anatomy II, Sapporo Medical College; *Kofun:* 4 specimens, Department of Anatomy, Medical School, Kyushu University and Department of Anatomy, School of Medicine, Tohoku University; *Yayoi:* 21 specimens, Fukuoka and Doigahama, Department of Anatomy, Medical School, Kyushu University, Fukuoka; *Jōmon:* 12 specimens (Early Jōmon 1, Middle Jōmon 2, Late Jōmon 6 specimens), Department of Anatomy II, Sapporo Medical College and Laboratory of Physical Anthropology, Faculty of Science, Kyoto University, Kyoto; Nagasaki "Yayoi," 3 specimens, Department of Anatomy, Nagasaki University School of Medicine; *Chinese:* 398 specimens; East Coast, 174 specimens, Biology Section, Department of Biology, Fudan University, Shanghai, People's Republic of China; North China, 40 specimens, University Museum, University of Tokyo; Western China (Sichuan), 69 specimens, Department of Anatomy, Chengdu College of Traditional Chinese Medicine, Chengdu, Sichuan, People's Republic of China; Southwest China (Yunnan), 64 specimens, Institute of Vertebrate Paleontology and Paleoanthropology, People's Republic of China; South China, 70 specimens, Department of Anatomy, Guangxi Medical College, Nanning, Guangxi Zhuang Autonomous Region, People's Republic of China; Southeast China (Hong Kong), 45 specimens, Department of Oral Anatomy, Prince Philip Dental Hospital, Hong Kong; *North Chinese Neolithic:* 18 specimens, Institute of Vertebrate Paleontology and Paleoanthropology, Beijing; *Koreans:* 17

specimens, University Museum, University of Tokyo; *Mongols:* 11 specimens, Department of Anthropology, American Museum of Natural History, New York; *Micronesians:* 55 specimens (Guam 36), Department of Anthropology, Bernice P. Bishop Museum, Honolulu, HI (Yap 5, Palau 5, Mortlock 4, Carolines 1, Chamorro 1, Jaluit 1, Naru 1, Tari-Tari 1) von Luschan Collection, American Museum of Natural History, New York; *Philippinos:* 21 specimens (Visayas), Museum of Anthropology, University of Michigan, Ann Arbor, MI; *Polynesians:* 131 specimens (Easter Island 11, New Zealand 25, Marquesas 26 specimens), American Museum of Natural History, New York; Hawaiian: 69, Bernice P. Bishop Museum, Honolulu, HI; *Thai:* 65 specimens, Department of Anatomy, Siriraj Hospital, Mahidol University, Bangkok, Thailand; *Thai Neolithic:* 2 specimens, Sood Sangvichien Museum of Prehistory, Siriraj Hospital, Bangkok, Thailand; *Vietnamese:* 5 specimens, Musée de l'Homme, Paris, France.

DATA COLLECTED

In previous studies where broad sweeps of time and long-term changes in selective forces were the objects of concern, a simple focus on dental metrics was sufficient to demonstrate major trends in the course of hominid evolution (Brace, 1979a and b; Brace et al., 1987). Where this approach was essayed to demonstrate the selective-force differences in the backgrounds of a series of contemporary modern populations—for example, in Australia and Oceania (Brace, 1980; Brace and Hinton, 1981)—the question could be legitimately raised as to whether the differences observed were really indicators of the differential operation of selective forces or whether they might indicate that the groups under consideration had come from widely separate areas in the recent past where genetic drift or some other such mechanism had produced different effects.

When the dental metrics of both moderns and their predecessors in the recent past were collected in both Japan and China (Brace and Nagai, 1982; Brace et al., 1984), an attempt to check for the possibility of immigration vs. continuity through time was made by assessing aspects of craniofacial form. In the case of Japan, the obvious differences between the Jōmon and the modern Japanese were noted at the same time that it was realized that the contrast in form between the Japanese and the Ainu involved exactly the same traits. These points were first made by Koganei (1927, 1937), whose discussion remains a model of accurate assessment. The argument can always be made, however, that this kind of morphological assessment is subjective at bottom and therefore unscientific. Fortunately, the quantitative treatments of non-metric aspects of the dentition (Turner, 1976, 1979, 1983, 1985a and b, 1986, in press) and skull (Dodo, 1986; Ossenberg, 1986) have reached exactly the same conclusions.

Craniofacial Metrics

With this in mind, we attempted to quantify those aspects of craniofacial morphology which had been the basis of the earlier subjective assessment of group relationships and differences, noting that Yamaguchi had done this successfully on a more limited set of samples (1967, 1982) and that Howells has repeatedly demonstrated that multivariate statistics elegJōmonantly confirm the conclusions reached by Koganei well over half a century ago (Howells, 1966, 1986). Evidently this approach works for much the same reason that massive DNA comparisons work (cf. Sibley and Ahlquist, 1984, 1986); i.e., if enough individual pieces of information are accumulated, the degree of similarity in pattern will reflect the degree of genetic relationship in spite of the particular effects of differences in selective force history. This is apparently why different workers using different sets of measurements on similar population samples come to the same general conclusions in regard to population relationships and distinctions (Howells, 1966, 1973, 1986, in press; Pietrusewsky, 1971, 1979, 1981, 1983, 1984, in press; Brace et al., in press).

The list of measurements we applied to the samples mentioned above is to be found in Table 10-1. Well over half of the 18 measurements included deal with aspects of nasal elevation and elongation since it was our preliminary observation that it was in these traits that the most obvious distinctions between the Jōmon and the Japanese and between the north and the south Chinese were to be found. As it happened, essentially the same roster was also successful in assessing the relationships of the peoples of Oceania, Australia, and continental Asia (Brace et al., in press).

Odontometrics

Mesial-distal and buccal-lingual measurements were made for all of the available teeth—maxillary and mandibular, right and left—for all of the individuals available in the samples used for the present study. The measurement techniques have been previously discussed in detail (Brace, 1979b, 1980). Since the right and left antimeres are phenotypic expressions of the same underlying genotype, the best expression of the latter is an average of the two. Individual dimensions for each tooth class, then, were calculated from the

Table 10-1 Craniofacial Measurements

Variable No.	Description
1	Nasal height (Martin No. 55)
2	Nasal bone height (Martin No. 56 [2])
3	Nasion prosthion (Martin No. 44 [1])
4	Nasion basion (Martin No. 5)
5	Basion prosthion (Martin No. 40)
6	Superior nasal bone width (Martin No. 57 [2])
7	Minimum nasal bone width
8	Inferior nasal bone width (Martin No. 57 [3])
9	Nasal breadth (Martin No. 54)
10	Simotic subtense (Howells)
11	Height of rhinion over measurement number 8
12	IOW subtense at nasion (Woo and Morant)
13	MOW subtense at rhinion (Woo and Morant)
14	Bizygomatic width (Martin No. 45)
15	Glabella opisthocranion (Martin No. 1)
16	Maximum cranial breadth (Martin No. 8)
17	Basion bregma (Martin No. 17)
18	Basion rhinion

means of the antimere measurements. To produce a sample figure for a given tooth class dimension, the midsex mean was used—that is, the sum of the mean male and the mean female dimensions divided by two (Brace et al., 1987). In this fashion, the mean mesial-distal and mean buccolingual dimensions of each of the 16 tooth classes were calculated for each sample. The result yielded 32 figures for each group considered.

To simplify this, cross sectional areas were produced by taking the product of the mesial-distal and buccolingual dimensions for each tooth class. As was the case for the individual mesial-distal and buccal-lingual dimensions, the sample figure was considered to be the midsex mean of the cross sectional area for each tooth class.

This still leaves 16 data points per sample, and while this provides a very effective means of comparing two or three groups at a time, there can be real confusion when the number of groups being compared rises to 10 or more. Under the latter circumstances, a crude but effective measure is provided by the use of the summary tooth-size figure, TS. This is simply the sum of the mean cross sectional areas of all the tooth categories in a single sample (Brace, 1978, 1979b, 1980). As with the means for individual measurement and cross sectional areas, the mean TS of a sample is a midsex mean.

Table 10-2 displays the TS figures for the samples used in this study arranged in order of magnitude. Since each TS figure is based on a summary of mean individual tooth cross sectional areas and since each of these has a different N, there is no way to calculate a variance for the TS figures presented here. As was noted in a previous study which included the analysis of

Table 10-2 Summary Tooth Size Measurements (TS) in mm^2

Sample	TS	Mean N	Range of N
Micronesia, Guam	1,311	70	(38–88)
China, North	1,261	26	(12–35)
Sendai	1,250	23	(12–37)
Kofun	1,245	29	(12–71)
Japan, Chiba	1,240	57	(32–68)
China, Neolithic	1,236	152	(57–278)
Yayoi	1,232	9	(3–18)
Korea	1,229	22	(14–44)
Japan, Edo	1,222	42	(7–89)
Thai, Neolithic	1,222	46	(30–61)
Thai	1,222	27	(23–31)
China, Sichuan	1,208	37	(2–90)
China, Yunnan	1,206	65	(4–168)
Jōmon, Early	1 205	5	(3–8)
Kamakura	1,197	43	(30–50)
China, Shanghai	1,197	107	(25–234)
Japan, Nagasaki	1,188	30	(17–38)
China, Guangxi	1,186	46	(27–63)
Polynesia	1,172	138	(104–170)
Vietnam	1,169	9	(2–21)
China, Hong Kong	1,154	37	(29–45)
Jōmon, Middle	1,152	18	(7–30)
Jōmon, Late	1,151	47	(18–73)
Ainu	1,141	83	(53–106)
Nagasaki, "Yayoi"	1,093	6	(5–8)

complete individuals where such variance figures could be calculated, "a summary tooth-size difference of 50 mm^2 between groups compared is probably meaningful, and a difference of 100 mm^2 or more almost certainly has some basic biological meaning" (Brace, 1980; Brace and Ryan, 1980).

ANALYSIS

In our use of the craniofacial measurements listed in Table 10-1, we have followed the procedures for the treatment of variables described by Howells (1986). This is an attempt to minimize the effects of major size differences when comparing diverse populations. The first step in this procedure is to convert individual unweighted measurements into sex-specific Z-scores where each Z-score represents the number of standard deviation units by which the value in question departs from the grand mean for each separate dimension of all the samples used in a given analysis. This can be represented as:

$$Z_{ij} = \frac{(Xij - \overline{Xj})}{\sigma_1} \tag{1}$$

where: i = number of the measurement (e.g. 1...18); j = number of the individual; X_{ij} = value of measurement "i" for individual "j"; $\overline{X}_i$ = overall sex specific average value for measurement "i"; and σ_i = overall sex specific standard deviation for measurement "i".

The use of Z-scores by themselves does not eliminate the problem of size. To deal with the matter of relative proportion or "shape" of the craniofacial features with which we are concerned, some kind of proportional transformation would be desirable. Recently, Howells (1986) has proposed the use of the C-score statistic to accomplish this purpose. C-scores are similar to ratios in that they both are measures of relative size. The advantage of a C-score over a simple ratio is that the C-score reflects relative size of a given feature in comparison to the size of all the other traits used, while a ratio can only reflect relative size in comparison to a single referent. C-scores are calculated as the difference between the Z-score of a single measurement for a given individual and the mean Z-score of that individual for all the measurements used in the analysis.

The mean Z-score for a single individual is calculated in the following fashion:

$$\overline{Z}j = \frac{\sum Zij}{N} \tag{2}$$

where: Z_j = the average Z-score for all the variables for individual "j"; and N = the number of variables used (e.g., 18 if all are represented).

Given this, then, the C-score is:

$$Cij = Zij - \overline{Zj} \qquad (3)$$

The C-scores were then used as the basis for constructing dendrograms representing the relationships of the various groups sampled. Actually, we made a great many trial dendrograms. Initially we used the untransformed data. Subsequently we repeated these trials using Z-scores, and finally we settled on the use of C-scores as defined above. We also made trials without the use of frequently missing variables in an attempt to maximize our sample sizes. In the final analysis, however, we used an approach that maximized discrimination even though it had the effect of reducing our sample sizes. This seemed to produce the most reliable results where reliability was determined by the consistency with which samples known to be related were put into the same cluster after the addition or subtraction of other samples in the course of constructing our various trial dendrograms.

The dendrograms we have produced are hierarchical trees based on calculations of Euclidean distance, a procedure that produces results similar to those achieved by Ossenberg (1986) and by Dodo and Ishida (1987) using Mean Measures of Distance of nonmetric cranial variables. The logic is discussed in Sneath and Sokal (1973), and the computation procedure is the one specified in Fox and Guire (1976). This is a multivariate procedure which requires values for all of the variables used in the analysis. In our case, since the calculation of C-scores requires that a Z-score value be present for each variable for each individual included, this means that we could only use individuals on whom a complete set of measurements could be made. And because of the problem of artificially maximizing common variance that occurs when regression procedures are used to estimate missing data, we avoided the use of any kind of interpolation to fill in missing variables. This is why the N for many of our samples is as small as it is, especially for the often-fragmentary prehistoric groups.

Before constructing each dendrogram, the program evaluates the importance of each variable by a stepwise linear multiple discriminant procedure. The variable with the greatest power of discrimination is used first. Subsequent variables are then added in order of importance until it is determined that the contribution to reliability has a *P* value of ≥ .05. Since this procedure is done automatically each time a dendrogram is constructed, there is always the possibility that dendrograms with different samples will have been built with the use of slightly differing sets of variables. Indeed, this is the case for the three dendrograms we have presented here—namely, Figures 10-1, 10-2, and 10-3. For example, six of the first seven variables that contributed to the dendrogram illustrated in Figure 10-1, numbers 2, 12, 14, 18, 8, and 7, were related to the nose. The first five variables that contributed to the construction of the dendrogram in Figure 10-2 were also measures of nasal elongation and projection. And the first eight variables that contribute to the picture shown in Figure 10-3 are also related to the nose. The lists of variables in the order that they were used in the construction of Figures 10-1 to 10-3, plus their F-statistics and significance values, are shown in Tables 10-3 to 10-5.

After constructing our dendrograms, we used the same samples and the same variables to construct a matrix of Mahalanobis distance (D^2) figures (Fox and Guire, 1976). These are presented in Tables 10-6 through 10-8. In essence these provide a numerical version of the relationships visually evident in Figures 10-1 to 10-3.

It is clear from the data in Figure 10-1 and an appraisal of the form shown in Figures 10-4 and 10-5 that the various levels of Jōmon and the modern Ainu

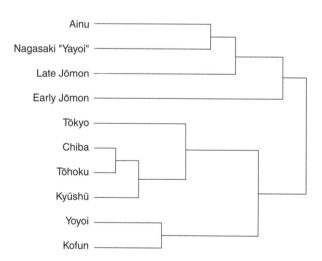

Figure 10-1 A Euclidean distance dendrogram showing the relationships between modern and prehistoric groups from the Japanese archipelago. A numerical expression of these relationships can be seen in Table 10-6.

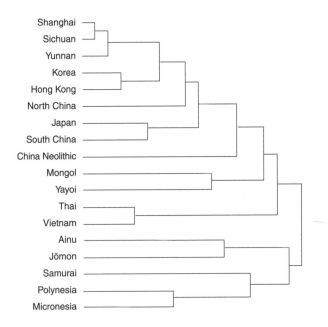

Figure 10-2 A Euclidean distance dendrogram showing the relationships between prehistoric and combined modern Japanese groups, combined Polynesians, combined Micronesians, and a series of mainland Asian groups. A numerical expression of these relationships can be seen in Table 10-7.

are basically the same kind of thing, so we have some reason to consider that they represent the continuity of a single lineage through time. For that reason, we feel justified in treating the evident odontometric reduction through time as a picture of real evolutionary change. Figure 10-6 shows the regression line produced when tooth size data are entered for the appropriate time levels. Early Jōmon is assigned an antiquity of 7000 B.P., Middle Jōmon an age of 4000 B.P., Late Jōmon an age of 2000 B.P., and we gave the Ainu burials a date of A.D. 1000. The Jōmon-to-Ainu regression line has a slope of –0.0090 mm²/yr and an *r* value of .631 (P=.09). This makes a reasonable comparison with the Mesolithic-to-Neolithic-to-modern slopes in Europe (–0.0123, *r*=.888, P=.0003), China (-0.0129, *r*=.922, P=.003), Southeast Asia (–0.017, *r*=.947, *P*<.001), and the Middle East (–0.0165, P=.04) (Brace et al., in press). Those groups called Late Jōmon are often only marginally more recent than those called Middle Jōmon and, as can be seen from Table 10-2, the TS of both is effectively the same. The one group that was archaeologically judged to be

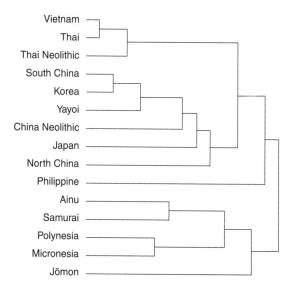

Figure 10-3 A Euclidean distance dendrogram showing the relationships between the various distinct Japanese and Oceanic samples with a spectrum of mainland Asian samples simplified by combining the coastal, southern, and western Chinese into a single "South" Chinese group. A numerical expression of these relationships can be seen in Table 10-8.

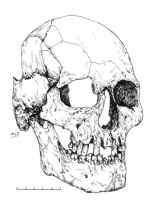

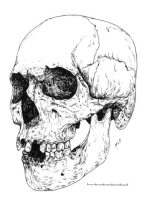

Figure 10-4 A Middle Jōmon male from the Ohta site (No. 668B) in the collection of the Laboratory of Physical Anthropology, Kyoto University. Drawn with the permission of Professor Jiro Ikeda.

Figure 10-5 An Ainu male (No. 1367) in the Koganei collection, University Museum, University of Tokyo. Drawn with the permission of Professor Kazuro Hanihara.

Table 10-3 Sequence of Entry of Variables Used to Produce Figure 10-1

No.	Variable Name	F-statistic	Significance
2	Nasal bone height	26.180	.0000
12	IOW subtense at nasion	8.922	.0000
14	Bizygomatic width	6.150	.0000
18	Basion rhinion	5.767	.000
8	Inferior nasal bone width	3.428	.005
7	Minimum nasal bone width	2.961	.002
13	MOW subtense at rhinion	2.365	.013

Table 10-4 Sequence of Entry of Variables Used to Produce Figure 10-2

No.	Variable Name	F-statistic	Significance
18	Basion rhinion	36.170	.0000
2	Nasal bone height	12.784	.0000
1	Nasal height	12.211	.0000
12	IOW subtense at nasion	9.259	.0000
9	Inferior nasal bone width	7.896	.0000
16	Maximum cranial breadth	7.158	.0000
17	Basion bregma	7.046	.0000
14	Bizygomatic breadth	6.687	.0000
3	Nasion prosthion	6.286	.0000
8	Inferior nasal bone width	5.448	.0000
13	MOW subtense at rhinion	5.563	.0000
15	Glabella opisthocranion	4.725	.0000
5	Basion prosthion	3.412	.0000
4	Nasion basion	2.530	.0006
10	Simotic subtense	2.186	.0036
6	Superior nasal bone width	2.408	.0011

"Middle/Late" Jōmon was given a date of 3500 B.P.—that is, between the rather crudely determined general dates for Middle and Late Jōmon. Since there was no way to get a direct date for the skeletal samples used, we had to adopt an arbitrary designation of time based on general archaeological assessment. If this is both arbitrary and lacking in the kind of precision for which we could wish, it is the best that could be done under the circumstances and we hope that it yields a reasonable model for the overall situation.

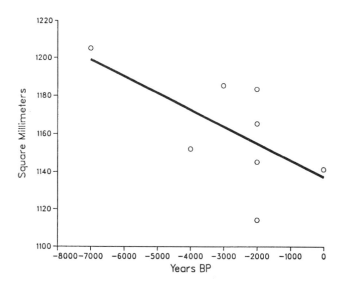

Figure 10-6 Total Tooth Size vs Time in Japan. The regression of total tooth size (TS) in situ in Japan from Early Jōmon through the modern Ainu (Brace et al., n.d. b). The combined measurements from which this was plotted can be found in Table 10-2.

Table 10-5 Sequence of Entry of Variable Used to Produce Figure 10-3

No.	Variable Name	F-statistic	Significance
18	Basion rhinion	44.627	.0000
2	Nasal bone height	16.329	.0000
1	Nasal height	13.337	.0000
3	Nasion prosthion	12.352	.0000
12	IOW subtense at nasion	10.403	.0000
13	MOW subtense at rhinion	9.067	.0000
8	Inferior nasal bone width	7.882	.0000
9	Nasal breadth	7.778	.0000
15	Glabella opisthocranion	7.089	.0000
17	Basion bregma	3.935	.0000
5	Basion prosthion	3.794	.0000
14	Bizygomatic width	4.012	.0000
16	Maximum cranial breadth	4.362	.0000
10	Simotic subtense	3.221	.0001
6	Superior nasal bone width	3.135	.0001
4	Nasion basion	2.431	.0023
7	Minimum nasal bone width	1.952	.0186

Table 10-6 Craniofacial D^2 Figures for the Modern and Prehistoric Samples from Japan Population

Sample	Kofun	Nagas "Yayoi"	Japan Kyushu	Japan Tohoku	Early Yayoi	Late Jōmon	Japan Jōmon	Japan Chiba	Jap Tok.	Ai
Kofun	—									
Nagasaki "Yayoi"	8.89	—								
Japan, Kyushu	10.59	14.22	—							
Japan, Tohoku	4.46	11.61	1.44	—						
Yayoi	2.49	10.94	5.27	2.06	—					
Early Jōmon	10.96	3.66	12.52	11.18	11.43	—				
Late Jōmon	8.43	2.95	14.41	11.66	9.91	5.05	—			
Japan, Chiba	5.50	11.91	1.04	0.19	2.39	10.14	11.33	—		
Japan, Tokyo	5.12	9.12	2.35	1.13	2.47	11.15	11.19	1.71	—	
Ainu	5.31	1.73	10.72	7.46	7.26	6.59	3.81	8.29	6.13	—

Table 10-7 Craniofacial D^2 Figures for a Series of Prehistoric and Combined Modern Japanese, Asian, and Oceanic Populations

Sample	Viet	Thai	Yun	Sich	Micro	Poly	Yayoi	Mongol	Samur	Guang	H Kong	Jōmon	Chn Neo	N Chin	Korea	Japan	Ainu	S Chin
Vietnam	—																	
Thai	3.24	—																
Yunnan	7.72	5.83	—															
Sichuan	6.90	4.56	1.58	—														
Micronesia	7.98	6.61	7.35	7.18	—													
Polynesia	9.12	6.66	7.69	8.44	4.33	—												
Yayoi	8.75	7.24	6.56	4.99	8.96	9.38	—											
Mongol	10.63	8.11	5.78	4.00	13.26	10.84	4.10	—										
Samurai	4.91	6.91	8.41	7.94	5.70	5.80	5.61	9.69										
Guangxi	3.89	4.53	2.71	2.83	5.35	6.36	4.87	7.43	3.52	—								
Hong Kong	4.83	3.95	3.52	2.82	6.86	6.77	6.58	8.74	6.31	1.86	—							
Jōmon	16.39	16.55	16.35	15.61	10.78	9.32	12.29	18.00	9.18	11.40	15.01	—						
China Neo	5.72	7.73	6.31	5.40	9.41	10.79	4.68	8.92	7.37	3.98	3.94	8.92	—					
N. China	10.32	8.47	3.42	2.71	9.89	8.07	5.83	6.96	9.42	4.15	2.60	16.43	4.66	—				
Korea	6.77	4.99	3.64	2.75	10.19	9.54	4.10	5.81	7.42	2.57	1.70	18.04	2.97	2.12	—			
Japan	5.95	4.79	4.86	3.06	5.16	4.13	4.60	7.30	4.98	2.26	2.01	10.42	4.91	2.86	3.14	—		
Ainu	13.29	13.15	13.09	13.66	8.65	4.78	9.06	14.71	4.15	8.17	11.32	4.31	13.94	13.03	13.33	7.19	—	
S. China	6.31	3.67	1.22	0.82	5.47	5.59	4.43	3.96	6.56	2.11	1.95	14.40	4.59	2.20	2.03	2.06	10.86	—

Table 10-8 Craniofacial D^2 Figures for a Series of Japanese, Oceanic, Combined Chinese and Asian Samples

Sample	Samurai	Korea	Yayoi	Chin	Philip	Thai New	Thai	Micro	Poly	Jōmon	Japan	Ainu	N Chin	S Chin	Viet
Samurai	—														
Korea	7.41	—													
Yayoi	5.51	4.12	—												
China Neo	7.55	3.06	4.72	—											
Philippine	11.12	13.60	13.46	15.12	—										
Thai Neol	19.80	12.01	16.20	11.64	14.79	—									
Thai	7.20	5.41	7.18	8.22	7.31	16.02	—								
Micronesia	5.65	10.24	8.71	9.61	7.48	22.18	6.50	—							
Polynes	5.87	10.04	9.35	10.93	11.30	27.34	7.03	4.20	—						
Jōmon	7.89	16.87	11.95	19.06	20.40	34.29	15.12	11.50	8.40	—					
Japan	5.12	3.39	4.57	5.05	13.69	18.17	4.88	5.05	4.12	10.38	—				
Ainu	4.14	13.27	9.74	14.00	17.96	32.46	13.20	8.47	4.59	3.16	7.18	—			
North China	9.66	2.52	5.85	4.74	18.26	18.61	8.62	9.86	8.40	17.58	2.87	13.24	—		
South China	6.84	2.28	4.31	4.88	10.08	14.64	4.08	5.81	6.71	14.41	2.56	11.47	2.44	—	
Vietnam	4.87	6.69	8.47	5.78	9.94	12.05	3.43	7.84	9.14	14.87	5.96	13.03	10.33	6.21	—

DISCUSSION

The principal points that emerge from our analysis are graphically displayed in Figures 10-1 to 10-3 and 10-6. A numerical version of these relationships and differences is recorded in the D^2 values in Tables 10-6 through 10-8 and in the TS values in Table 10-2, but it is easiest to make our appraisals from the figures.

Jōmon-Ainu Continuity

Figure 10-1 shows the relationships and distinctions between the samples from the Japanese islands alone. Two clear-cut and distinct clusters are represented—one including all the modern Japanese groups plus the Kofun and the Yayoi. From a craniological standpoint, the idea that the Kofun is simply a continuation of the Yayoi expressed in recent archaeological work (Barnes, 1986; H. Kanaseki, 1986) is clearly substantiated. Both, in sequence, can clearly be regarded as the ancestors of the modern Japanese.

The second cluster in Figure 10-1 obviously lumps the various levels of Jōmon and the Ainu together and indicates that they have very little in common with the Yayoi rice farmers or the recent Japanese. This is very much in line with the view that emerged from the multivariate work of Howells (1966,

1986), Yamaguchi (1967), Dodo (1986), and Dodo and Ishida (1987). It is also very much in line with the assessment of dental morphology so elegantly demonstrated by Turner (1976, 1979, 1983, 1986, in press; Turner and Hanihara, 1977) and in the nonmetric cranial treatment by Ossenberg (1986).

The one group in Figure 10-1 that may seem out of place is the sample labeled Nagasaki "Yayoi." As can be seen, this is included in the Ainu-Jōmon cluster and, morphologically, is obviously unrelated to the Yayoi in the modern Japanese cluster. Equally obvious is the fact that it does not cluster with the modern specimens from Kyushu, most of which came from the dissecting rooms at Nagasaki University School of Medicine.

This sample was excavated from northwestern Kyushu between 1964 and 1969 by Professor Yoshiatsu Naito. It dates from the early to middle Yayoi and has been taken as proof that that the Yayoi biological configuration developed in situ right out of the preceding Jōmon population as an example of "microevolution" (Suzuki, 1969; Naito, 1971; Akazawa, 1982b). However, the only reason it is called Yayoi at all is because of its association with Yayoi pottery. Unlike the Yayoi sites at Doigahama in western Honshu and around Fukuoka in the core of Kyushu, where the subsistence economy was characterized by the practice of intensive, irrigated rice agriculture (Ushijima, 1954; Kanaseki and Kai, 1955; Kanaseki et al., 1960), the "Yayoi" people of northwestern Kyushu were fishers and gatherers using a lithic technology and pursuing a subsistence strategy that was indistinguishable from that of the Jōmon people wherever they are found in Japan. Since they are skeletally indistinguishable from the Jōmon as well, we suggest that they were simply representatives of the indigenous Jōmon of Kyushu who adopted the turned pottery of their Yayoi neighbors. When we use a lumped Jōmon sample for our subsequent clusters (Figures 10-2 and 10-3), we feel justified in including these individuals to increase our sample size. We should note, however, that, whether they are included or not, the rest of the relationships displayed in those clusters are unaffected.

Certainly we feel that the arrangement visible in Figure 10-1 justifies our treatment of continuity from Early Jōmon right on up to the modern Ainu as an example of a continuing evolutionary lineage. If we consider the change in tooth size through time displayed within this lineage, we get the regression line portrayed in Figure 10-6. Since there is no comparable reduction in cranial dimensions over that same span of time, it has been considered as an example of the point where tooth size and body size have become notably "decoupled" in recent human evolution (Brace et al., 1987). The reduction in tooth size evidently proceeded at approximately the same rate (1 percent per thousand years) as it did in Europe and elsewhere in the post-Pleistocene. If, as has been suggested, this is the consequence of the adoption of improved food preparation practices, then it is no surprise to discover not only that the Jōmon-Ainu continuum in Japan shows the same trends found elsewhere but also that the smallest teeth in all of Asia are to be found in the Ainu of Japan: they, after all, are the direct descendants of the makers of the oldest pottery tradition in the world (Bleed, 1978; Ikawa-Smith, 1986), and it may well have been the use of pottery, which reduced the selective pressures maintaining usable tooth substance, that consequently allowed dental reduction to occur (Brace, 1978, 1988; Brace et al., 1987).

Japan vis-à-vis Asia and Oceania

We have taken the clustering of modern Japanese visible in Figure 10-1 as justification for lumping them together as a single group with a larger sample size for purposes of comparison with other mainland Asian and a couple of Oceanic samples. The results can be seen in Figures 10-2 and 10-3. Figure 10-2 shows the lumped modern Japanese, the lumped Jōmon, the Ainu, and a group labeled Kamakura "Samurai" compared to a maximum diversity of mainland Asian samples and a combined Polynesian and a combined Micronesian set. The Kamakura Samurai are a most interesting case, and we shall defer treatment until the end of this discussion. In Figure 10-2, as in Figure 10-1, two broad clusters can be seen: one that lumps the Ainu, the Jōmon, and the Samurai with the peoples of the island Pacific, and the other that includes the Yayoi and the modern Japanese with the peoples of mainland Asia. When these two broad clusters were first noted in a treatment of Asia, Oceania, and Australo-Melanesia, they were respectively referred to as the Jōmon-Pacific cluster and the Mainland-Asian cluster (Brace et al., in press).

In Figure 10-2, the Thai and the Vietnamese, though clearly related to each other, are the most remote members of the Mainland Asian cluster. Slightly less remote and also tied to each other are the Yayoi and the Mongols, something that may pique the interests of the linguists who posit an interior north Asian origin for the Korean and Japanese languages (Miller, 1986). When the small sample of Mongols is removed and the various Chinese are condensed as in Figure 10-3, however, the Yayoi form a tighter subcluster with the coastal Chinese, Koreans, Chinese Neolithic, and modern Japanese, which certainly is in line with the visual impressions the observer gets when handling the material.

When this lumping of southern and coastal Chinese is made, as shown in Figure 10-3, the two main clusters still remain distinct, and the samples within them are arranged in a manner that is intuitively satisfying and easy to interpret. We added a Philippine sample, and it comes as close as the program allows to being a perfect intermediary between the Mainland-Asian and the Jōmon-Pacific cluster, which is just what it ought to do, the Philippines being right at the edge of the Pacific Basin with a long history of influence from the Asian mainland and yet populated by people who speak Austronesian languages related to those of the island Pacific (Heine-Geldern, 1932; Beyer, 1947, 1948; Solheim, 1972; Hutterer, 1974; Jocano, 1975). The Vietnamese and Thai still remain something of an outlier of the Mainland-Asian cluster. The core of this cluster is composed of Koreans, coastal Chinese, Yayoi, the Chinese Neolithic, and the modern Japanese, with the north Chinese at another remove. The Jōmon-Pacific cluster still retains the same members, but, in this manifestation, the Jōmon themselves are the least tightly included, and the Ainu display a closer association with the group we have called "Samurai."

Yayoi-Kofun-Japanese Continuity

As can be seen in Figure 10-1, the various groups of modern Japanese cluster with the Kofun and the Yayoi, all of which are distinct from the Ainu-Jōmon cluster. When other Oceanic and mainland Asian groups are included, the Yayoi (Figure 10-7) and the Japanese (Figure 10-8) consistently are grouped with mainland samples—note their association with Koreans, southern Chinese, and the Chinese Neolithic in Figure 10-3 and their continued separation from the cluster that includes Ainu, Jōmon, and Oceanic samples. The evidence seems to indicate that the Yayoi arrived as invaders—from southern Korea as many have suggested (Ohno, 1970; Befu, 1971; Bowles, 1977; Aikens and Higuchi, 1982) and that they then replaced the indigenous Jōmon and went on via their Kofun descendants and give rise to the majority of the modern Japanese.

While it has been said that "skeletal changes from the latter half of the end of the Jōmon period to the Tomb period and on into modern times are not drastic enough to prove the conquest of Japan by a foreign race" (Ohno, 1970:81), and more recent work has noted that "research on skeletal remains of the Yayoi period has not offered any substantial evidence for supporting this kind of a working model" (Akazawa, 1982b:166; and see a similar view

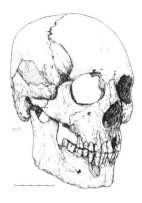 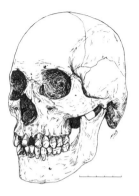

Figure 10-7 A Yayoi male from the Doigahama site (No. 140) in the Department of Anatomy, Kyushu University School of Medicine. Drawn with the permission of Professor Masafumi Nagai.

Figure 10-8 A Japanese male from Tokyo (No. 234) in the Koganei collection at the University Museum, University of Tokyo. Drawn with the permission of Professor Kazuro Hanihara.

in H. Kanaseki, 1986:317), we suggest that our current analysis and the results of all previous systematically comparative work (Howells, 1966, 1986; Yamaguchi, 1967, 1982; Turner, 1976, 1979, 1983, 1986, in press; Dodo, 1986; Dodo and Ishida, 1987; Ossenberg, 1986) make precisely this interpretation the most likely model for the origins of the modern Japanese.

One of the objections from the archaeological standpoint is that there are no surviving indications of major armed conflict (Akazawa, 1982a and b). Our counter to this is that the replacement may simply have been accomplished by the reproductive success of the incoming Yayoi population. The most generous estimate for the total Jōmon population of Japan puts it at 120,000 people in all (Howells, 1986:87). In contrast, the Yayoi had achieved a minimum of between 1 and 2 million within 300 of their arrival—again a minimum estimate (Tsukada, 1986:50). This yields a Yayoi numerical superiority of 10:1. And if we take the model of Aoki and Omoto (1980), the terminal Jōmon population was 14,000 all told vs. a total of 2.8 million for the Yayoi—a Yayoi superiority of 200:1. Any way it is calculated (and note the various simulations proposed by Hanihara, 1987), the Yayoi achieved an overwhelming numerical superiority in a very short space of time.

We grant that Aoki and Omoto prefer to regard the Yayoi population level as having been achieved as the result of an increase in numbers by acculturated Jōmon people, but it could just as well have been a comparable increase in an immigrant population. In fact, this is exactly what has occurred on the island of Hokkaido only within the last century, and we suggest that this was simply the last act in the triumph of the Japanese expansion which began in the west with the Yayoi invasion of 300 B.C. Furthermore, such a model is the only way we can account for the nature of the clusters shown in Figures 10-1 to 10-3.

We should also note that there is indeed legendary and historical evidence for a clash between those coming from the western part of Japan with the resident populace farther east. The chronicles of the emergence of feudal Japan demonstrate an important phase of this long-playing drama, and we present a key aspect of this when we consider the emergence of the Samurai ideal.

The Source of the Samurai

The sample that we have chosen to call "Samurai" (Figure 10-9) is such an interesting example of the intersection of the historical and the biological that we shall take some time to consider it. The skeletons themselves are the remains of the victims of the attack on Kamakura City by Nitta Yoshisada in the summer of A.D. 1333 (Suzuki, 1956; Sansom, 1961). That particular battle may have marked the end of the Kamakura Shogunate (1185–1333) per se, but the governing structure that had been set up by its founder, Minamoto Yoritomo, was so entrenched by that time that it set the pattern for the military rule of Japan for the succeeding 600 years (Murdoch, 1903; Asakawa, 1933; Sansom, 1958; Shinoda, 1960).

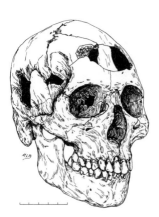

Figure 10-9 A "Samurai" male, one of the victims of the battle at Kamakura City in 1333. No. 190 in the University Museum, University of Tokyo. Drawn with the permission of Professor Kazuro Hanihara.

276

When Yoritomo set up the model in A.D. 1185 for what was to be the continuing Shogunate, he did so with an army of retainers whom he had brought with him from "the east," where his forebears had previously served as frontier administrators (Asakawa, 1933; Storry, 1978). As was so often the case when the emperor in Kyoto sent administrators to try to pacify the unruly inhabitants at the eastern frontier, the armies raised to accomplish this task were often recruited from the very residents the provincial administration was charged with controlling. The latter were traditionally referred to in Japanese historical accounts as "Emishi" (e.g., in Sansom, 1958, 1961), a derogatory term that was replaced by "Ainu" following the Meiji restoration in 1868. Consistent with this tradition, Yoritomo assembled a following with promises of land and emoluments, and it was with these expectations that they accompanied him to Kamakura in 1180 whence he launched the campaigns that brought him undisputed military power in A.D. 1185. The "east" from which his army was recruited was the Kanto district, the area surrounding what is now Tokyo, a region famous for the warlike qualities of its inhabitants (Sansom, 1958; Shinoda, 1960; Storry, 1978). It was also the area where much of the unrest was caused by contention for control with the Ainu, who were still a force in northeastern Japan, and it is a good guess that Yoritomo, by recruiting from the very population that was the source of that contention, basically acquired an army that was in large part of Ainu (Emishi) origin. Is it any surprise, then, that the descendants of his supporters who lost their lives in the battle at Kamakura in 1333 should so consistently fall into the Ainu-Jōmon cluster as they do in Figures 10-2 and 10-3?

To be sure, Suzuki specifically regards them as a local variant of modern Japanese and denies that they could be Ainu (Suzuki, 1956) even while he mentions certain traits that are more characteristically Ainu than Japanese. In our analysis also they fall into the Japanese cluster under some circumstances. When we used untransformed measurements, they fell into the Japanese cluster when we included bizygomatic breadth and into the Ainu cluster when we left it out. And when we leave out Mainland Asian and Oceanic samples as in Figure 10-1, they fall in with the Yayoi and the Kofun. It would seem that under some circumstances they can be regarded as Ainu, and under other conditions they rank as Japanese: but this is just what we should expect for a population that had been right at the frontier between those two contending elements for a prolonged period of time.

All of this may well have had some impact on the physical characteristics of people of different status in Japan as well as on Japanese ideals in regard to personal appearance. The effect of Yoritomo's brief regime was to give an enduring measure of power and prestige to a warrior class of eastern origin (Asakawa, 1933; Sansom, 1958, 1961; Shinoda, 1960; Storry, 1978). In turn, the form of their facial features became a kind of high-status criterion and could very well account for the fact that the "Samurai" stereotype idealized in Japanese art is so unlike the average appearance of the typical person encountered on the Japanese street—or in the medical-school dissecting rooms from Kyushu to Tohoku. The kabuki actors, courtesans, and samurai portrayed so often in paintings, screens, kites, and wood block prints (cf. Streeter, 1974; Neuer et al., 1979; Halloran, 1986) all tend to display the elevated nasal skeleton, the slight swelling at the center of the brow, the point on the chin and the flat-sided cheeks that set apart Ainu form from that of the typical Japanese. The first European to write a serious history of Japan, the seventeenth-century German physician Engelbert Kaempfer, also noted that a "higher, more European-like nose" was to be found among the nobility and important state officials (Kaempfer, 1964 [1777–1779]:110, though the earlier English translation of 1727 only mentions that the "countenance" in the "noblest families, of the Princes and Lords of the Empire" was "more like Europeans" 1906 [1727]:151).

One could even suggest that the lighter skin color documented for the higher social classes in Japan (Hulse, 1967) had its origin in the same manner, for the early observers often remarked that skin color in the Ainu was noticeably lighter than in the Japanese (Batchelor, 1892). Even the characteristic tonsure of the samurai, with the shaved section at the front, is recorded by earlier observers to have been an Ainu custom (Batchelor, 1892; Sternberg, 1929), though it is conceivable that this could have been copied by the Ainu from their oppressors. Still, it is just possible that it might be part of the legacy that the samurai received from the obviously Ainu part of their ancestry. The Jōmon-Ainu legacy might also be the source of those culinary traditions wherein the Japanese differ to such a striking extent from the Chinese and, in fact, from all the other cuisines of Asia (cf. Lin and Lin, 1972; Solomon, 1976; Tsuji, 1980).

There is more than a little irony in this whole picture: where the Ainu, so looked down upon in the traditional Japanese conception of the social spectrum (Takaki, 1987), have had a genetic effect on the ruling classes of Japan that would be completely unexpected for a conquered and despised people presumed to have been exterminated—and whose very prior existence has been denied for much of Japan (cf. the synopsis of these denials in Ohno, 1970).

CONCLUSIONS

The casual observer of the features of the modern Japanese invariably notes that in general they share so much in common with the other inhabitants of eastern Asia that it is not possible to make broad regional or national distinctions on the basis of an assessment of those features alone. Occasionally a particularly observant appraiser may remark that sometimes there are nuances of brow form, eye socket shape, nasal bridge elevation, and chin-and-jaw definition that are not shared with other well-known Asian populations. The results of our multivariate analysis of a set of craniofacial variables are quite in line with the conclusions of that hypothetical "casual observer," as are those of previous, if less extensive, studies. Biologically, the Japanese evidently are closely similar to continental Asians from Korea and throughout coastal, southern, and western China. From our treatment of the available evidence from all of the various major groups to inhabit the Japanese islands past and present, and a sampling of continental Asian and Oceanic populations, these are the points with which we can conclude:

1   The modern Japanese belong to what can be termed the Mainland-Asian cluster.

2   The advent of this Mainland-Asian manifestation in Japan was the immigration in 300 B.C. of the Yayoi rice agriculturalists, and its modern representatives reflect little from the indigenous Jōmon inhabitants of the Japanese archipelago.

3   The Jōmon fishing-hunting-collecting people of prehistoric Japan are the direct ancestors of the Ainu, once spread throughout the islands but now restricted to dwindling numbers only on Hokkaido.

4   The dental reduction demonstrable for the continuing line from Early Jōmon to the modern Ainu has been proceeding at the same rate as the one documented for Europe, the Middle East, and elsewhere in the world during the post-Pleistocene. Since we suggest that this reduction was the result of the relaxation of the forces of selection consequent on the use of pottery in food preparation, and since Jōmon pottery is the oldest in Asia and perhaps the world, it is consistent to note that the Ainu in fact have the smallest teeth in all of modern Asia.

5   Jōmon form is closely allied to that visible in Polynesia and Micronesia, constituting an important part of and perhaps a point of origin for what can be called the Jōmon-Pacific cluster. This in turn is essentially unrelated to the Mainland-Asian cluster.

6   Because of the actual course of history and the regional shifts of power that occurred as the feudal system emerged in Medieval Japan, the genetic characteristics derived from the Jōmon-Ainu continuum came to constitute a significant part of the biological makeup of the dominant military class. This has been unconsciously perpetuated in the artistic canons used to depict Samurai form in the various manifestations of Japanese graphic art.

7   To the extent that these elements are part of modern Japan, their physical heritage may be said to depart from the Mainland-Asian configuration and to reflect a survival of the aboriginal but otherwise unrelated Jōmon-Pacific set of characteristics. The biological relationship between the Jōmon-to-Ainu line in Japan and the peoples of island Oceania should lend credence to the possibility of an Austronesian element or "substratum" in the Japanese language, but this is a matter for separate study by a different group of scholars.

ACKNOWLEDGMENTS

The research on which this project is based was refused support by the National Science Foundation in 1973, 1981, and 1985. Partial support was provided by the Horace H. Rackham School of Graduate Studies at the University of Michigan in 1973, 1977, 1980, and 1983; by the University of Auckland, Auckland, New Zealand, in 1973–1974; by the Committee on Scholarly Communication with the People's Republic of China, National Academy of Sciences, in 1980 and 1985; by the University of Michigan Museum of Anthropology Field Research Fund in 1984, 1985, and 1986; by the L. S. B. Leakey Foundation in 1986; and by Diana Blaban Holt in 1987. Essential assistance has also been given by Mark A. Gordon and Chacma, Inc., of New York; by Professor Hiroshi Kanaseki, Tenri University, Nara; by Professor Takeshi Kanaseki, Kyushu University; by Dr. Gina L. Barnes, Cambridge University; by Professors Ben R. Finney and Wilhelm G. Solheim, II, University of Hawaii; by Roger C. Brace of Ann Arbor, MI; by G. Brace of Nanterre, France; and by Lono. Important financial support was also provided by the late E. B. Hoagland and by the late Professor and Mrs. G. W. Brace.

For access to and help in the various collections under their care, we are grateful to Professor Kazuro Hanihara, University of Tokyo; Dr. Jean-Louis Heim, Musée de l'Homme, Paris; Professor Jiro Ikeda, Kyoto University; Professor Toshihiro Ishii, Tohoku University; Professor Nina Jablonski, University of Hong Kong; Professors Kohei Mitsuhashi and Yukio Dodo, Sapporo Medical College, Professor Masafumi Nagai, Kyushu University; Professor Yoshiatsu Naito, Nagasaki University; Professor Michael Pietrusewsky, University of Hawaii; Professor Shao Xiang-qing, Anthropology Section, Department of Biology, Fudan University, Shanghai, People's Republic of China; Dr. Yoshihiko Sinoto, B. P. Bishop Museum, Honolulu, HI; Dr. Ian Tattersall, American Museum of Natural History; Dr. Wei Boyuan, Guangxi Medical College; and Professor Wu Jukang, Professor Wu Xinzhi and Zhang Zhenbiao, Institute of Vertebrate Paleontology and Paleoanthropology, Academia Sinica, Beijing, People's Republic of China.

We are also grateful to Charles L. Brace, Professor Kazuro Hanihara, Professor Frederick S. Hulse, and Margot Massey for references, advice, and guidance in some of the more difficult aspects of Japanese history. We are also indebted to Dr. Gina L. Barnes, Department of Archaeology and Anthropology, Cambridge University, and to Professor Karl L. Hutterer and Masao Nishimura, Museum of Anthropology, University of Michigan, Ann Arbor, for guidance in matters of Japanese prehistory; and to Professor Hitoshi Watanabe, Waseda University, Tokyo, and Professor Masakazu Yoshizaki, Hokkaido University, Sapporo, for valuable perspectives on matters pertaining to the Ainu, past and present.

∾   ∾

Epilogue

Since the work reported here was accomplished, the attempt to test clusters and relationships was extended by adding more samples from eastern Asia and representative samples from the original populations of the western hemisphere. The formidable task of helping to collect the data and analyzing them for the Americas was done by A. Russell Nelson in his doctoral dissertation (Nelson, 1998). Access to further Chinese Neolithic and Bronze Age and Manchu samples was made possible by Pan Qifeng of the Institute of Archaeology at the Chinese Academy of Social Sciences in Beijing. When we put this all together, we came up with a picture of the relationship of particular New World groups to specific Asian populations. One of the things we were able to show was that the unity of the New World samples is more myth than reality. In other words, if you have seen one Indian, you have by no means seen them all. One of the ties we found was that the Jōmon of Japan are closely related to one of the major groupings of New World populations but not at all related to the first major entrants into the hemisphere. Since the Polynesians and one major set of New World inhabitants are clearly tied to the older and continuing manifestations of Jōmon Japan, we have renamed that cluster the Jōmon-Derived cluster. This is just another answer to the "What next?" question posed in Chapter 9. It has been submitted for publication, but it would be premature to say more about our findings until they have appeared in print (Brace, Nelson, and Pan, submitted).

CHAPTER 11

A Four-Letter Word Called "Race"
(1996)

Prologue

The very genesis of the field of biological anthropology was rooted in the assumption that there are valid biological entities that can be called "races," and that these then are legitimate targets of anthropological study. Biological anthropologists have often been somewhat slower than others to realize that those "entities" do not have coherent biological reality. This has been particularly true in America where the concept of "race" was more an ancillary result of the circumstances of the human settlement of the hemisphere and how this affected the way people think about things than a consequence of the study of the real nature and dimensions of human biological variation.

The first biological anthropologist in America to bring this to the attention of the reading public was a transplanted Englishman, Ashley Montagu, who settled in the United States in 1930, the very year that I was born, and has remained here ever since (Brace, 1997). Montagu's most influential work, *Man's Most Dangerous Myth: The Fallacy of Race* (Montagu, 1942), has had a turbulent history. In the past, much of biological anthropology tended to treat it as though it were a manifestation of what we now refer to as P.C.—political correctness—in this case a kind of "feel-good" manifestation of liberal wishful thinking (for example, Shipman, 1994; but see the critique of that by Brace, 1995).

The approach may indeed be compatible with liberal social thought, but it is actually based on a solid grasp of the biological nature of human variation. As the synthetic theory of evolution began to have its impact on some parts of biological anthropology in the decade after the end of World War II, there were some who realized that we could only make real biological sense out of the nature of human variation after the concept of "race" was junked and we started over from scratch. I was one of the people who came to that realization when I started teaching at the Santa Barbara campus of the University of California. I had been able to get Ashley Montagu to speak to our undergraduate anthropology club there, and I was successful in getting him brought to the campus in 1963 as Regent's Lecturer for our winter term. In turn he invited me to contribute a chapter for the volume *The Concept of Race,* which he was editing to appear in 1964 (Brace, 1964). In that chapter, I tried to show how to handle the study of the nature of human biological variation after the "race" concept had been dispensed with.

That was a third of a century ago, however, and there has been more than a bit of back-sliding in the world of biological anthropology. Some of that is evident in the outlook of the colleague Frank Livingstone and I brought in to the Department of Anthropology at the University of Michigan a quarter century ago in hopes of giving some momentum to an evolutionary perspective, namely Milford Wolpoff. Before it could be housebroken, the big friendly puppy had burgeoned into the dimensions of an oversized Saint Bernard with the proclivities often attributed to a pit bull. In spite of all the time he has been in Ann Arbor, Wolpoff has still not gotten the concept of cline right and persists in defining it in oxymoronic fashion as if it were an "isogene" or "isomorph" (Wolpoff, 1996:816; Wolpoff and Caspari, 1997:356, 399—with no mention of the role played by Livingstone in bringing the concept to the attention of anthropology and providing both the theory and the data by which it can be applied). A cline in fact is a gradient by definition, though Wolpoff has chosen to redefine it as the extent of the unchanging expression of a trait. One is reminded of the *Looking Glass* world of Lewis Carroll, and Humpty Dumpty's claim that a word "means just what I choose it to mean—neither more nor less." When a 250-pound pit bull chooses to interpret the command to "sit" as "sic 'em," one is reminded of Humpty Dumpty's admonition to Alice, "The question is…which is to be master— that's all" (Carroll, 1872:124).

Because of the intellectual sluggishness displayed by so much of biological anthropology, it seems appropriate to reopen the approach that many of us hoped we had successfully gotten under way a third of a century ago. With that in mind, Larry Reynolds and Leonard Lieberman, of Central Michigan University, prepared a volume of essays in honor of Ashley Montagu's ninetieth year, and, to my great plea-sure, they invited me to be one of the contributors. This gave me the opportunity to completely revamp and update the approach I had taken in 1964 with the addition of the quantities of information and insight that have accumulated since that time. Actually, since so many biological anthropologists still have not gotten much beyond the point of trying to justify the application of "racial" names to human individuals and groups, the information relating to the distribution of the separate aspects of human adaptation has not accumulated as rapidly as it could have. Hope springs eternal, and, this time around, just maybe the idea will take root and a new genera-tion will make the effort to go and get the information we need to document the pic-ture of what I present here in outline form (Brace, 1996).

When I presented a version of this paper to the Canadian Association of Physical Anthropologists in Windsor, Ontario, on October 28, 1994, I was able to get the assistance of Humbert O. Echo, another member of that extraordinary faculty in the Department of Homopathic Anthropopoetics at the University of Southern North Dakota at Hoople. Echo had previously been of assistance by rendering some of the gambits I have essayed in versified form, and he had allowed me to use that particu-lar piece as an addendum to a comment, "What shall we call 'Them'?", which I pub-lished in 1996 (Echo, 1996). This is attached here:

The Name of a Race

When we ponder on the contours in the features of a face
That resembles all the others which are from a given place,

What potential harm would follow if we use a single name,
To denote a group of people when we think they look the same?

But there are no implications that a common shape will bear,
Beyond the clear reminder of the kinship that they share;

For selection's not delimited by groups of kin alone,
Or confined within the boundaries of a continental zone.

Pigment in the skin will give protection from the sun,
But it doesn't give a clue to how another trait will run;

Both the desert and the arctic take the moisture from the air,
And people from both places have a nose with length to spare.

Features cannot tell us who is mad and who is sane,
Or nuance of the forehead say a thing about the brain.

Each trait that is adaptive will pursue a separate course,
Determined by the nature of its own selective force

Which crosses all the others in a fashion that defines
A pattern without meaning made of independent clines.

Since each selected feature has a different place of birth,
The mix within a region can have no collective worth.

When thoughtlessly we verbalize without the proper care,
Our words can make an entity that isn't really there;

How much pigment or how little will suffice to give the right
To warrant the conferral of the label "Black" or "White"?

And beware the added meaning in the tag we lightly give;
For it oftentimes determines who may have the right to live.

Acceptance of the concept, and all that it can mean,
Gives credence to an image that could best be called obscene;

To use the very word is to be captured by its spell:
That which we call a "race," by any other name would smell…

≈   ≈

INTRODUCTION

All good people agree,
  And all good people say,
All nice people, like us, are We
  And everyone else is they.

—Rudyard Kipling, *We and They*

The issues dealt with here are so important that they should transcend the involvement and pronouncements of any single individual or school of thought. If there is a possible exception to that generalization, it would have to be illustrated by the life and work of Ashley Montagu. For more than half a century now, he has stood for the view not only that "race" is a "myth," but that it is our *Most Dangerous Myth,* to quote from the title of one of his most influential books, first written in 1942. The insights in that seminal work remain as true today as when he first phrased them, and they can serve as a solid point of departure for my own efforts in this paper written to celebrate the career and accomplishments of the author of that signal contribution. This gives me the opportunity to update my own first attempt (Brace, 1964) to deal with the question of "race" written some 30 years ago at the specific request of the very person in whose honor I am writing now—Ashley Montagu.

I am going to begin with the conclusion: "race" is a social construct derived mainly from perceptions conditioned by the events of recorded history, and it has no basic biological reality. Quite simply, there is no useful entity that corresponds to what is popularly intended by the term "race." This was explicitly noted in regard to the case of Americans of African ancestry by no less a figure than the late Gunnar Myrdal—that extraordinary Swedish economist and author of one of the most perceptive books ever written about the way things are in the United States, *An American Dilemma* (1944:115). To much of the reading public, this will seem like a complete absurdity. The average literate citizen of the western world reacts with frank disbelief when told that there is no such thing as "race." "Why, it's as plain as the nose on your face!" is one of the partially facetious reactions. When the anthropologist continues to insist that there is no human biological category that can be called "race," the skeptical layman will shake his head and just regard this as further evidence of the innate silliness of those who call themselves intellectuals.

This feeling has been seconded by some biological anthropologists who have gone so far as to say that denials of the biological reality of "race" are simply the products of their well-meaning colleagues' abhorrence of the ills and injustices that have arisen in its name. In this view, the denial that "race" has a biological reality is itself the result of socially conditioned perceptions. Myrdal, for instance, was a social scientist and not recognized as an authority on biological matters. However well-intentioned they may be, then, such denials themselves presumably have no biological justification and therefore lack validity. The cry of both professional and nonprofessional skeptics goes like this: "If there are no 'races,' how come people are so good at identifying them?" (and see how that rhetorical question is asked—and answered!—in Sauer, 1992).

But what is this "them" that we are so good at recognizing? It is true that people are reasonably good at being able to tell what part of the world someone comes from in a general kind of way. Unless a person has parents from very different parts of the world, it is not hard to tell whether a person's family roots were in eastern Asia, western Europe, or southern India. In addition, most Americans would feel confident that they could detect the presence of African ancestry, though in fact they are quite unable to tell whether a person comes from West Africa or the eastern end of New Guinea. There are reasons for that particular confusion which will be treated later, but, though it introduces a touch of uncertainty, it does not really blunt the general conviction that it is not all that difficult to tell at a glance the part of the world from which a person's ancestors originally came.

TRADITIONAL "RACES"

So far, however, I have said nothing about "race"—I have just mentioned the characteristic appearance associated with geographic areas. Well, you may ask, why isn't that recognizable appearance an indicator of the presence of something legitimately called "race"? To answer that, we have to come to grips with what it is that produces those configurations that we can associate with given areas, and we have to consider the biological significance of each such configuration.

One of the most enduring schemes of "racial" designation divides the peoples of the world into three large categories crudely conceptualized as "black," "white," and "yellow," or in more orotund and polysyllabic form, "Negroid," "Caucasoid," and "Mongoloid." Early in the nineteenth century, this scheme was advocated by Georges Cuvier (1769–1832), one of the most influential figures in the history of French science, though it was neither original with him nor offered in anything more than the most casual of terms (Cuvier, 1817:1:94; 1829:1:80). Some of Cuvier's readers interpreted these three "races" as the respective descendants of the three sons of the Biblical Noah—Ham, Shem, and Japheth (Murray, 1834:255; Morton, 1839:2).

For many of the beneficiaries of the traditions of "western civilization," this formulation was eminently satisfying because it drew strength from its apparent roots in the Bible, the most honored written work in existence in the minds of the Christian faithful who made up the overwhelming majority of the representatives of that "western civilization." In addition, it evoked the sanctity of what westerners regarded as that most mystically sacred of quantities, the number three—also long associated with the Christian "Trinity" even though that baffling concept can only be vaguely and somewhat tortuously squeezed out of the actual phraseology of the Bible.

Now let us take a closer look at what it is that makes us think that we can understand something about human variation if we divide the world up into those three categories. Are they really comparable in the sense of being equally distinctive? And is there something about each that justifies its identification as a category, and what is the biological significance of that "something" if indeed it exists?

Negroid

The very name "Negroid" derives from the Latin word for black—*niger*— and the word used to denote that color in modern Italian, Spanish, and Portuguese is *negro*. Because southern Europe is closer to Africa than the other European countries, it was inevitable that contacts between the peoples of southern Europe and Africa began earlier and were carried on more continuously than was true between Africans and more northerly European nations. Eventually when northern Europeans extended their contacts toward the south, they tended to adopt the terms already in use by their Mediterranean neighbors. Early in the history of English involvement in the growing trade of enslaved Africans, and long before there were any English-speaking settlers in the western hemisphere, the term "Negro" entered the English language to mean a native inhabitant of the African continent south of the Sahara (Pope-Hennessy, 1968:46). The identification of native Africans as "Negroes" served to focus the attention of would-be categorizers on a single descriptive attribute—skin color. The presence of sufficient melanin in the skin to warrant using a term such as "Negro" or "Black," however, is not restricted to the people of Africa alone. The native inhabitants of southern India, New Guinea and adjacent islands, and northern Australia all possess equivalent amounts of melanin in their skins. If a word meaning "Black" is warranted as a description for people of African origin, then it is also equally appropriate for those others.

The use of the term "Negroid" obviously cannot distinguish between the long-term equatorial inhabitants from one end of the Old World to the other. In fact, melanin in the skin is an adaptation that shields the possessor from the damaging effects of the ultraviolet component of sunlight, and all human populations whose immediate ancestors had been continuous dwellers of the tropics for 100,000 years or more possess that adaptation to an equal extent even if they are only remotely related to each other. As Darwin explicitly realized, any trait that is under the control of selective forces is "almost valueless" for purposes of tracing population relationships (Darwin, 1859:427). Obviously a classification based on a trait whose manifestation is under the control of selection will tell us much about the distribution of the relevant selective force, but it will tell us little about the degree of relationship of those populations that display similar degrees of development of the trait in question.

Traditionalists unwilling to give up so soon may raise points concerning the presence of other traits visible in people with elevated levels of melanin in the skin, and suggest that these hang together to indicate the presence of some kind of fundamental underlying entity. Dark skin tends to be associated with tightly curled hair, for example, and dark-skinned people often have large jaws and teeth. However, hair form is the product of the same kinds of selective forces that are associated with skin color. Jaws and teeth, on the other hand, vary according to quite different rules as we shall see later. For the dark-skinned people of New Guinea and Australia, for example, jaw and tooth size actually increases as the intensity of skin pigmentation decreases grading from the North of Australia down to its southern edge (Brace, 1980; Brace et al., 1991). Clearly the idea of a "Negroid race" has so many flaws that it is best simply to drop it and start on another tack. More of that later.

Caucasoid

All right, you may say with some reluctance, if an essentially descriptive word does not work to categorize human populations, how about a word that is relatively abstract—"Caucasoid" for example? What could be wrong with using that presumably innocuous term to stand for the people in the northwestern quadrant of human habitation? The history of the application and use of the term "Caucasoid," however, introduces still further problems. The word derives from the Caucasus, that isthmus of land that separates the Black and the Caspian Seas and joins Russia and the Middle East. Its use to denote human physical appearance dates from the "racial" scheme offered by the

German physician Johann Friedrich Blumenbach (1752–1840) in his doctoral dissertation of 1775, *De Generis Humani Varietate Nativa* (*On the Natural Varieties of Mankind*) best known from the revised and enlarged third edition of 1795 (translated and edited by Thomas Bendyshe in 1865 and republished in 1969).

The initial reason for the focus on that part of the world was the assumption that, as the biblical flood subsided, Noah's Ark landed at Mount Ararat in the mountains of the Caucasus. Although the idea was not original with him, Blumenbach claimed that the living people of that region comprise "the most beautiful race of men" with "the most beautiful form of the skull, from which, as from a mean and primeval type, the others diverge by most easy gradations on both sides" (Blumenbach in Bendyshe [ed.], 1865:269). Adding to this assumption of pristine beauty, Blumenbach went on to claim that "white… we may fairly assume to have been the primitive colour of mankind" (idem).

Blumenbach evidently assumed that "Caucasoids" were the least modified descendants of the people who allegedly got off the Ark at Mount Ararat and therefore the best representatives of what God intended when He created human beings in the first place. Other "races" were said to have departed from the form of God's original intent by a process of "degeneration" in proportion to their geographical distance from the mountains of the Caucasus and the differences in the circumstances under which they now find themselves.

I have actually written an overly simplistic synopsis of Blumenbach's thoughtful treatise, and I have left out many of the positive things that it contained. My purpose is not to fault Blumenbach but to highlight the absurdity of the term "Caucasoid." One could go even further by noting that Mount Ararat is actually in Turkish Armenia, and, if there were any justification in using point geographic designations to refer to broadly related human populations, it could be argued that the term "Armenoid" should be preferable to the term "Caucasoid." Of course, the designation "Armenoid" was used for somewhat different purposes in other "racial" classifications a couple of generations ago (Coon, 1939:628–629), and this makes it as tainted as "Caucasoid." Again, the best thing to do is to abandon the use of any narrow regional designation as a means of encompassing the perceived similarities of human groups distributed across widespread geographic expanses. The related morphological pattern that we can see running from Scandinavia to the Middle East is poorly served by trying to indicate this by using a narrowly local term, whether that be "Armenoid," "Norwegioid," or "Caucasoid."

Mongoloid

All right, so descriptive terms and narrow regional designations fail to serve our purposes, but what about names derived from human groups? What could be wrong with the use of the term "Mongoloids" to refer to all the related people of eastern Asia? In fact, it has all of the flaws present in narrow regional designations plus some others as well. Just as the Norse or Armenians are inappropriate to use as representatives of all of the people who extend between Norway and Armenia, the Mongols are inappropriate to stand for all of the people who extend from Mongolia to Indonesia.

Adding further less-than-positive connotations to the term "Mongoloid" is the long-time usage of that term to refer to the visible features associated with an inherited syndrome that occurs as a result of irregularities in the transmission of chromosome 21. The first full description was published in 1866 by the English physician John Langdon Down (Patterson, 1987).

When the syndrome recognized by Dr. Down was first described, it was noted that the English children in whom it was observed were afflicted with developmental defects that influenced a series of systems. These included the growth and ossification of the interorbital portion of the face as well as the normally expected path of intellectual maturation. Affected children are also observed to display an alteration in the expected course of pigment production giving a slightly yellowish cast to their appearance. In the European mind, all of these manifestations reminded them of their stereotypic picture of the inhabitants of eastern Asia—flattish of face, yellowish in color, and mentally dull and lethargic. The inherited interference with development observed by Dr. Down then was duly labeled "Mongolism" or, in more pejorative fashion, "Mongoloid idiocy." Implicit in this was the feeling that the genetic defect which caused the syndrome was related to the hereditary reasons why the people of eastern Asia differ in general appearance from the people of western Europe. Subsequent generations of geneticists and physicians have recognized the blatant racism behind such attitudes and have sought to correct this by eliminating the term "Mongoloid" from the description of that suite of inherited developmental defects and describing it simply as "Down's syndrome." More recently, the possessive has been eliminated, and it has come to be called "Down syndrome" or "Down disease," and no mention is made of the supposed similarity in appearance between those who are afflicted and the inhabitants of Asia. The memory lingers on in a large segment of the public in the western world, and, if for no other reason, this alone would make the use of the term "Mongoloid" an unfortunate choice of words to describe the population of a major segment of the earth.

However, there is more than just the taint of that racism in the terms of yesteryear to illustrate the fact that the designation "Mongoloid" is misleading at best when used in descriptive fashion. The Mongols, as it happens, display systematic morphological differences from the rest of the people in Asia to such a degree that they could be regarded as the most untypical of that whole set of related populations (Li et al., 1991:278). This is not just an off-handed judgment. A standard set of two dozen craniofacial measurements (the measurements and the techniques used are described at much greater length in Chapter 10, "Reflections on the Face of Japan") was made on samples chosen from all the available localities in eastern Asia. These were used to construct a tree diagram—the "dendrogram" shown in Figure 11-1— where the length of the stem of each twig is proportional to the morphological relationship with the other twigs to which it is connected. A short stem running from a named twig to the next connecting link means a close relationship. The longer the stem on the twig, the more remote the relationship.

In Figure 11-1, the twig connecting the Mongols to the rest of the samples from eastern Asia is the longest unlinked branch in the entire dendrogram. Other studies using slightly different techniques have come to the same conclusions (Pietrusewsky, 1992:42; Pietrusewsky et al., 1992:552). Mongols, then, are as morphologically remote from the other inhabitants of eastern Asia as it

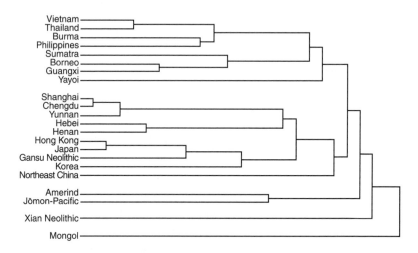

Figure 11-1 A Euclidean Distance dendrogram or cluster diagram demonstrating the atypical status of Mongols when compared with representative samples of the other inhabitants of East Asia. The values for the measurements were converted into C scores and compared by Unweighted Matched Pair Group Analysis (UMPGA). The procedure was pioneered by Howells (1986) and is described in greater detail in Brace and Hunt (1990).

is possible to be and yet still count as related (Brace and Tracer, 1992:459). To use the Mongols as though they could stand for something essential to all of the related populations of eastern Asia is to run the risk of serious misrepresentation at best. Of course, the assumption that there is some sort of "essence" that we should be looking for is itself fundamentally misguided.

CLINES

A generation ago, Frank Livingstone produced the aphorism "There are no races, there are only clines" (Livingstone, 1962:279). This fit in nicely with he assumptions of the neo-Darwinian or synthetic theory of evolution that characterized much of the outlook of the biological sciences that arose in the middle third of the twentieth century. One of the most important figures in that synthesis was the late Sir Ronald A. Fisher (1890–1962), an English biological statistician whose quirky genius occasionally led him into positions of dogmatic intransigence (Box, 1978). His long-running feud with the American geneticist Sewall Wright (1889–1998) was a case in point.

Wright had entertained the possibility that biological evolution could be conditioned by a number of different factors including chance alone—especially when population size is small (Wright, 1931). Fisher simply refused to acknowledge the actual mechanisms Wright proposed (Fisher and Ford, 1950; Wright, 1951). Their argument narrowed down to whether genetic drift could or could not play a role in addition to the effects of natural selection. Fisher had taken the view that selection is all (Fisher, 1930), and that in those instances where we could not see how it had its effect, the fault was in our finite and limited powers of observation and understanding. Biologists who accepted this conclusion were put in the position of assuming that all discernible inherited traits and configurations owed their various manifestations to the controlling effects of selection. Our duty, then, was to determine the nature of the selective forces involved and to demonstrate just how these work to control variation in the particular traits that respond to changes in the intensity of their operation. If all traits respond to the graded influence of their particular selective forces, the intersection of their various manifestations to make identifiable configurations in given individuals or populations has no intrinsic significance. This in brief is the intellectual background behind the phrase "there are no races, there are only clines." Whenever separate adaptively significant traits are controlled by separate and unrelated selective forces, this still remains true.

Hemoglobin S

Let me give a concrete example using variation in human populations. Before Livingstone coined that portentous phrase, he had shown that the frequency of the gene for hemoglobin S—the source of human sickle-cell anemia—is controlled by the intensity of infestation with falciparum malaria (Livingstone, 1958). Populations in the malarial areas of tropical Africa, the Middle East, and on into India all show high percentages of hemoglobin S even though a certain number of S genes are taken out of circulation each generation because of deaths due to sickle cell anemia.

The distribution of hemoglobin S, then, is unrelated to human population boundaries. It is not an automatic marker for African ancestry as has often been assumed, though many of the Americans who possess it did inherit it from African ancestors. Africa itself probably received hemoglobin S from the Middle East via Arab trade routes across the Sahara, up the Nile, and down the east coast (Livingstone, 1989b). The circumstances that led to the infestation by *Plasmodium falciparum,* the mosquito-transmitted microbe that causes falciparum malaria, are associated with the increase in human population size and the environmental modifications produced by successful agricultural practices in areas where that malaria-producing parasite can flourish. Those areas originally included the tropical, subtropical, and temperate parts of the Old World with enough water to allow propagation of the mosquito vector and where the winter was not so severe that they could not survive from one season to the next.

Figure 11-2 shows the distribution of hemoglobin S in the Old World. In its areas of highest frequency, falciparum malaria also reaches high levels of intensity. If falciparum malaria is the reason for the high frequency of hemoglobin S, one might expect that there would be a one-to-one correlation between malaria intensity and hemoglobin S, but this is not exactly the case. In Southeast Asia, for example, falciparum malaria constitutes a very serious health problem, but hemoglobin S fades out and disappears. The reason for this is the presence of another abnormal hemoglobin—hemoglobin E—which, as it happens, also enables its possessors to cope with malarial infestation but which does not have quite such serious consequences in its homozygous—EE—state (Livingstone, 1989a).

Skin Color

The abnormal hemoglobins, then, are distributed among the world's populations strictly in accordance with the history of their involvement with malaria

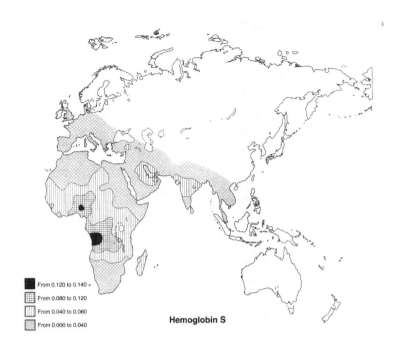

From 0.120 to 0.140 +
From 0.080 to 0.120
From 0.040 to 0.080
From 0.000 to 0.040

Hemoglobin S

Figure 11-2 The distribution of hemoglobin S according to its different frequencies in the populations of the Old World. Adapted from Bodmer and Cavalli-Sforza (1976:310). The various shadings represent the different indicated gene frequencies for hemoglobin S.

of various kinds and without reference to any other manifestations such as geographical, cultural, or political boundaries or anything like face form or pigmentation (Livingstone, 1967, 1985). In fact, this is the classic pattern for the distribution of any trait under selective force control. And when we turn to a consideration of pigment, that too shows a pattern of gradation which is independent of the distribution of any other trait not directly related to the intensity of solar radiation. Figure 11-3 shows the distribution of skin color in the human populations of the world.

Melanin in the skin exists for one purpose only, and that is to prevent the penetration of the ultraviolet component in sunlight. Attempts to suggest that melanin has any relation to mental function—pro or con—are nothing less than unwarranted manifestations of racism (Ortiz de Montellano, 1991, 1992). However, it is the 290 to 320 millimicron ultraviolet range, "mid-UV," "middlewave UV" or "UV-B"—either alone or, as is usually the case, in conjunction with UV-A—that causes the most trouble (Potter, 1985; Kligman, 1986). The "trouble" caused by UV-B is cancer. Particularly affected are the

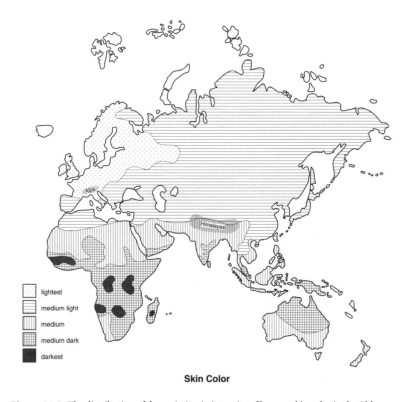

Figure 11-3 The distribution of the variation in intensity of human skin color in the Old World. Adapted from Biasutti (1959:I:Table IV [pp.192–193]) by Brace and Montagu (1977:392), revised from Brace 1964:109).

cells at the bottom of the epidermis at the interface between this layer and the underlying dermis itself. These cells give rise to the outermost portion of the skin in a continued process of renewal that has a three- to four-week turnover (Daniels et al., 1968). UV-B can cause damage that leads to cancer in the basal cells and the derived overlying squamous cells that form the surface of the skin.

In the United States alone in the late 1970s, European Americans contracted over 400,000 cases of basal cell skin cancer, which amounted to an incidence of over 232 cases per every 100,000 people. At the same time, less than 3.5 cases per 100,000 occurred among Americans of African origin (Ackerman and del Regato, 1985:180). At that time, the average number of Americans who died per year from the effects of skin cancer was some 5,000 (interview with Dr. Tim Johnson on ABC television, April 10, 1978).

Carefully designed and controlled laboratory tests have clearly demonstrated the role played by UV-B in leading to skin cancer and have shown that the effects are augmented when both UV-A and UV-B are involved, which of course they are in the case of people and animals exposed to natural sunlight. It has also long been known that "white" skin will allow the penetration of ultraviolet radiation right down through the epidermis to the underlying dermis (Daniels, 1969; Kligman, 1969; Pathak and Stratton, 1969), but that the skin of well-tanned or naturally pigmented individuals will block up to 95 percent of the penetration of UV-B (Daniels et al., 1968:41; Holick, 1987:1879). And in the occasional person of African ancestry in whom a mutation has occurred that blocks the formation of skin pigment—a condition known as albinism—the skin will allow the penetration of ultraviolet radiation in the same manner as in "whites." African albinos are susceptible to skin cancer in the same manner as Europeans (Blum, 1959; Friedman et al., 1991:10). From the accumulation of the experimental and clinical evidence, it is impossible to avoid the conclusion that the sole function of melanin in the skin is as the first line of defense against the possible cancer-producing effects of ultraviolet radiation from the sun.

That being the case, the distribution of human skin pigmentation in the world should correspond to the distribution of the intensity of ultraviolet radiation, or, roughly speaking, to latitude: i.e., dark skin color should be concentrated in the tropics where it is adaptively advantageous. From Figure 11-3, it is clear that the dark-skinned populations of the world are all located in the tropics. However, it is also clear that not all tropic dwellers *are* dark skinned. The people of mainland Southeast Asia and most of island Indonesia plus the remote islands of Oceania are nowhere near so heavily pigmented as the indigenous populations of tropical Africa, southern India, New Guinea, or northern Australia. And finally, there were no indigenous dark-skinned people in the tropics of the western hemisphere.

The obvious reason for this apparent discrepancy is that the relatively light-skinned inhabitants now in those tropical regions must be comparatively recent arrivals. This suspicion is amply confirmed by the evidence available from history, linguistics, and archaeology (Benedict, 1942; Barth, 1952; Bellwood, 1979, 1986, 1991; Solheim, 1981; Bulbeck, 1982). Historical records, for example, show that there has been a continuing movement of peoples southward from the older centers of settled agriculture in China to what had been uncut forest lands in Southeast Asia. Even where there are no written records, the oral traditions of a northern origin and the trail of related languages all tend to confirm this general picture. The web of what is obviously recent linguistic divergence extends all the way out into the islands of the Pacific where archaeology tells us that settlers had reached the Philippines 5,000 years ago but had not gotten as far as Easter Island and Hawaii in Remote Oceania until about 1,500 years ago (Bellwood, 1986:107 ff., 1991; Pawley and Green, 1973; Tuggle, 1979:189).

As for the western hemisphere, though the crucial events occurred long before writing was thought of, and so far back that linguistic evidence is equivocal at best (Nichols, 1990:513; Greenberg and Ruhlen, 1992:94), archaeology tells us that the first inhabitants came over from the northeast edge of Asia by the end of the Pleistocene almost 12,000 years ago (Haynes, 1982:383; Hoffecker et al., 1993:51). The possibility still exists that people may have reached the New World somewhat earlier, but the signs are all tenuous and equivocal. From 11,500 years ago on, however, the evidence is clear and widespread, and it leaves most professional students of the matter with the reasonably comfortable feeling that the ancestors of the "Native Americans" did not arrive in the western hemisphere much before 12,000.

The ancestors of the modern inhabitants of the tropics in Southeast Asia, Polynesia, and South America all came from the nontropical portions of eastern Asia no earlier than the latter part of the Pleistocene. We can assume, then, that the skin color of those ancestors was not significantly different from that of the inhabitants of the temperate parts of eastern Asia today. The reason why they should have been characterized by that particular hue is a different matter that will be considered shortly. For the moment, however, what this tells us is that it takes a lot longer than 10,000 years for the selective effects of UV-B in tropical sunshine to produce the intensity of pigmentation seen in the skin of such modern people as the inhabitants of New Guinea or tropical Africa.

The related question is why people who live in the northern portions of the world have as little skin pigment as they do. All the available fossil and archaeological evidence indicates that ultimate human origins were in the tropics of Africa, and that even after spreading out from that base at the end of the lower Pleistocene a million years ago, humans remained tropic dwellers with only temporary northward forays for much of the rest of their existence (Brace, 1991b, and in press). Humans still have the basic physiological characteristics and responses of tropical mammals, and we can guess that the common tropic-dwelling human ancestor of half a million years ago had a degree of skin pigmentation fully comparable to that found today among the inhabitants of equatorial Africa, India, and New Guinea. This brings us back to the question of why some modern people are less heavily pigmented than others.

Since all of the long-term inhabitants of the north temperate zone are markedly less pigmented than long-term tropic dwellers, and since we can assume that the common human ancestor was dark, it follows that there must be something about living north of the tropics that leads to a reduction in skin pigment. There are in fact two possible explanations. One suggests that a lessening in the amount of pigment is adaptively advantageous in the north, and the other argues that depigmentation is simply the result of a reduction in the intensity of selection for the maintenance of epidermal melanin.

Those who prefer to see pigment reduction as the result of the positive action of selection point to the evidence indicating that heavily pigmented people are more likely to suffer the effects of vitamin D deficiency in the north temperate zone than is true for people with lesser amounts of skin pigment (Holick, 1987). As it happens, those very UV-B wave lengths that lead to skin cancer after prolonged doses are also an essential part of the process that leads to the synthesis of vitamin D. The absorption and incorporation of calcium necessary for proper bone growth is mediated by vitamin D, and a lack of that crucial substance will result in abnormalities and stunting of skeletal development known as rickets.

Rickets, however, is a distinct rarity among the cats, dogs, cows, horses, sheep, rodents, birds, and others of the animal world that were native inhabitants of the north temperate zone in spite of the fact that few if any indulged themselves with codfish livers and that the skin in all of these creatures is well protected from any possible ultraviolet penetration by virtue of being thoroughly covered by fur or feathers. There is one more oddity about this whole picture, and this is the fact that there is no pigment in the skin of those thoroughly protected creatures. And finally, it only requires a brief exposure to generate all the vitamin D one needs, and summer sunshine in the north temperate zone is more than adequate even for heavily pigmented skin to provide a supply of vitamin D that can be stored up in fat and muscle tissue in sufficient quantities to last the rest of the year (Robins, 1991:203, 205, 208).

From my perspective, it would seem that the reason for the absence of pigment in the skin of most furred and feathered creatures is the absence of selection for its presence. And I would argue that the same thing may well be true for the human inhabitants of the north temperate zone. Since there is just not enough intensity of UV-B to generate cancers that would shorten possible life spans, there was nothing that would maintain skin pigment at the level which had characterized the tropical forebears of the long-term human inhabitants of the north. A generation ago, I argued that when selection is reduced or suspended, any trait that had been maintained by a formerly active selective force should undergo reduction in proportion to the length of time that selection had been held in abeyance. Under such conditions, the reductions would be the results of mutations alone—a process I referred to as "The Probable Mutation Effect" (Brace, 1963—reprinted here as Chapter 5, "Structural Reduction in Evolution").

A more detailed defense of the "PME" is presented elsewhere (Brace et al., 1991:41–46, and included here as Chapter 6, "What Big Teeth You Had, Grandma!"). Here we need only note that those areas where the archaeological evidence indicates that human habitation of the north temperate zone has been continuous for the longest periods of time are also just those areas where modern human populations display the least amount of pigment in the skin. In a zone running from the Middle East to the Atlantic Ocean in northwest Europe, there is reason to believe that human habitation has been continuous for the last 250,000 years (Straus, 1989; Mercier et al., 1992). It is in just that stretch where the living inhabitants include people with the least amount of pigmentation among the living populations of the world.

At comparable latitudes in the northeast end of human occupation in the Old World, the continuous archaeological record is only about half as old. From this, it would follow that relaxation of selective pressures to maintain skin pigmentation at fully tropical levels has been in effect only half as long, and depigmentation should not have proceeded to the same extent as in the comparable latitudes in the West. Indeed, the modern inhabitants of Northeast Asia are notably less pigmented than the populations who have continued to live in the tropics without break, but pigment reduction has not proceeded to quite the same extent as that visible at the northwestern edge of the human range.

Actually, it does not matter which attempt at explanation is correct since both propose reasons why pigment reduction should occur in areas where ultraviolet radiation is markedly reduced from the levels of its intensity in the tropics. Either would account for the existence and extent of depigmentation in the north temperate zones both east and west in the Old World, and both offer reasons why the relatively recent movement of people from the latitude of China south into Southeast Asia and equatorial Indonesia introduced people with lesser amounts of skin pigmentation than one would otherwise expect to find for people living in the tropics.

At the same time, the movement of agriculturally based populations out of the Middle East during the Neolithic and Bronze Age was predominantly an East-to-West phenomenon rather than a North-to-South one (Brace and Tracer, 1992). The result was that the North-to-South gradation or cline in skin color was not disrupted. To this day, skin color grades by imperceptible means from Europe southward around the eastern end of the Mediterranean and up the Nile into Africa. From one end of this range to the other, there is no hint of a skin color boundary, and yet the spectrum runs from the lightest in the world at the northern edge to as dark as it is possible for humans to be at the equator.

South of the equator, the cline reverses, and skin color becomes lighter away from the tropics toward the south. In Africa, this lightening is more pronounced than the comparable case in Australia, and the aboriginal inhabitants of the southern tip of Africa—the San people once called by the derogatory term "Bushmen"—are no darker than the people by the shores of the Mediterranean who are about the same distance north of the equator as the San are south of it. Skin pigment also lightens toward the south in Australia, but not quite to the same extent as in the African example. Australia, however, has only been occupied for the last 50,000 years (Roberts et al., 1990), and evidently the process of pigment reduction has not had time enough to proceed to the extent evident at the comparable latitudes in Africa.

From all of this, it can be seen that human skin pigmentation is distributed in clinal fashion among those people who have remained in the latitudes where they are found for a period of time on the order of 50,000 years or more. Where skin pigmentation is at variance with our expectations of clinal variation such as Southeast Asia and the New World, we have reason to suspect that such anomalies in human appearance are due to population movements within the last 20,000 years or so. So far, all such suspected instances are confirmed by the available archaeological evidence.

Finally, it is clear that the distributions shown in Figures 11-2 and 11-3 are following different sets of rules. Evidently neither one can be understood if one uses the old-fashioned concept of "race" as a starting point, and yet both display vital but unrelated aspects of human biological variation. Each evidently is clinal in nature, but the clines have little to do with each other. Each can be readily understood when studied separately, but the pattern made by the intersection between these two has no "meaning" in and of itself. And when one adds a third trait or a fourth or more, the configurations that emerge tell us nothing whatsoever about the nature and significance of human biological variation.

Tooth Size

The third trait that I am going to deal with is tooth size. It is neither more instructive nor in other ways "better" than any other trait one could use, but it serves the purpose, and I can use the information that I have been collecting myself for the past several decades to demonstrate the nature of modern human tooth size differences.

There has long been a vague kind of perception on the part of European observers that "other races" had larger jaws and teeth than those found in Europe. Along with this perception of greater size in jaw and tooth was a related assumption of smaller size of head and brain. These were interpreted in a hierarchical fashion which assumed European superiority as a given, and the mere presence of a large dentition automatically led to the conclusion that the associated brain was therefore smaller and that the position of the possessor in the world was consequently "lower." None other than the eminent nineteenth century biologist and defender of Darwin, Thomas Henry Huxley, declared that "no rational man...believes that the average negro is the equal, still less the superior, of the average white man." He went on to say that "it is simply incredible that...our prognathous relative...will be able to compete successfully with his bigger-brained and smaller-jawed rival, in a contest which is to be carried on by thoughts and not by bites" (Huxley, 1865:561).

Before I go on to deal with tooth size and the circumstances that relate to size differences between human populations, I should first dispel the idea that large teeth entail small brains. There is absolutely no relationship between brain size and tooth size (Brace et al., 1991:37). As with other traits of adaptive value, the selective forces appropriate to the control of one are completely unrelated to the forces responsible for the control of the other. People do not chew with their brains or think with their teeth. Consequently, variation in one trait is completely unrelated to variation in the other. Second, there is absolutely nothing to sustain the idea that "other" people have smaller brains than Europeans. When brain size is corrected for body size, there is no demonstrable difference between any of the populations of the world (Jensen, 1984:54-55; Brace et al.. 1991:37—i.e., Chapter 6).

If Huxley was wrong in his assumption that the African brain is significantly smaller than the European brain, he was quite correct in his recognition of the fact that Europeans have smaller jaws and teeth. Oddly enough, that "fact" had not been demonstrated by any systematic quantitative study before he produced his declaration, and very little attention has been devoted to the matter since that time. As it happens, the issue of tooth-size differences between human populations past and present has been largely ignored by the dental and anthropological sciences.

No living human population has teeth that are as large on the average as their predecessors in the Middle Pleistocene, so it is evident that dental reduction has taken place over the last 100,000 years or more in the lines that have led to all of the regional human inhabitants of the world. Reduction has amounted to at least 40–45 percent in those who live in the north temperate zone between Europe and the Middle East. This is the maximum amount of dental reduction visible in modern *Homo sapiens,* though it is equaled in spots in eastern Asia such as Hong Kong and the northern island of Hokkaido in Japan. The least amount of reduction is evident in Australia where it runs between 10 and 15 percent (Brace, 1980). In sub-Saharan Africa, the amount of reduction in the groups in the Congo Basin and in West Africa with the largest jaws and teeth is around 25 percent, but it runs up to 40 percent in the Horn of East Africa.

The documented reductions in the dentition have all taken place as "archaic" human form—what I would call regional representatives of the Neanderthal Stage—becomes transformed into "modern" *Homo sapiens* (Brace, 1991b:170; 1994). We are not accustomed to thinking of the Neanderthals as cultural innovators, but the very real possibility exists that they may have been "the ones who pioneered the use of cooking as a regular means of preparing food" (Brace, 1991b:155). Survival in the north during the onset of glacial conditions depended on the control of fire. Among other things, there would have been no point in going to the trouble of bringing down a large Pleistocene prey animal if the thing would become unusable within a day or so by virtue of having frozen solid. "Obligatory cooking" (Brace, 1994a and b), then, was a part of the cultural traditions of those who survived through the last two glacial maxima along the northwestern edge of human habitation in the Old World, and it has been suggested that the extensive hearth residues that characterized the Mousterian sites occupied by the Neanderthals were actually the remains of earth ovens in which they regularly thawed the products of the chase simply in order to make them edible (Brace and Montagu, 1977:335–336; Brace, 1978:214, 1979:545–546, 1992:16–17; Brace et al., 1987:713–714, 1991:46–51).

Cooking not only made it possible to eat what previously had been frozen, but it reduced the amount of chewing necessary to get anything so treated into swallowable consistency. The regular use of cooking, then, reduced the amount of mandatory chewing. A reduction in the amount of tooth use over a lifetime meant that teeth did not wear out quite so fast, and also that a person did not need quite such a large dentition to be able to survive for the otherwise expectable human span. Under such conditions, mutations affecting tooth size could accumulate without being automatically weeded out by selection, and, since most such mutations produce a reduction in size, the predictable long-term results would be dental diminution. Today, the largest number of the people with the smallest teeth in the world are those who live in that stretch that runs from the Middle East through to the Atlantic Coast of Western Europe—just that area where the cooking of food has been in continuous use for the longest period of time.

Figure 11-4 shows a crude picture of relative tooth size among the modern populations of the Old World. The reader will remember that it was in just that stretch running from the Middle East to the west and north that pigment reduction began earliest and has gone to its greatest extent. Pigment, however, is related to the intensity of ultraviolet radiation, and teeth are only related to the nature of the tasks required to process food. Of course, food is more likely to freeze in areas of limited solar radiation, so there is a degree to

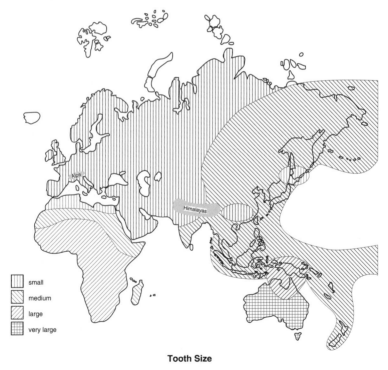

small

medium

large

very large

Tooth Size

Figure 11-4 The distribution of human tooth size among the populations of the Old World. A sampling of those data is reported in Brace et al. (1991).

which the value of maintaining skin pigmentation and the value of maintaining a dentition that could cope with uncooked food covary to a certain extent. Some of this is apparent when Figure 11-4 is compared with Figure 11-3, but it is also apparent that there are areas where the traits are completely uncorrelated.

The evident value of cooking at northern latitudes meant that it spread into the northeastern areas more readily than it did to the south. Dental reduction then followed suit, and tooth size in Eastern Asia followed the same track that it had taken starting somewhat earlier in the northwestern parts of the Old World. Eventually, of course, it spread south because, though it was not necessary to thaw food in the tropics, the repeated application of heat to the ripening results of a previous kill could partially delay and counteract the noxious effects of the various microorganisms that would otherwise render the decaying products of earlier hunting activities unfit for human consumption.

Cooking was adopted last in Australia, and dental reduction is least evident among the aborigines who were encountered by the Europeans who settled there over the last two centuries. Earth oven cookery had spread to Australia perhaps before the end of the Pleistocene, but, in any case, the kind of reduction in chewing stress that it represented got into Australia later than anywhere else in the world. Not only that, but it spread slowly south in the continent and never did get to Tasmania before the terminal Pleistocene rise in sea level turned it into an island. As a consequence, there is a tooth-size gradient in Australia running from the North down to the South where people had the largest-sized teeth of any living human beings. Even so, tooth size had begun to reduce from the Middle Pleistocene–sized levels that were displayed only 10,000 years ago (Brace, 1980:147).

Some of that recent reduction may have been as a result of gene flow from areas to the north where reduction had already taken place, but some may have been because of the relaxation of selection that followed the adoption of cooking techniques. At the moment, it is not possible to say how much of which led to that recent reduction. In any case, the pigment cline is reversed and skin color in the south lightens in just those areas where tooth size gets to its maximum. This is just another instance of the general principle that separate traits will respond to the changes in the intensity of the selective force that is responsible for their individual manifestation, and that each will go its own way without regard to what any other trait is doing unless that other trait is responding to that self-same selective force.

Late in the overall picture of dental reduction, another event occurred which completely changed things as far as the teeth were concerned. This was the invention of pottery. Archaeological reputations have been made and lost as a result of the analysis of pottery, but few have noted what the presence of the humble pot meant to the inventors and users. It meant that teeth were no longer necessary at all. Of course, we dearly enjoy the process of chewing the culinary delights that we savor, and we tend to think that the toothless are less attractive than those who are dentally well-endowed, but as soon as pots became available it was possible to reduce nourishment to drinkable consistency. From that point on, the edentulous could survive as well as anybody else. Since selection for the maintenance of tooth size all but ceased at that point, one would predict that recent human tooth size reduction should have accelerated to its maximum. From the evidence available from the several places in the world where pottery had more or less independent beginnings, this indeed appears to be the case.

For various reasons, that post-Pleistocene change has been entirely overlooked in the anthropological world, and we still hear that somewhat self-satisfied statement that once "modern man" had emerged, maybe 35,000 years ago, all biological evolution ceased and the only subsequent changes were in the cultural realm (R. Leakey in Fisher, 1983:145; Diamond, 1990:26; Klein, 1992:12). A quick perusal of the actual evidence, however, shows that this is simply not so. Not only have jaws and teeth undergone a change of up to 20 percent since that time, but there has been an equally clear-cut reduction in the indications for muscularity and robustness in the postcranial skeleton as well. Cultural change certainly has been important. In fact, it was the reduction in environmentally imposed selective forces created by those very cultural developments that led to the changes visible in the human physique.

When other genetically controlled aspects of human variation are mapped, they also tend to show unrelated distributions that are as independent of each other as those shown in Figures 11-2, 11-3, and 11-4. For example, when aspects of the common variance in the expression of some 95 genes are plotted on a world map in terms of principal component loadings, the distributions of the first three components are completely independent of each other (Cavalli-Sforza et al., 1993). One such map will show the greatest intensity of loadings in Africa with decreasing effects strictly proportional to distance. The authors have chosen to regard this as indications of an actual migration out of Africa at an unknown date in the past with modern differences being proportional to the time of separation. Another such map plotting the next independent residuum of common variance shows the greatest intensity of loadings in South America with decreases proportional to distance from that spot. Again, this distribution is presumed to illustrate the results of migration. The same is assumed to be true for plots of the remaining independent residuals of common variance.

The problem with trying to invoke migration as the explanation for such gradients in the manifestations of genetic likeness is that, while it might work to explain an initial distribution, the traces of that pattern would be completely altered by just one later migration from a separate center. The independent and noncoincident patterns of genetic distributions can only be the results of the operations of unrelated selective force gradients and the further complications added by genetic drift. At the moment, it is impossible to say how much of which has contributed to the picture of independent regional manifestations of genetic difference shown by the separate principal component maps. The only thing we can say for certain is that migrations cannot possibly be invoked to explain the distributions observed, and that the pattern is completely compatible with what would be expected if separate and unrelated selective force gradients were involved.

Intelligence

Of all the traits that have played a role in ensuring the survival and success of *Homo sapiens* as a species, innate brain power clearly must be accorded a position of prime importance. Just as the order Primates as a whole is distinguished from the rest of the animal kingdom by a greater average degree of intelligence and a corresponding expansion of the organ from which that emanates—the brain—so humans transcend their Primate relatives in this regard by yet another order of magnitude (Donald, 1991:98–100). The human brain underwent a near-threefold expansion from the essentially chimpanzee-sized brain of our Australopithecine ancestors 1.5 to 2.0 million years ago. It stands to reason, then, that this illustrates the results of the continuing effects of strong forces selecting for the increase in intelligence. One might also think it logical that intelligence in the human world would be distributed in a manner analogous to that of other traits under strong selective force control, that is, not in terms of population boundaries but according to the pattern of distribution of the relevant selective force. As we shall see, this is probably not the case. There are unexpectedly difficult problems involved in assessing both the selective forces involved and the nature of the distribution of intelligence.

Unfortunately, "intelligence" is another of those words like "race" that people use with glib facility but which proves to be extremely hard to define. I am not going to offer my own definition because it would be just another in a list that is as long as the number of people involved in comparing themselves to others. At bottom, "intelligence" is a completely subjective category. It has no clearly identifiable reality like a pigment or a hemoglobin molecule, and it has no tangible measurable form like a tooth. Its existence as a category at all is an example of the creative capacity inherent in one of the most powerful tools at human disposal—language. The words we use are analogues of a real world that is vastly more graded and complicated than our verbal rendition. Of course we gain much of our power to deal with the infinite complexities of that graded reality by reducing it to a finite and manageable linguistic analogue. However, the danger always exists that our linguistic simplifications may just create categories where none really exist. "Race" clearly is an example of just that. "Intelligence" comes close to being another.

One of the problems stems from the essentially subjective way in which we perceive the phenomenon. Virtually all living human beings compare themselves to the people with whom they interact on what they perceive as a scale of relative cleverness. We all are perfectly convinced that we can assess relative intellectual ability, and each of us uses our own capacities as the basic yardstick. Consequently there are as many standards as there are individuals involved in the debate. Nor have the professional scholars involved in the assessment of intelligence provided much assistance. Possibly the most opaque and unhelpful nondescription ever offered was the one coined by the distinguished psychologist Edwin G. Boring: "Intelligence is what the tests test" (Boring, 1923:35). That simply expands the possible scales of measurement beyond the number of individuals doing the evaluating by the amount of tests that professional ingenuity can concoct.

It has long been realized that the increase in brain size during the evolution of the mammals was certainly related to an increase in intelligence (Radinsky, 1967, 1979). In parallel fashion, the increase in human brain size from the Pliocene through the Middle Pleistocene was also evidence of the increase in intelligence (Van Valen, 1974). Relative brain size between living species also is associated with degrees of intelligence (Brace and Brace, 1976). With this as a general background, there has been a repeated attempt to associate differences in brain size between the living human populations with differences in their intellectual abilities.

Before the American Civil War, the claim was made that the institution of slavery was justifiable on the basis of supposed differences in brain size and intelligence between African Americans and European Americans (Nott, 1849:35–36, 1858:77; Nott and Gliddon, 1854). There are still psychologists who maintain that "among humans, crude brain size does have some relation to intelligence" (Rushton, 1984:12), and that the best way to determine a person's intelligence is to "take a tape measure, put it around people's heads, [and] measure the head circumference" (Rushton, 1989).

The thing that is left out of these attempts to assess the relative brain power of living members of the same species is any correction for body size. From my own measurements of the crania of samples representing all of the major living populations of the world, I can show that the average difference between the largest and smallest heads is not significantly different from the average difference between male and female brain case size. In the latter instance in any given population, the male/female size difference is entirely in proportion to the difference in body size.

If one is going to argue that larger head size within a single species such as *Homo sapiens* really indicates greater intellectual power, then one will also have to support the proposition that, on the average, men are smarter than women. There is absolutely nothing to sustain such a conclusion, and the suspicion arises that those who are continuing to pursue research relating to the average "racial" differences in brain size are simply engaging in an exercise in applied bigotry.

Conscientious scholars in the intelligence-evaluation business have devoted much effort and ingenuity to the process of making intelligence tests "culture-free" or "fair" in a variety of ways, and one such has written a ponderous tome filled with numbers and formulae called *Bias in Mental Testing* (Jensen, 1980). The basic assumption behind that work is that bias can be eliminated by proper procedural means. Beyond the subjectivity inherent in the assessment of individuals, however, there is the added problem associated with evaluations projected on whole groups. Professionals involved in the testing of intelligence simply accept the biological reality of "race" in the first place and go on to presume that it is reasonable that "racial" differences in intelligence are simply there to be discovered (Jensen, 1969a:80, 1969b:14; Neary, 1970:62). This is nothing less than bias itself, and no amount of statistical manipulation can eliminate it. Although it is presented with all the trappings of serious scientific scholarship, it is just a gussied-up version of the universal ethnocentric assumption held by every living human society that "we" are better than "they."

In equally simplistic fashion, the further assumption has been gratuitously added that intelligence is the ability to adapt to "civilization," and that "races" differ in intellectual ability in conjunction with the civilizations with which they are associated. This was one of the undocumented items of faith at the core of the Eugenics movement early in the century (Popenoe and Johnson, 1918:285, 292), and it was shared with equally unjustified enthusiasm by the contemporary supporters of geographic determinism (Huntington, 1915, 1924:1). One recent advocate of such a view feels that the Stanford-Binet I.Q. test measures the inherent ability to adapt to "Western civilization" (Jensen, 1969b:14).

Nothing could better illustrate the dangers of making judgments about the relative worth of whole populations in the absence of the basic facts than potentially harmful and certainly irresponsible claims such as that. As we have seen above, even a relatively simple and clearly adaptive trait such as skin color shows only minimal response to alterations in selective force intensity that have been in effect for no more than 10,000 to 15,000 years. Our vaunted "Western civilization" has a time depth of only a small fraction of that span, and most of those who now reap its benefits are descended from ancestors who, only a few centuries back, were peasant farmers untrained in the niceties of reading and writing.

Even more to the point, there is not a single society in the world today that pursues a way of life like that of its ancestors 10,000 years ago. Even the few groups who lived by hunting and gathering until quite recently have all acquired steel tips for their spears and arrows, steel knives and axes, plastic containers, synthetic fiber cordage, and firearms. Given the pace at which selection works on something as elusively complex as intelligence, a much more plausible case could be made for the view that virtually no living population is mentally adapted to the society with which it is now associated.

Now turn things around and look at them from the perspective of the conditions under which our mental capacities actually were shaped. Ten thousand years ago, agriculture had yet to be invented. There were no sedentary farming communities, and subsistence was gained by foraging for what could be acquired by hunting and gathering activities. From that point on back for the previous million to 1.5 million years, hunting and gathering was the common heritage shared by all human beings. Surely it was that long-term situation which played the major controlling role in shaping human intellectual capabilities.

Of course, objections have been raised that the environment and the availability of specific resources was radically different in the disparate parts of the world. The geographic determinists of two or three generations ago were fond of contrasting the supposedly indolent life in the tropics where goodies were available for the plucking from a plethora of fruiting trees and bushes with what was purported to be the bracing rigor of more northerly climes where survival was said to depend more on ingenuity and disciplined effort.

Aside from the lesser chance of freezing to death, however, there is virtually no evidence to suggest that it is any easier to gain a living by gleaning from the land in the tropics than it is in the temperate portions of the world. The knowledge of what is edible and what is not, what ripens where at which time of the year, and the detailed habits of potential prey animals is every bit as difficult to come by at the equator as in the North. Wherever professional scientists have had extensive contacts with local populations who live off the land—whether it be Eskimos in the arctic, Australian aborigines in the "outback," or the inhabitants of the New Guinea highlands barely south of the equator—they have come away with the realization that the people they have gotten to know all understand their local natural history with a sophistication and detail that is fully the equivalent of what would be required of a doctoral candidate defending a Ph.D. dissertation on aspects of the area in question. In the preliterate world of the hunter-gatherer, evidently the penalty for stupidity is starvation.

Nothing can illustrate this point more graphically than the saga of the elderly Australian who led his group on a six-month trek to escape the consequences of the drought of 1943 in the outback of Western Australia. His first goal was the fallback waterhole at the extreme northwestern corner of the tribal territory which he had visited only once in his youth more than half a century earlier. When the resources there started to fail, he led them off westwards again through territory known to him only through the verses of a song cycle sung at totemic ceremonies and depicting the legendary wanderings of "ancestral beings." The trek led on through a sequence of more than 50 waterholes until the little band finally emerged at Mandora Station on the coast of Western Australia more than 600 kilometers from where they had started (Birdsell, 1979:147–148). If he had been wrong just once in his sequence, that would have been it for the whole group. Evidently the "myths" that constituted those tribal ceremonies actually represented the transmitted knowledge of previous generations, and, as the story shows, this could literally be of life or death significance. One would be hard put to come up with any instance in the literate world where survival was so directly dependent upon such a feat of human memory.

In their reliance on a major hunting element in their subsistence activities, ancestral humans depended on a most un-Primate-like kind of behavior. Even for those other Primates that occasionally catch and eat animal prey, there are none in which this kind of behavior is essential to their very survival. Prehistoric human beings, on the other hand, clearly relied on the products of the chase for their survival. And yet our basic anatomy gives almost no hint of a capacity for successful hunting activities. There is not a trace of specialization toward effective capture and disabling of prey to be found in the shape and the size of our teeth, and human locomotor capabilities are such that we cannot outrun anything larger than a rabbit.

Finally, human beings exploit a spectrum of plant foods that is orders of magnitude beyond the list relied on by even our cleverest nonhuman relatives. A fair portion of these would be of no value unless subjected to extensive preparation prior to ingestion. Human beings are the only creatures that cook their food, but, beyond that, no other animal has made more than the most rudimentary start at the ingenious roster of peeling, shelling, pounding, grating, grinding, soaking, leaching, and the many other techniques that people have used to render some of the most unlikely items capable of yielding nourishment.

Surely it is these accomplishments and the capabilities that made them possible that are behind the successful spread of humans into such an extraordinary variety of locales. The ingenuity necessary to extract sustenance in the most unlikely areas and by the most unlikely means was an essential element in the human success story. That ingenuity was certainly taxed by the need to maintain a network of supportive relationships and deal with potential human competitors. It had to have been a combination of these factors that constituted the selective pressures that led to the expansion of the human brain starting at the beginning of the Pleistocene 2 million years ago.

These circumstances, however, were a constant for human beings pursuing a hunting and gathering mode of subsistence at any time during the Pleistocene and throughout the length and breadth of their occupation. With the nature of selection for intellectual development held constant, the response should have been a constant also. Under such circumstances, there should have been no differential response. This is why human intelligence, though an adaptive trait of utmost importance, should not be expected to have a clinal distribution. If there is one faint exception to the expectation that there should be no significant difference between the intellectual capabilities of any of the human populations living in the world today, it would be of a most unexpected nature. It is a common prejudice of representatives of groups with long and sophisticated written traditions to regard their nonliterate contemporaries with a kind of self-satisfied contempt. The denigrations run from regarding such people as "barbarians" or "benighted savages" to evaluations that barely consider them human. Almost invariably, their manifestations of what is considered to be cultural inferiority are assumed to be innate, and they are consigned to a state of genetically determined intellectual inferiority.

On the other hand, as the previously mentioned Australian saga abundantly demonstrated, it surely requires more basic smarts to survive in a world where one cannot go and look up the answers to crucial questions in a book. For those of us who can consult reference works in a library, it is simply less important that we keep that information stored in our heads. It is just possible, then, that those whose ancestry has the longest continuous tie with literate civilization are the recipients of a heritage where selection for intelligence has been least stringent. Now recall that the rationale of the Probable Mutation Effect suggests that where the strength of selection maintaining a given trait is relaxed, there should be a consequent reduction in that trait itself. If indeed there is any difference in intelligence among the living populations of the world, then the greatest innate wit should be found among those who have most recently emerged from a nonliterate past.

No representatives of a tradition of continuous literacy, however, have been able to enjoy its benefits for much more than 5,000 years at the most. As we have been able to see, tooth size may have changed as much as 5 percent during that time, but that figure is so close to measurement error that we cannot take it as proof of real biological difference. And no discernible skin color difference has arisen during that time even though some populations have moved into areas where selection operating over much longer periods of time has produced highly visible consequences. Therefore, even though the PME suggests that there might be a slight difference in intellectual capability between living human groups in the opposite direction from that so commonly assumed, the problems associated with assessing the amount of innate intelligence both within and between human populations are so sticky that it is unlikely that we shall ever be able to put such a possibility to the test. At the moment, we have no reason to suspect that there are any group-specific differences in intelligence, and we have no way to test for them even if we did.

CLUSTERS

There are other traits that are distributed according to the graded effects of the selective forces that influence their appearance. The relative length of the lower arm and leg in proportion to the upper arm and leg, and limb length in proportion to trunk length, are related to conditions of heat and cold. Average length and elevation of the nose on its part is related to the relative lack of moisture in the air. With the sole exception of intelligence, which is equally important everywhere and consequently everywhere the same, it would seem that every trait that is really important for human survival is distributed in conjunction with the intensity of the controlling selective force, and that these on their part are distributed completely without regard for human population boundaries.

From this it follows that the traits which are distributed across population boundaries as though they did not exist are the only ones that have real biological significance, while those that are constrained by population boundaries have no differential survival value. Although the more orthodox of R. A. Fisher's followers still feel that we are obliged to assume that every biological trait is determined by a controlling selective force even if we cannot figure out what that might be, others are increasingly coming to the realization that there are many configurations that have no particular adaptive value in and of themselves. Those who have claimed that the failure to find adaptive meaning in certain traits is simply due to limitations in our powers of understanding have been called "hyperselectionists" and compared to "foolish Dr. Pangloss" of Voltaire's eighteenth century satire *Candide* (Gould and Lewontin, 1979; Gould, 1980:40). In Dr. Pangloss's philosophy, "all is for the best in this the best of all possible worlds," even if it is beyond our capacity to understand what might be good about it.

As disaster after disaster befell the unfortunate Candide, it became quite apparent that there was not always some unappreciated "good" behind the events of the world. In like fashion, it is evident that many biological configurations are that way just because of chance circumstances and not because of any unappreciated benefit conferred on their possessors. This realization had been reinforced by the discovery that there are substantial sequences of DNA in the genome that are just there and serve no functional purpose—"junk DNA," in the words of one geneticist (Ohno, 1972).

In the absence of selective force control, certain variants may increase or decrease in frequency in various regions simply by chance. The process referred to by Sewall Wright as "genetic drift" can produce local differences in inherited features particularly where the populations are relatively small and partially isolated from their neighbors—circumstances that were generally the rule for the human condition prior to the advent of agriculture (Wright, 1943). The significant expansion in numbers by those groups that adopted a farming mode of subsistence subsequently established certain of those chance local variants as the characteristic regional morphological conformation in the various areas where agriculture had led to that notable expansion in population size. The ensuing perpetuation of identifiable regional configurations then occurred for the simple reason that the pattern was already present—not because it conveyed any particular adaptive advantage.

We can identify many such aspects of morphology associated with the configuration of the heads and faces of people in various parts of the world. Some of these coexist with features that are legitimately under selective force control, and we have to make an effort to separate the two categories. For example, nasal form in the long-term inhabitants of the colder portions of the world runs to the high-bridged and elongate. The Native Americans in the northernmost portions of the New World were famous for having noses that were just as prominent as those of northern Europeans. However, in the other details of the face—for instance, the jut of the cheekbones and the relative forward placement of the lateral borders of the eye sockets—they were quite distinct from characteristic European form though they could not be differentiated from the positioning of cheekbones and lateral orbital margins of the living people of northeast Asia.

Nasal form is adaptive and responds to the forces of selection, but there is nothing particularly adaptive about nuances of cheekbone form or shape of the eye socket. What possible advantage could it be to have high rounded eye sockets as opposed to low wide rectangular ones (Brace and Hunt, 1990:344)? And why would it be better to have cheekbones that are hollowed out below the lower margin of the orbit as opposed to ones that drop straight down to present the appearance of a relatively flat face? Differences in the details of facial form of this nature are clearly associated with different regions of the world, but it is hard to see the faintest reason why any one should be any "better" than any other. And yet each region shows a continuity running from the present back into the past to the point where general morphology ceases to look "modern." In fact, some of those very aspects of cheekbone and eye socket morphology that show different configurations in different regions of the world today were also characteristic of facial form for the archaic inhabitants of the same parts of the world going back into the Middle Pleistocene.

The same sort of thing is true for the form of the rest of the skull. For example, the characteristic general cranial shape at the northwest edge of Europe is long and low with a tendency toward the presence of a marked bulge or "bun" at the rear, while the characteristic form in eastern Europe is toward a skull that is short, wide, and almost flat behind (Brace, 1991a). But, again, there is absolutely no reason why one such shape is "better" than another, and, despite undocumented claims to the contrary (Cavalli-Sforza et al., 1993:641), no possible set of selective forces can be imagined that would have led to the special development of either one. It really does not matter what shape the brain case takes so long as it is large enough to encompass the brain. At best, we are left to assume that the different local patterns were simply the products of genetic drift (Lynch, 1989:13). Once established, these are perpetuated because that is what the local gene pool has to contribute to subsequent generations.

What is true for so many aspects of the bones of the head is also the case for many of the details of its fleshy covering. The external shape of the eye opening differs from one human population to another. For example, it is widely recognized that people of eastern Asian ancestry are likely to display a particular and recognizable configuration. However, there is no evidence that it has any effect whatsoever on the ability to see. At one time, it was suggested that the people of eastern Asia had been shaped by prolonged exposure to intense cold during the last glaciation, and that this led to the developments of eyelid form that played a protective role (Coon et al., 1950:71). However, the ancestors of Europeans survived the effects of the last two glaciations without ever developing the eyelid form characteristic of modern eastern Asians, and there is no indication that the characteristic form of the European eye opening puts them at any disadvantage even when subject to prolonged exposure to conditions of intense cold. The form of the external ear also differs in characteristic fashion from region to region. But again, there is virtually no evidence to suggest that there is an associated difference in the ability to hear or that selection is involved. And the same thing can be said for the fleshy portions of the lips and nose.

It is by an appraisal of features such as these that we can recognize the portion of the world to which the ancestors of a given person are likely to have belonged. When we take a standard set of measurements on representatives of people from all parts of the world, the different samples will show patterns of regional association. All the samples from a given region will cluster with each other as opposed to samples from another region unless, of course, a given sample actually is composed of migrants from somewhere else. When that is the case, the migrant sample will cluster with samples from the region from which it originally came.

In an effort to create a picture of clusters for all of the major regions of the world, I have made measurements on crania from as many samples as I could get access to over the last dozen years. These were then converted into standard scores as Howells recommended (Howells, 1986). Sample means were compared by an unweighted pair grouping method analysis (UPGMA) and used to create a Euclidean Distance dendrogram (Romesburg, 1984:15; Brace and Hunt, 1990:347). This is the same procedure that was used to generate the pattern shown in Figure 11-1.

When samples from all over the world were treated in this fashion, the picture that emerged is that seen in Figure 11-5. At that, it is greatly simplified from the much larger cluster diagram that was generated when I used more than twice as many groups as are depicted in Figure 11-5. Even so, it is obvious that the samples from each region tend to cluster with each other. When the various samples from each region were merged with their nearest neighbors so that only a single pooled group was left and a Euclidean Distance dendrogram was produced, what emerged was the picture seen in Figure 11-6. In this, the individual twigs stand for the regional clusters from which they were formed and can be called by the name of the region with which it is associated.

So we can refer to an African cluster, an East Asian cluster, a European cluster, and so forth. It would be a mistake to say that this is just another name for "race," since nothing held in common by the members of any cluster allows us to say anything about the adaptations of its components. The only thing that ties members of a given cluster together is the common inheritance of traits of no adaptive value whatsoever. A cluster by its very nature

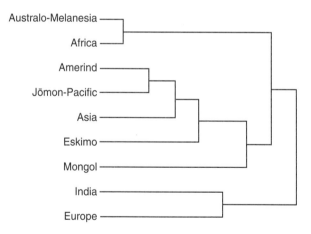

Figure 11-5 A cluster diagram showing the relationships of samplings from the major regions of the world. The measurements used, and the samples, are reported in Brace and Hunt (1990) and Brace and Tracer (1992). Variable transformation procedures were those used in Li et al. (1991) and Brace and Tracer (1992), while the cluster algorithm is the same as that used to generate Figure 10-1.

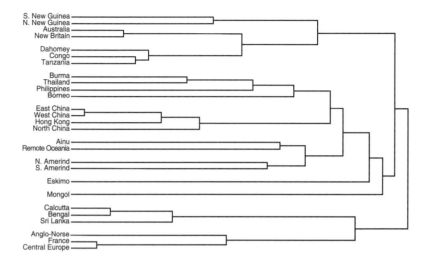

Figure 11-6 A cluster diagram constructed by merging samples of each region to generate separate branches representing the cluster associated with each of the major geographic regions of the world. The procedure is the same as that used to generate Figures 11-1 and 11-5. The Mongols were left in, not because they represent a "major geographic region," but simply to reinforce the point that they cannot be used to typify the inhabitants of eastern Asia.

cannot be assessed in terms of ability, intelligence, resistance to disease, or anything else that could be placed on a hierarchy of value since the only thing that holds a cluster together in an analytical sense is the complete triviality of the traits by which it is defined.

Nor is there any significance to the mean figures calculated by generating the central tendencies of the clusters as is done to construct Figure 11-6. It is important to note that those "central tendencies" do not reflect any kind of "essence" or aspect of common variance. The farther away from the center of a geographic region one goes, the less the peripheral members of that cluster share with the others in an opposite direction and the more they share with members of the immediately adjacent geographic region. Major regional cluster names, then, are simply convenient labels for describing people who differ in utterly unimportant ways. The convenience offered by geographic names is that there is no possible loading with the hint of the often covert implications included when descriptive or ethnic labels are used. Finally, geographic names can be easily amended by directional modifiers. Asia can be sharpened by specifying Central Asia, Western Asia, South Asia, Southeast Asia, and the like. The same is also true for the other major clusters such as Africa, Amerind, Australia, Europe, Pacific-Ainu, and Siberia-Eskimo.

CONCLUSIONS

Where *Homo sapiens* is concerned, the concept of "race" does not correspond to any biological entity. Not only does it have at least as many flaws as the concept of subspecies (Wilson and Brown, 1953; Brown and Wilson, 1954), but it also has been invoked as a platform for the purpose of sustaining invidious value judgments that stem largely from unwarranted prejudice. Its existence arises entirely from the human tendency to categorize when dealing with what is perceived to be the nature of the world. In this case, the category "race" is a misperception of the reality of human biological variation.

That variation exists, and it is real and significant. However, those aspects that have arisen in response to the effects of natural selection cannot be perceived or understood if we take popularly assumed "races" as our starting points. Only by tracing the distribution of each trait separately can we discern its association with the relevant selective force. Since selective forces themselves have distributions that are unrelated to human population boundaries, traits that are under selective force control, and hence that are biologically significant, will also be distributed without relation to those human population boundaries. More than one modern anthropologist has clearly perceived these matters and treated them with admirable sophistication (Bermann, 1992; Sauer, 1992).

Where traits are constrained by human population boundaries, the dynamics by which they are controlled are entirely the result of inheritance and local breeding behavior. The manifestation and distribution of such traits is unrelated to the forces of natural selection and therefore will have no adaptive value. As a consequence, they cannot be ranked as "better" or "worse" when populations are compared with each other. At most, they can be seen as "different" and as illustrating what has been perpetuated by chance in the different areas of human habitation.

Regional configurations observed in the clusters of samples from given parts of the world cannot be labeled by using aspects of variation that are under selective force control. Designations such as "Negroid," for example, fail to specify people from a given circumscribed area. Ethnic designations are no better. "Mongoloid," for instance, is a word derived from the Mongols who are both geographically and morphologically peripheral to the other populations with whom they are tied. "Caucasoid" refers to the people living in the locale where, according to the Biblical narrative, Noah's Ark disgorged its contents after the retreat of the scriptural flood, and its use in a broader context implies acceptance of a whole series of assumptions that have no scientific basis.

The only really useful means of referring to the various regional configurations visible in the world is by using broad geographical terms to designate the appropriate inhabitants. The people of Europe are properly referred to as Europeans, the people of Africa are Africans, the people of Australia are Australians, and so forth. This can be narrowed down by referring to people as South Asians, Northwest Europeans, Southwest Australians, and the like. That way no "ethnic" or behavioral attributes are indicated, and no confusion or hidden implications can result from the labels given.

Finally, if indeed that all-important but hopelessly undefinable phenomenon, "intelligence," has the adaptive significance for human survival that we have reason to assume it does, then it has to be apportioned according to the distribution of its controlling selective force. Further, if the latter is distributed in a manner analogous to that of other forces affecting human survival, it is clear that we have no right to base our expectations concerning intellectual capability on a distribution that is limited by the boundaries marking the area of extent of any given population. Beyond that, no human population now lives under anything like the kind of circumstances that shaped human capabilities through that million-years-plus stretch of the Pleistocene during which they were established.

However, until 10,000 years ago or less, all humans everywhere were pursuing the same kind of subsistence strategy, whatever the latitude. This meant that the selective pressures influencing intellectual development at any given time were identical for all living humans over a span of more than a million years. Only within the last 10,000 years have things changed to the extent that it requires substantially more—or less—intelligence to make a go of it in some parts of the world as opposed to others. That relatively short post-Pleistocene stretch is not enough to produce a measurable difference between the intellectual capacities of the various surviving populations of the world.

Given all of this, we have no right to expect that there is any innate difference of intelligence between the various regional clusters and configurations of modern human beings. The only possible reason behind efforts to test for differences in "racial" intelligence is an assumption—whether covert or overt—that some groups are brighter and therefore better than others and that one's own group can be shown to be the brightest and best. Since the configurations present in regional clusters are nothing more than "family resemblance writ large" and have no other biological meanings, any attempt to assess "racial" difference in any aspect at all with the expectation of finding something of significance beyond an otiose catalogue of trivia can only be based on invidious expectations that themselves can have no scientific justification.

"Race" at best is just another four-letter word, empty of any biological significance. Biological differences do exist among modern humans, and an investigation of these differences is interesting and valuable. But this can only be accomplished by abandoning the "race" concept and tracing the traits to be studied according to their own distributions as they reflect the selective forces that have influenced the variation observed. Insofar as the assumption remains that regionally circumscribed peoples possess an essential nature defined by associated abilities, this is just a continuing manifestation of the use of the concept of "race" in the absence of the use of the name. The continuation of such an outlook can only result in scientific futility and social harm. As a concept without redeeming social or scientific value, "race" indeed deserves to be ranked with the roster of those four-letter words that merits the designation "obscenity." It is too much to expect that what I say here will have much influence on the public at large, but at least I hope that it will be read and understood by the anthropological community and that they will respond by consigning the term and the concept to the oblivion that it deserves.

Rudyard Kipling, known as a jingoistic apologist for the British Empire, also had another side that reflected a deeper understanding of and sympathy for the essential humanity of the various manifestations of the "other" with which he had come in contact. Some of this is expressed in the conclusion of the verse that stands at the head of my Introduction, and it can serve as a fitting note on which to conclude:

> But if you live over the sea,
> Instead of over the way,
> You may end by (think of it!) looking on We
> As only a sort of They!

ACKNOWLEDGMENTS

This manuscript is condensed from parts of a book in preparation entitled *Race Is a Four-Letter Word*. Like the present paper, that book, when completed, is dedicated to Ashley Montagu, not only in honor of the splendid example he has set for us in an extraordinary lifetime of accomplishments motivated by the highest and most admirable of ideals, but also for the kindness and support that he has shown to me personally. I also wish to express my gratitude to Professors Larry J. Reynolds and Leonard Lieberman for giving me the opportunity of being part of this tribute to Ashley Montagu. The world is a better place because of him, and he continues to be an inspiration to us all.

CHAPTER 12

The Cultural Ecological Niche

Prologue

The story of human evolution has a seductive fascination because it is our own story. Inevitably the specter of subjectivism intrudes to such an extent that an aura of suspicion gets attached to anyone who would try to tell its tale. We take for granted the dominant role played by *Homo sapiens* in the world today, and that leads us to perceive the course of human history as a kind of success story. At the moment we are indeed the most numerous of the large animals of the world, though if we stop to reflect, we realize that there are a great deal more insects than people. Even so, it comes as a bit of a surprise to learn that the sheer weight of insects is orders of magnitude beyond that of humans. In the estimate of one of the world experts, E. O. Wilson, ants alone make up fully one-third of the biomass of the Amazon Basin in South America (Royte, 1990:21).

Aspects of the tale of human evolution have attracted writers of all kinds: paleontologists (Romer, 1954; Stringer and Gamble, 1993; Gould, 1997); physiologists (Diamond, 1992; von Hippel, 1995); psychologists (Donald, 1991; Humphrey, 1992); primatologists (Tattersall, 1995, 1997; Dunbar, 1996); anthropologists of course (Rightmire, 1990; Brace, 1995; Howells, 1997); and inevitably, journalists (Lewin, 1993; Shreeve, 1995). There are many, many others as well. There seems to be the feeling that since we are all equally human, we are all equally qualified to tell the story of our species.

In telling that story, we are using that human creation which has been the key to our success as a species—language. It seems almost trite to say that the existence of language is a prerequisite for the ability to tell a story at all, and each one of the accounts mentioned above is a narrative tale (and see Landau, 1991). Yet it is useful to remind ourselves what language is and how this distorts the picture being portrayed. Language is basically a verbal analogue of the world as a whole, a shorthand rendering of the larger graded reality where whole complex dimensions of that world are represented by arbitrarily assigned words. The reduction of the infinitely graded reality of the world at large to a finite set of verbal symbols that can be grasped and shared by all human beings is what has given *Homo sapiens* an unparalleled edge over the rest of the animate world. It is so extraordinarily convenient and useful that we sometimes forget that the words we use as finite means of dealing with the infinite are simplifications of the larger reality, and, as simplifications, run the risk of misrepresenting it. Nowhere is that more evident than in the use of a set of finite categories to represent the gradual emergence of humankind, as we know it in the world today, from its nonhuman ancestry.

I started this prologue with a caution about how the use of verbal categories sometimes may lead us into an oversimplification of reality. Having said that and given an example, I am now going to turn around and make the case that a consideration of the cultural realm, of which language is the essential core, is mandatory if we would make any coherent sense out of the course of human evolution. Yet in virtually all the renderings of that story currently in print, it is treated in such simplistic fashion as to be more of a caricature than a contribution to our understanding. The temptation to lampoon the more egregious inanities is irresistible, but there is a serious point to be made, and I have tried to conclude this chapter with its development and application.

≈   ≈

HOMINID CATASTROPHISM

Over the past some years, a whole series of writers have cashed in on a gambit that could be called folklore repackaged as "science." This is the portrayal of the latter portion of the course of human evolution as "a good old-fashioned melodrama" where Neanderthals are cast as the embodiment of the villain, "hairy, strong and dangerous, violent and bestial, dwarfed and physically 'inferior,' and crafty but not really intelligent." Then enter Cro-Magnon the hero, stage right: "Sweeping into Europe from out of the East came a new type of man, tall and straight, with strong but finely formed limbs, whose superiority is proclaimed in the smooth brow and lofty forehead, and whose firm and prominent chin bespeaks a mentality in no way inferior to ourselves. In this fine and virile race we can recognize our own ancestors who suddenly appear on the scene and replace the degenerate and inferior Neanderthals, perhaps as a result of bloody conflict in which the superior mentality and physique of the newcomers tipped the balance. Whatever the cause, the lowly Neanderthals disappear forever and the land henceforth becomes the never-to-be-relinquished home of our own lineage, the creator of the culture which is our own patrimony, and the originator of what has been built to the heights of Western civilization" (Brace, 1995:242–243, and in all four previous editions back to 1967).

If this sounds like improbable hyperbole, my reply is the same as the one of that extraordinary soprano manquée Anna Russell, in her spoof of Wagner's Ring operas, "You know, I'm not making this up!" (Russell, 1985). I actually generated my version as a parody of the views and the style of expression of Marcellin Boule's writings of over 70 years ago (Boule, 1913, 1921). That imagery captivated writers of fiction from H. G. Wells and his "Grisly Folk" (1927[1966]) to the steamy pot-boilers of Jean Auel written over a half-century later (Auel, 1980, 1985). In spite of the fact that my own satire, dating from 30 years ago, noted that the impetus for such derogatory portrayals was rooted in the traditional morality dramas of European folklore in which, despite adversities, "good prevails and evil is vanquished," yet the overwhelming majority of "scientists" writing on the topic of human evolution still continue to perpetuate this mythology in all seriousness if with less literary flamboyance.

As was noted in the Prologue to Chapter 2, "The Fate of the 'Classic' Neanderthals," William Golding also built on that stereotype and elevated it—lowered it?—to a caricature in *The Inheritors* (1955). As that book shows, even a distinguished writer will be defeated in the attempt to create scintillating dialogue if he starts with the assumption that his characters can only converse in monosyllables and grunts. When he was subsequently awarded the Nobel Prize in literature (1983), it would appear that the Nobel Committee chose to overlook the lumpen prose in that eminently forgettable volume.

All of these and many others like them are simply variations on a theme established by the French paleontologist Marcellin Boule (1861–1942), in the first quarter of our now-waning century. As Boule described Neanderthal capabilities, he declared, "It is probable that *Homo Neanderthalensis* could only have possessed a rudimentary psychic nature, superior certainly to that of the anthropoid apes, but notably inferior to that of any living race whatsoever" (Boule, 1913:227). He repeated those words subsequently and added, "Without doubt he had only the rudiments of articulate speech" (1921:237), a denigration which has been referred to as a depiction of Neanderthal as "The Unspeakable" (Brace, 1995:217). Boule went on to expound with relish on the "brutal caste of the heavy, vigorous body, of the bony skull with its robust jaws which affirm the predominance of the purely vegetative or bestial over cerebral functions" (1913:227; 1921:238). He concluded that, "Perhaps one could go so far as to say that it was a degenerate species" (1921:245).

Finally, in splendidly bombastic fashion he opined: "What a contrast with the men of the following geological and archaeological period, the men of the type of Cro-Magnon with a more elegant body, a finer head, a broad and upright forehead who, in the caves where they lived, left such evidences of their manual skills, of the resources of their inventive spirit, their artistic and religious preoccupations, their faculties of abstraction, and who were the first to merit the glorious title *Homo sapiens*" (Boule, 1913:227; 1921:248). Years later, this passage was repeated verbatim by the equally orotund Sir Arthur Keith writing with one of his American protégés (McCown and Keith, 1939:360–361). Keith (1866–1955) was the most prominent British paleoanthropologist of his generation, and, after the "conversion experience" that occurred as a result of his visit to France in September of 1911 just after the first installment of Boule's treatment of the French Neanderthal, the La Chapelle-aux-Saints skeleton, had been published, he championed Boule's interpretation for much of the rest of his life (Keith, 1950, esp. p. 319 ff.). This then became the standard outlook in the English-speaking world, and has remained so ever since.

Since Boule was a paleontologist by training and Keith was an anatomist and physician, neither had the background that would have qualified them to comment with insight on the implications of the archaeological record. In this realm again, Boule set the precedent that has been followed by just about everyone who has subsequently dealt with the Neanderthal "Problem."

Writing about the Mousterian tools with which the known Neanderthal skeletons are associated, he declared, "There is hardly a more rudimentary or more miserable industry than that of our Mousterian man. The use of a single basic material, stone (outside of wood and perhaps bone), the uniformity, the simplicity and crudity of his lithic tools, the probable absence of all traces of concern of an esthetic order or of a moral order" all served to confirm his judgments based on anatomical features of the "brutal," "bestial," and "inferior" nature of the Neanderthals (Boule, 1913:227; 1921:238).

In the cultural as in the biological realm, the possibility of a transformation in situ of the Mousterian into subsequent more recent traditions or of Neanderthal into living human form was simply denied a priori. As Boule concluded, "no living human type could be considered a direct descendant, even modified, of the Neanderthal type" (Boule, 1921:248). Neither Boule nor Keith accepted Darwin's mechanism of natural selection operating on chance mutations as the main engine driving the course of organic evolution. Change occurred when new forms appeared from somewhere else replacing what had previously been there. No effort is ever made to explain how the succeeding forms arose. In effect, it is a form of creationism right in line with the catastrophism attributed to Cuvier that I discussed in Chapter 2. As was true over a generation ago, most of the students of human "evolution" today spend far more time trying to deny the possibility of evolution than in trying to figure out what actually happened and why.

From the time of Boule on, the import of "culture" in the anthropological sense, as both the consequence and the cause of the human condition, is something that is almost completely missing from what counts as current orthodoxy in the study of human evolution. Even the impact of separate adaptive aspects of the cultural realm as treated in Chapter 8, "Deriving the Quick from the Dead," is not mentioned in any of the recent treatments of human evolution. Beyond that, the concept of culture as a milieu created by human beings and essential for their very survival is never included as part of the picture. As Rob Foley, one of the prominent members of the current English school has phrased it, culture is "an unnecessary and not particularly useful concept" (Foley, 1987:5). More recently, the same author has advocated the value of dealing with human evolution in a manner that is "probably superfluous to any Darwinian approach" (Foley, 1996:196).

One of the other most prominent figures in that school, Chris Stringer, even though writing in collaboration with an archaeologist, has dealt with Neanderthal technological capabilities in exactly the same fashion as

Marcellin Boule even while denying that this was what he was doing (Stringer and Gamble, 1993:26). For example, he has derided Neanderthal habitations as more the equivalents of the "nests" of birds than the symbolic "homes" of "modern" humans. In similar fashion, when it was shown that Neanderthals were making the same kinds of tools that are found in the succeeding Aurignacian, he conceded that they could be considered capable of "emulation, for change, but not for symbolism" (ibid., p. 207). This evident failure to understand the nature and importance of culture in the anthropological sense may be related to why the English school of paleoanthropology has been unable to offer any insight into the actual processes and dynamics by which human evolution took place.

Following up on Boule's lead, there has been what almost looks like a competition to devise ever more ingenious ways in which to denigrate the Neanderthals. As one recent commentator has observed, "the esteem accorded to the Neandertals is at its lowest nadir since Marcellin Boule's (1911–1913) early portrayals of them as semi-simian brutes" (Hayden, 1993:114). One technically competent American anthropologist, observing that the muscle attachments on the Neanderthal skeleton were especially well developed to resist lateral movements, attributed this to their presumably congenital inability to run in a straight line (Trinkaus, 1986:204–206). Since it has been assumed that, unlike the canids—the wolves—with whom they were competing for edible game, they were unable to make plans to coordinate hunting activities, the suggestion was made that they charged forth in witless fashion like hyperactive inebriates, "scrambling around on the landscape, rather than strolling or walking briskly from place to place" (Trinkaus and Shipman, 1992:368).

One of my former students christened this "the hunter-blunderer hypothesis," and it led to a bit of versified blundering by the ever-skeptical I. Wright Drivell, that indubitably cross cousin of I. Doolittle Wright, and his colleague in the Department of Homopathic Anthropopoetics at the University of Southern North Dakota at Hoople:

> In a common view that's offered now,
> Nature never did endow
> Neanderthals with brains enow
>   To frame the thought
> Of hunting plans that would allow
>   For dinner caught.

In addled search to gain his fare,
He rushes forth he knows not where,
Blunders here and stumbles there,
    And hopes, this way,
By random luck and wear and tear,
    To find his prey.

But random hunts are ever vain;
And surely that expanded brain
Suggests there was no mental strain
    Behind the hunch
That let them plan the means to gain
    That sought-for lunch.

Quoted in Brace, 1995:238

The most prolonged of the recent attempts to perpetuate Boule's treatment of the Neanderthals has been by Christopher B. Stringer, an anthropologist in the Department of Palaeontology at the Natural History Museum (formerly the British Museum [Natural History]) in London (Stringer, 1987b, 1990; Stringer and Andrews, 1988; Stringer and Gamble, 1993; Stringer and McKie, 1997). It is actually quite fitting that the Natural History Museum in South Kensington should be the locus of those most prominently involved in trying to downplay the efforts to deal with the evidence for human evolution from the perspective of mechanisms and causes (Stringer, 1994:168). The museum, as an entity separate from the British Museum in Bloomsbury, was brought into being by the efforts of the eminent Victorian anatomist Sir Richard Owen (1804–1892) (Rupke, 1994).

Owen produced a huge output of studies in comparative anatomy and paleontology. Quantities of these were very fine contributions (and see the recognition of the role he played in establishing the comparative anatomy of teeth as recounted in Türp, Brace, and Alt, 1997), but he spoiled our memory of his positive impact by his self-promotion and "personal pettiness" (Di Gregorio, 1984:35). Darwin had given the vertebrate fossils from the *Beagle* expedition to Owen to describe, and then, after he had done so, Owen spent much of the rest of his life denying the magnitude of Darwin's achievements (Browne, 1994). The gist of his denunciation of Darwin's synthesis was of the sort that goes: "It is not true; everybody knows it anyway; and besides, I said it first" (MacLeod, 1965:278) .

Chris Stringer and his colleagues at the Natural History Museum show none of the Owen strain of nastiness at the personal level. They do, however, display his commitment to the neo-Platonic essentialism of his role model, Georges Cuvier in France. The elevation of a single Neanderthal specimen, La Chapelle-aux-Saints, and a single early "modern" specimen, Cro-Magnon, to the level of invariant and essentially distinct icons is right in the intellectual tradition represented by Cuvier, Owen, and Boule and quite at variance with the kind of "population thinking" that grew in evolutionary biology start-ing in the decade before World War II. The absence of anything of more than lip-service concern for the mechanisms by which biological change occurs is also characteristic of the outlook that has continued in paleoanthropology from the time of Cuvier early in the nineteenth century right up to the present day.

The dynamics by which evolutionary change takes place are generally avoided, and what counts as change is attributed to replacements of earlier by later populations who had invaded from somewhere else. This was what earned Cuvier's views the designation "catastrophism" by the English philos-opher of science William Whewell (1794–1866) in 1832, a label that was never used in a French milieu (Whewell, 1831, but, more especially, 1832:126). Oddly enough, it was really a characteristically English mind-set that insisted on the intellectual distinctions and the labels implied in what we call "uniformitarianism" and "catastrophism" (Rudwick, 1972:132; Wilson, 1972:350; Grayson, 1983:49; Hallam, 1983:23). By the late nineteenth century, the scenario of invasion and replacement was designated "evolution" in the French literature, whereas the idea of the operation of natural forces to gener-ate change was called "Darwinism." To deal with the latter was to presuppose that one could predict the intents of "l'auteur du Monde," and this was not considered an appropriate realm for human investigation (Topinard, 1888:473).

Marcellin Boule followed right in the same tradition when he established the field of paleoanthropology in France starting just after the turn of the century. The idea of continuity and change by natural means in situ was rejected in favor of invasions and replacements. In the absence of any actual evidence, the source of the invaders who were assumed to have replaced the Neanderthals—people of the Aurignacian culture (which includes Cro-Magnon)—was somewhat offhandedly placed as farther to the east: the Mediterranean and, ultimately, Africa (Boule, 1921:274). This tradition con-tinues today in the "out-of-Africa" views of Chris Stringer, who has laid claims to being their originator. He evidently is honestly unaware that these had in actual fact been established as the core paradigm of paleoanthropology nearly half a century prior to his birth (Stringer, 1994; Stringer and McKie, 1997a and b). Except for a few figures discussed in Chapter 1, such as Aleš Hrdlička

(1869–1943) at the Smithsonian and Franz Weidenreich (1873–1948) latterly at the American Museum of Natural History in New York, the intellectual tradition that derives from Cuvier is alive and well and continues to represent what the late Thomas Kuhn would have called the "paradigm of normal science" in biological anthropology today (Kuhn, 1962; and see for example Stringer and Gamble, 1993; Stringer and McKie, 1997a; Klein, 1995; Tattersall, 1997; Tattersall and Schwartz, 1999). A third of a century ago, I called this "hominid catastrophism" (see Chapter 2), and, though that has drawn a recent if belated harrumph (Gould, 1997:23), the label is still apt.

A SNAIL'S-EYE VIEW OF HUMAN EVOLUTION, OR, THE OUTLOOK OF THE "GOULDEN AGE"

This manifestation of the reigning orthodoxy received a major boost from a powerful figure in the April 1997 issue of the magazine *Natural History*. Stephen Jay Gould, the celebrated Harvard paleontologist-zoologist and science writer, and now President of the American Association for the Advancement of Science, devoted his monthly column, "This View of Life," to what he perceives as the unexpected unity that currently characterizes the condition of the human species (Gould, 1997). In Gould's view, we should have been expecting to recognize a plethora of species in the human fossil record at any one time in the past. Gould's own research specialty is the world of Caribbean land snails where each island throughout the region has a separate species. By analogy, it is his expectation that there should have been a distinct hominid species for each geographical division in each geological time segment. The relationships of such local and temporal manifestations can be plotted in a diagram that resembles a bush where each twig is awarded a separate specific name.

As a vision, it is a kind of apotheosis of nominophilia (and see Chapter 4, "Punctuationism, Cladistics, and the Legacy of Medieval Neoplatonism"). In Gould's words, the expectation that the human fossil record was characterized by a "substantial bushiness throughout most of hominid history" is a "new" realization that has grown up to replace "the traditional linear view" (Gould, 1997:21). In actuality, however, this has given a major shot in the arm to the eighteenth-century conception of what science is all about, i.e., demonstrating the richness and variety of God's creation by discovering and naming the multitude of His creatures. The manifestation of this in paleoanthropology is illustrated by the statement that "it would be better for the comprehensiveness of our understanding of the human fossil record that, if err we must, we err (within reason!) on the side of recognizing too many rather than, as is the tendency, too few species units" (Tattersall, 1986:168; Lieberman, 1997). The guiding philosophy clearly is that of Saint Thomas Aquinas who argued that "the multiplication of species adds more to the goodness of the universe than the multitude of individuals in one species" (Aquinas, 1923 [originally 1259–1264]:207).

Now, to anyone who has followed my argument so far, there ought to be a substantial double-take at this point and a query concerning how anyone who knows anything about the field at all could have labeled the traditional view "linear." That is astonishing enough, but the biggest surprise of all is the fact that Gould identifies the source of that supposedly traditional view as *me!* As he presents his case, the embodiment of "the traditional linear view" was to be found in *Human Evolution,* the book I wrote with Ashley Montagu (second edition, 1977). This Gould identifies as "the leading basic textbook in physical anthropology at the time" (Gould, 1997:23), and its "cardinal error of linearization" was caused by a "disabling cultural bias" (ibid., pp. 21–22). He does not spell out what the latter might be, but it appears to be a kind of euphemism for what is now being subsumed under the label "political correctness." My initial rueful reaction was to reflect that the only thing in which our book could have been judged as "leading" was the speed with which it went out of print.

Summing up his appraisal, Gould observed that "of all alterations in thinking about human evolution that have occurred during my professional lifetime, none has been more transforming, or further ranging in implications, than the increasing documentation of substantial bushiness throughout most of hominid history. Our recent reality of one worldwide species is the oddity, not the norm—and we have been fooled by our bad habit of generalizing a transient and contingent present" (ibid., p 23). What Gould had observed concerning the history of thinking about human evolution, however, was not the replacement of an old view by a new one. Instead it was actually the failure of my effort to introduce an element of Darwinian processual thinking into a field that was traditionally dominated by a pre-Darwinian, typological mind-set. I had been engaged in the attempt to drag paleoanthropology "kicking and screaming into the twentieth century," to borrow a phrase from the late Adlai Stevenson, and, as the preponderance of current writing clearly shows, my efforts in paleoanthropology were no more successful than were Stevenson's in politics.

The glorification of the bush which Gould finds so "transforming," rather than being fraught with possibilities for the future, is in fact simply a manifestation of the typological essentialism which has been at the core of the field since its inception. I can make the case that it is this, rather than "linearization," that is the result of a "cultural bias," though whether that can be regarded as "disabling" or not is another rather subjective judgment. The "transforming alteration" that Gould had observed was real enough, but it was in fact a manifestation of "The Great Leap Backward" that I discuss in Chapters 3 and 4 since its roots are not merely pre-Darwinian but positively medieval.

Somehow, Gould has generalized the time, dating from his own intellectual maturation in the 1960s, to the twentieth century as a whole. Summing up his picture of the latest of evolutionary thinking a decade ago, Gould declared at that time, "evolution is a bush, not a ladder" (1986:69). It was not a new idea at the time. In fact, it is a marvelous example of what the historian of ideas Arthur O. Lovejoy identified as a concept originally offered in defense of the ruling set of ideas of a previous age held over and offered in service of the diametrically opposed ideas of the age that follows. Lovejoy's example was the concept of the "missing link," originally forged in service of the frame of reference of the static and unchanging "Great Chain of Being" but later incorporated into the expectations generated by a Darwinian view of organic evolution where individual fossil representatives of related forms separated by strata through time would eventually be linked together in a continuum when the remains of their intervening relatives were eventually discovered (Lovejoy, 1936).

Early in the nineteenth century, Georges Cuvier promoted the view that "life was a bush, not a ladder" in his own attack on the unity of the Great Chain of Being of the previous age (Eiseley, 1958:88). His bushes did not imply the genetic relationship of adjacent branches, however, and the world depicted had no place for the expectation of continuity with change through time—descent with modification, as Darwin termed it—i.e. organic evolution in the parlance of today. The similarities of the twigs were assumed to be due to the fact that they were manifestations of similar thoughts in the mind of God. Each twig, no matter how similar it might be to another, was created separately and remained distinct through time—"stasis," as Gould likes to express his expectations of the normal nature of the organic world (Gould, 1982a:85). To be sure, he has recognized the grammatical problem in the phrase that he coined, "stasis is data" (Gould, 1993:15), but, to a mind committed to stasis, even the overwhelming documentation of gradual change through time presented by the fossil hominid evidence is apportioned into distinct categories and labeled "static."

Cuvier's intellectual descendants in paleontology and paleoanthropology in France early in the current century adopted the imagery of the "bush" and applied it in an archaeological and an anthropological context. In the textbook of physical anthropology that really was the most influential in this century, and whose influence remains unrecognized but undimmed as the century has drawn to a close, *Les Hommes Fossiles,* Marcellin Boule declared that "Each grouping of beings related to one another…may be compared to a tree or a bush more or less branched" (Boule, 1921, as updated in Boule and Vallois, 1957:54). Where human fossils were concerned, however, those that differed in form from living humans were declared to be "specializations" that died out without issue. The human fossil record, then, was sprinkled with a plethora of "aberrant" forms each allotted its own specific label and of unknown relationship to the others, a picture I have described as "a collection of dead twigs and no trunk" (Brace et al., 1979:168). Not to demean the American brewing industry, but there is something comparable in the dissatisfaction felt in the contemplation of such a disembodied bush to the feelings of the bibulous symposium participant who discovers that the only available postmeetings tipple is restricted to the products of an Anheuser-Busch. It is the bushy, and not the linear view, that properly qualifies as the "dominant tradition" among students of human "evolution," and it was explicitly labeled "evolution buissonante" by Boule's successor in France, Henri-Victor Vallois (Vallois, 1950:70). Sir Arthur Keith in England in 1915 and 1925 developed this at length; his student Earnest Albert Hooton brought it to Harvard and introduced it to America in 1931 and 1946; his student in turn, W. W. Howells, perpetuated this in a series of versions from 1944 to 1997; and Christopher Stringer and assorted others including, now, Stephen Jay Gould, have picked up the same theme and made sure that it will be alive and well as the new millennium gets under way.

Yes, it is true that the majority of life forms that ever existed in the past eventually died out without evolving into something else, though many gave rise to offshoots that did continue in different directions (Stanley, 1987). The philosopher Daniel Dennett has pointed out that Gould, by concentrating on the density of "bushes of unactualized possibility," may himself be making a mistake by overlooking the "rather sparse twigs" of actual continuity of exploitation (Dennett, 1995:260–261). As Gould himself has said, the matter should be decided on "the contingent and empirical data of actual history, not preferences of theory [laden with a complex range of unconscious biases]" (1997:70). And so it should. The unconscious biases of an island land-snail specialist should not be our guide in trying to make sense out of the scattered bits of evidence bearing on early human existence.

More than one observer has noted that Gould's own approach to evolutionary theory has more than a bit of what could only be called "bias." In the delightfully crafted critique of the "hyperselectionism" in neo-Darwinism, "The Spandrels of San Marco and the Panglossian Paradigm," Gould and his coauthor, Richard C. Lewontin, after chiding attempts to stretch the implications of Darwinian selection to levels of undocumentable faith, then extend themselves on to denounce evolutionary biology for assigning any role to selection at all (Gould and Lewontin, 1979). In an equally amusing spoof of that overextension, "The Spaniels of St. Marx and the Panglossian Paradox," David Quellar, after offering his demurrer "Of course, I do not mean to imply that Gould and Lewontin are dogs," goes on to say that, "it is their well-known devotion to Marxist thought that might be construed as spaniel-like" (Quellar, 1995:486). He concludes, "When a narrative is woven with political woof it is worth keeping an eye out for biological warp" (idem).

Having told us that he had "learned his Marxism, literally at his daddy's knee" (Gould and Eldredge, 1977:146), Gould then declared of himself, "A strict Darwinian—I am not one" (Gould, 1982b:20). Not only that, Daniel Dennett has demonstrated that "America's evolutionist laureate has always been uncomfortable with the fundamental core of Darwinism" (Dennett, 1995:266). "Gould's ultimate target is Darwin's dangerous idea itself; he is opposed to the very idea that evolution is, in the end, just an algorithmic process" (idem). In advocating the expectation that the normal course of evolutionary change is the periodic sudden appearance of biological novelty for no discernible reason, after which a period of stasis ensues to be followed by another sudden change—"punctuated equilibria"—the idea of natural selection has been entirely eliminated from a role in organic evolution (Eldredge and Gould, 1972). As Daniel Dennett puts it, Gould posits the existence of "skyhooks" as an alternative to Darwinian mechanism. The same line of thinking led one bemused zoologist to note that, after all the evidence for natural mechanism is discounted, we are left with no alternative but to believe that "And then a miracle occurs" (Kellog, 1988). The chief public defender of "scientific" creationism reacted to the proposal of Eldredge and Gould's "alternative" to Darwin with the observation, "Eliminate the words 'evolutionary burst' and substitute the words 'burst of creation' and one would think he was reading an article by a creationist" (Gish, 1979:177).

There is one other consideration of at least equal importance. That involves taking into account the life-ways of the creatures in question. This is a matter of assessing the nature of the ecological niches occupied by the species being considered. When comparing the picture of within as opposed to between group variation, it is of even greater import to take into account the effects of the circumstances to which they must adapt than it is to calculate the simple existence of their genetic relationships. Human beings are obviously more closely related to Madagascar lemurs than they are to Caribbean land snails, and closer yet to African chimpanzees. However, the genetic differences between groups of lemurs and even between groups of chimpanzees should have properties that resemble the kinds of genetic distinctions between various island snail populations to a greater extent than they do different populations of living human beings, and such is indeed the case (Lewontin, 1972; D'Andrade and Morin, 1996; Deinard and Kidd, 1997; Gagneaux et al., 1999). Stephen Jay Gould, looking at this, marvels at the "Unusual Unity" displayed by modern *Homo sapiens*. The present human condition is what he regards as the "oddity," a "transient and contingent present" (Gould, 1997:23). I am going on to develop the position that the contingent present is not as transient as Gould assumes, and that it is a full consideration of this that should lead us to realize why human unity is not in the least bit "odd," and why we can project that realization back into the past and use it not only to cast light on the duration of that unity but also to explain the reason for and the time of the uniform emergence of "modern" humans throughout the whole of the inhabited world and not just in one local segment.

Before that, however, I have to consider one remaining component of Gould's "bias" against such expectations. This involves his objections to using an understanding of the present to make sense out of the past. It was one of the tenets of Scottish Realism in the eighteenth century that the laws of Nature have remained uniform in their application throughout time and were the same in the past as they are now and shall be in the future (and see Chapter 1, "The Intellectual Standing of Charles Darwin"). This was the assumption that the Scottish geologist James Hutton (1726–1797) used as a guide to understanding the nature of geological processes, and it was built on by his Scottish successor Sir Charles Lyell (1797–1875), who quoted from John Playfair's *Illustrations of the Huttonian Theory* (Playfair, 1802) in the epigraph to the first volume of his seminal contribution, *Principles of Geology* (Lyell, 1830), a book that had such fundamental importance to shaping the thought processes of Charles Darwin. Later christened "Uniformitarianism," it was the source of the watch words "The present is the key to the past" and has served as a guide to the geologists and evolutionary biologists who have added to our knowledge in the generations that have elapsed since that time.

It is an approach, however, that has been regarded with profound suspicion by Stephen Jay Gould, who has complained that "I have long regarded Lyell's argument as deeply unfair in principle, however brilliant in rhetoric" (Gould, 1994:12). To be sure, he had made a useful distinction between what he has referred to as "substantive uniformitarianism," with its patently false assumption that rates of change in the past have been constant, and "methodological uniformitarianism" which posits the unchanging continuity of the laws of Nature (Gould, 1965:224). As Lyell and Darwin both clearly realized, our knowledge of the processes which serve to shape the geological and biological domains has to be established by our experience with the extant world (Ruse, 1975:168). Only then can we turn our attention to the surviving pieces of evidence of the world of the past and attempt to see how those processes served to shape the changes discernible in that preserved record, and how the past was consequently transformed to produce the present of our immediate experience.

By recommending that the term uniformitarianism in its "methodological" sense be "honorably retired" (Gould, 1965:227), Gould in effect has sanctioned the neglect of a concern for evolutionary dynamics—the processes by which organic changes have occurred. The mere use of the label "punctuation event" or its cladistic equivalent, "speciation event," says nothing at all about the processes by which such an occurrence was brought about. At this point, I am going to suggest that a concern for processes, as is shown in Chapters 5, 6, and 8, can provide some major assistance to our efforts to figure out what happened in the past and why. A focus on the contemporary human condition and how it emerged should be able to tell us some of the reasons why *Homo sapiens* is a single world-wide species.

LIFE-WAY AND THE BACKGROUND OF HUMAN UNITY: THE LARGE CARNIVORE GUILD

The concept of "ecological niche" has been used by biologists to describe the circumstances exploited by a given species to make a go of it in the world. As one of them generalized, "Every species has its niche, its place in the grand scheme of things." "The niche is an animal's (or plant's) profession" (Colvinaux, 1978:10). This is a peculiarly human way of looking at things, but, as humans trying to make sense out of the world we inhabit, it has its uses for us even if it sometimes requires an exercise of intellectual gymnastics to use a single term to encompass things as diverse as the survival strategy of the blue whale on the one hand, ploughing across thousands of square miles of the plankton-bearing oceans of the world, and the malaria parasite on the other with its focus on the stomach and salivary glands of a particular kind of mosquito alternated with the liver and red blood cells of human beings.

The zoological Order, Primates, to which we belong, arose in the first place to exploit the resources of the tree-branch tips in tropical rain forests. The nature of those resources includes tree-going insects as well as the fruits and leaves of the tropical trees themselves. These in turn can be subdivided into niches characterized by a focus on different kinds of insects, fruits, and so forth, and those species that concentrate on each particular resource can be said to be exploiting a particular ecological niche of which that resource is a characteristic part. The large terrestrial herbivores of the world exploit various aspects of the grassland ecological niche, and the species that prey on them display various adaptations to the carnivorous ecological niche.

The very first thing to note is that human beings are not island-dwelling land snails. It is also clear that they are not rain forest canopy lemurs. The circumstances that produced the condition of many distinct contemporary species in snails and monkeys have not applied to the hominid line since it ceased being arboreal between 5 and 7 million years ago. On the other hand, it is clear that terrestrial hominids between that time and somewhere near 2 million years ago were indeed divided into a series of separate local species. At that point, however, the rules of the game changed, and with it also the picture of hominids as local plant-foraging, specifically distinct species. What happened was the extension of hominids into the realm of terrestrial carnivores—the "large carnivore guild" in Alan Walker's words (Walker, 1984:144).

That change in life-way was somewhat comparable to the transformation of a 50 million year old Eocene condylarth from an opportunistic terrestrial scavenger/hunter into a whale as documented by the work of my colleague Philip D. Gingerich in the University of Michigan Museum of Paleontology (Gingerich, Smith, and Simons, 1990). Before there was any fossil evidence for it, the creationist Duane Gish had regarded that change as so unlikely that he regularly lampooned it with a series of somewhat crass cartoons that he used in his appearances, as he did in his "debate" with me in 1982. Phil Gingerich, however, has spent years mining the Eocene deposits of Pakistan and Egypt, and has now documented that transition in an abundant series of fossil finds (Gingerich, 1994; Gingerich and Uhlen, 1997). The full metamorphosis of a land quadruped to a flippered whale is even more extraordinary than the retooling of something like a chimpanzee into a human being, and, not surprisingly, it took quite a lot longer.

The emergence of a terrestrial hunting hominid from a tree-going vege-
tarian also was not accomplished overnight. From the quantities of chipped
stone flakes surrounding large animal skeletons in Pliocene deposits in Africa
such as at Olduvai Gorge in Tanzania, it is clear that their makers were scavenging the flesh of elephant-sized animals that had died a natural death. No
living carnivores, whether lions or hyenas, have the dental equipment to get
through the skin of an adult pachyderm. The cutting edge of a freshly chipped
flake of rock, however, will do the job even when wielded by the relatively
weak hands of a living human being (Stanford et al., 1981). Evidently our
stronger-fingered relatives of the genus *Australopithecus* had discovered this
well over 2 million years ago and regularly supplemented their vegetable food
supply by scavenging from the carcasses of large animals. The evidence is
there in African savanna deposits in the widespread distribution of those
stone flakes and the cores from which they had been chipped—Oldowan tools
as they have been named in honor of Olduvai Gorge where Louis Leakey first
found them in 1931 (Toth, 1985, 1987; Schick and Toth, 1993).

Although these are the oldest tools preserved, there is good reason to
suspect that hominids had been relying on hand-held tools for survival going
back another several million years. Our Australopithecine relatives, back to
the time when they diverged from a common ancestor with the chimpanzee,
had lacked the normal projection of canine teeth beyond the level of the surface of the rest of the dentition. None other than Charles Darwin suggested
that this indicated that human ancestors must have relied on hand-held
implements for defensive purposes, and that this had taken away the selective
force pressure maintaining canine tooth projection (Darwin, 1871:I:138). He
also realized that the advantage conveyed by using hand-held tools provided
the initial pressure favoring the adoption of a bipedal mode of locomotion.
One cannot effectively take along one's defensive weapons if one is using all
four appendages for purposes of locomotion. The ancestors of those stone
flake–wielding Australopithecines then had to have been accustomed to using
tools of perishable materials for the previous several million years.

Scavenging is one thing, but deliberate hunting is quite another. The evidence shows that living chimpanzees will occasionally prey upon monkeys
that live in the same area, and that they will also prey on the newborn of such
creatures as bush pigs and antelopes when they are encountered. Certainly the
early Australopithecines must have done so as well. We can guess that a taste
for baby gazelle on the part of those early hominids could have induced them
to chase slightly older infants. Hominids then and now have no chance of
out-sprinting a grown impala or even a wart hog, but the young of those

animals, even though they become mobile very quickly, cannot run very far for some days after birth. A persistent early hominid, even though out-sprinted for the first hundred yards or two, could easily have discovered that the young antelope cannot keep it up for a half mile or more.

Not only that, the larger adult antelopes run into problems if they try to keep up to speed over longer distances during the full sun of tropical daylight hours. Hominids, of course, were constrained to concentrate their activities during the sunny parts of the day since, as is true for all primates, we are relatively night blind. Somewhat inadvertently, those early hominids discovered that there was no member of the large carnivore guild that functioned during broad daylight, and the prey animals of the world are less well equipped to cope with flight from predation during the heat of the tropical day. All have fur coats, and the heat build-up caused by prolonged flight from pursuing predators will actually cause heat prostration. Somewhere in Africa around 2 million years ago, one of the various Australopithecine groups discovered that it could count on a meal by the laborious process of chasing an otherwise much fleeter quadruped through the heat of the day until it was forced to stop or face collapse from its heat build-up.

Our bipedal mode of locomotion may not make us very fast, but it does allow us to cover long distances with less energy expenditure than is true for similar-sized quadrupeds (Watanabe, 1971; Carrier, 1984; Devine, 1985). Persistence hunting, used by all hunting-and-gathering human groups right up into the twentieth century, selected for heat-dissipation characteristics in our early forebears, and the result was the elimination of the fur coat that is characteristic for the average terrestrial mammal. It also encouraged the increase in the number of sweat glands per unit skin area to the extent that human beings have more than any other creature in the world (Kuno, 1956; Macfarlane, 1976; Zihlman and Cohn, 1988). A hairless and sweaty skin is one of the most visible distinctions between a human and a chimpanzee, and it was almost certainly the result of the effect of the selective forces that operated to shape those early ancestors who worked themselves into the otherwise unoccupied diurnal portion of the life-way of the large carnivore guild.

In pondering on the implications of this change in food resource focus, Walker has noted that a dependence on particular kinds of plant foods restricts the exploiting species to the regions where those particular plants can be found. The toxins and other problems that have to be overcome in order to digest uncooked and unprocessed plants can be quite constraining. In contrast, meat is meat, and it is just as easy to catch—and digest—an African bongo as it is an Indonesian bintang. Once those early hominids learned to add a major hunting component to their subsistence activities, there was nothing to stop them from spreading throughout the entire Old World tropical grasslands and forest margins that supported exploitable game species.

Of course, the transition from scavenging to hunting was hardly instantaneous, but by around 2 million years ago it is clear that hominid hunters had spread throughout the Old World tropics. It is such an atypical way of life for a primate that the probability of more than one species having made that adaptation in successful fashion is vanishingly small. Even so, it is not out of the question that more than one early hominid species made an initial stab at it. By just under 2 million years ago, however, there was a single hunting hominid adaptation spread throughout the tropics of the Old World. Butchering tools are scattered from the African locus of their first appearance all the way to China in the East (Clark, 1993; Larick and Ciochon, 1996). Even in the absence of convincing skeletal evidence, the likelihood is that these were the products of a single if regionally variable hominid species.

The life-way analogy that supports such an expectation is the comparable phenomenon in the north temperate zone—that of the wolf. *Canis lupus* today is a single species whose range extends from the Atlantic coast of Europe across the Old World to Siberia and, because of the periodic past coalescence of Alaska with the Asian continent, from there across North America to Greenland. Not only is it a single species today, but it has been so throughout the 5 to 7 million year history of the genus (Macdonald, 1992).

The size of territory occupied by a successful wolf pack, the exchange of mates between groups promoting gene flow throughout the entire range occupied by the species, and the dynamics of intergroup relationships are all strikingly similar to those of hunting-and-gathering human populations (Mech, 1970; Stains, 1975; Livingstone, 1992). These are the reasons that we should expect that the hunting hominids constituted a single species from late in the Pliocene right on up to the present day.

That is the hunting argument, and it derives as much from a full understanding of the dynamics of living wolf (and human) populations as from anything else. The wolf of the present certainly is a key to understanding the wolf of the past, and it should provide provocative insights into what to expect for the human past as well. Although it was more a reflection of the grim pessimism with which he viewed the human condition, Thomas Hobbes's dictum *"Homo homini lupus est"*—man is a wolf to all mankind—actually represents a most appropriate analogy for the circumstances of human existence throughout much of the span of our duration (Thompson, 1978:557). Given all of this, there is plausibility in the argument that there was a single hominid species dating from the time that systematic hunting first became a regular and important component of hominid subsistence activities.

But what species would that have been? The first fossil representative of that stage of human evolution was the famous specimen found in Java by the Dutch army physician Eugène Dubois and named by him *"Pithecanthropus" erectus* in 1894. In his view, his famous fossil was distinct from living humans at both the generic as well as the specific levels (Dubois, 1894). Certainly the difference in life-way from that of any of the other primates was so profound that it warranted generic distinction from all other nonhuman relatives. Members of the geologically older genus *Australopithecus* did not begin to be discovered for another 30 years, but our assessment today recognizes separation at the level of the genus.

However, Dubois's attempt to attribute his material to genus *"Pithecanthropus"* has not generally been accepted by paleoanthropologists, and most have chosen to include those early hunting hominids in the genus *Homo*. Again, most practitioners have been happy to separate them from *Australopithecus* at the generic level and from *sapiens* at the specific level. Many have been willing to accept Dubois's specific designation which makes the post-Australopithecine and presapient hominids of the Lower Pleistocene *Homo erectus*. Although it has been slow in coming, many also regard this as the species that subsequently gave rise to *Homo sapiens*.

One of the pieces of awkwardness in giving names to segments of an ancestral lineage is that it makes arbitrary categories out of what is actually a continuum. Where late *Australopithecus* grades into early *Homo* somewhere around 2 million years ago, this is reflected in the various specimens attributed to Louis Leakey's *Homo "habilis"* (Leakey, Tobias, and Napier, 1964). Leakey's biographer cited the comment made by one of his colleagues that, as an entity, *"habilis* had been launched mainly by the power of Louis's personality" (Cole, 1975:256). It is true that it was a category created more by the will to believe than by anything generated from the actual data at hand. Louis Leakey had long been one of the most enthusiastic exponents of nominophilia, and was a pioneer in the now resurgent paleoanthropological tradition of giving every new-found scrap of ancient hominid a new specific if not generic name. In fact, however, he crossed us up badly in this one. He created a new name, all right, but he then used it as a designation for a whole series of specimens that really were specifically distinct. The result is a terminological muddle which, if not terminal, shows no signs of approaching a clarifying resolution.

If our understanding of the beginnings of the genus *Homo* is still fuzzy, the evidence demonstrating the nature of its life-way throughout the Lower Pleistocene, from nearly 2 million to just under 800,000 years ago, and the Middle Pleistocene, lasting another half a million years or so, should be reasonably clear. That evidence is largely in the form of stone tools. Unlike the skeletons themselves, these do not decay and disappear. Those stone tools were largely related to the processes of butchering the animals that their makers had hunted. To be sure, the information gained from the study of hunter/gatherers whose life-way had survived up to the twentieth century has shown that hunting only provided a part of the subsistence base, and often not even the major part. We can suspect that the overwhelming reliance on meat, as was the case in the recent Eskimo on the one hand, and the ingenious ways of making even the most unpromising plant material edible, as practiced by the inhabitants of the Kalahari Desert in South Africa and in the Outback of Australia on the other, represent a spectrum of subsistence activities that are relatively recent specializations and do not tell us a great deal about the average strategies of our common ancestors in the Lower and Middle Pleistocene.

The distribution of the game-processing tools of *Homo erectus* shows us more than just where people were living across the extent of the Old World from Africa through the Indian subcontinent to Southeast Asia and intermittently northwards in Europe, Central Asia, and the Far East (and see the depiction of their spread across the tropics of the Old World in Figure 12-1). They also tell us that the way of life was essentially the same from one end of human habitation to the other, and that there were no boundaries between one human group and another. The current enthusiasm among paleoanthropologists for ignoring the continuity in life-way and concentrating on trivial anatomical squiggles to justify specific distinctions such as *"heidelbergensis"* and *"ergaster"* is just one of those illustrations of what can happen when the cultural dimensions are left out of an assessment of prehistoric population relationships. The life-way indicated by that archaeological continuity did not involve elaborate preparation of plant foods, fire was not applied for the processing of either plant or animal food or for warmth and defense, and the use of traps, nets, and projectiles in the course of hunting was unknown.

During this stretch of a million-and-a-half years or more, cultural change was very slow. The same categories of tools were manufactured and used throughout, though local differences in available raw material sometimes meant that the same functional tool categories could look a bit different from

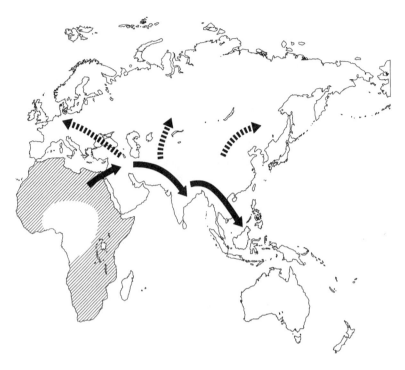

Figure 12-1 The spread of tools out-of-Africa from about 2 million years ago (from Brace, Fig. 11-12, 1995:167). The dashed lines extending northward show their temporary extent into the temperate latitudes during recurring interglacials.

place to place. Although there were differences in the annual temperature from one place to another, and some places were drier while others were wetter, the basic problems faced in making a go of it were essentially the same throughout the entire geographic expanse of human occupation. This means that the main selective pressures were the same on all human populations. Since specific unity was maintained through regular mate exchanges between adjacent groups throughout the entire range of habitation, and since selection was the same throughout, it stands to reason that the common Pleistocene heritage of all living human groups is essentially identical. That ancestral hunting hominid can properly be considered as belonging in the genus *Homo*, but, for reasons discussed in the next section, it could not yet be considered *sapiens*. Considering everything that has been discussed so far, it is most usefully designated *Homo erectus*.

CULTURE AND CULTURAL ELEMENTS
AS KEYS TO HOMINID SURVIVAL

From the time that *Homo erectus* first appeared—signaled by a brain that was arguably larger than that of *Australopithecus*—and continuing over the next million years or more, brain size slowly increased until it reached levels within the normal range of living *Homo sapiens.* This had been accomplished somewhere between 300,000 and 200,000 years ago. Quite obviously the business of retooling a bipedal foraging Australopithecine, dependent on the hand-held pointed stick both for fending off predators and for delving for edibles below ground surface, into a foraging-and-hunting creature, slow of foot but able to sustain the enduring pursuit of a persistence hunter, involved selection for increased levels of brainpower.

What transformed *erectus* into *sapiens,* however, was more than just the increase in brains alone. Entering the niche of the large carnivore guild as a diurnal hunter provided circumstances that led to the transformation of *Australopithecus* into *Homo,* and that unlikely event almost certainly occurred only once. Subsequently it was the creation of and entry into the realm of the cultural ecological niche that generated what we would now regard as the fully human. The manufacture of tools is not simply a manifestation of a genetically encoded set of instructions designed to result in their fabrication. Tools are not independently invented and produced by each generation. Instead, they represent the continuity of learned behavior transmitted from one generation to the next. In this sense, tools are cultural elements in the anthropological sense.

Louis Leakey's protégée the primatologist Jane Goodall demonstrated that the chimpanzees of the Gombe National Park in Tanzania in East Africa practice rudimentary but clear-cut tool manufacture and use. The technique of selection and defoliation of twigs appropriate for insertion into termite hills is learned by young chimpanzees imitating their mothers, and it represents a behavioral tradition passed from one generation to the next among her East African chimpanzees (Goodall, 1964). Subsequently it has been shown that chimpanzees in the Taï National Park of the Ivory Coast of West Africa use selected hammer stones and anvils to crack open edible nuts (Boesch and Boesch, 1981). Again, this is learned by succeeding generations. The tool traditions of the East African and the West African chimpanzees are clearly different and reflect the transmission of different learned behavior in different places (Whiten et al., 1999). By definition, this is cultural behavior (and see in McGrew, 1992; and de Waal, 1999). In neither of these places nor in the others where chimpanzee tool manufacture has been observed, however, is it essential for chimpanzee survival. Chimpanzees, then, have the rudiments of cultural behavior, but one could not regard them as being dependent on aspects of culture for their very existence.

It was otherwise for the hominids dating from the beginning of genus *Australopithecus*. A weaponless biped on the African savannas would simply have been an easy meal for any of the resident carnivores. Even the subsequent persistence hunters of herbivorous quadrupeds could not have survived if they had relied on their locomotor capabilities to avoid being dinner for a leopard or a pack of hyenas. Trotting patiently after an antelope for a matter of hours or even days is one thing, but survival chances are absolutely zero if one turns around and tries to trot away from a charging lion or a dozen hungry hyenas.

Bipedal locomotion had been established several million years before persistence hunting changed *Australopithecus* into *Homo*. The appearance of bipedalism coincides with the reduction in canine tooth projection. Bipedalism may be slow, but it is energy-efficient and it removes the locomotor role of the fore-limbs. As Darwin perceived, the wielding of hand-held weapons more than compensates for the loss of foot speed. Further, it reduces the value of projecting canine teeth to insignificance. The likelihood of deterring a hungry leopard by actually grabbing it and biting it is far less than by poking it in the eye with five or six feet of tough acacia tree branch. And if the leopard throws caution to the wind and charges, one need only plant the butt of the branch on the ground and aim the point at the oncoming predator, which will literally impale itself—a technique the Masai still use in dealing with lions on the Serengeti Plain of East Africa. Admittedly the Masai use wrought-iron-tipped spears for the purpose, but the principle is the same.

At the point where hand-held weaponry became essential for survival to the extent that the mode of locomotion and the normal mammalian dental defenses became permanently altered, we have to concede that at least one element of culture had become an integral part of the hominid way of life. The perishable tools on which early hominids had been dependent ever since they first became bipedal, and the stone ones that accompanied their adoption first of scavenging and then of regular hunting, certainly count as items of culture in the anthropological sense, but the big change in that cultural realm occurred when it acquired a linguistic dimension. I am suggesting that this was what converted a series of crucial adjuncts to human survival activities into an entire realm which exerted its own pressures on those who would take advantage of its benefits. When the elements subsumed under the term "culture" can be collectively regarded as part of a whole complex whose mastery is essential for survival, then they can be seen as constituting an adaptive realm in and of itself, usefully designated the cultural ecological niche.

At this point, it becomes important to stop and consider just what it is that the anthropologist means by the term "culture." The first Professor of Anthropology at Oxford, Edward Burnett Tylor (1832–1917), offered his definition in full Victorian prolixity.

> Culture or Civilization, taken in its wide ethnographic sense, is that complex whole which includes knowledge, belief, art, morals, law, customs, and any other capabilities and habits acquired by man as a member of society (Tylor, 1871:1).

This can be somewhat generalized to read:

> Culture is "*all those aspects of learning and experience accumulated by previous generations that people acquire by virtue of being members of a continuing society*" (adapted from Brace, 1995:114, italics in the original).

The survival value given by culture, considered in the anthropological sense, is that its beneficiaries are no longer faced with the necessity of having to "reinvent the wheel" each generation, so to speak. Of course, the cynics of the elder generation are ever wont to complain that they can advise their juniors until they are blue in the face and it does no good until the lessens offered are reinforced by the "school of hard knocks." However, though they may not follow the advice proffered, the younger generation invariably learns the techniques of articulation by which it can argue about the dimensions of the message their elders are trying to convey. Language itself is the single most important and remarkable dimension of what the anthropologist means by culture, and it is invariably transmitted from one generation to the next in spite of all the harrumphs about "traditional" grammatical niceties as opposed to the neologisms of youthful slang.

Before going on to treat the broader implications inherent in the use of the concept of culture as an ecological niche, I should at least give some consideration to the ambiguities raised whenever the word "culture" is used outside of the context defined above. For example, the farmer practices agri-"culture" by cultivating his fields, the biochemist sustains a "culture" of microorganisms in a flask or a Petri dish, and the brewer pays especial care to maintaining his yeast "culture."

Then there is the use of "culture" to indicate esthetic refinement and discriminating good taste in matters of artistic sensibility. An extension of this is sometimes indicated by the attachment of an adjective indicating hierarchical social value: thus, "high culture" and perhaps, conversely, "pop culture." At some of the middling but aspiring levels of social stratification in the western world, "culture" even takes on implications of gender. Attendance at a concert or a visit to an art museum is considered time devoted to "culture" and is often associated with the feminine. To maintain a suitably macho degree of self-respect, many middle-class males will approach such functions as a matter of duty befitting the civically responsible but with overt manifestations of reluctance lest they be considered effeminate.

The perception of "culture" as a manifestation of esthetic value and social status can be traced back to the Victorian poet, critic, and arbiter of education Matthew Arnold (1822–1888) who had held the chair of poetry at Oxford a full generation before Tylor received his appointment in anthropology. The difference in emphasis placed on the structure of the educational process by Arnold and his good friend, Darwin's "bulldog," Thomas Henry Huxley (1825–1895), was expressed in successive years in their Rede Lectures at Cambridge University in the late spring of 1882 and 1883 as well as in their speeches at the Royal Academy in 1881 and 1883 (Armytage, 1953; Roos, 1977). In 1869, in his famous *Culture and Anarchy,* Arnold had defined culture as "the best which has been thought and said in the world" (1869:xi). His Rede Lecture of 1882, "Literature and Science," has been called "perhaps the classic defense of the humanistic tradition against the attacks of positivism and science" with Huxley identified as the principal assailant (Trilling, 1939:371).

This, however, is a misreading of the positions of both Arnold and Huxley. Arnold had included the findings of science among "the best which has been thought and said," and Huxley, in his own Rede Lecture of 1883, "Science and Literature," affirmed the classics of literature as essentials to the production of an educated citizen. (Parenthetically, his friend Matthew Arnold was present in Cambridge on the same day, June 13, 1883, to receive an honorary degree for the Rede Lecture he had delivered the year before.) It was not a case of science versus literature or the other way around, it was simply a matter of emphasis. Arnold was convinced that a fully rounded literary background would equip a person to understand virtually anything. Huxley took the stand that polished literacy alone was not sufficient, and that an educated "man" (and they were virtually all "men" in that world) needed training in science as well as letters to deal with the workings of the world. The American university world, with its "distribution" requirements, has tended to come down on Huxley's side of their "debate," while Arnold has prevailed to a greater extent in the structure of the British university curriculum. In both worlds, however, there has been a kind of de facto acceptance to the equating of literary sophistication with "culture."

With so many different meanings conveyed by the term "culture," one might legitimately ask why we should not simply abandon it and use another word. After all, the language has plenty to spare. The main reason is that it has been used in Tylor's anthropological sense for just about as long as it has been used in Arnold's humanistic sense. At this late date, we simply cannot undo over a century of anthropological writing. The most productive thing to do is to start with the sense of Tylor's definition when we specify that we are using the concept of "culture" in the anthropological sense, and go on from there. Discussions building on that start were most specifically promoted by the late American anthropologist Alfred L. Kroeber (1876–1960), whose article "The Superorganic" expanded on Tylor's foundation (Kroeber, 1917). The point made is that culture is not a simple outgrowth or product of human biology, and it is more than just the tangible elements documented by archaeology and in the record of contemporary human technologies. The title of Kroeber's article, however, suggested a possible transcendental aspect as in Nietzsche's *"Übermensch."* This clearly was not part of his intent, and he expended considerable effort in his long and productive career in trying to combat efforts to read an element of the mystical into his treatment. The result, however, was an ever-increasing quantity of words with the consequence that things were somewhat muddied rather than clarified, as for example in the prolonged discourse he coauthored with Clyde Kluckhohn (Kroeber and Kluckhohn, 1952).

The segment of anthropology called "ethnology" or "cultural anthropology," by far the largest component of the field as a whole, takes as its focus the realm of "culture" in the larger anthropological sense, and its practitioners tend to focus on the particular "cultures" of specific and locally circumscribed groups of people. With the expansion of Euro-American settlements and economic political hegemony into many portions of the world during the era of colonization, the encounters with the aboriginal inhabitants in various parts of the world led to an interest in just how they had been making a go of it up to that point. Their languages, customs, and modes of subsistence—their "cultures"—became objects of interest both on the part of authorities intent on maintaining a position of dominance for the colonizing country and on the part of those scholars interested in seeing what light the various local cultural manifestations could throw on the phenomenon of culture as a whole. In many respects, there was an implicit assumption of comparative hierarchical worth built into much of traditional cultural or social anthropology. Anthropologists were said to study "primitive" people, and these were often thought to exemplify stages in sociocultural evolution that were left-overs of what had preceded the emergence of the supposedly "superior" life-ways of the self-satisfied colonizers. The image of ethnology as the handmaiden of colonial exploitation has been responsible for a long-lasting case of guilty conscience on the part of many social anthropologists (Stauder, 1993).

As with many of the dimensions of human biological variation, so in the cultural realm there are things that are under selective force constraints. The cultural traditions of each group have to provide for subsistence needs or else the group itself and the culture it sustains will fail to survive. Adequate means of acquiring food, shelter from the elements, mates for the production of off-spring, defense against hostile actions of competing groups, and other such requirements are universal needs. There is no single best means by which each of these needs can be met, and different cultures display a fascinating spectrum of equally successful solutions to these common problems.

There are many other dimensions of culture that have much less stringent—if any—guiding constraints. Aspects of graphic artistry, music, dance, drama, narrative, and a host of other portions of culture display an endless range of variation and elaboration to fascinate their creators and their constituents as well as anthropologists and other observers. Many anthropologists concentrate on those cultural manifestations that are unrelated to the mechanics of sheer survival to such an extent that they approach a kind of relativistic and postmodernist extreme where the unconstrained is regarded as being all that counts in anthropology. The idiosyncratic is indeed a fascinating realm, but human survival has always had to deal with the problems of coping with the constraints of the world—the "reality" which Scottish Realism assumed to be there. The various means by which this is done remain just as valid a portion of anthropology as the part that revels in the purely subjective. From the perspective of the student of human biological evolution, it is of fundamental importance to understand those aspects of culture that have changed the force of the constraints which have impinged on human chances for survival.

I have already noted that, unlike our nearest relatives the chimpanzees, the hominids ever since they became bipedal were dependent for their survival on elements of culture. Even up through the level of the hunters of the Lower and Middle Pleistocene, lasting up to nearly 200,000 years ago, these key aspects of culture could easily have been transmitted from one generation to the next simply by demonstration and observation. All that was needed was clever mimicry and the understanding of what works.

At about that time, however, a threshold was achieved that changed the nature of the game. Previously, the same technology was distributed throughout the entire range of human occupation. The initial spread of *Homo erectus* out of Africa across the tropics of the Old World nearly 2 million years ago was chiefly demonstrated by the spread of flake tools used for butchering purposes. Then just a shade under 1.5 million years ago, the famous hand-axe was invented somewhere in Africa and was adopted by the inhabitants of that continent (Clark, 1975). From there its usage spread across the rest of the Old World, and it has been found in Lower Pleistocene strata from Europe to India, Southeast Asia, China and Japan (Bordes, 1968:82; Ikawa-Smith, 1982:16; and see a European example in Figure 12-2; and note the area of occupation indicated in Figure 12-3).

Since this picture is mostly made up of the distribution of the tools themselves, there is room for more than one way to interpret how that came about. Followers of the catastrophist tradition, as might be expected, tend to see the picture as the result of hand-axe makers spreading out of Africa and doing in the flake users who had preceded them. The other way to account for it is to see the local residents simply adopting the new ideas of their neighbors on one side, and then their neighbors on the other side copying them in turn. From this point of view, the picture is one of a spread of tools and not of people. My own preference is very much for this second interpretation.

The reason is an assessment of what the hand-axe meant to its possessors. It was not a weapon that was wielded in combat, nor was it a projectile whose tear-drop shape was designed for aerodynamic efficiency. After all, even our more muscular Pleistocene ancestors would have found it impossible to hurl a five- or ten-pound chunk of rock with enough velocity so that its

Figure 12-2 A biface or hand-axe from St. Acheul in northwestern France, the location that gave its name to a whole category of Middle Pleistocene tools. (Drawn by M. L. Brace from a specimen given to Charles L. Brace by Sir Charles Lyell. From Brace, 1995:14.)

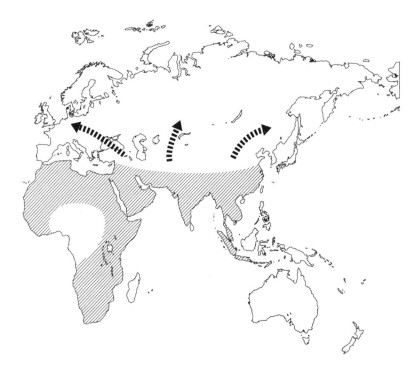

Figure 12-3 The permanent zone occupied by the hominid members of the large carnivore guild between about 2 million years ago and 250,000 years ago. The dotted arrows show the direction of temporary interglacial incursions into the Temperate Zone (from Figure 11-13, Brace, 1995:168).

shape would have had any discernible effect on its trajectory. And then there is the wondrous suggestion that it was propelled like a discus so that it whirled through the air like a kind of "killer frisbee" (Calvin, 1990:276). Hurled into a herd of grazing animals, presumably it might just hit one, though the probability of doing anything more than bruising the frightened creature struck by chance in such a fashion is so low that it would hardly have warranted the time and effort obviously devoted to the construction of the countless examples of such tools known to date. All of the rest of the tool kit of its users shows that the way of life they pursued was exactly the same as was that of the groups who did not have it. The same animals were being hunted, the same localities were being exploited, and population density was no different.

The chipping and battering around the pointed portion of the hand-axe suggests that this was the business end. Documentary films of living hunter-gatherers butchering large animals, even with the aid of steel knives, shows them holding the handle with two hands and chonking downward with the point to get through the large leg joints of the creature being dismembered. Lacking metal tools, Pleistocene hunters could well have accomplished the same effect by holding the blunt end of a hand-axe in two hands and chonking downward in just the same fashion. The result would be just the same, if slower, and the battering of the pointed end would be one of the side effects. The benefit to the user, as shown by those ethnographic films, is that the meat-bearing segments of animal limbs can be separated from the portion that is mostly bone and gristle so that one can walk off with the usable parts without having to lug along the whole thing. It is something of a convenience, but it would hardly have given its users a significant competitive edge over those who had not yet adopted it.

The same scenario was probably true for virtually every technological innovation prior to the invention of agriculture about 10,000 years ago. Only then did some populations clearly gain the advantage over the previous residents in a given area, and the advantage gained was solely that of numbers. The ability to till the ground did not give the first farmers a technological edge over their hunting neighbors in any potential situation of actual confrontation. Farming, however, could sustain many more people in a given area, and their advantage over their nonfarming neighbors was that they could simply put more combatants in the field at any given time.

THE CULTURAL ECOLOGICAL NICHE AND LANGUAGE: THE CLINCHER OF HUMAN UNITY

Not all that long after agriculture had become well established, the discovery of metallurgy did give those societies sustained by crop cultivation a real edge in weaponry over those who continued to gain their livelihoods by hunting and gathering. At about the same time, the rise of literacy gave the former the ability to write about their experiences. At that point, we have clear evidence that human intellectual capabilities were essentially what they are today. That record shows *Homo sapiens* as articulate creatures whose success in the world was largely dependent on following and building on the ways of life that had been successful for their predecessors: that is, reaping the benefits of life within the cultural ecological niche. The key to the ability to do that is tied to their mastery of the most central and unique component of that realm— language. The single most dramatic behavioral distinction between a chimpanzee and a human being is the presence of articulate speech in the latter. Chimpanzees are as clever as animals get, but, despite prolonged and patient efforts of instruction, no one has ever come close to teaching one to speak (Terrace, 1979; Terrace et al., 1979).

All normal human beings master the art of verbal communication between the ages of 2 and 12. Those who are unable to do so for whatever reason are never fully able to participate in the human experience. Within any given human group there are individual differences in the skill with which language is used, but there is no hint that there are average differences in verbal ability when any such group is compared with any other. All human languages are constructed on the same principles, there are no differences in grammatical complexity, and all are equally effective in dealing with objects, actions, places, and time. All are equally able to deal with abstractions as well as with the concrete (Swadesh, 1971; Hockett, 1978; Pinker and Bloom, 1990; Pinker, 1994). There is no difference in the size of the working vocabulary between speakers of one language and those of another. Of course, those languages that are preserved in written form will accumulate a far larger vocabulary than those that exist only in the minds of their living speakers, and those languages that have the longest continuous written record, such as Chinese, will have a proportionately greater list of words than those that have only been recorded within the span of living memory. When we assess the living peoples of the world, there is no evidence that the number of words actively used by the average speaker of any of the thousands of languages currently spoken differs between any of the known groups.

If this, then, is a measure of the common human condition as it exists in the world today, there is still the matter of the where, the when, and the why language emerged. This clearly occurred long before the first written records, but how long? Obviously we cannot test this by what has been written, but there is another more indirect kind of check. The tools that go back over 2 million years, and the regularly shaped hand-axes that continued from 1.5 million years, indicate traditions that have been passed on from generation to generation, century to century, and millennium to millennium. But the point has been made often enough that sheer imitation should have been sufficient for the perpetuation of something that so evidently works. The continuity of tools alone, then, does not necessarily indicate the presence of language as we know it.

However, when tools begin to differ in the nuances of construction—not in the major uses to which they are put—then we begin to get the idea that something more than their demonstrably self-evident effectiveness is involved. When those nuances in the style of their formation begin to show clear-cut differences from one region to another, then there is reason to suspect that there are implications of "we do it this way" involved. Starting somewhere around 250,000 years ago, differing local styles of tool manufacture begin to become apparent between areas such as the Cape of Good Hope in South Africa, the Horn of East Africa, the Mediterranean lands of North Africa, France, and adjacent areas of Western Europe, Southern Russia, the Arabian Peninsula, the Tigris-Euphrates drainage area of the Middle East, and less well studied but comparable aspects of territory in South Asia/India and in East Asia. This is not intended as a comprehensive list. Instead, it is just an illustration of the kinds of areas within which regional differences in shared stylistic manifestations of stone tool manufacture can be found (Clark and Schick, 1988; Clark, 1993; Bar-Yosef, 1991–1992). Interestingly enough, this is just about the same time that evidence for the control of fire can be documented (Straus, 1989), and one can make the case that perpetuating knowledge about how to make and sustain fire almost had to involve language (Ronen, 1998:445).

As we look at it from the perspective of another quarter-of-a-million years down the road, we begin to suspect that a sense of collective identity was emerging for the first time among the hunting bands who lived adjacent to each other in larger but topographically circumscribed geographic provinces. When the interpolated distributions of the style characteristics of those late Middle Pleistocene tools are plotted on the map, they are eerily reminiscent of the distributions one would plot for linguistic relationships of more recent human groups (see Figure 12-4). It is hard to see how we can ever get much beyond the subjective nature of the suspicions which this puts into our minds, but it would be equally unproductive to banish that suspicion just because we can never subject it to a definitive test.

The nature of the distribution of the styles of those tools and the ubiquitous evidence for the control of fire leads us to suspect that this was the point where the rudiments of language as we know it had begun to become manifest as a common human property. It was not that a single language was universally distributed. Rather, it was linguistic capability that was present throughout. Nor is there any evidence that this started in one locally identifiable region and spread elsewhere. Instead, it would appear that this emerged effectively simultaneously throughout the entire extent of human occupation. Evidently the amount of genetic exchange between adjacent groups was sufficient so that the circumstances of the human hunting and gathering life-way selected for what was intellectually advantageous everywhere to the same degree, and what became linguistic behavior emerged as a species-wide phenomenon.

Figure 12-4 A schematic depiction of the extent of areally shared stylistic elements in the Mousterian and Mousterian-related cultures of the Old World. The number of question marks in the Far Eastern area of "shared" elements is really the result of absence of information since much less systematic research has been pursued in eastern Asia than elsewhere. (Modified from Brace, 1995:220, which had used the old Mercator projection.)

It is also clear that this was not an instantaneous event. Throughout the course of the Lower Paleolithic from 2 million to just over 200,000 years ago, there was very little in the way of evident cultural "advance." Hand-axes had been added to the tool kit, but that would seem to have made little difference in the major aspects of the subsistence activities pursued. This does remind us, however, that we are making our assessments of Pleistocene hominid life-ways on the basis of a small portion of the tip of the figurative cultural iceberg. Stone tools, important as they were, represent only a tiny fraction of the technological capabilities of their employers, and butchered animal bones are the products of what had to be substantially less than half of the subsistence activities pursued.

We can guess that, throughout the Lower Paleolithic, there had to have been a growth in those aspects of cultural sophistication represented by items that have not been preserved. As a cautionary example, the contrast between the relative simplicity and uniformity of the stone tools now being studied by archaeologists in Australia, a continent where a hunting-and-gathering means of subsistence was ubiquitous at the time English colonization began late in the eighteenth century, gives no hint of the extraordinary sophistication of the perishable aspects of Australian technology visible in the material in Australian museums contributed by living Aborigines in the recent past. That in turn gives only the most tantalizing suggestion of the quantities of detailed information possessed by the average Aborigine. That knowledge, as is true for the detail and accuracy of the information controlled by the hunters of highland New Guinea, the Amazon Basin of South America, the San of the Kalahari Desert in South Africa, or the Eskimo in the Arctic, represents an intellectual achievement for each of the aspects of natural history on a par with what is expected of a Ph.D. candidate at a major research university in the western world (Dornan, 1925; Poliakov, 1974:346 [quoting from Trubetskoy]; Stephenson, 1982; Diamond, 1989; Hill and Hurtado, 1996). The doctoral student, however, only focuses on one specific phenomenon such as a particular category of insects, or birds, or plants, or soil—or whatever—while the unlettered people making a go of it in their own part of the world have doctoral-level sophistication in their knowledge of all such categories simultaneously. Furthermore, this is not discovered anew each generation. Instead, it is verbally transmitted and then reinforced by experience.

Darwin's contemporary Alfred Russel Wallace (1823–1913) articulated the quaintly ethnocentric idea that, unlike that self-declared paragon the Victorian "gentleman," the "savage" in the Amazon Basin or Borneo, or wherever, needed only a fraction of the full complement of human intelligence to survive. Natural selection, he then concluded, could not account for the evolution of the human brain (Wallace, 1875:355–356). The same kind of ethnocentrism still governs the assumptions that the large-brained Neanderthals were only capable of "minimally directed movement during the food quest" and so were reduced to flailing around aimlessly "on the landscape" to get their next meal (Trinkaus, 1986:204–206; Trinkaus and Shipman, 1992:368). In like fashion, and despite the fact that the one well-preserved Neanderthal voice box—the hyoid bone—is morphologically indistinguishable from that of a living human one (Arensberg et al., 1990), Chris Stringer has declared that "Neanderthals lacked complex spoken language because they did not need it" (Stringer and Gamble, 1993:217).

At this point I am impelled to editorialize that what is needed here is a good, solid dose of the full four-fold anthropological perspective. Within the anthropological business itself, this is referred to as the "four-field" approach, and has been a built-in aspect of the graduate student training programs in the stronger academic departments of anthropology in the United States for much of the twentieth century. This requires that each student acquire a basic grounding in the fields of ethnology, archaeology, biological anthropology, and linguistics before going on to specialize in one particular area. Despite his staunch opposition to Darwinian views, it was the vision held by the founder of anthropology in France, Paul Broca (1824–1880), though, there, it did not long survive his death (Williams, 1923; Schiller, 1979). "Anthropology" on the Continent now means largely the anatomical focus of biological anthropology. In England, "anthropology" generally is identified with "social anthropology" (which may encompass linguistics), while archaeology and biological anthropology tend to be shunted off into departments of their own. To get some kind of control over how human groups were able to survive in the past, we need to have an understanding of the interaction between the various elements of the human condition at the present. In effect, we need to have a better perspective on the full nature of the cultural ecological niche and the selective pressures this imposes on those who would take advantage of what it offers.

Archaeologists in America, in contrast to other kinds of anthropologists, have often displayed a greater consciousness of this requirement, though, since their work inevitably is narrowly object-centered, the subtleties of those objects sometimes take on a significance to the scholar that may be out of proportion to what they would have meant to the original makers. As many archaeologists have realized, the way to put this into proper perspective is to become thoroughly familiar with the outlook of the remaining traditional tool-makers whose products have not yet been supplanted by the gaudier gadgetry that emanates with ever-greater effect from the industrialized world. The information about tools, traditions, life-ways, and what people say about them is all part of the cultural ecological niche, and all aspects of this are necessary for the basic possibility of human survival. It is from the archaeological evidence that we can project such expectations back into the past. The biological anthropologist, then, can use this to make some kind of sense out of the anatomical evidence provided by ancient skeletons and the trajectory of change by which the archaic becomes transformed into "modern" aspects of form.

If the style changes seen, as the Lower Paleolithic gives way to the Middle Paleolithic over 200,000 years ago, suggest the beginnings of linguistic behavior, then we can suspect that the cultural ecological niche had begun to exert still greater pressures to adapt on those who attempted to take full advantage of its benefits. Interestingly enough, the human brain, which had slowly doubled in size over the previous two million years, ceased to increase from that point on. Relative to body size, it has remained the same ever since. That long-term record of brain expansion should mean that neurological changes necessary for language had a long, slow course of development. This argues against the idea promoted by the linguists Noam Chomsky and Derek Bickerton that the capacity for language was the result of a single mutation at some unknown time in the past (Chomsky, 1975:53, 1988:170; Bickerton, 1990:174, 192). Like the cladists and the punctuationists, this smacks of the "and then a miracle occurs" school of thought, and it has been treated with well-deserved skepticism by other commentators (Pinker and Bloom, 1990; Pinker, 1994; Dennett, 1995; Deacon, 1997).

Almost predictably, those anthropologists who represent the continuity of hominid catastrophism have preferred to regard the acquisition of linguistic capabilities as having been comparable to "the flick of a switch and *not* the slow upward movement of a symbolic dimmer" (Stringer and Gamble, 1993:204). As even that mutation enthusiast Derek Bickerton has noted, this kind of treatment overlooks the complexity of the neurological basis that makes language possible. Simple-minded appraisals such as this exemplify what he would regard as "the Flintstones approach to language origins [which] totally ignores the vast amount of preadaptation that was necessary before you could even get to that point, and equally ignores the vast amount of postadaptation that was necessary in order to get from that point to fully developed human language" (Bickerton, 1981:215).

The slow increase in brain size from the 700 cubic centimeters or so of early *Homo erectus* to the 1200 to 1500 cc. levels achieved by the time it stabilized over 200,000 years ago should provide a hint of that "preadaptation." Of course, this is only the grossest kind of index and can tell us nothing about the details of the interconnections of neurons in the various areas of the cortex that are all essential before language is possible. The suggestion has been made that one of the forces driving the development of language was the need to deal with other clever competitors, namely other groups of equally intelligent hominids (Humphrey, 1976, 1992; Alexander, 1990). The same logic ought to apply equally to chimpanzees, orangs, and others of our primate relatives, and yet none of them display even the simplest rudiments of what could count as linguistic behavior. A related argument has suggested that brain size and language coevolved as a kind of verbal extension of the grooming behavior that cements social relationships in primate groups. Verbal exchanges, many simply in the form of gossip, allow a much larger extension of interindividual networks to be maintained (Dunbar, 1993, 1996). Larger cooperative networks should be advantageous for the participants in comparison to those going it alone or limited to the number of others with whom one can maintain a mutual fur-combing relationship.

Extending this further, the linguistic world allows us to retain a role in group membership for individuals who are physically removed, either in place or in time—a previous generation, for example. During their colonization of Australia, Europeans often found it quaintly amusing that Australian aboriginal groups, on encountering each other for the first time, would sit down and discuss kinship before doing anything else. But if they could ferret out some ancestral figures shared in common, then the confronting groups could be regarded as kinfolk and not simply strangers presumed to be hostile. The same kind of behavior characterized the colonizers of the American Midwestern frontier as they tried to find out possible relationships with each other: "And who's your mother's brother?" or, "Who's your father's mother?" or, "Who's your…?" to such an extent that the settlers in what is now the state of Missouri acquired the name of "Hoosiers." The survival value of this kind of capability is obviously considerable, but was this the key to the development of language as a discrete phenomenon? Probably not, in and of itself. No judgment can be anything more than an informed guess, but it seems likely that the circumstances that led to the evolution of our linguistic capabilities were a combination of all of the above and perhaps more.

Just exactly when the coalescence of capabilities occurred that allowed the first version of language as we know it is something we shall probably never know. It may not have been identifiable as a single obvious occurrence as it took place. Today it seems self-evident to us that there is a categorical distinction between the human linguistic capability and its lack in other organisms, but that long, slow period of increase in brain size during the Lower Paleolithic, and the slow gain in the momentum of increasing technological sophistication after modern sizes of brain had been achieved over 200,000 years ago just at the time that the control of fire became a human universal, suggests that the development of language was indeed a gradual phenomenon and not "the flick of a switch." If it really was the acquisition of a version of language that was indicated by the transformation of the Lower Paleolithic into the Middle Paleolithic late in the Middle Pleistocene, it was apparently engendered by the life-way of the hunting-and-gathering makers of those tools. Since that life-way was essentially the same from one end of human occupation to the other, and since specific unity was maintained by genetic exchange—gene flow—between adjacent groups subject to essentially identical pressures of selection, it seems likely that the capacity for language developed simultaneously throughout the entire extent of the species.

By the time that capacity had been achieved, a new specific label would seem to be warranted for those who had attained it. This we can properly indicate by using the specific designation *sapiens*. But those representatives of *Homo sapiens* merit that label by brain size and cultural capacity alone. In all other anatomical details, they still displayed the robustness and muscularity of their *erectus* predecessors. Earlier in this century, Aleš Hrdlička and Franz Weidenreich had pointed out that the first human fossil to have been discovered displaying these characteristics was the one discovered in 1856 in a valley—the Neanderthal—in the western part of Germany, and they both proposed that the term "Neanderthal" be used to indicate a stage of premodern robustness which preceded and evolved into what we designate "modern" human form. Following their lead, I have continued to find it useful to recognize a Neanderthal Stage in human evolution (Brace, 1995, Chapter 13).

To be sure, my own honored mentor, W. W. Howells, has objected, with an almost palpable shudder of disdain, that broadening the definition of Neanderthal to include all Late Pleistocene premodern human form would result in "a monster of which the morphological character is merely large cranial size and large brows, and of which the range of variation is simply illegitimate" (Howells, 1974:9). Exactly the same objection could be raised to calling all the people living in the world at the present time by the same term, "modern." The range of tooth size alone exhibited between the living populations of the world is greater than the average difference between that of the Neanderthals and some groups of living humans, but that is just because variation in living human populations is at least as great as variation between the various samples dating from the end of the Middle Pleistocene on into the Late Pleistocene (see Figures 12-5 and 12-6). If living populations can all be encompassed by the same term, I would defend the view that there is nothing illegitimate in referring to their more robust predecessors as *Homo sapiens neanderthalensis,* that is, regional representatives of an earlier manifestation of Pleistocene robustness, or a Neanderthal Stage in human evolution (Brace, 1995, Chapter 13).

As with the emergence of language according to the way we define it, the transition from *Homo erectus* to *Homo sapiens* was also a gradual phenomenon without any absolute and set boundary. Because of the spotty and incomplete record, anything we choose to do in recognizing these distinctions is going to have an element of the arbitrary to it, and there will continue to be emotionally charged disagreements between the scholars who have invested their professional careers and reputations on divergent interpretations. Human brain size had reached modern levels at just that time when the control of fire and local stylistic embellishments became evident on what was functionally the same kind of tool kit just beyond 200,000 years ago, and I am

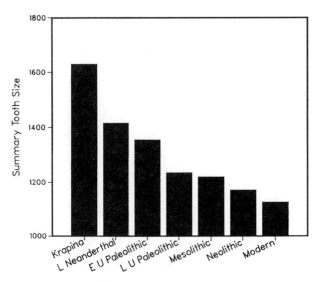

Figure 12-5 European Tooth Size Change. Summary tooth size figures made by adding up the cross-sectional areas of each category of tooth for a given individual and then making an average for the group named. The picture shown demonstrates the change of tooth size in situ over a span of 50,000 years in Europe. The data and the references are cited in Chapter 6, though Dave Frayer has told me that, each time a version of this diagram is used, he wants separate citation for the measurements he made on the Late Upper Paleolithic European specimens for his doctoral dissertation (Frayer, 1976).

making the case that at this point we can recognize the beginning of *Homo sapiens*. I am also suggesting that this marks the beginning of culture as a full-scale ecological niche in and of itself.

Aspects that have to be called "cultural" had existed for the previous several million years and had become increasingly essential for human survival, but, somewhere late in the Middle Pleistocene, the addition of what can be called language to the cultural repertoire added a kind of selective force imperative that had its effect on all the various human groups wherever they lived. Survival had become closely tied to the ability to learn the traditions of one's natal group, and this could only be done by learning their language. The nature of the selective forces associated with the requirement of learning a language is very different from the kinds of forces that impinge on nonverbal species. The very matter of human survival is involved, and selection for the ability to master linguistic basics is intense, but it is also the same for all human beings and it has been so for approximately a quarter-of-a-million years.

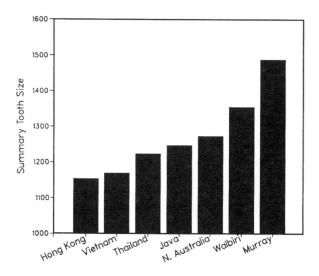

Figure 12-6 Australasian Tooth Size. Summary tooth size figures for a series of living human populations distributed from Southeast Asia out to South Australia. The spectrum is exactly the equivalent of 50,000 years of change in situ following the adoption of cooking as a means of food preparation. The picture shown here suggests that it took an equivalent length of time for that kind of food-preparation technology to spread south on the Asian mainland and out through the Indonesian archipelago to Australia. The data and sources used are presented in Chapter 6.

The pressures involved in entering the cultural ecological niche, at least initially, can be compared to those involved for creatures that would exploit a version of the aerial ecological niche. The floors of bat-roosting caves are littered with the bodies of young bats that just could not master the requirements of flight. The greatest mortality among young birds also comes at the point where they have to learn how to fly. In the past, humans who could not learn the rudiments of verbal communication simply were not able to grow up and raise a successful family. And their inherited characteristics were not passed on to the succeeding generations. Those who could gain command of the verbal world had instant access to the experience of previous generations and of contemporaries who could relay the lessons from events not directly experienced by any others. The survival value of this kind of vicarious experience is the most important benefit conveyed by living within the cultural ecological niche.

The unity of the human species, far from being a recent and unexpected phenomenon, is the product of that long pre-*sapiens* stretch as the only primate member of the large carnivore guild, and this was reinforced by the subsequent species-wide entry into the cultural ecological niche. Human ancestors then continued to share a similar life-way until the beginning of farming some 10,000 years ago. This put neither more nor less stress on the need to be enculturated into ancestral ways of doing things. The accumulation of the codified experience of previous generations made possible by the invention of writing gave people a much larger information base to work with, but it also meant that less of this had to be carried around in the head. Instead, one could go and look it up.

This raises the possibility that, if there might indeed be a residue of difference in average intellectual capacity between living human populations, it could be proportional to the length of time that literacy has been a factor in survival strategy. If there is anything to such a possibility, however, it would be the reverse of the assumptions so often articulated by the literate as they contrast themselves to what they usually perceive as the state of "benighted savagery." On the other hand, the length of time that a given group has enjoyed the benefits of literacy might just indicate how long the selective pressures maintaining brain power have been reduced, allowing a consequent erosion in average capacity. Even if there is an off chance that the acuteness of memory may have faded, the pressures maintaining linguistic capability have remained as strong as ever and virtually identical throughout the human world, literate or not. In any case, the actual amount of time that has elapsed since the acquisition of written records has been so extremely short when viewed from the longer perspective of human evolution that it is almost certain that no discernible difference in intellectual capacity could have arisen between then and now. Selection for skin color differences has been unable to produce any discernible differences in two to three times that length of time. The obvious conclusion to all of this is that there should be absolutely no difference in the average intellectual ability between any of the living populations of the world.

All of this has clear-cut implications for the debate involving the pros and cons of affirmative action in present-day America. If average ability is the same for all human groups, then members of each should be present in desirable school programs and jobs in numbers that mirror the proportions that each such group constitutes of the population as a whole. If this is not the case, then there is clearly bias involved in the criteria used for selection. Scores on tests of "ability" or "achievement" are clearly different for different social classes. The most overriding determinant of social class in America, however, is the hold-over from two centuries of slavery and a subsequent century of legal racial segregation. The bottom of the American social hierarchy is made up of people whose ancestors had been forcibly removed from Africa. If their inherent capabilities are exactly the same as those of any other group, and yet an "ability" test shows a lower average ranking for them than for another group, then it is clear that the "ability" test is measuring the effects of that social status and not innate capacity. Despite what anyone might say, "ability" tests are actually selecting for the products of privilege—"race"—even though the word is not used and the intent may be denied. The abolition of affirmative action programs means that "racial preference" will return in full force in spite of all the pious invocations of "color-blind justice." Like the notorious *Bell Curve*, this is nothing less than hypocrisy on the part of a privileged elite applied in an effort to maintain its own superiority in income and social status at the expense of a racial minority (see the manifestations of that in Herrnstein and Murray, 1994; and Bolick, 1996).

THE CULTURAL ECOLOGICAL NICHE ≠ BIOLOGICAL DIFFERENCES

As has been developed at some length above, the most important dimension of the cultural ecological niche is language. The selective pressures exerted by the need to learn a language have been the same for all human beings ever since linguistic behavior became an integral and defining part of the niche as a whole. This has been a constant ever since humans acquired their sapience, and it is clearly the reason why human intelligence on the average is the same wherever there are human beings. This, however, is the only dimension of the cultural ecological niche that is the same throughout.

It is Chris Stringer's view that humans are all Africans under the skin (Stringer, 1997a and b), but the contribution made by Africa to the human condition was not unique to that continent. The shaping effect exerted was that of the tropics. This could just as easily have been done in southern India or Southeast Asia, but the evidence shows that it was accomplished by the tropics in Africa. Physiologically speaking, we are tropical mammals, and no human can survive the rigors of winter in the temperate zone without substantial cultural assistance. Clothing, shelter, and heat in the form of the control of fire are essentials. The archaeological record shows that these had all become available for use at just that time when brain size stopped expanding and the rudiments of language had been acquired. In fact, the planning necessary for a physiologically tropical hominid to surmount the problems of survival in the colder parts of the temperate zone would have been almost inconceivable in the absence of language. And who were the first humans to face that challenge successfully? None other than Chris Stringer's Neanderthals. So much for the idea that they had no language "because they did not need it" (Stringer and Gamble, 1993:217).

It seems probable that Neanderthals, whom I have defined as the more robust but equally brainy predecessors—the ancestors—of "modern" humans, were the first to operate within what can be called the cultural ecological niche as that is characterized by the presence of its key linguistic component. The tools with which they were associated have been called Mousterian, and one can use that term to describe the culture of the northwestern Neanderthals. The Mousterian proper is distributed throughout Europe, southern Russia, the Balkans, and the Middle East, and it has an antiquity that goes back to around 250,000 years ago and possibly more (Straus, 1989:489–490). There are counterparts eastward all the way to China and Japan (Bordes, 1978:ix; Tanaka et al., 1995:2; though see the doubts by Clark and Schick, 1988:445), in the "Middle Palaeolithic" of India (Ghosh, ed., 1989:28–29), and the "Middle Stone Age" of Africa (Bar-Yosef, 1992:197, 1993:139; Klein, 1996:188). Archaeologists in each of these major geographic areas have concluded that these Mousterian-like or Middle Paleolithic complexes arose independently from local Lower Paleolithic predecessors and did not represent the spread from a single identifiable locality, whether African, European, or any other. This is the archaeological support for the idea that entry by humans into the cultural ecological niche occurred effectively simultaneously throughout the entire inhabited world.

There is no evidence to suggest that the Middle Paleolithic people living in one part of the world were more sophisticated in any significant way than those living anywhere else. At the northwestern edge of that zone of habitation, the preparation of skins for use as clothing is attested to by the proliferation of Mousterian scrapers, largely absent from Middle Paleolithic assemblages elsewhere (Bordes, 1961). Post holes and mammoth-bone implantings show that they were constructing shelters (Chard, 1969; though see the problems concerning the evidence mentioned by Soffer, 1994:108). Ashes, burnt bone, and fire-blackened rocks confirm the fact that they were regularly making fires and cooking their food (Straus, 1989; Bar-Yosef et al., 1992). Clearly, the products of the chase would have frozen within a day or so in a Europe in the grip of a glaciation, so, as mentioned in Chapters 6 through 8, cooking was essential to their survival. Their shelter-constructing ability and the preparation of hearths has been denigrated by the intellectual heirs to the tradition of Marcellin Boule (Stringer and Gamble, 1993:155, 207), but one should realize that there is no evidence at all for shelter or hearth-making activities going on at that time anywhere else in the world. Whatever was being done was being done by Neanderthals.

The deliberate burial of the dead with symbolic grave-goods suggests a concern for spiritual values and notions of an afterlife (Smirnov, 1989:228; Bar-Yosef, 1994:45), though, again, the proponents of the idea of Neanderthals as beasts have dismissed such practices as merely "corpse disposal" (Stringer and Gamble, 1993:160). Another possible indicator of Neanderthal capabilities is the discovery of a fragment of a bear leg bone found in a Mousterian site in Slovenia with holes carved in it suggesting that it was a flute constructed to be able to reproduce the notes of a minor diatonic scale (Wilford, 1996; Wong, 1997). For all the attempts to demote the Neanderthals to represent the embodiment of Thomas Hobbes's misanthropic caricature of human life—"nasty, brutish, and short"—the hunting capabilities and domestic arrangements of the bearers of the Mousterian culture were the equal of those of their contemporaries anywhere else in the world. The symbolic content and nature of Middle Paleolithic culture was the same everywhere, and the selective pressures on its makers to adapt to a niche that demanded linguistic capability was a uniform requirement.

This did not mean that all Middle Paleolithic cultures were identical in all details. The requirements of life in the northern reaches of human habitation put much more stress on clothing, cooking, and shelter. As noted in several of the previous chapters, one of the results of what might be called the beginnings of "the culinary revolution" was that the selective forces maintaining Middle Pleistocene levels of tooth size were relaxed, allowing mutations to accumulate, and resulting in the reduction of tooth size amongst those long-term practitioners of cooking. The smallest teeth in the world today occur in just those areas where the archaeological evidence shows us that cooking was practiced earlier than anywhere else. In Chapters 7 and 8, the evidence was surveyed for the earliest appearance of thrown projectiles in Africa in the Middle Stone Age perhaps as far back as 200,000 years. Recently, the discovery of wooden spears in a Middle Pleistocene site in Germany has raised the possibility of projectile use dating back to 400,000 years ago (Thieme, 1997), but the sheer heft of those shafts suggests that they were too weighty to have been hurled and served instead as hand-held thrusting spears. Later on, the invention of the thrown projectile had the effect of taking the pressure off the previously required degree of muscularity and robustness from the neck on down. As the manufacture and use of projectiles spread to other parts of the world, parallel degrees of reduction developed, and eventually all the people who had acquired that aspect of technology became "modern" in form (and see Chapter 8).

Skin Color as an Index of Time in Place

One aspect of human biological difference that varies dramatically between populations is skin color. This is unrelated to variations in the cultural ecological niche as such, but it is a very good index of the intensity of natural selection associated with differences in latitude. Differences in skin pigment can also serve as a measure of how long a given population has been at the latitude where it is currently found. Variation in the color of the human skin is principally caused by differences in the amount of the pigment melanin inherited by each individual (Robins, 1991).

The role of melanin in the skin is to prevent the penetration of ultraviolet rays. Small doses of ultraviolet radiation play a valuable role in helping synthesize vitamin D, necessary for normal bone growth, but added ultraviolet impact can have damaging effects. The most dangerous of these is skin cancer. Ultraviolet radiation is most intense at the equator and between the Tropics of Cancer and Capricorn. Because of factors involving the tilt of the earth's axis of rotation, there are differences in the intensity of solar radiation reaching the portions of the earth's surface to the south of the equator in contrast to those in the northern hemisphere. The south gets a greater average dosage (Relethford, 1997). Residents in Cape Town in South Africa need somewhat more protection than those in Jerusalem, though both are about equally distant from the equator.

When *Homo erectus* became a member of the large carnivore guild some 2 million years ago, the life of a persistence hunter on the African savannas all the way from Ethiopia down to South Africa was possible only by the elimination of the fur coat that had been part of our ancestral primate heritage. That exposed the skin to the effects of ultraviolet radiation, and this constituted the selective force which led to the development of a uniform distribution of melanin in the skin. The common human ancestor, then, had a skin as heavily pigmented as that of the darkest color visible in human beings living today.

Departure from that ancestral condition has been directly proportional to the length of time that current populations have been living in regions removed from the areas of maximum ultraviolet ray intensity in the tropics. There have been repeated attempts to view the reduction of pigment in the skin of nontropical peoples as the results of some sort of beneficial selection. It has been suggested that reductions of pigmentation in northern latitudes helped utilize what little UV gets through the atmosphere to the skin in the synthesis of vitamin D (Murray, 1934; Loomis, 1967). As it happens, however, vitamin D is a fat-soluble substance, and a few good doses of exposure during the summer, even if one has a fully pigmented skin, generates enough to be stored in fat and muscle tissue for usage the rest of the year (Robins, 1991:203–208). Northern fur-covered quadrupeds such as deer and our old competitors the wolves get enough UV radiation through the exposed, even-if-pigmented, patch of skin on the nose to satisfy their requirements. At that, the rest of the skin under their fur coats, where it cannot react to ultraviolet light, is entirely devoid of pigment.

Obviously the selective-force argument does not explain why skin pigment is reduced in northern populations. I am thrown back to the same kind of explanation that accounts for reduction in human tooth size. That is, in the absence of selection maintaining a trait, mutations alone, accumulating through time, will produce a reduction in the trait in question. It is the operation of the Probable Mutation Effect (see Chapter 5, and the considerations in Chapter 6). Those populations that have existed for the longest periods in areas of low ultraviolet intensity will show the greatest amount of pigment reduction. Depigmentation, then, is an index of the amount of time spent at a remove from the tropics (Brace, Henneberg, and Relethford, 1999).

As with the picture shown by DNA haplotype similarities and differences, there is the question of calibrating this index. There are a number of examples which demonstrate how this can be done. Perhaps the most convincing example of how to start this calibration is to consider the original human extension into the western hemisphere. The first Native Americans to arrive came from Northeast Asia no more than about 15,000 years ago and rapidly spread throughout the entire hemisphere from the Arctic Circle to the equator and on down to a latitude that is as far south of the equator as Hudson's Bay is north (Meltzer, 1993, 1997). And yet there is no faint hint of a gradient or cline of pigmentation varying with latitude in the western hemisphere. Instead, pigment is effectively the same as that of the still-living populations of Northeast Asia. Evidently, 15,000 years is just not enough time for differences in the intensity of ultraviolet radiation to have any effect on human skin pigmentation.

A consideration of the case of Australia can add a bit more to our assessment. As with the example of the western hemisphere, there is a similar uncertainty about nailing down the exact date of the initial populating of the continent. From several lines of evidence, however, many archaeologists are comfortable with a date of about 50,000 years (Roberts et al., 1994; Morell, 1995). Unlike the New World examples, there is a pigment gradient from the northern tip of Australia, well north of the Tropic of Capricorn, to Tasmania which is well south of the latitude of the Cape of Good Hope at the southern-most tip of Africa (Birdsell, 1967:120; 1993:186). The Australian skin color gradient runs all the way from tropical African degrees of darkness in the north to a kind of medium-dark brown in the south. Depigmentation has taken place in Australia over the span of 50,000 years, but it has not pro-ceeded to the same extent as that visible in the comparable stretch of Africa from the equator south to the Cape of Good Hope. In Africa, the equatorial inhabitants are every bit as dark as the Australians of North Queensland, but the San of the southern tip of the continent are a lighter brown than the Australians at the southern edge of their own continent.

One thing this example can tell us is that 50,000 years simply will not do to account for the reduction of European levels of pigmentation from an ancestor of tropical African hue. Even if one projects that African exodus back to 100,000 years, it would be difficult to produce the spectrum of pig-mentation observed. However, if one accepts the Mousterian archaeological evidence for the antiquity of in situ European continuity and faces the fright-ening thought of (gasp!) a Neanderthal ancestry for living Europeans, one has 250,000 years to deal with, and this should easily do the trick.

The remaining instance of skin pigment as an index of time in situ is the comparison of peoples at the same latitude in the North Temperate Zone. None of the indigenous peoples of that area show anything like the amount of skin pigmentation seen in long-term tropic dwellers such as the inhabitants of Nigeria or New Guinea. At both the western and eastern edges of the Old World, there is a skin color gradient that runs from south to north (see Figure 11-3). Skin pigment gradually lightens as one proceeds from Sicily to Scandi-navia (or Cairo to Cracow) in the West, and from Shanghai to Siberia (or Malaysia to Mongolia) in the East. However, the extent of depigmentation is more marked amongst the northern inhabitants of the West than is true for the East. The natives of Sweden are noticeably lighter than the natives of Siberia, and the citizens of Barcelona are lighter than the population of Beijing though the latitudes in question are the same. This suggests that the ancestors of Europeans must have been living at that latitude longer than the ancestors of the North Chinese. As the archaeological record of the Mousterian shows, the control of fire allowed permanent habitation in the western parts of the Temperate Zone to have extended from over 200,000 years ago. The

Figure 12-7 The extent of the earliest continuous occupation of the North Temperate Zone based on a combined assessment of the evidence from Middle Paleolithic archaeological continuity and modern skin pigment distribution. (Modified from Figure 13-16 in Brace, 1995:223.)

archaeological record for the comparable latitudes of eastern Asia is not so easy to assess, principally because much less work has been done (Figures 12-4, 12-7). One can guess that the northern parts of the Far East have been continuously occupied for about 150,000 years, but this needs to be tested by good, datable archaeological evidence.

∾ ∾

Epilogue

Chris Stringer has presented the case that "we are all Africans under the skin" (Stringer and McKie, 1997a and b). The presumed recency of the dispersal of the various regionally identifiable populations of the world from an African origin is offered as the reason why human capabilities the world around are more alike than different. The good intentions behind this view are laudable indeed, even if they have more in common with the outlook of the creationists than with evolutionary biology. Actually, this is one of those instances where the conclusions of religious fundamentalism are not at variance with those of science, even if the means by which those conclusions are reached are quite different.

Darwin's initial guess that human origins would be found in Africa was right for the right reasons. The paleontological and archaeological evidence, unavailable during his lifetime, has provided incontrovertible support. More recently, the demonstration that humans share more than 98 percent of their genes with African chimpanzees adds further credibility to the case for a common African ancestor, not just for all human beings, but also for humans and their closest nonhuman kin (King and Wilson, 1975).

Still more recently, the findings of molecular geneticists that the greatest amount of genetic diversity among human populations is found among and between various groups of Africans, and that diversity drops the farther away from Africa the sample tested is located, provides added support for a picture of dispersal from an original African home (Tishkoff et al., 1996). The questions remain, then, how recently or how remotely did that dispersal take place? Was it only one, or was it a repeated phenomenon?

Curiously enough, the answer to the question of time, however interesting it may be, is not really very important. From the evidence available, a dispersal from Africa 50,000 years ago, or even 100,000 years ago, just will not work. Given what we can deduce about how much time it had to have taken to produce the regional variation in human skin color now visible, a date of 200,000 years or more would allow the differences visible between living human populations sufficient time to have arisen where they now are in the Old World. Although this would work, there is no compelling evidence to establish this as of yet, and the archaeology gives us quite a different picture. What is missing is any reliable evidence for the actual date of an African exodus more recent than the archaeological documentation of the spread of *Homo erectus* around 2 million years ago.

The biological differentiation evident today could all have been produced in a bit over 200,000 years. Even if the original movement of *Homo erectus* out of Africa was the only such episode, it was the northward expansion made possible by cultural developments 250,000 years ago that led to the pigment differentiation that is now so evident. The food-preparation practices that made life in the north a possibility also played a role in generating some of the differences in face form now visible, and these also could easily have arisen within that time span. In similar fashion, differences in nose and body proportions and in aspects of metabolism such as resistance to frostbite and salt-retention capabilities could easily have been selected for in that same stretch of time.

None of these, however, has even the faintest connection with the essential nature of the human mind, though this has been a long-running expectation on the part of many in the intelligence-testing business. The quotas allotted to different "races" and nations in framing the United States immigration restriction legislation in 1924 were based on the assumption that, just as populations differ in physical appearance, so we should expect them to differ in mental ability. (This whole sorry episode is surveyed in depth by Chase, 1977.) The effort to demonstrate the reality of that expectation has been a long-running and inconclusive one. Over half a century after the testing of immigrants was initiated in America, the University of California educational psychologist Arthur R. Jensen declared: "everything else that's ever been examined has shown differences and why should the brain be an exception? It's not an unreasonable proposition, but it has not been proved in any scientifically acceptable way. I think it *could* be" (quoted by Neary, 1970:62).

That expectation, however, is not based on science. At bottom it is generated by racial prejudice as it was in the case of the Stanford psychologist Lewis M. Terman (1877–1956) who developed the idea of I.Q.—the Intelligence Quotient— and who assumed that the figures derived from the tests he devised demonstrated the "dullness" which occurs "with such extraordinary frequency among Indians, Mexicans, and negroes," and he concluded that "Their dullness seems to be racial" (Terman, 1916:91). The same assumptions clearly underlie the efforts to justify the racial differences in income today by noting the correlations with "intelligence" test scores and concluding that a "racial" difference in intelligence is only what one would expect (cf. Herrnstein and Murray, 1994).

Intelligence, however it may be defined, has absolutely nothing to do with the capacity to prevent the penetration of ultraviolet radiation, i.e., there is absolutely no genetic or environmental link between cognitive capability and skin color. Likewise, intelligence has nothing whatsoever to do with the greater air-moistening capacity of a long, high-bridged nose as compared with a short, low-bridged nose. Nor is intelligence involved in determining salt-retention capabilities or the temperature at which cold-induced shivering signals an elevation of metabolic rate. There are latitude-related differences in each of these aspects of human biology, and each is the result of a very specific aspect of environmentally imposed selection, but not one of those selective force dimensions has any relation to brains.

The expectation that intelligence will vary between groups because pigment and some other specific biological traits vary is tantamount to assuming that intelligence also responds in predictable fashion to changes in ultraviolet light intensity, humidity, or ambient temperature. There is no shred of evidence to suggest why there should be a tie between brains and sunlight, or brains and moisture, or brains and the thermometer. Yes, it is true that the self-satisfied and ethnocentric

Euro-Americans of a generation or two past were convinced that the pinnacle of human intelligence was generated by long-term adaptation to the rigors of life in the North Temperate zone, and that life in the tropics was one of indolence and ease, lacking in the kind of stimulus that produced high intellectual capabilities (Huntington, 1915; Matthew, 1915; Osborn, 1926; and summarized in Horsman, 1981). Strains of that bigotry are alive and flourishing at the present time (Jensen, 1960; Herrnstein and Murray, 1994; Itzkoff, 1994; Rushton, 1995; Bolick, 1996).

A good dose of the full anthropological perspective is what is needed to counter the narrow ethnocentrism represented in this tradition, and special care has to be given to avoid the manifestations of *anthropologie naïve* that are so frequently cited in its support (and see the cautions voiced in Stoczkowski, 1994). It is not enough to say that we are all Africans under the skin and that a recent divergence from a common ancestral condition is why we are basically more alike than different. Yes, we are indeed more alike than different, but what makes us alike is the fact that all living human beings have been shaped by a common heritage that has exerted its controlling effects for the past 2 million years in general and, most specifically and importantly, over the last 250,000 years in particular. That latter and key stretch has been dominated by the realm of the cultural ecological niche. The common pressure of having to learn the language and lore of the nurturing group has been the legacy of all human beings. Differences in latitude and temperature are absolutely unrelated to the importance of language acquisition.

Wherever people have made a go of it, the fundamental need to acquire the knowledge of previous generations and to benefit vicariously from the experiences of their contemporaries by verbal means is the essence of the common human condition. There are individual differences in mental capacity in each human group, past and present, but the survival problems faced by each group have been absolutely identical. Hot or cold, humid or arid, groups survive only when their average members learn to speak well enough to absorb the lessons passed on by previous generations. The human condition is both the producer and the product of that phenomenon of its own creation, the cultural ecological niche. The differences within it are superficial and trivial, and its basic nature is profound and unifying. This is a lesson that anthropology can contribute for the edification and benefit of all.

∽ References Cited ∽

When I printed out the whole list of the references cited in the chapters included here, it ran to some 250 pages. This would have made the manuscript half again as long as what the good people at AltaMira Press were willing to publish. Since all but the last chapter have appeared previously in print, I decided that the reader who really wants to check up the sources mentioned could go to the published versions to get the full reference information. I have listed here the full publication data for the papers that are reprinted here, and I have also added full references for the sources mentioned in the Prologues and the Epilogues, and also for the last chapter.

Alexander, Richard D., 1990. How Did Humans Evolve? Reflections on the Uniquely Unique Species. *Museum of Zoology, University of Michigan Special Publications* no. 1, pp. 1–38.

Aquinas, Saint Thomas, 1923. *The Summa Contra Gentiles.* Literally Translated by the English Dominican Fathers from the latest Leonine Edition. Vol. II. Burns, Oates & Washbourne, Ltd., London. 305 pp.

Arensburg, B., A.-M. Tillier, B. Vandermeersch, H. Duday, L. Schepartz, and Y. Rak, 1989. A Middle Palaeolithic human hyoid bone. *Nature* 338:758–760.

Arensburg, Baruch, Lynn A. Schepartz, Anne-Marie Tillier, Bernard Vandermeersch, and Yoel Rak, 1990. A reappraisal of the anatomical basis for speech in Middle Pleistocene hominids. *American Journal of Physical Anthropology* 83(2):137–146.

Armytage, W. H. G., 1953. Matthew Arnold and T. H. Huxley: Some new letters. *Review of English Studies* 4(16):346–353.

Arnold, Matthew, 1869. *Culture and Anarchy: An Essay in Political and Social Criticism.* Smith, Elder and Co., London. 212 pp.

Auel, Jean M., 1980. *The Clan of the Cave Bear: Earth's Children.* Crown Publishers, New York. 468 pp.

_____ , 1985. *The Mammoth Hunters.* Crown Publishers, New York. 645 pp.

Bar-Yosef, Ofer, 1990–91. Mousterian adaptations—A global view. *Quaternaria Nova* 1:515–591.

_____ , 1992. Middle Paleolithic Human Adaptations in the Mediterranean Levant. *In* Takeru Akazawa, Kenichi Aoki, and Tasuku Kimura (eds.), *The Evolution and Dispersal of Modern Humans in Asia.* Hokusen-Sha, Tokyo. Pp. 189–215.

_____ , 1993. The Role of Western Asia in Modern Human Origins. *In* M. J. Aikens, C. B. Stringer, and P. A. Mellars (eds.), *The Origins of Modern Humans and the Impact of Chronometric Dating.* Princeton University Press, Princeton, N.J. Pp. 132–147.

_____ , 1994. The Contributions of Southwest Asia to the Study of the Origin of Modern Humans. *In* Matthew H. Nitecki and Doris V. Nitecki (eds.), *Origins of Anatomically Modern Humans.* Plenum, New York. Pp. 23–66.

Bar-Yosef, O., B. Vandermeersch, B. Arensburg, A. Belfer-Cohen, P. Goldberg, H. Laville, L. Meignen, Y. Rak, J. D. Speth, E. Tchernov, A.-M. Tillier, and S. Weiner, 1992. The excavations in Kebara Cave, Mt. Carmel. *Current Anthropology* 33(5):497–550.

Bickerton, Derek, 1981. *Roots of Language.* Karoma Publishers, Ann Arbor, Mich. 351 pp.

_____ , 1990. *Language and Species.* University of Chicago Press, Chicago. 297 pp.

Birdsell, Joseph B., 1967. Preliminary data on the trihybrid origin of the Australian aborigines. *Archaeology and Physical Anthropology in Oceania* 2(2):100–155.

Boesch, Christophe, and Hedwige Boesch, 1991. Sex differences in the use of natural hammers by wild chimpanzees: A preliminary report. *Journal of Human Evolution* 10(7):585–593.

Bolick, Clint, 1996. *The Affirmative Action Frauds: Can We Restore the American Civil Rights Vision?* Cato Institute, Washington, D.C. 170 pp.

Bordes, François, 1968. *The Old Stone Age.* Trans. from the French by J. E. Anderson. McGraw-Hill, New York. 255 pp.

_____ , 1978. Foreword. *In* Fumiko Ikawa-Smith (ed.), *Early Paleolithic in South and East Asia.* Mouton, The Hague. Pp. ix–x.

Boule, Marcellin, 1913. *L'Homme Fossile de La Chapelle-aux-Saints.* Reprinted from *Annales de Paléontologie,* vols. 6–8. Masson & Cie., Paris. 278 pp.

_____ , 1921. *Les Hommes Fossiles. Éléments de Paléontologie Humaine.* Masson et Cie., Paris. 491 pp.

Boule, Marcellin, and Henri-Victor Vallois, 1957. *Fossil Men.* Michael Bullock, trans. Dryden Press, New York. 535 pp.

Brace, C. Loring, 1963. Structural reduction in evolution. *The American Naturalist* 97:39–49.

_____ , 1964a. The fate of the "classic" Neanderthals: A consideration of hominid catastrophism. *Current Anthropology* 5(1):1–41.

_____ , 1964b. A Non-Racial Approach Towards the Understanding of Human Diversity. *In* Ashley Montagu (ed.), The Concept of Race. The Free Press of Glencoe, New York. Pp. 103–152.

_____ , 1967. Environment, tooth form and size in the Pleistocene. *Journal of Dental Research* 46 (Supplement to no. 5):809–816.

_____ , 1976. Tooth reduction in the Orient. *Asian Perspectives* 19(2):203–219 (actually published in 1978).

_____ , 1980. Australian tooth size clines and the death of a stereotype. *Current Anthropology* 21(2):141–164.

_____ , 1981. Tales of the phylogenetic woods: The evolution and significance of phylogenetic trees. *American Journal of Physical Anthropology* 56(4):411–429.

_____ , 1982. The roots of the race concept in American physical anthropology. *In* Frank Spencer (ed.), *A History of American Physical Anthropology 1930–1980*. Academic Press, New York. Pp. 11–29.

_____ , 1988. Punctuationism, cladistics and the legacy of medieval neoplatonism. *Human Evolution* 3(3):121–138.

_____ , 1992. *Modern Human Origins*: Narrow Focus or Broad Spectrum? The David Skomp Lecture, April 16, 1992. Department of Anthropology, Indiana University, Bloomington, Ind. 30 pp.

_____ , 1995a. Bio-cultural interaction and the mechanism of mosaic evolution in the emergence of "modern" morphology. *American Anthropologist* 97(4):1–11.

_____ , 1995b. Review of *The Evolution of Racism: Human Differences and the Use and Abuse of Science,* by Pat Shipman. *American Journal of Physical Anthropology* 96(2):204–210.

_____ , 1995c. *The Stages of Human Evolution*, 5th ed. Prentice-Hall, Englewood Cliffs, N.J. 371 pp.

_____ , 1996a. Cro-Magnon and Qafzeh—vive la différence. *Dental Anthropology Newsletter* 10(3):2–9.

_____ , 1996b. A four-letter word called "race." In Larry J. Reynolds and Leonard Lieberman (eds.), *Race and Other Miscalculations, and Mismeasures: Papers in Honor of Ashley Montagu in his Ninetieth Year*. General Hall, Publishers, Dix Hills, N.Y. Pp. 106–141.

_____ , 1997a. The intellectual standing of Charles Darwin and the legacy of the "Scottish Enlightenment" in biological thought. *Yearbook of Physical Anthropology* 40:91–111.

_____ , 1997b. Montagu, Ashley (1905–). *In* Frank Spencer (ed.), History of Physical Anthropology: An Encyclopedia. Garland, New York. Pp. 683–685.

_____ , 1997c. Neanderthals "Я" Us? *Anthropology Newsletter* 38(8):1, 4.

Brace, C. Loring, Mary L. Brace, and William R. Leonard, 1989. Reflections on the face of Japan: A multivariate and odontometric perspective. *American Journal of Physical Anthropology* 78(1):93–113.

Brace, C. Loring, Maciej Henneberg, and John H. Relethford, 1999. Skin color as an index of timing in human evolution. *American Journal of Physical Anthropology*, Supplement 28 (annual Meetings Issue): 95–96.

Brace, C. Loring, and Kevin D. Hunt, 1990. A non-racial craniofacial perspective on human variation: A(ustralia) to Z(uni). *American Journal of Physical Anthropology* 82(3):341–360.

Brace, C. Loring, and Paul E. Mahler, 1971. Post Pleistocene changes in the human dentition. *American Journal of Physical Anthropology* 34(2):191–204.

Brace, C. Loring, and Ashley Montagu, 1977. *Human Evolution,* 2d ed. Macmillan, New York. 493 pp.

Brace, C. L., and Masafumi Nagai, 1982. Japanese tooth size, past and present. *American Journal of Physical Anthropology* 59(4):399–411.

Brace, C. Loring, A. Russell Nelson, and Pan Qifeng, Submitted. Peopling of the New World: A comparative craniofacial view. *Proceedings of the National Academy of Sciences of the United States of America.*

Brace, C. Loring, Harry Nelson, Noel Korn, and Mary L. Brace, 1979. *Atlas of Human Evolution,* 2d ed. Holt Rinehart and Winston, New York. 175 pp.

Brace, C. L., Shao Xiang-qing, and Zhang Zhen-biao, 1984. Prehistoric and Modern Tooth Size in China. *In* F. H. Smith and F. Spencer (eds.), *The Origins of Modern Humans: A World Survey of the Fossil Evidence.* Alan R. Liss, New York. Pp. 485–516.

Brace, C. Loring, Shelley L. Smith, and Kevin D. Hunt, 1991. What Big Teeth You Had, Grandma! Human Tooth Size, Past and Present. *In* Marc A. Kelley and Clark S. Larsen (eds.), *Advances in Dental Anthropology.* Wiley-Liss, New York. Pp. 33–57.

Brace, C. L., and Virginia J. Vitzthum, 1984. Human tooth size at Mesolithic, Neolithic and modern levels at Niah Cave, Sarawak: Comparisons with other Asian populations. *Sarawak Museum Journal* 33(54):75–82.

Browne, Janet, 1994. Natural causes, Review of *Richard Owen: Victorian Naturalist,* by Nicolaas A. Rupke. *Times Literary Supplement,* Aug. 12. Pp. 3–4.

_____ , 1995. *Charles Darwin: Voyaging:* Vol. I of a Biography. Knopf, New York. 605 pp.

Calvin, William, 1990. *The Ascent of Mind: Ice Age Climates and the Evolution of Intelligence.* Bantam Books, New York. 302 pp.

Carrier, David R., 1984. The energetic paradox of human running and hominid evolution. *Current Anthropology* 25(4):483–495.

Carroll, Lewis, 1972. *Through the Looking Glass and What Alice Found There.* Macmillan and Co., London. 224 pp.

Chard, Chester S., 1969. Archaeology in the Soviet Union. *Science* 163:774–779.

Chase, Allan, 1977. *The Legacy of Malthus: The Social Costs of the New Scientific Racism.* Knopf, New York. 686 pp.

Chomsky, Noam, 1975. *Reflections on Language.* Random House, New York. 269 pp.

_____ , 1988. *Language and Problems of Knowledge: The Managua Lectures.* MIT Press, Cambridge, Mass. 205 pp.

Clark, Geoffrey, and Catherine M. Willermet (eds.), 1997. *Conceptual Issues in Modern Human Origins Research.* Aldine de Gruyter, New York. 508 pp.

Clark, J. Desmond, 1975. Africa in prehistory: Peripheral or paramount? *Man* 10(2):175–198.

_____ , 1993. African and Asian Perspectives on the Origins of Modern Humans. *In* M. J. Aitkens, C. B. Stringer, and P. A. Mellars (eds.), *The Origins of Modern Humans and the Impact of Chronometric Dating.* Princeton University Press, Princeton, N.J. Pp. 148–178.

Clark, J. Desmond, and Kathy D. Schick, 1988. Context and content: Impressions of Palaeolithic sites and assemblages in the People's Republic of China. *Journal of Human Evolution* 17(4):439–448.

Clark, W. E. Le Gros, 1955. *The Fossil Evidence for Human Evolution: An Introduction to the Study of Paleoanthropology.* University of Chicago Press, Chicago.

Cole, Sonia, 1975. *Leakey's Luck: The Life of Louis Seymour Bazett Leakey.* Harcourt Brace Jovanovich, New York. 448 pp.

Colvinaux, Paul A., 1978. *Why Big Fierce Animals are Rare: An Ecologist's Perspective.* Princeton University Press, Princeton, N.J. 256 pp.

Crow, James F., 1999. The odds of losing at genetic roulette. *Nature* 397:293–294.

Culver, David C., 1982. *Cave Life: Evolution and Ecology.* Harvard University Press, Cambridge, Mass. 190 pp.

D'Andrade, Roy, and Phillip A. Morin, 1996. Chimpanzee and human mitochondrial DNA: A principal components and individual-by-site analysis. *American Anthropologist* 98(2):352–370.

Darnton, John, 1996. *Neanderthal.* Random House, New York. 366 pp.

Darwin, Charles R., 1859. *On the Origin of Species by Means of Natural Selection, or the Preservation of Favoured Races in the Struggle for Life.* John Murray, London. 502 pp. (See reprint of 1st ed., Philosophical Library, New York, 1951.)

————, 1871. *The Descent of Man and Selection in Relation to Sex.* 2 vols. John Murray, London.

Deacon, Terrence W., 1997. *The Symbolic Species:* The Co-Evolution of Language and the Brain. W. W. Norton, New York. 527 pp.

Deinard, A. S., and Kenneth K. Kidd, 1997. Identifying conservation units within chimpanzee populations. *American Journal of Physical Anthropology,* Supplement 24, Annual Meeting Issue. P. 100.

Denby, David, 1997. In Darwin's wake. *The New Yorker* 73(20):50–62.

Dennett, Daniel C., 1995. Darwin's Dangerous Idea: Evolution and the Meanings of Life. Simon & Schuster, New York. 586 pp.

Devine, John, 1985. The versatility of human locomotion. *American Anthropologist* 87(3):550–570.

Diamond, Jared, 1989. This-fellow frog, name belong-him dakwo. *Natural History* 4:16–23.

————, 1992. *The Third Chimpanzee: The Evolution and Future of the Human Animal.* Harper Collins, New York. 407 pp.

Di Gregorio, Mario A., 1984. *T. H. Huxley's Place in Natural Science.* Yale University Press, New Haven, Conn. 248 pp.

Donald, Merlin, 1991. *Origins of the Modern Mind: Three Stages in the Evolution of Culture and Cognition.* Harvard University Press, Cambridge, Mass. 413 pp.

Dornan, S. S., 1925. *Pygmies & Bushmen of the Kalahari: An Account of the Tribes Inhabiting the Great Arid Plateau of the Kalahari Desert, Their Precarious Manner of Living, Their Habits, Customs & Beliefs, With Some Reference to Bushman Art, both Early & of Recent Date, & to the Neighboring African Tribes.* Seeley, Service & Co., London. 318 pp.

Dubois, Eugène, 1894. *Pithecanthropus erectus, eine menschenänliche Uebergangsform aus Java.* Batavia Landes Druckerei, Java. 40 pp.

Dunbar, Robin I. M., 1993. Co-evolution of neocortex size, group size and language in humans. *Behavioral and Brain Sciences* 16(4):681–694.

————, 1996. *Grooming, Gossip and the Evolution of Language.* Harvard University Press, Cambridge, Mass. 230 pp.

Echo, Humbert O., 1996. The name of a race. *The Connective Tissue* 12(1):5.

Eco, Umberto, 1984. *Semiotics and the Philosophy of Language.* Macmillan, London. 242 pp.

Eiseley, Loren C., 1958. *Darwin's Century: Evolution and the Men Who Discovered It.* Doubleday & Company, Garden City, N.Y. 378 pp.

Eldredge, Niles, and Stephen Jay Gould, 1972. Punctuated Equilibria: An Alternative to Phyletic Gradualism. *In* T. J. M. Schopf (ed.), Models in Paleobiology. Freeman, Cooper & Co., San Francisco. Pp. 82–115.

Eyre-Walker, Adam, and Peter Keightley, 1999. High genomic deleterious mutation rates in hominids. *Nature* 397:344–347.

Foley, Robert, 1987. *Another Unique Species: Patterns in Human Evolution.* Wiley, New York. 313 pp.

_____ , 1996. The adaptive legacy of human evolution: A search for the environment of evolutionary adaptedness. *Evolutionary Anthropology* 4(6):194–203.

Frayer, David W., 1976. *Evolutionary Dental Changes in Upper Paleolithic and Mesolithic Human Populations.* Ph.D. Dissertation, Anthropology, University of Michigan, Ann Arbor. 529 pp.

Gagneau, Pascal, Christopher Wills, Ulrike Gerloff, Diethart Tautz, Philip A. Morin, Christophe Boesch, Barbara Fruth, Gottfried Hohmann, Oliver A. Ryder, and David S. Woodruff, 1999. Mitochondrial sequences show diverse evolutionary histories of African hominoids. *Proceedings of the National Academy of Sciences USA* 96(9):5077–5082.

Ghiselin, Michael T., 1969. *The Triumph of the Darwinian Method.* University of California Press, Berkeley. 287 pp.

Ghosh, A. (ed.), 1989. *An Encyclopaedia of Indian Archaeology.* Munshiram Manoharlal Publishers, New Delhi. Vol. I, 413 pp.

Gillespie, John H., 1997. Evolutionary basics, Review of *Molecular Evolution,* by Wen-Hsiung Li. *Science* 277:906–907.

Gingerich, Philip D., 1994. The whales of Tethys. *Natural History* 103(4):86–88.

Gingerich, Philip D., B. Holly Smith, and Elwyn L. Simons, 1990. Hind limbs of Eocene *Basilosaurus:* Evidence of feet in whales. *Science* 249:154–157.

Gingerich, Philip D., and Mark D. Uhen, 1997. The evolution of whales. *LSA Magazine* (University of Michigan) 20(2):7–10.

Gish, Duane T., 1979. *Evolution: The Fossils Say No!* Creation Life Publishers, San Diego, Calif. 198 pp.

Golding, William, 1955. *The Inheritors.* Faber and Faber, London. 233 pp.

Goodall, Jane, 1964. Tool using and aimed throwing in a community of free-living chimpanzees. *Nature* 201:1264–1266.

Gould, Stephen Jay, 1965. Is uniformitarianism necessary? *American Journal of Science* 263(3):223–228.

_____, 1981. What, if anything, is a zebra? *Natural History* 90(7):6–12.

_____, 1982a. The Meaning of Punctuated Equilibrium and its Role in Validating a Hierarchical Approach to Macroevolution. *In* Roger Milkman (ed.), Perspectives on Evolution. Sinauer Associates, Sunderland, Mass. Pp. 83–104.

_____, 1982b. The oddball human male. *Natural History* 91(7):14–22.

_____, 1986. Evolution and triumph of homology, or why history matters. *American Scientist* 74(1):60–69.

_____, 1993. Cordelia's dilemma. *Natural History* 102(2):10–18.

_____, 1994. Jove's thunderbolts. *Natural History* 103(10):6–12.

_____, 1997. Unusual unity. *Natural History* 106(3):20–23, 69–71.

Gould, Stephen Jay, and Niles Eldredge, 1977. Punctuated equilibria: The tempo and mode of evolution reconsidered. *Paleobiology* 3(2):115–151.

Gould, Stephen Jay, and Richard C. Lewontin, 1979. The Spandrels of San Marco and the Panglossian Paradigm: A Critique of the Adaptationist Programme. *Proceedings of the Royal Society of London,* B 205:581–598.

Grayson, Donald K., 1983. *The Establishment of Human Antiquity.* Academic Press, New York. 262 pp.

Greene, John C., 1959. *The Death of Adam: Evolution and Its Impact on Western Thought.* Iowa State University Press, Ames. 288 pp.

Hallam, Anthony, 1983. *Great Geological Controversies.* Oxford University Press, New York. 190 pp.

Hanihara, Kazuro, 1986. The Origin of the Japanese in Relation to Other Ethnic Groups in East Asia. *In* Richard J. Pearson, Gina L. Barnes, and Karl L. Hutterer (eds)., *Windows on the Japanese Past: Studies in Archaeology and Prehistory.* Center for Japanese Studies, University of Michigan, Ann Arbor. Pp. 75–83.

Hayden, Brian, 1993. The cultural capacities of Neandertals: A review and re-evaluation. *Journal of Human Evolution* 24(2):113–146.

Hendriks, W., J. Leunissen, E. Nevo, H. Bloemendal, and W.W. de Jong, 1987. The lens protein α A-crystallin of the blind mole rat, *Spalax ehrenbergi:* Evolutionary change and functional constraints. *Proceedings of the National Academy of Sciences USA* 94(15):5320-5324.

Hennig, Willi, 1966. *Phylogenetic Systematics.* Trans. by D. Dwight Davis and Rainer Zangerl. University of Illinois Press, Urbana. 263 pp.

Herrnstein, Richard J., and Charles Murray, 1994. *The Bell Curve: Intelligence and Class Structure in America.* The Free Press, New York. 845 pp.

Hill, Kim, and A. Magdalena Hurtado, 1996. *Ache Life History: The Ecology and Demography of a Foraging People.* Aldine de Gruyter, New York. 561 pp.

Hockett, Charles F., 1978. In search of Jove's brow. *American Speech* 153(4):243–313.

Horsman, Reginald, 1981. *Race and Manifest Destiny: The Origins of American Anglo-Saxonism.* Harvard University Press, Cambridge, Mass. 367 pp.

Howells, William W., 1973. *Cranial Variation in Man: A Study by Multivariate Analysis of Patterns of Difference Among Recent Human Populations.* Papers of the Peabody Museum of Archaeology and Ethnology, Harvard University, Cambridge, Mass. Vol. 67. 260 pp.

_____ , 1974. Neanderthal man: Facts and figures. *Yearbook of Physical Anthropology* 18:7–18.

_____ , 1997. *Getting Here: The Story of Human Evolution.* New ed. The Compass Press, Washington, D.C. 267 pp.

Humphrey, Nicholas K., 1976. The Social Function of Intellect. *In* Paul P. G. Bateson and Robert A. Hinde (eds.), *Growing Points in Ethology.* Cambridge University Press, New York. Pp. 303–318.

_____ , 1992. *A History of Mind.* Chatto Windus, London. 230 pp.

Huntington, Ellsworth, 1915. *Civilization and Climate.* Yale University Press, New Haven, Conn. 333 pp.

Ikawa-Smith, Fumiko, 1982. Early Prehistory of the Americas as Seen from Northeast Asia. *In* J. E. Ericson, R. E. Taylor, and R. Berger (eds.), *Peopling of the New World.* Ballena Press Anthropological Papers no. 23, Ballena Press, Los Altos, Calif. Pp. 15–33.

Itzkoff, Seymour W., 1994. *The Decline of Intelligence in America: A Strategy for National Renewal.* Praeger, Westport, Conn. 242 pp.

Jensen, Arthur R., 1980. *Bias in Mental Testing.* The Free Press, New York. 786 pp.

Kanaseki, Takeo, Masafumi Nagai, and Hajime Sano, 1960. Craniological studies of the Yayoi-Period ancients excavated at the Doigahama Site, Yamaguchi Prefecture. *The Quarterly Journal of Anthropology (Jinruigaku-Kenkyu)* 7(Supplement):1–36. In Japanese, English summary, pp. 1–2.

Kellog, Davida E., 1988. "And then a miracle occurs"—weak links in the chain from punctuation to hierarchy. *Biology and Philosophy* 3(1):3–28.

King, Mary-Claire, and Allan C. Wilson, 1975. Evolution at two levels in humans and chimpanzees. *Science* 188:107–116.

Klein, Richard G., 1995. Anatomy, behaviour, and modern human origins. *Journal of World History* 9(2):167–198.

_____, 1996. Neanderthals and modern humans in west Asia: A conference summary. *Evolutionary Anthropology* 4(6):187–193.

Krings, Matthias, Helga Geisert, Ralf W. Schmitz, Heike Krainitzki, and Svante Pääbo, 1999. DNA sequence of the mitochondrial region II from the Neandertal type specimen. *Proceedings of the National Academy of Sciences USA* 96(10):5581–5585.

Krings, Matthias, Anne Stone, Ralf W. Schmitz, Heike Krainitzki, Mark Stoneking, and Svante Pääbo, 1997. Neandertal DNA sequences and the origin of modern humans. *Cell* 90(1):19–31.

Kroeber, Alfred L., 1917. The superorganic. *American Anthropologist* 19(2):163–213.

Kroeber, Alfred L., and Clyde Kluckhohn, 1952. *Culture: A Critical Review of Concepts and Definitions.* Papers of the Peabody Museum of American Archaeology and Ethnology, Harvard University. Vol. 47, no. 1. 228 pp.

Kuhn, Thomas S., 1962. *The Structure of Scientific Revolutions.* University of Chicago Press, Chicago. 172 pp.

Kuno, Yas, 1956. *Human Perspiration.* C. C. Thomas, Springfield, Ill. 416 pp.

Landau, Misia, 1991. *Narratives of Human Evolution.* Yale University Press, New Haven, Conn. 202 pp.

Larick, Roy, and Russell L. Ciochon, 1996. The African emergence of early Asian dispersals of the genus *Homo. American Scientist* 84:538–551.

Larson, James L., 1971. *Reason and Experience: The Representation of Natural Order in the Work of Carl von Linné.* University of California Press, Berkeley. 172 pp.

Leakey, Louis S. B., Phillip V. Tobias, and John R. Napier, 1964. A new species of the genus *Homo* from Olduvai Gorge, *Nature* 202:7–9.

Lewin, Roger, 1989. *In the Age of Mankind: A Smithsonian Book of Human Evolution.* Smithsonian Institution Press, Washington, D.C. 256 pp.

_____, 1993. *Human Evolution: An Illustrated Introduction*, 3rd ed. Blackwell Scientific Publications, Boston, Mass. 208 pp.

Lewontin, Richard C., 1972. The apportionment of human diversity. *In* Th. Dobzhansky, M. K. Hecht, and W. C. Steere (eds.), *Evolutionary Biology* 16:381–398.

Lieberman, Daniel E., 1997. A developmental approach to defining modern humans. *American Journal of Physical Anthropology*, Supplement 24:155–156. Annual Meeting Issue.

Livingstone, Frank B., 1992. Gene flow in the Pleistocene. *Human Biology* 64(1):67–80.

Loomis, W. Farnsworth, 1967. Skin-pigment regulation of vitamin-D biosynthesis in man. *Science* 157:501–506.

Lovejoy, Arthur O., 1936. *The Great Chain of Being: A Study in the History of an Idea.* The William James Lectures, Delivered at Harvard University, 1933. Harvard University Press, Cambridge, Mass. 382 pp.

McCown, Theodore D., and Sir Arthur Keith, 1938. *The Stone Age of Mount Carmel.* Vol. II. The Fossil Human Remains from the Levalloiso-Mousterian. The Clarendon Press, Oxford. 390 pp.

Macdonald, David W., 1992. *The Velvet Claw: A Natural History of the Carnivores.* BBC Books, London. 256 pp.

Macfarlane, W. V., 1976. Aboriginal palaeophysiology. *In* Robert L. Kirk and Alan G. Thorne (eds.), *The Origin of the Australians.* Australian Institute for Aboriginal Studies, Human Biology Series No. 6, Canberra, Australia. Pp. 183–194.

McGrew, William C., 1992. *Chimpanzee Material Culture: Implications for Human Evolution.* Cambridge University Press, New York. 277 pp.

MacLeod, Roy M., 1965. Evolutionism and Richard Owen 1830–1868: An episode in Darwin's century. *Isis* 56(3):259–280.

Matthew, William Diller, 1915. *Climate and Evolution.* The Academy of Sciences, Special Publication, New York. Pp. 171–318.

Mech, L. David, 1970. *The Wolf: The Ecology and Behavior of an Endangered Species.* The Natural History Press, Garden City, N.Y. 384 pp.

Meltzer, David J., 1993. Pleistocene peopling of the Americas. *Evolutionary Anthropology* 1(5):157–169.

———, 1997. Monte Verde and the Pleistocene peopling of the Americas. *Science* 276:754–755.

Montagu, M. F. Ashley, 1942. *Man's Most Dangerous Myth: The Fallacy of Race.* Columbia University Press, New York. 216 pp.

Morell, Virginia, 1995. The earliest art becomes older—and more common. *Science* 267:1908–1909.

Murray, Frederick G., 1934. Pigmentation, sunlight, and nutritional disease. *American Anthropologist* 36(3):438–445.

Neary, John, 1970. A scientist's variations on a disturbing racial theme. *Life* 69(22):58 B, C, D; 61, 62, 64, 65.

Nei, Masatoshi, 1975. *Molecular Population Genetics and Evolution.* Elsevier, New York. 288 pp.

Nelson, A. Russell, 1998. *A Craniofacial Perspective on North American Indian Population Affinity and Relations.* Ph.D. Dissertation, Anthropology, University of Michigan, Ann Arbor. 344 pp.

Ohta, Tomoko, and Kenichi Aoki (eds.), 1985. *Population Genetics and Molecular Evolution*: Papers Marking the Sixtieth Birthday of Motoo Kimura. Japan Scientific Societies Press, Tokyo. 503 pp.

Omoto, Keichi, and Naruya Saito, 1997. Genetic origins of the Japanese: A partial support for the dual structure hypothesis. *American Journal of Physical Anthropology* 102(4):437–446.

Osborn, Henry Fairfield, 1916. 2d ed. *Men of the Old Stone Age: Their Environment, Life and Art.* New York: Charles Scribner's Sons. 545 pp.

_____ , 1926. Why Central Asia? *Natural History* 26(3):263–269.

Pinker, Steven, 1994. *The Language Instinct: How the Mind Creates Language.* William Morrow, New York. 494 pp.

Pinker, Steven, and Paul Bloom, 1990. Natural selection and natural language. *Behavioral and Brain Sciences* 13 (4):707–784.

Poliakov, Léon, 1974. *Aryan Myth: A History of Racist and Nationalist Ideas in Europe.* Trans. by Edmund Howard. Basic Books, New York. 388 pp.

Popescu, Petru, 1996. *Almost Human.* William Morrow, New York. 544 pp.

Quellar, David C., 1995. The spaniels of St. Marx and the Panglossian paradox: A critique of a rhetorical programme. *Quarterly Review of Biology* 70(4):485–489.

Relethford, John H., 1997. Hemispheric difference in ultraviolet radiation and geographic distribution of human skin color. *American Journal of Physical Anthropology* 104(4):449–457.

Rightmire, G. Philip, 1990. *The Evolution of* Homo Erectus: *Comparative Anatomical Studies of an Extinct Human Species.* Cambridge University Press, Cambridge. 260 pp.

Roberts, R. G., R. Jones, N. A. Spooner, M. J. Head, A. S. Murray, and M. A. Smith, 1994. The human colonisation of Australia: Optical dates of 53,000 and 60,000 years bracket human arrival at Deaf Adder Gorge, Northern Territory. *Quaternary Science Reviews* 13(5–7):575–586.

Robins, Ashley H., 1991. *Biological Perspectives on Human Pigmentation.* Cambridge Studies in Biological Anthropology, 7. Cambridge University Press, New York. 253 pp.

Romer, Alfred S., 1954. *Man and the Vertebrates.* Penguin Books, Harmondsworth, Middlesex, England. 2 vols.

Ronen, Avaraham, 1998. Domestic Fire as Evidence for Language. *In* T. Akazawa, K. Aoki, and O. Bar-Yosef (eds.), *Neandertals and Modern Humans in Western Asia.* Plenum Press, New York. Pp. 439–447.

Roos, David A., 1977. Matthew Arnold and Thomas Henry Huxley: Two speeches at the Royal Academy, 1881 and 1883. *Modern Philology* 74(3):316–324.

Royte, Elizabeth, 1990. The ant man. *New York Times Magazine,* July 22. Pp. 16–21, 38–39.

Rudwick, Martin J. S., 1972. *The Meaning of Fossils: Episodes in the History of Palaeontology.* Macdonald, London. 287 pp.

Rupke, Nicolaas A., 1994. *Richard Owen: Victorian Naturalist.* Yale University Press, New Haven, Conn. 462 pp.

Ruse, Michael, 1975. Darwin's debt to philosophy: An examination of the influence of the philosophical ideas of J. F. W. Herschel and W. Whewell on the development of Charles Darwin's theory of evolution. *Studies in History and Philosophy of Science* 6(2):159–181.

Rushton, J. Philippe, 1995. *Race, Evolution and Behavior: A Life History Behavior Perspective.* Transaction Publishers, New Brunswick, N.J. 334 pp.

Russell, Anna, 1985. *I'm Not Making This Up, You Know. The Autobiography of the Queen of Musical Parody.* Continuum, New York. 246 pp.

Sahlins, Marshall D., and Elman R. Service (eds.), 1960. *Evolution and Culture.* University of Michigan Press, Ann Arbor. 131 pp.

Schick, Kathy D., and Nicholas Toth, 1993. *Making Silent Stones Speak: Human Evolution and the Dawn of Technology.* Simon & Schuster, New York. 351 pp.

Schiller, Francis, M.D., 1979. *Paul Broca: Founder of French Anthropology, Explorer of the Brain.* University of California Press, Berkeley. 350 pp.

Schuman, E. L., and C. L. Brace, 1954. Metric and morphologic variations in the dentition of the Liberian chimpanzee: Comparisons with anthropoid and human dentitions. *Human Biology* 26(3):239–267.

Shipman, Pat, 1994. *The Evolution of Racism: Human Differences and the Use and Abuse of Science.* Simon & Schuster, New York. 318 pp.

Shreeve, James, 1995. *The Neanderthal Enigma: Solving the Mystery of Modern Human Origins.* William Morrow, New York. 369 pp.

Smedley, Audrey, 1993. *Race in North America: Origin and Evolution of a World View.* Westview Press, Boulder, Colo. 340 pp.

Smirnov, Yuri, 1989. Intentional human burial: Middle Paleolithic (last glaciation) beginnings. *Journal of World Prehistory* 3(2):199–233.

Soffer, Olga, 1994. Ancestral lifeways in Eurasia—The Middle and Upper Paleolithic records. *In* Matthew H. Nitecki and Doris V. Nitecki (eds.), *Origins of Anatomically Modern Humans.* Plenum, New York. Pp. 101–119.

Stains, Howard J., 1975. Distribution and Taxonomy of the Canidae. *In* Michael J. Fox (ed.), The Wild Canids: Their Systematics, Behavioral Ecology and Evolution. Van Nostrand Reinhold, New York. Pp. 3–26.

Stanford, Dennis, Robson Bonnichsen, and Richard E. Moral, 1981. The Ginsberg experiment: Modern and prehistoric evidence of a bone-flaking technology. *Science* 212:438–440.

Stanley, Steven M., 1987. *Extinction.* Scientific American Books: Distributor, W. H. Freeman and Co., New York. 242 pp.

Stauder, Jack, 1993. The "relevance" of anthropology to colonialism and imperialism. *In* Sandra Harding (ed.), *The "Racial" Economy of Science: Toward a Democratic Future.* Indiana University Press, Bloomington. Pp. 408–427.

Stephenson, Robert O., 1981. Nunamiut Eskimos: Wildlife Biologists and Wolves. *In* Fred H. Harrington and Paul C. Paquet (eds.), *Wolves of the World: Perspectives of Behavior, Ecology, and Conservation.* Noyes Publications, Park Ridge, N.J. Pp. 434–440.

Stoczkowski, Wiktor, 1994. *Anthropologie naïve, Anthropologie savante. De l'origine de l'homme, de l'imagination et des idées reçues.* CNRS Éditions, Paris. 242 pp.

Straus, Lawrence Guy, 1989. On early hominid use of fire. *Current Anthropology* 30(4):488–491.

Stringer, Christopher B., 1987. A numerical cladistic analysis for the genus *Homo. Journal of Human Evolution* 16(1):135–146.

_____ , 1990. The emergence of modern humans. *Scientific American* 263(6):98–104.

_____ , 1994. Out of Africa—A Personal History. *In* Matthew H. Nitecki and Doris V. Nitecki (eds.), *Origins of Anatomically Modern Humans.* Plenum, New York. Pp. 149–172.

Stringer, Chris, and Peter Andrews, 1988. Modern human origins. *Science* 241:773–774.

Stringer, Christopher, and Clive Gamble, 1993. *In Search of the Neanderthals*: Solving the Puzzle of Human Origins. Thames and Hudson, London. 247 pp.

Stringer, Christopher, and Robin McKie, 1997a. *African Genesis: The Origins of Modern Humans.* Henry Holt, New York. 282 pp.

_____ , 1997b. Neanderthals on the run. *New York Times,* Op-Ed, July 17. E15.

Swadesh, Morris, 1971. *Origin and Diversification of Language,* Joel Scherzer, ed. Routledge and K. Paul, London. 350 pp.

Tanaka, Migaku, Sasaki Ken'ichi, and Sagawa Musatoshi, 1995. Japanese Archaeology. *In* M. Tanaka, K. Sasaki, and M. Sagawa (eds.), *An Introductory Bibliography for Japanese Studies* 9(2):1–30.

Tattersall, Ian, 1986. Species recognition in human paleontology. *Journal of Human Evolution* 15(3):165–175.

_____ , 1995. *The Last Neanderthal: The Rise, Success, and Mysterious Extinction of Our Closest Human Relatives.* Macmillan, New York. 208 pp.

_____ , 1997. Out of Africa again…and again? *Scientific American* 274(4):60–67.

Tattersall, I., and Jeffrey Schwartz, 1999. Commentary: Hominids and hybrids: The place of Neanderthals in human evolution. *Proceedings of the National Academy of Sciences USA* 96(13):7117–7119.

Terman, Lewis M., 1916. *The Measurement of Intelligence: An Explanation of and a Complete Guide for the Use of the Stanford Revision and Extension of the Binet-Simon Intelligence Scale.* Houghton-Mifflin, Boston. 362 pp.

Terrace, Herbert S., 1979. *Nim: A Chimpanzee Who Learned Sign Language.* Knopf, New York. 303 pp.

Terrace, Herbert S., L. A. Petitto, R. J. Sanders, and T. G. Bever, 1979. Can an ape create a sentence? *Science* 206:891–902.

Theunissen, Bert, 1989. *Eugène Dubois and the Ape-Man from Java: The History of the First "Missing Link" and Its Discoverer.* Trans. from the Dutch by Enid Perlin-West. Kluwer Academic Publishers, Dordrecht. 216 pp.

Thieme, Hartmut, 1997. Lower Palaeolithic hunting spears from Germany. *Nature* 385:807–810.

Tishkoff, Sarah A., E. Dietzsch, W. Speed, A. J. Pakstis, J. R. Kidd, K. Cheung, B. Bonné-Tamir, A. S. Santachiara-Benerecetti, P. Moral, M. Krings, S. Pääbo, E. Watson, N. Risch, T. Jenkins, and K. K. Kidd, 1996. Global patterns of linkage disequilibrium at the CD4 locus and modern human origins. *Science* 271:1380–1387.

Topinard, Paul, 1888. Review of *Les ancêtres de nos animaux dans les temps géologiques* by Albert Gaudry. *Revue d'Anthropologie* 3e série, t. III, pp. 472–474.

Toth, Nicholas, 1985. The Oldowan reassessed: A closer look at stone artifacts. *Journal of Archaeological Science* 12(2):101–120.

_____ , 1987. The first technology. *Scientific American* 256(4):112–121.

Trilling, Lionel, 1939. *Matthew Arnold.* W. W. Norton, New York. 465 pp.

Trinkaus, Erik, 1986. The Neandertals and modern human origins. *Annual Review of Anthropology* 15:193–218.

Trinkaus, Erik, and Pat Shipman, 1992. *The Neandertals: Changing the Image of Mankind.* Alfred A. Knopf, New York. 454 pp.

Türp, Jens C., C. Loring Brace, and Kurt W. Alt, 1997. Richard Owen and the comparative anatomy of teeth. *Bulletin of the History of Dentistry* 45(1):11–16.

Tylor, Edward Burnett, 1871. *Primitive Culture: Researches Into the Development of Mythology, Philosophy, Religion, Language, Art, and Custom,* Vol. I. John Murray, London. 453 pp.

Valladas, Hélène, and Georges Valladas, 1991. Datation par la thermolumiscence de silex chauffés des grottes de Kebara et de Qafzeh. *In* O. Bar-Yosef and B. Vandermeersch (eds.), *Le Squelette Moustérien de Kebara 2.* Cahiers de Paléoanthropologie, Éditions du Centre National de la Recherche Scientifique, Paris. pp. 43–47.

Valladas, Hélène, and Georges Valladas, 1991. Datation par la thermolumiscence de silex chauffés des grottes de Kebara et de Qafzeh. *In* O. Bar-Yosef and B. Vandermeersch (eds.), *Le Squelette Moustérien de Kebara 2.* Cahiers de Paléoanthropologie, Éditions du Centre National de la Recherche Scientifique, Paris. pp. 43–47.

Vallois, Henri-Victor, 1950. La paléontologie et l'origine de l'homme. In *Les Processus de l'Hominisation.* Centre National Pour la Recherche Scientifique, Paris. Pp. 53–86.

Vandermeersch, Bernard, 1981. *Les Hommes Fossiles de Qafzeh (Israël).* Centre National de la Recherche Scientifique, Paros. 319 pp.

_____ , 1997. The Near East and Europe: Continuity or Discontinuity? *In* G. A. Clark and C. M. Willermet (eds.), *Conceptual Issues in Modern Human Origins Research.* Aldine de Gruyter, New York. Pp. 107–116.

Von Hippel, Arndt, 1995. *Human Evolutionary Biology: Human Anatomy and Physiology from an Evolutionary Perspective.* The Stone Age Press, Anchorage, Alaska. 548 pp.

de Waal, Frans B. M., 1999. Animal behaviour: Cultural primatology comes of age. *Nature* 399:635–636.

Walker, Alan, 1984. Extinction in Hominid Evolution. *In* Matthew H. Nitecki (ed.), Extinctions. University of Chicago Press, Chicago. Pp. 119–152.

Wallace, Alfred Russel, 1875. *Contributions to the Theory of Natural Selection: A Series of Essays.* Macmillan, London. 384 pp.

Washburn, Sherwood L., 1959. Speculations on the interrelations of the history of tools and biological evolution. *In* J. N. Skpuhlar (ed.), *The Evolution of Man's Capacity for Culture.* Wayne State University Press, Detroit. pp. 21–31.

_____ , 1960. Tools and human evolution. *Scientific American* 203(3):63–75.

Watanabe, Hitoshi, 1971. Running, creeping and climbing: A new ecological and evolutionary perspective on human locomotion. *Mankind* 8(1):1–13.

Weinert, Hans, 1947. *Menschen der Vorzeit: Ein Überblick über die altsteinzeitlichen Menschenreste*, 2d ed., revised. Ferdinand Enke, Stuttgart. 188 pp.

Wells, H. G., 1966. The Grisly Folk. In *The Complete Short Stories of H. G. Wells* (first published in 1927). Ernest Bann, London. Pp. 607–621.

Whewell, William, 1831. Review of *Principles of Geology; being an Attempt to Explain the former Changes of the Earth's Surface by reference to Causes now in operation,* vol. I, by Charles Lyell. *British Critic, Quarterly Theological Review and Ecclesiastical Record* 9(17):180–206.

_____ , 1832. Review of *The Principles of Geology,* vol. II, by Charles Lyell. *The Quarterly Review* 47:103–132.

White, Leslie A., 1959. *The Evolution of Culture.* McGraw-Hill, New York. 378 pp.

Whiten, Andrew, Jane Goodall, William C. McGrew, T. Nishida, Vernon Reynolds, S. Sugiyama, C. E. G. Tutin, Richard W. Wrangham, and Christopohe Boesch, 1999. Culture in chimpanzees. *Nature* 399:682–685.

Wiley, Edward O., 1981. *Phylogenetics: The Theory and Practice of Phylogenetic Systematics.* Wiley-Interscience, New York. 440 pp.

Wilford, John Noble, 1996. Playing of flute may have graced Neanderthal fire. *New York Times,* Oct. 29. Pp. B5, B9.

Williams, Henry Smith, 1923. *The Story of Modern Science,* vol. VII, *Bettering the Race.* Funk & Wagnalls, New York. 212 pp.

Wolpoff, Milford H., 1996. *Human Evolution.* McGraw Hill, New York. 921 pp.

Wolpoff, Milford H., and Rachel Caspari, 1997. *Race and Human Evolution: A Fatal Attraction.* Simon & Schuster, New York. 462 pp.

Wong, Kate, 1997. Neanderthal notes. *Scientific American* 277(3):28–29.

Wright, Sewall B., 1964. Pleiotropy in the evolution of structural reduction and of dominance. *The American Naturalist* 97:65–69.

Zihlman, Adrienne L., and B. A. Cohn, 1988. The adaptive response of human skin to the savanna. *Human Evolution* 3(5):397–409.

Index

The following typographical conventions are used in this index: *f* and *t* identify figures and tables, respectively.